Java Language Reference

THE JAVA SERIES™

Exploring Java

Java Threads

Java Network Programming

Java Virtual Machine

Java AWT Reference

Java Language Reference

Java Fundamental Classes Reference

Database Programming with JDBC and Java

Developing Java Beans

Also from O'Reilly

Java in a Nutshell

Java in a Nutshell, Deluxe Edition

Java Language Reference
Second Edition

Mark Grand

O'REILLY™

Cambridge · Köln · Paris · Sebastopol · Tokyo

Java Language Reference, Second Edition
by Mark Grand

Copyright © 1997 O'Reilly & Associates, Inc. All rights reserved.
Printed in the United States of America.

Published by O'Reilly & Associates, Inc., 101 Morris Street, Sebastopol, CA 95472.

Editor: Paula Ferguson

Production Editor: Nicole Gipson Arigo

Printing History:

January 1997:	First Edition.
July 1997:	Second Edition. Updated for Java 1.1.

This book is printed on acid-free paper with 85% recycled content, 15% post-consumer waste. O'Reilly & Associates is committed to using paper with the highest recycled content available consistent with high quality.

ISBN: 1-56592-326-X

Table of Contents

Preface

This book is a reference manual for the Java programming language; it covers Version 1.1 of the Java language. It provides a complete description of all of the constructs in the language, so that programmers can write Java programs that function exactly as expected. This book is not meant to teach you the Java language, although you could probably use it for that purpose if you are already fluent in a number of other programming languages.

This is an exciting time in the development of Java. Version 1.1 is a huge new release that more than doubles the size of the core Java APIs. Fortunately, the Java language itself contains relatively few changes for Java 1.1. The new features of the language are significant, however, both in terms of the useful functionality and the elegance they add to the language. This book covers all of the new language constructs in Java 1.1. Here's a quick list of the new features:

- Inner classes, which include nested top-level classes and interfaces, member classes, local classes, and anonymous classes

- `final` local variables, method parameters, and `catch` clause parameters

- Instance initializers

- Blank finals, or `final` variable declarations that do not include initializers

- Class literals for obtaining `Class` objects

- Anonymous arrays, or arrays created and initialized without a variable initializer

Audience

This book is for serious Java programmers. If you are such a programmer, you often need to know precisely how the language works in particular situations. This reference manual provides that information in an easy-to-use form. So, for example, if you need to know exactly how Java selects the method to be invoked by a method call expression, you can find a detailed explanation in this book. Or, if you need to know precisely how the multiplication operator behaves with floating-point data, you can find the details here.

However, if you are actually implementing a Java compiler, this book is not meant for you. In some cases, we've simplified the grammar to make it easier for programmers to understand. These simplifications don't detract from the precision of the book; they simply omit details that aren't important unless you are developing a Java compiler. If you are implementing a compiler or other Java environment, you'll want to get *The Java Language Specification* written by James Gosling, Bill Joy, and Guy Steele, published by Addison-Wesley.

Using This Book

This book is not meant to be read from cover to cover. Instead, it is meant to be used as a reference manual for the syntax and lexical structure of the Java language. The language is presented in a bottom-up order. The text starts with lexical analysis and works up through data types, expressions, declarations, statements, and overall program structure. The book also covers threads and exception handling in detail. The final chapter presents reference information on the classes in the `java.lang` package, since these classes are essential to the Java language.

When you need to know the details about a particular Java construct, you can find the appropriate section and read everything you need to know about that aspect of the language. For every construct, there is a railroad diagram that presents its syntax in an easy-to-understand, visual fashion. The text also provides many examples to illustrate subtle features of the language.

The book includes numerous cross-references to help you move quickly between related topics. A cross-reference shown in italic type specifies the location of a railroad diagram related to the current diagram, while cross-references in plain text specify other sections of the book.

The *Java Language Reference* is broken down into ten chapters and an appendix as follows:

Chapter 1

Introduction provides a quick introduction to the Java programming language by way of a "Hello World" example. The chapter also describes the notational conventions of the railroad diagrams that are used to define the syntax and lexical structure of the Java language.

Chapter 2

Lexical Analysis describes the process by which the Java compiler reads the characters in a Java source file and looks for sequences that form identifiers, keywords, literals, and operators.

Chapter 3

Data Types discusses all of the different data types provided by the Java language.

Chapter 4

Expressions presents the syntax of Java expressions and describes the function of each operator in the language.

Chapter 5

Declarations covers the syntax of class, interface, method, and variable declarations. The chapter also provides a detailed look at the object-oriented aspects of the Java language.

Chapter 6

Statements and Control Structures describes each of the available statements in Java.

Chapter 7

Program Structure presents the syntax of Java compilation units and also covers the two common types of Java programs: stand-alone applications and applets.

Chapter 8

Threads discusses how to create and control threads in a Java program, as well as how to synchronize multiple threads.

Chapter 9

Exception Handling describes how to generate, declare, and handle exceptions in Java. The chapter also covers the hierarchy of exception classes provided in the java.lang package.

Chapter 10

The java.lang Package provides reference information on each of the classes in java.lang.

Appendix

The Unicode 2.0 Character Set lists the character sets that comprise the Unicode standard.

Related Books

O'Reilly & Associates is developing an entire series of books on Java. This series consists of introductory books, reference manuals, and advanced programming guides.

The following books on Java are currently available or due to be released soon from O'Reilly & Associates:

Exploring Java, by Patrick Niemeyer and Joshua Peck

A comprehensive tutorial that provides a practical, hands-on approach to learning Java.

Java AWT Reference, by John Zukowski

A comprehensive reference manual for the AWT-related packages in the core Java API.

Java Fundamental Classes Reference, by Mark Grand and Jonathan Knudsen

A complete reference manual for the `java.lang`, `java.io`, `java.util`, and `java.net` packages, among others, in the core Java API.

Java Virtual Machine, by Jon Meyer and Troy Downing

A programming guide and reference manual for the Java virtual machine.

Java in a Nutshell, by David Flanagan

A quick-reference guide to Java that lists all of the classes, methods, and variables in the core Java API.

Java Threads, by Scott Oaks and Henry Wong

An advanced programming guide to working with threads in Java.

Java Network Programming, by Elliotte Rusty Harold

A complete guide to writing sophisticated network applications.

Database Programming with JDBC and Java, by George Reese

An advanced tutorial on JDBC that presents a robust model for developing Java database programs.

Developing Java Beans, by Robert Englander

A complete guide to writing components that work with the JavaBeans API.

Look for additional advanced programming guides on such topics as distributed computing and electronic commerce from O'Reilly in the near future.

Online Resources

There are many sources for information about Java. Sun Microsystems's official Web site for Java topics is *http://www.javasoft.com/*. You should look here for the latest news, updates, and Java releases. This site is where you'll find the Java Development Kit (JDK), which includes the compiler, the interpreter, and other tools.

The various *comp.lang.java.** newsgroups can be a good source of information about Java. The *comp.lang.java.announce* newsgroup is for announcements that may be of interest to Java developers. The *comp.lang.java.programmer* newsgroup is for discussion of the Java language; it's also a good place to ask intelligent questions. There are a number of other Java newsgroups for various kinds of specialized discussions. You should read the FAQ to find out more. The FAQ is maintained on the Web at *http://sunsite.unc.edu/javafaq/javafaq.html*.

You should also visit O'Reilly & Associates' Java site on the Web at *http://www.ora.com/publishing/java*. There you'll find information about other books in O'Reilly's Java series.

Conventions Used in This Book

Italic is used for:

- The names of syntactic constructs and lexical structures in the Java language

- New terms where they are defined

- Pathnames, filenames, and program names

- Internet addresses, such as domain names and URLs

`Typewriter` Font is used for:

- Anything that might appear in a Java program, including keywords, operators, data types, constants, method names, variable names, class names, and interface names

- Command lines and options that should be typed verbatim on the screen

- Tags that might appear in an HTML document

Request for Comments

We invite you to help us improve our books. If you have an idea that could make this a more useful language reference, or if you find a bug in an example or an error in the text, let us know by sending mail to *bookquestions@ora.com*.

Acknowledgments

I wish to acknowledge the patience of my wife, Ginni, and my daughters, Rachel, Shana, and Sossa, during the long hours I spent writing this book.

I also want to thank Mike Loukides and Andy Cohen for their valuable suggestions on the content of this book. I particularly want to thank Paula Ferguson, who spent many long hours above and beyond the call of duty poring over the details of this book to edit it into its final form.

Thanks also to the staff at O'Reilly & Associates. Nicole Gipson Arigo was the production editor and project manager. Kismet McDonough-Chan proofread the book. Ellie Fountain Maden and Sheryl Avruch performed quality control checks. Seth Maislin wrote the index. Erik Ray, Ellen Siever, and Lenny Muellner worked with the tools to create the book. Robert Romano fine-tuned the figures. Nancy Priest designed the interior book layout, and Edie Freedman designed the front cover.

1

Introduction

Java is a relatively new programming language. However, many of the features that make up the language are not new at all. Java's designers borrowed features from a variety of older languages, such as Smalltalk and Lisp, in order to achieve their design goals.

Java is designed to be both robust and secure, so that it can be used to write small, hosted programs, or *applets*, that can be run safely by hosting programs such as Web browsers and cellular phones. Java also needs to be portable, so that these programs can run on many different kinds of systems. What follows is a list of the important features that Java's designers included to create a robust, secure, and portable language.

- Java is a simple language. It borrows most of its syntax from C/C++, so it is easy for C/C++ programmers to understand the syntax of Java code. But that is where the similarities end. Java does not support troublesome features from C/C++, so it is much simpler than either of those languages. In fact, if you examine the features of Java, you'll see that it has more in common with languages like Smalltalk and Lisp.

- Java is a statically typed language, like C/C++. This means that the Java compiler can perform static type checking and enforce a number of usage rules.

- Java is fully runtime-typed as well. The Java runtime system keeps track of all the objects in the system, which makes it possible to determine their types at runtime. For example, casts from one object type to another are verified at runtime. Runtime typing also makes it possible to use completely new, dynamically loaded objects with some amount of type safety.

- Java is a late-binding language, like Smalltalk, which means that it binds method calls to their definitions at runtime. Runtime binding is essential for an object-oriented language, where a subclass can override methods in its superclass, and only the runtime system can determine which method should be invoked. However, Java also supports the performance benefits of early binding. When the compiler can determine that a method cannot be overridden by subclassing, the method definition is bound to the method call at compile-time.

- Java takes care of memory management for applications, which is unlike C/C++, where the programmer is responsible for explicit memory management. Java supports the dynamic allocation of arrays and objects, and then takes care of reclaiming the storage for objects and arrays when it is safe to do so, using a technique called *garbage collection*. This eliminates one of the largest sources of bugs in C/C++ programs.

- Java supports object references, which are like pointers in C/C++. However, Java does not allow any manipulation of references. For example, there is no way that a programmer can explicitly dereference a reference or use pointer arithmetic. Java implicitly handles dereferencing references, which means that they can be used to do most of the legitimate things that C/C++ pointers can do.

- Java uses a single-inheritance class model, rather than the error-prone multiple-inheritance model used by C++. Instead, Java provides a feature called an *interface* (borrowed from Objective C) that specifies the behavior of an object without defining its implementation. Java supports multiple inheritance of interfaces, which provides many of the benefits of multiple inheritance, without the associated problems.

- Java has support for multiple threads of execution built into the language, so there are mechanisms for thread synchronization and explicit waiting and signaling between threads.

- Java has a powerful exception-handling mechanism, somewhat like that in newer implementations of C++. Exception handling provides a way to separate error-handling code from normal code, which leads to cleaner, more robust applications.

- Java is both a compiled and an interpreted language. Java code is compiled to Java byte-codes, which are then executed by a Java runtime environment, called the Java virtual machine. The specifications of the Java language and the virtual machine are fully defined; there are no implementation-dependent details. This architecture makes Java an extremely portable language.

- Java uses a three-layer security model to protect a system from untrusted Java code. The byte-code verifier reads byte-codes before they are run and makes sure that they obey the basic rules of the Java language. The class loader takes care of bringing compiled Java classes into the runtime interpreter. The security manager handles application-level security, by controlling whether or not a program can access resources like the filesystem, network ports, external processes, and the windowing system.

As you can see, Java has quite a list of interesting features. If you are a C/C++ programmer, many of the constructs of the Java language that are covered in this book should look familiar to you. Just be warned that you shouldn't take all of these constructs at face value, since many of them are different in Java than they are in C/C++.

1.1 A "Hello World" Program

Before diving into the various constructs provided by the Java language, you should have at least a general understanding of the Java programming environment. In the fine tradition of all language reference manuals, here is a short Java program that outputs "Hello world!" and then exits:

```
/*
 * Sample program to print "Hello World"
 */

class HelloWorld {              // Declare class HelloWorld
    public static void main(String argv[]) {
        System.out.println("Hello World!");
    }
}
```

This example begins with a comment that starts with /* and ends with */. This type of comment is called a *C-style comment*. The example also uses another kind of comment that begins with // and ends at the end of the line. This kind of comment is called a *single-line comment*; it is identical to that style of comment in C++. Java supports a third type of comment, called a *documentation comment*, that provides for the extraction of comment text into a machine-generated document.

Comments aside, the example consists of a single class declaration for the class called HelloWorld. If you are unfamiliar with classes, you can think of a class as a collection of variables and pieces of executable code called *methods* for the purposes of this discussion. In Java, most executable code is part of a method. Methods are identical to virtual member functions in C++, except that they can exist only as part of a class. Methods are also similar to functions, procedures, and subroutines in other programming languages.

The `HelloWorld` class contains a single method named `main()`. When you ask the Java interpreter to run a Java program, you tell it what code to run by giving it the name of a class. The Java interpreter then loads the class and searches it for a method named `main()` that has the same attributes and parameters as shown in the example. The interpreter then calls that `main()` method.

In the declaration of `main()`, the name `main` is preceded by the three keywords: `public`, `static`, and `void`. The `public` modifier makes the `main()` method accessible from any class. The `static` modifier, when applied to a method, means that the method can be called independently of an instance of a class. The `void` keyword means that the method returns no value. The `main()` method of an application should always be declared with these three keywords. Although the meanings of these keywords is similar to their meanings in C++, there are some differences in the meaning of the keyword `static` as used in Java and C++.

The `main()` method contains a single line of executable code that calls the `println()` method of the object `System.out`. Passing the argument `"Hello World!"` to the `println()` method results in "Hello World!" being output. `System.out` is an object that encapsulates an application's standard output. It is similar in purpose to `stdout` in C and `cout` in C++. Java also has `System.in` and `System.err` objects that are similar in purpose to `stdin` and `stderr` in C and `cin` and `cerr` in C++, respectively.

1.2 New Language Features in Java 1.1

Although Java 1.1 is a massive new release, there are relatively few changes to the Java language in this version. The new features of the language are quite significant, however, as they add useful functionality and make the Java language even more elegant. Here is a brief summary of the new features of the Java language in Java 1.1:

- The addition of inner classes is the largest change to the Java language in Java 1.1. With this new feature, classes can be defined as members of other classes, just like variables and methods. Classes can also be defined within blocks of Java code, just like local variables. A class that is declared inside of another class may have access to the instance variables of the enclosing class; a class declared within a block may have access to the local variables and/or formal parameters of that block.

  Inner classes include: nested top-level classes and interfaces, member classes, local classes, and anonymous classes. The various types of inner clases are described in 5.3.7 Inner Classes. The syntax for nested top-level and member classes is covered in 5.4.11 Nested Top-Level and Member Classes, while the syntax for nested top-level interfaces is covered in 5.5.7 Nested Top-Level

Interfaces. The syntax for local classes is described in 6.1.2 Local Classes. The syntax for an anonymous class is part of an allocation expression, as covered in 4.2 Allocation Expressions.

- Java 1.1 provides the ability to declare `final` local variables, method parameters, and `catch` clause parameters. `final` local variables, method parameters, and `catch` parameters are needed to allow local classes to access these entities within the scope of their blocks. The syntax for `final` local variables is described in 6.1.1 Local Variables, while `final` method parameters are covered in 5.4.6.4 Method formal parameters. The new syntax for the `catch` clause is described in 6.12 The try Statement.

- Instance initializers are blocks of code that execute when an instance of a class is created. Instance initializers have been added in Java 1.1 to allow anonymous classes to perform any necessary initialization, since anonymous classes can not define any constructors. The syntax for instance initializers is covered in 5.4.10 Instance Initializers.

- As of Java 1.1, `final` variable declarations do not have to include initializers. A `final` variable declaration that does not include an initializer is called a blank final. The functionality of blank finals is described in 5.4.5.1 Variable modifiers and 6.1.1.1 Final local variables.

- A class literal is a new kind of primary expression that can be used to obtain a `Class` object for a particular data type. Class literals have been added to support the new Reflection API in Java 1.1. The syntax for class literals is covered in 4.1.9 Class Literals.

- An anonymous array is an array created and initialized without using a variable initializer. The syntax for an anonymous array is part of an allocation expression, as described in 4.2 Allocation Expressions.

1.3 Compiling a Java Source File

The interface for the Java compiler in Sun's Java Development Kit (JDK) is the command line. To compile a Java program, run the program *javac* with the name of the source file specified as a command-line argument. For example, to compile the "Hello World" program, issue the following command:

```
C:\> javac HelloWorld.java
```

The Java compiler, *javac*, requires that the name of a Java source file end with a *.java* extension. If the source file contains a class or interface that is declared with the keyword `public`, the filename must be the name of that class or interface. There can be at most one such class or interface in a source file.

In an environment such as Windows 95 that does not distinguish between upper-case and lowercase letters in a filename, you still need to be sure that the case of the filename exactly matches the case used in the `public` class or interface declaration. If you use a filename with the incorrect case, the compiler will be able to compile the file but it will complain about an incorrect filename.

The compiler produces a compiled class file with the same name as the `public` class or interface declaration; the file extension used for a compiled Java file is *.class.*

If the *javac* compiler complains that it is unable to find some classes, it may mean that an environment variable named `CLASSPATH` has not been set properly. The exact setting needed for `CLASSPATH` varies depending on the operating system and its directory structure. However, the value of `CLASSPATH` always specifies a list of directories in which the compiler should search for Java classes.

1.4 Running a Java Application

To run a Java application, you invoke the Java interpreter, *java*, with one or more arguments. The first argument is always the name of a Java class. Here is how to run the "Hello World" application:

```
C:\> java HelloWorld
```

The capitalization of the class name must match the name used in the class declaration in the source file. The interpreter loads the specified class and then calls its `main()` method.

A class can belong to a particular package. This allows the class to prevent classes in other packages from accessing its declared variables and methods. If a class is not specified as part of a package, it automatically becomes part of the default package. Because the `HelloWorld` class is part of the default package, you do not need to include the package name as part of the class name on the command line. If the `HelloWorld` class were part of a package called `student.language`, however, you would have to include the package name on the command line. For example, you would run the application as follows:

```
C:\> java student.language.HelloWorld
```

Any additional arguments specified on the command line are passed to the `main()` method in its `String[]` parameter. For the "Hello World" application, the `String[]` parameter is an empty array. If, however, there were command-line arguments, the first array element, `String[0]`, would correspond to the first command-line argument specified after the class name, `String[1]` would correspond to the next command-line element, and so on. The name of the class does not appear as an element in the array of parameters passed to the `main()` method. This is different than in C/C++, where the first element in the array of command-line arguments identifies the program name and the second element is the first command-line argument.

1.5 *Notational Conventions*

One of the topics of this manual is the *syntax* of Java: the way that identifiers such as `foobar`, operators such as +, and punctuation such as ; can be put together to form a valid Java program. This book also talks about *lexical structure*: the sequences of characters that can be put together to form valid numbers, identifiers, operators, and the like.

To describe syntax and lexical structure, many language reference manuals use a notation called BNF. BNF notation is very helpful to language implementors because it defines language constructs in a way that can easily be turned into a working language parser. Unfortunately, however, BNF can be difficult for human beings to understand. This reference manual uses a different notation, called a *railroad diagram,* to describe syntax and lexical structure. Railroad diagrams are much easier for people to understand. A railroad diagram provides a visual means of specifying the sequence of words, symbols, and punctuation that can be used to write a syntactic construct or a lexical structure.

Here is a simple example:

The idea is to follow the lines from left to right. The sequence of words or symbols that you pass along the way is the sequence of words or symbols that the railroad diagram specifies. The primary rule when navigating railroad diagrams is that you can follow lines from left to right only, unless there is an arrow pointing to the left. In the above example, there are no arrows, so there is only one way to navigate through the diagram. Therefore, the above railroad diagram specifies exactly one sequence of words: ROW YOUR BOAT.

The next example provides you with a choice of sequences:

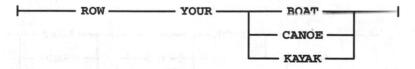

You can navigate the above diagram with one of three sequences:

- ROW YOUR BOAT

- ROW YOUR CANOE

- ROW YOUR KAYAK

The following example contains an arrow:

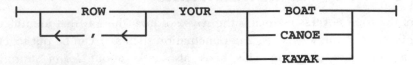

In the above diagram, there is a left-pointing arrow on the line under the word ROW. That arrow means that the line can only be traversed from right to left. The line with the arrow provides a loop that allows the word ROW to be repeated one or more times, separated by commas. This allows a sequence like: ROW,ROW,ROW YOUR BOAT.

The railroad diagrams shown so far lack a feature that is typically needed to make them useful: a name. A name allows one railroad diagram to refer to another diagram. The following railroad diagram defines a construct named *color*:

To further illustrate this point, let's look at two more railroad diagrams. The first diagram defines a construct named *size*:

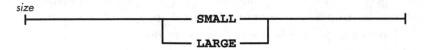

The second railroad diagram is similar to previous ones except that now it allows an optional color or size to precede BOAT, CANOE, or KAYAK. The diagram does this by referring to the names of the railroad diagrams that define these things:

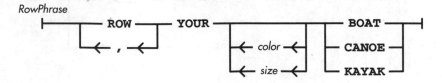

In the diagrams in this book, the font for words such as ROW that are directly contained in railroad diagrams is different from the font used for words like *color* that
are names of railroad diagrams. The preceding railroad diagram allows *size* and
color to occur more than once. The next diagram limits size and color to at most
one occurrence:

RowPhrase2

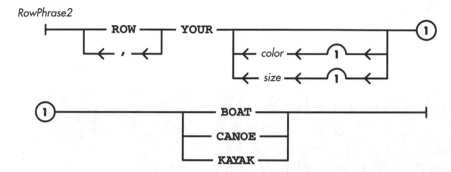

The lines that refer to the *size* and *color* diagrams both have semi-circles with the
number one under them. The semi-circles represent bridges that collapse if
crossed more than a certain number of times. The number under the semi-circle is
the number of times a bridge can be crossed. Adding bridges that can be crossed
only once creates a railroad diagram that permits no more than one occurrence of
color and *size*.

The other new feature introduced in the above railroad diagram is a circle enclosing a number. These circles are connectors used when a diagram does not fit
across a page. The numbered connector at the right end of one part of a railroad
diagram attaches to a connector with a matching number at the left end of
another part of the railroad diagram.

2

In this chapter:
- *Pre-Processing*
- *Tokenization*

Lexical Analysis

When the Java compiler compiles a program, the first thing it does is determine the structure of the program. The compiler reads the characters in the program source and then applies rules to recognize progressively larger chunks of the file, such as identifiers, expressions, statements, and classes. The process of discovering the organization of the program is divided into two components:

- The *lexical analyzer.* This component looks for sequences of characters called *tokens* that form identifiers, literals, operators, and the like.

- The *parser.* This component is responsible for discovering higher levels of organization in the sequences of tokens discovered by lexical analysis.

This chapter describes the rules governing the lexical analysis of Java programs. The rules governing the parsing of Java programs are described over the course of subsequent chapters.

The lexical analysis rules for Java can appear slightly ambiguous. Where ambiguity occurs, the rules for interpreting character sequences specify that conflicts are resolved in favor of the interpretation that matches the most characters. That's a bit confusing, so an example should help. Take the character sequence:

    +++

The ambiguity is that the sequence could potentially be interpreted as either + followed by ++ or the other way around; both are valid tokens. But according to the lexical analysis rules that insist that tokenization favor the longest character match, Java interprets the character sequence as:

    ++ +

Because ++ is longer than +, Java first recognizes the token ++ and then the +.

These rules can produce undesired results when character sequences are not separated by white space. For example, the following sequence is ambiguous:

x++y

The programmer probably intended this sequence to mean "x + (+y)", but the lexical analyzer always produces the token sequence "x ++ y". This sequence is syntactically incorrect.

Java lexical analysis consists of two phases: pre-processing and tokenization. The pre-processing phase is discussed in the following section. The tokenization phase is responsible for recognizing the tokens in the pre-processed input and is discussed later in this chapter.

2.1 Pre-Processing

A Java program is a sequence of characters. These characters are represented using 16-bit numeric codes defined by the Unicode standard.[*] Unicode is a 16-bit character encoding standard that includes representations for all of the characters needed to write all major natural languages, as well as special symbols for mathematics. Unicode defines the codes 0 through 127 to be consistent with ASCII. Because of that consistency, Java programs can be written in ASCII without any need for programmers to be aware of Unicode.

Java is based on Unicode to allow Java programs to be useful in as many parts of the world as possible. Internally, Java programs store characters as 16-bit Unicode characters. The benefits of using Unicode are currently difficult to realize, however, because most operating environments do not support Unicode. And those environments that do support Unicode generally do not include fonts that cover more than a small subset of the Unicode character set.

Since most operating environments do not support Unicode, Java uses a pre-processing phase to make sure that all of the characters of a program are in Unicode. This pre-processing comprises two steps:

- Translate the program source into Unicode characters if it is in an encoding other than Unicode. Java defines escape sequences that allow all characters that can be represented in Unicode to be represented in other character encodings, such as ASCII or EBCDIC. The escape sequences are recognized by the compiler, even if the program is already represented in Unicode.

---

* Unicode is defined by an organization called the Unicode Consortium. The defining document for Unicode is *The Unicode Standard, Version 2.0* (published by Addison-Wesley, ISBN 0-201-48345-9). More recent information about Unicode is available at *http://unicode.org*.

- Divide the stream of Unicode characters into lines.

2.1.1 Conversion to Unicode

The first thing a Java compiler does is translate its input from the source character encoding (e.g., ASCII or EBCDIC) into Unicode. During the conversion process, Java translates escape sequences of the form \u followed by four hexadecimal digits into the Unicode characters indicated by the given hexadecimal values. These escape sequences let you represent Unicode characters in whatever character set you are using for your source code, even if it is not Unicode. For example, \u0000 is a way of representing the NUL character.

More formally, the compiler input is converted from a stream of *EscapedSourceCharacters* into a stream of Unicode characters. *EscapedSourceCharacter* is defined as:

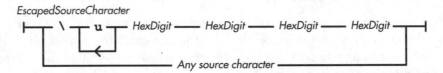

HexDigit is either a *Digit* or one of the following letters: A, a, B, b, C, c, D, d, E, e, F, or f.

A *Digit* is one of the following characters: 0, 1, 2, 3, 4, 5, 6, 7, 8, or 9.

As you can see, the definition of *EscapedSourceCharacter* specifies that the 'u' in the escape sequence can occur multiple times. Multiple occurrences have the same meaning as a single occurrence of 'u'.

If the program source is already in Unicode, this conversion step is still performed in order to process these \u escapes.

The Java language specification recommends, but does not require, that the classes that come with Java use the \u*xxxx* escapes when called upon to display a character that would not otherwise be displayable.

2.1.2 Division of the Input Stream into Lines

The second step of pre-processing is responsible for recognizing sequences of characters that terminate lines. The character sequence that indicates the end of a line varies with the operating environment. By recognizing end-of-line character sequences during pre-processing, Java makes sure that subsequent compilation steps do not need to be concerned with multiple representations for the end of a line.

In this step, the lexical analyzer recognizes the combinations of carriage return (\u000D) and line feed (\u000A) characters that are in widespread use as end-of-line indicators:

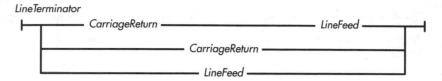

As always, ambiguities in lexical rules are resolved by matching the longest possible sequence of characters. That means that the sequence of a carriage return character followed by a linefeed character is always recognized as a one-line terminator, never as two.

2.2 Tokenization

The tokenization phase of lexical analysis in Java handles breaking down the lines of Unicode source code into comments, white space, and tokens. The rule that defines the overall lexical organization of Java programs is *TokenStream:*

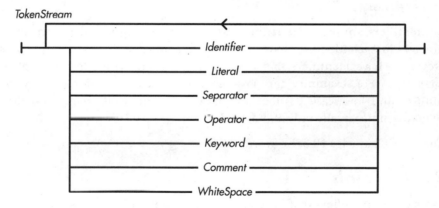

References *Comment* 2.2.6; *Identifier* 2.2.1; *Keyword* 2.2.2; *Literal* 2.2.3; *Operator* 2.2.5; *Separator* 2.2.4; *WhiteSpace* 2.2.7

2.2.1 Identifiers

An *identifier* is generally used as the name for a thing in a program. A few identifiers are reserved by Java for special uses; these are called *keywords.*

From the viewpoint of lexical analysis, an identifier is a sequence of one or more Unicode characters. The first character must be a letter, underscore, or dollar sign.

The other characters must be letters, numbers, underscores, or dollar signs. An identifier can't have the same Unicode character sequence as a keyword:

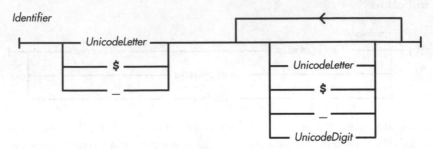

For example, foo21, _foo, and $foo are all valid identifiers; 3foo is not a valid identifier. There is no limit to the length of an identifier in Java. Although $ is a legal character in an identifier, you should avoid using it to eliminate confusion with compiler-generated identifiers.

A *UnicodeDigit* is a Unicode character that is classified as a digit by Character.isDigit().

A *UnicodeLetter* is a Unicode character code that is classified as a letter by Character.isLetter().

Two identifiers are the same if they have the same length and if corresponding characters in each identifier have the same Unicode character code. It is possible, however, to have identifiers that are distinct to a Java compiler, but not to the human eye. For example, the Java compiler recognizes lowercase Latin 'a' (\u0061) and lowercase Cyrillic 'a' (\u0430) as different characters, although they may well be visually indistinguishable.

References Character 10.3; Keywords 2.2.2

2.2.2 Keywords

Keywords are identifiers that have a special meaning to Java. Because of their special meanings, keywords are not available for use as names of things defined in programs. A *Keyword* is one of the following:

Keyword

abstract	default	goto	null	synchronized
boolean	do	if	package	this
break	double	implements	private	throw
byte	else	import	protected	throws
case	extends	instanceof	public	transient

catch	false	int	return	true
char	final	interface	short	try
class	finally	long	static	void
const	float	native	super	volatile
continue	for	new	switch	while

The keywords const and goto are not currently used for any purpose in Java, although they may be assigned meaning in future versions of the Java language.

References Identifiers 2.2.1

2.2.3 Literals

A *literal* is a token that represents a constant value of a primitive data type or a String object:

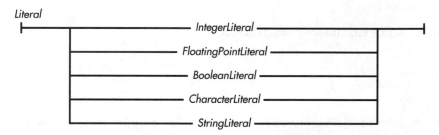

References *BooleanLiteral* 2.2.3.3; *CharacterLiteral* 2.2.3.4; *FloatingPointLiteral* 2.2.3.2; *IntegerLiteral* 2.2.3.1; *StringLiteral* 2.2.3.5

2.2.3.1 Integer literals

An integer literal represents an integer constant:

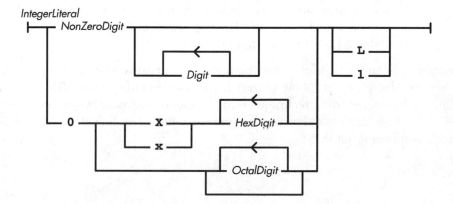

NonZeroDigit is defined as one of the following characters: 1, 2, 3, 4, 5, 6, 7, 8, or 9.

OctalDigit is defined as one of the following characters: 0, 1, 2, 3, 4, 5, 6, or 7.

Integer literals that begin with a non-zero digit are in base 10 and are called *decimal literals*. Integer literals that begin with 0x are in base 16 and are called *hexadecimal literals*. Integer literals that begin with 0 followed by 0–7 are in base 8 and are called *octal literals*.

If an integer literal ends with L or l, its type is long; otherwise its type is int.

Integer literals cannot begin with a + or a -. If either of these characters precedes an integer literal, it is treated as a unary operator, a separate token in its own right.

Here are some examples of int literals:

```
0
92
0642
0xDeadBeef
```

Here are some examples of long literals:

```
0L
14142135623731
0x2000000000L
0752041
```

Note that the preceding examples end with either an uppercase or lowercase "L". They do not end with the digit 1 (one).

Decimal literals of type int may not be greater than 2147483647, which represents 2^{31}-1. Decimal literals of type long may not be greater than 9223372036854775807L, which represents 2^{63}-1. Decimal literals cannot be used directly to represent negative values. To represent negative values using a decimal literal, you must use the decimal literal in conjunction with the unary minus operator. For example, representing -321 requires the use of a unary minus and a decimal literal. To represent the int -2147483648, use 0x80000000. To represent the long -9223372036854775808L, use 0x8000000000000000L.

Hexadecimal and octal literals may be positive or negative because they represent either a 32-bit (int) or 64-bit (long) two's-complement quantity. Two's complement is a binary encoding technique that represents both positive and negative values. The range of values that can be represented by int hexadecimal and octal literals is shown in Table 2-1.

Table 2–1: Minimum and Maximum int Literals

Representation	Minimum Value	Maximum Value
Hexadecimal	0x80000000	0x7fffffff
Octal	020000000000	017777777777
Base 10 equivalent	-2147483648	2147483647

The range of values that can be represented by `long` hexadecimal and octal literals is shown in Table 2-2.

Table 2–2: Minimum and Maximum long Literals

Representation	Minimum Value	Maximum Value
Hexadecimal	0x8000000000000000L	0x7fffffffffffffffL
Octal	01000000000000000000000L	0777777777777777777777L
Base 10 equivalent	-9223372036854775808	9223372036854775807

References *Digit* 2.1.1; *HexDigit* 2.1.1; Integer types 3.1.1.1; Conversion to Unicode 2.1.1; Unary Operators 4.4

2.2.3.2 Floating-point literals

A floating-point literal represents a constant value of type `float` or `double`:

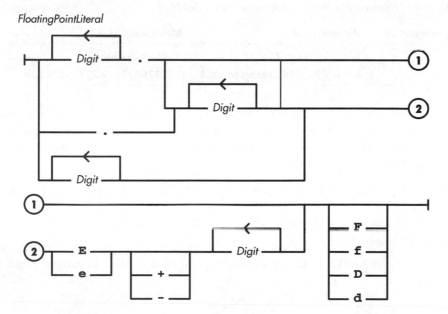

A floating-point literal must minimally contain at least one digit and either a decimal point or an exponent.

The data type of a floating-point literal is `float` if and only if the suffix `f` or `F` appears at the end of the literal. If there is no suffix or the suffix is `d` or `D`, the data type is `double`.

Floating-point literals cannot begin with a + or a -. If either of these precedes a floating-point literal, it is treated as a separate token, a unary operator.

Here are some examples of `float` literals:

```
23e4f
1.E2f
.31416e1F
2.717f
7.63e+9f
```

Here are some examples of `double` literals:

```
23e4
1.E2
.31415e1D
2.717
7.53e+9d
```

The ranges of values that can be represented by `float` and `double` literals are shown in Table 2-3.

Table 2–3: Minimum and Maximum Floating-Point Literals

Representation	Minimum Value	Maximum Value
float	1.40239846e-45f	3.40282347e38f
double	4.94065645841246544e-324	1.79769313486231570e308

Floating-point literals that exceed these limits are treated as errors by the Java compiler. The special floating-point values positive infinity, negative infinity, and not-a-number are available as predefined constants in Java, as part of the `Float` and `Double` classes.

References *Digit* 2.1.1; Floating-point types 3.1.1.2; Unary Operators 4.4; Double 10.8; Float 10.9

2.2.3.3 *Boolean literals*

There are two `boolean` literal values, represented by the keywords `true` and `false`:

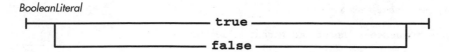

BooleanLiteral

References Boolean Type 3.1.2

2.2.3.4 Character literals

A character literal represents a constant value of type char (an unsigned 16-bit quantity). A character literal consists of either the character being represented, or an equivalent escape sequence, enclosed in single quotes:

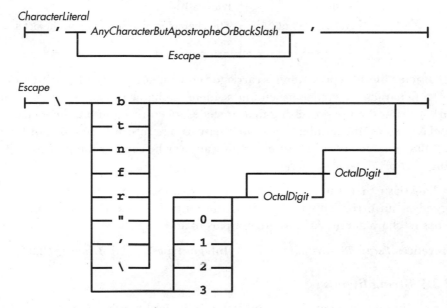

CharacterLiteral

Escape

Here are some examples of character literals:

```
'c'
'n'
'\\'
'\u0138'
```

The character sequence \u*xxxx* is not defined above as a valid *Escape*, even though it can be used as a legal character literal. This sequence of characters is defined as an *EscapedSourceCharacter*, which is handled during the pre-processing phase, before tokenization takes place. As a result, the tokenization phase never sees an *EscapedSourceCharacter*. Tokenization sees only the single Unicode character that replaces the *EscapedSourceCharacter* during pre-processing.

The translations of the different types of escape sequences supported in Java are shown in Table 2-4.

Table 2–4: Java Escape Sequences

Escape Sequence	Unicode Equivalent	Meaning
\b	\u0008	Backspace
\t	\u0009	Horizontal tab
\n	\u000a	Linefeed
\f	\u000c	Form feed
\r	\u000d	Carriage return
\"	\u0022	Double quote
\'	\u0027	Single quote
\\	\u005c	Backslash
\ *xxx*	\u0000 to \u00ff	The character corresponding to the octal value *xxx*

A character literal representing a carriage return character can be written only as '\r'; a character literal representing a linefeed character can be written only as '\n'. During the pre-processing that precedes token recognition, these characters are classified as line terminators, so neither carriage return (\u000d) nor linefeed (\u000a) characters in Java source code can ever be seen by the Java compiler as being part of a character literal.

If a backslash that is not part of a legal *Escape* appears in a character literal, it is flagged as an error. This is different from languages like C++ that ignore backslashes in character literals that are not part of an escape.

References *EscapedSourceCharacter* 2.1.1; Integer types 3.1.1.1; *OctalDigit* 2.2.3.1

2.2.3.5 String literals

A string literal represents a constant string value and consists of the characters in the string or the equivalent escapes:

StringLiteral

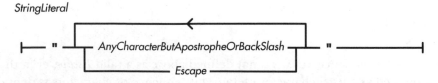

Here are some examples of string literals:

```
""                          // the empty string
"Hello World"
"This has \"escapes\"\n"    // a string literal with escapes
```

There is no primitive type for representing strings in Java. Instead, each string literal becomes a reference to a `String` object. If two or more string literals consist of the same sequence of characters, they refer to the same String object. Using one String object to represent multiple string literals works because, once created, the contents of a String object cannot be changed.

For a string literal to contain a carriage return or linefeed character, the carriage return or linefeed must be written as \r or \n. Neither carriage return (\u000d) nor linefeed (\u000a) characters in Java source code can ever be seen by the Java compiler as part of a string literal. These characters are classified as line terminators during the pre-processing phase that precedes token recognition. For the same reason, \u Unicode escapes for carriage return and linefeed characters cannot be directly used in string literals.

If a backslash that is not part of a legal *Escape* appears in a string literal it is flagged as an error. This is different from languages like C++ that ignore backslashes in string literals that are not part of an escape.

Because operations on strings are generally based on the length of the string, Java does not automatically supply a NUL character (\u0000) at the end of a string literal. For the same reason, it is not customary for Java programs to put a NUL character at the end of a string.

References *Escape* 2.2.3.4; Specially supported classes 3.2.1.1; String 10.20; StringBuffer 10.21; String Concatenation Operator + 4.6.3

2.2.4 Separators

A *separator* is any one of the punctuation tokens in the following railroad diagram:

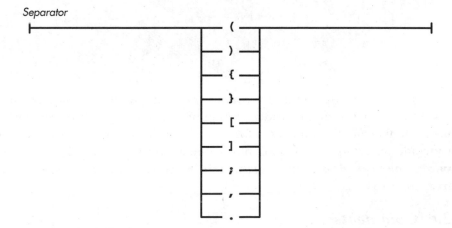

Separator tokens are used to separate other types of tokens. Thus, separators are a part of a higher-level syntactic construct. Although separators have syntactic significance, they do not imply any operation on data.

2.2.5 Operators

An operator is a token that implies an operation on data. Java has both assignment and non-assignment operators:

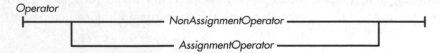

A *NonAssignmentOperator* is one of the following:

NonAssignmentOperator

+	–	<=	^	++
<	*	>=	%	–
	/	!=	?	>>
!	&	==	:	>>
~	|	&&	>>>	

An *AssignmentOperator* is one of the following:

AssignmentOperator

=	–=	*=
/=	|=	&=
^=	+=	%=
<<=	>>=	>>>=

Unlike C/C++, Java does not have a comma operator. Java does allow a comma to be used as a separator in the header portion of `for` statements, however. Java also omits a number of other operators found in C and C++. Most notably, Java does not include operators for accessing physical memory as an array of bytes, such as `sizeof`, unary `&` (address of), unary `*` (contents of), or `->` (contents of field).

2.2.6 Comments

Java supports three styles of comments:

- A standard C-style comment, where all of the characters between /* and */ are ignored.

- A single-line comment, where all of the characters from // to the end of the line are ignored.

- A documentation comment that begins with /** and ends with */. These comments are similar to standard C-style comments, but the contents of a documentation comment can be extracted to produce automatically generated documentation.

The formal definition of a comment is:

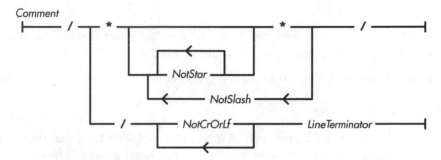

C-style comments and documentation comments do not nest. For example, consider the following arrangement of comments:

```
/*   ...   /*   ...   */   ...   */
```

The Java compiler interprets the first */ to be the end of the comment, so that what follows is a syntax error.

However, in a single-line comment (i.e., one that starts with //), the sequences /*, /**, and */ have no special meaning. Similarly, in a C-style comment or a documentation comment (i.e., comments that begin with /* or /**), the sequence // has no special meaning.

In order to comment out large chunks of code, you need to adopt a commenting style. The C/C++ practice of using #if to comment out multiple lines of code is not available for Java programs because Java does not have a conditional compilation mechanism. If you use C-style comments in your code, you'll need to use the // style of comment to comment out multiple lines of code:

```
///*
// * Prevent instantiation of RomanNumeral objects without
// * parameters.
// */
//    private RomanNumeral() {
//        super();
//    }
```

The /* */ style of comment cannot be used to comment out the lines in the above example because the example already contains that style of comment, and these comments do not nest.

If, however, you stick to using the // style of comment in your code, you can use C-style comments to comment out large blocks of code:

```
/*
*// Prevent instantiation of RomanNumeral objects without
*// parameters.
*    private RomanNumeral() {
*        super();
*    }
*/
```

Which style you choose is less important than using it consistently, so that you avoid inadvertently nesting comments in illegal ways.

References Documentation Comments 7.4; *LineTerminator* 2.1.2

2.2.7 *White Space*

White space denotes characters such as space, tab, and form feed that do not have corresponding glyphs, but alter the position of following glyphs. White space and comments are discarded. The purpose of white space is to separate tokens from each other:

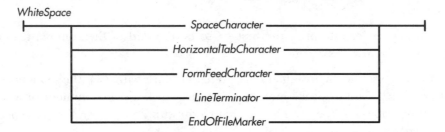

SpaceCharacter is equivalent to \u0020.

HorizontalTabCharacter is equivalent to \u0009 or \t.

FormFeedCharacter is equivalent to \u000C or \f.

EndOfFileMarker is defined as \u001A. Also known as Control-Z, this is the last character in a pre-processed compilation unit. It is treated as white space if it is the last character in a file, to enhance compatibility with older MS-DOS programs and other operating environments that recognize \u001A as an end-of-file marker.

References *LineTerminator* 2.1.2

In this chapter:
- *Primitive Types*
- *Reference Types*

3

Data Types

A *data type* defines the set of values that an expression can produce or a variable can contain. The data type of a variable or expression also defines the operations that can be performed on the variable or expression. The type of a variable is established by the variable's declaration, while the type of an expression is determined by the definitions of its operators and the types of their operands.

Conceptually, there are two types of data in Java programs: primitive types and reference types. The primitive types are self-contained values that can be contained in a variable. The primitive types are comprised of integer types, floating-point types, and the `boolean` type. Of these, the integer types and floating-point types are considered arithmetic types, since arithmetic can be performed on them. Reference types contain values that point to or identify arrays or objects. The syntax for specifying a type is:

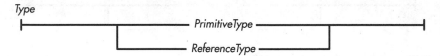

References Arithmetic Types 3.1.1; Boolean Type 3.1.2; Floating-point types 3.1.1.2; Integer types 3.1.1.1; Interface method return type 5.5.6.2; Interface Variables 5.5.5; Local Variables 6.1.1; Method return type 5.4.6.2; *PrimitiveType* 3.1; *ReferenceType* 3.2; Variables 5.4.5

3.1 Primitive Types

A primitive data type represents a single value, such as a number, a character, or a Boolean value. Java has primitive types for arithmetic and Boolean data:

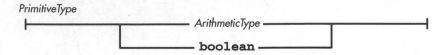

References *ArithmeticType* 3.1.1; Boolean Type 3.1.2

3.1.1 Arithmetic Types

Unlike in C/C++, all of the arithmetic data types in Java are specified to have representations that are independent of the particular computer running a Java program. This guarantees that numeric computations made by Java programs produce the same results on all platforms.

There are two kinds of arithmetic types: integer and floating-point.

The integer types are: `byte`, `short`, `int`, `long`, and `char`. Like C/C++, character data is considered an integer type because of its representation and because arithmetic operations can be performed on `char` data. Unlike C/C++, however, `short int` and `long int` are not valid data types in Java. In addition, `signed` and `unsigned` do not have any special meaning in Java.

The floating-point data types are `float` and `double`.

The formal definition of an arithmetic type is:

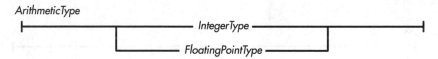

References *IntegerType* 3.1.1.1; *FloatingPointType* 3.1.1.2

3.1.1.1 Integer types

Java provides integer data types in a variety of sizes. Unlike C/C++, however, the sizes of these types are part of the language specification; they are not platform-dependent. Formally:

IntegerType

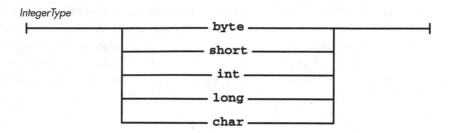

The values represented by these types are specified in Table 3-1. The representation shown is used on all platforms and is independent of the native platform architecture.

Table 3–1: Integer Types and Their Representations

Type	Representation	Range
byte	8-bit, signed, two's complement	-128 to 127
short	16-bit, signed, two's complement	-32768 to 32767
int	32-bit, signed, two's complement	-2147483648 to 2147483647
long	64-bit, signed, two's complement	-9223372036854775808 to 9223372036854775807
char	16-bit, unsigned, Unicode	'\u0000' to '\uffff'

All of the signed integer types in Java use a two's complement representation. Two's complement is a binary encoding for integers, which has the following properties:

- The leftmost bit is the sign bit. If the sign bit is 1, the number is negative.

- Positive numbers have the usual binary representation.

- Negating a number involves complementing all of the bits in the number and then adding 1 to the result.

- The most negative value does not have a positive equivalent.

The java.lang package includes the Byte, Short, Integer, Long, and Character classes. These classes provide object wrappers for byte, short, int, long, and char values, respectively. Each of these classes defines static MIN_VALUE and MAX_VALUE variables for its minimum and maximum values.

Java performs all integer arithmetic using int or long operations. A value that is of type byte, short, or char is widened to an int or a long before the arithmetic operation is performed.

A value of any integer type can be cast (i.e., converted) to a value of any other integer type. Integer types, however, cannot be cast to a boolean value, nor can the boolean type be cast to an integer-type value. A value of a signed integer type can be assigned to a value of the same or wider type without a cast. In this case, the value is automatically widened to the appropriate type. Table 3-2 shows whether an assignment from a particular integer type to another integer type can be done directly or if it requires a type cast.

Table 3–2: Assignment Compatibility Between Integer Types

To/From	byte	char	short	int	long
byte	Assignable	Cast needed	Cast needed	Cast needed	Cast needed
char	Cast needed	Assignable	Cast needed	Cast needed	Cast needed
short	Assignable	Cast needed	Assignable	Cast needed	Cast needed
int	Assignable	Assignable	Assignable	Assignable	Cast needed
long	Assignable	Assignable	Assignable	Assignable	Assignable

The principle underlying the above table is that assignments that do not lose information do not require a type cast. Assigning a short value to an int without a cast is allowed because all of the values that can be represented by a short can also be represented by int. However, assigning an int value to a short is not allowed without a cast because it involves going from a 32-bit signed quantity to a 16-bit signed quantity. Similarly, a byte value cannot be assigned to char without a cast. byte is an 8-bit signed quantity, so it can represent negative numbers. However, char is a 16-bit unsigned quantity, so it cannot represent negative numbers.

Java provides the following kinds of operators for integer values:

- Comparison operators
- Arithmetic operators
- Increment and decrement operators
- Bitwise logical operators

If all of the operands of an operator are of an integer type, the operation is performed as an integer operation. Normally, integer operations are performed with a precision of 32 bits. If at least one of the operands of an integer operation is a long, however, the operation is performed with a precision of 64 bits.

When an integer operation overflows or underflows, there is no indication given that the overflow or underflow occurred.

If the right-hand operand (the divisor) of a division or remainder operation is 0, Java throws an `ArithmeticException`. Division by zero is the only circumstance that can cause an integer operation to throw an exception.

References Additive Operators 4.6; Assignment Operators 4.13; Bitwise/Logical Operators 4.10; Byte 10.2; Character 10.3; Conditional Operator 4.12; Equality Comparison Operators 4.9; Increment/Decrement Operators 4.3; Integer 10.10; Integer literals 2.2.3.1; Long 10.11; Multiplicative Operators 4.5; Relational Comparison Operators 4.8; Runtime exceptions 9.4.1.1; Shift Operators 4.7; Short 10.19; Unary Operators 4.4

3.1.1.2 Floating-point types

Like C/C++, Java provides two sizes of floating-point numbers: single precision and double precision.

Formally:

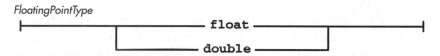

Java uses the single precision 32-bit IEEE 754 format to represent `float` data and the double precision 64-bit IEEE 754 format to represent `double` data.[*] These representations are used on all platforms, whether or not there is native support for the formats. The values represented by these types are shown in Table 3-3.

Table 3-3: Floating-Point Types and Their Representations

Type	Representation	Range
float	32-bit, IEEE 754	1.40239846e-45 to 3.40282347e+38
double	64-bit, IEEE 754	4.94065645841246544e-324 to 1.79769313486231570e+308

Normally, non-zero `float` values are represented as:

$$sign*mantissa*2^{exponent}$$

where `sign` is +1 or −1, `mantissa` is a positive integer less than 2^{24}, and `exponent` is an integer in the inclusive range −149 to 104.

---

[*] The IEEE 754 floating-point data representation and operations on it are defined in *IEEE Standard for Binary Floating-Point Arithmetic*, ANSI/IEEE Std. 754-1985 (IEEE, New York). The standard can be ordered by calling (908) 981-0060 or writing to IEEE, 445 Hoes Lane, PO Box 1331, Piscataway, NJ 08855-1331, USA.

Non-zero `double` values are represented as:

$$sign*mantissa*2^{exponent}$$

where `sign` is +1 or –1, `mantissa` is a positive integer less than 2^{53}, and `exponent` is an integer in the inclusive range –1045 to 1000.

In addition, the IEEE 754 standard defines three special values:

Positive infinity

> This value is produced when a `float` or `double` operation overflows, or a positive value is divided by zero. Positive infinity is by definition greater than any other `float` or `double` value.

Negative infinity

> This value is produced when a `float` or `double` operation overflows, or a negative value is divided by zero. Negative infinity is by definition less than any other `float` or `double` value.

Not-a-number (NaN)

> This value is produced by the `float` and `double` operations such as the division of zero by zero. When NaN is one of the operands for an operation, most arithmetic operations return NaN as the result. Since NaN is unordered, most comparison operators (e.g., <, <=, ==, >=, >) return `false` when one of their arguments is NaN. The exception is !=, which returns `true` when one of its arguments is NaN.

The `java.lang` package includes `Float` and `Double` classes that provide object wrappers for `float` and `double` values. Each class defines the three special values as symbolic constants: `POSITIVE_INFINITY`, `NEGATIVE_INFINITY`, and `NaN`. Each class also defines `MIN_VALUE` and `MAX_VALUE` constants for its minimum and maximum values.

Floating-point operations never throw exceptions. Operations that overflow produce positive or negative infinity. Operations that underflow produce positive or negative zero. Operations that have no defined result produce not-a-number.

Both `float` and `double` data types have distinct representations for positive and negative zero. These values compare as equal (`0.0 == -0.0`). Positive and negative zero do produce different results for some arithmetic operations, however: `1.0/0.0` produces positive infinity, while `1.0/-0.0` produces negative infinity.

A `float` value can be assigned to a `double` variable without using a type cast, but assigning a `double` value to a `float` variable does require a cast. Conversion from a `float` or `double` value to any other data type also requires a cast. Either of the floating-point data types can be cast to any other arithmetic type, but they cannot be cast to `boolean`. When a floating-point number is cast to an integer type, it is truncated (i.e., rounded toward zero).

Java provides the following kinds of operators for floating-point values:

- Comparison operators

- Arithmetic operators

- Increment and decrement operators

If any of the arguments of an operation are of a floating-point type, the operation is performed as a floating-point operation. In other words, any of the integer operands are converted to floating point before the operation takes place. Floating-point operations are normally performed with a precision of 32 bits. However, if at least one of the operands of the operation is a double, the operation is performed with a precision of 64 bits.

References Additive Operators 4.6; Assignment Operators 4.13; Conditional Operator 4.12; Equality Comparison Operators 4.9; Double 10.8; Float 10.9; Floating-point literals 2.2.3.2; Increment/Decrement Operators 4.3; Multiplicative Operators 4.5; Relational Comparison Operators 4.8; Unary Operators 4.4

3.1.2 Boolean Type

The boolean data type represents two values: true and false. These values are keywords in Java. The java.lang package includes a Boolean class that provides an object wrapper for boolean values. This Boolean class defines the constant objects Boolean.TRUE and Boolean.FALSE.

Java provides the following kinds of operators for boolean values:

- Equality and inequality operators

- Boolean logical operators

The following Java constructs require a boolean value to specify a condition:

- if

- while

- for

- do

- The conditional operator ? :

Unlike C/C++, any attempt to substitute a different type for boolean in these constructs is treated as an error by Java.

No other data type can be cast to or from boolean. In particular, using the integer 1 to represent true and 0 to represent false does not work in Java. Though Java does not provide conversions between `boolean` and other types, it is possible to provide explicit logic to accomplish the same thing:

```
int i;
i != 0              // This is true if i is not equal to zero
boolean b;
b ? 1 : 0           // If b is true produce 1; otherwise 0
```

References Boolean 10.1; Bitwise/Logical Operators 4.10; Boolean literals 2.2.3.3; Boolean Negation Operator ! 4.4.3; Boolean Operators 4.11; Conditional Operator 4.12; Equality Comparison Operators 4.9; The do Statement 6.7.2; The for Statement 6.7.3; The if Statement 6.5; The while Statement 6.7.1

3.2 Reference Types

Java is an object-oriented language. An object is a collection of variables and associated methods that is described by a class. The concepts in this section that relate to objects are discussed in detail in 5.3 Object-Orientation Java Style.

The name of a class can be used as a type, so you can declare an object-type variable or specify that a method returns an object. If you declare a variable using the name of a class for its type, that variable can contain a *reference* to an object of that class. Such a variable does not contain an actual object, but rather a reference to the class instance, or object, the variable refers to. Because using a class name as a type declares a reference to an object, such types are called *reference types*. Java also allows the use of an interface name to specify a reference type. In addition, array types in Java are reference types because Java treats arrays as objects.

The two main characteristics of objects in Java are that:

- Objects are always dynamically allocated. The lifetime of the storage occupied by an object is determined by the program's logic, not by the lifetime of a procedure call or the boundaries of a block. The lifetime of the storage occupied by an object refers to the span of time that begins when the object is created and ends at the earliest time it can be freed by the garbage collector.

- Objects are not contained by variables. Instead, a variable contains a reference to an object. A reference is similar to what is called a pointer in other languages. If there are two variables of the same reference type and one variable is assigned to the other, both variables refer to the same object. If the information in that object is changed, the change is visible through both variables.

Java references are very similar to pointers in C/C++, but they are not at all related to the C++ notion of a reference. The main difference between Java references and C++ pointers is that Java does not allow any arithmetic to be done with references. This, coupled with Java's lack of any way to explicitly deallocate the storage used by reference type values, guarantees that a reference can never point to an illegal address.

The formal definition of a reference type is:

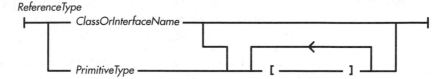

It is possible to cause a reference variable to contain a reference to nothing by assigning the special value represented by the keyword null to the variable. The value null can be assigned to any reference variable without a type cast.

Java does not allow reference types to be cast to primitive data types or primitive data types to be type cast to reference types. In particular, unlike C/C++, there is no conversion between integer values and references.

The only operation that Java provides for reference-type variables is the ability to fetch the referenced object. However, Java does not provide an operator to fetch the object referenced by a reference variable. Instead, the object fetch operation is performed implicitly by the following operations:

- A field expression that accesses a variable or method of a class or interface object

- A field expression that accesses an element of an array object

- A type comparison operation that uses the instanceof operator

References Array Types 3.2.3; *ClassOrInterfaceName* 4.1.6; Class Types 3.2.1; Field Expressions 4.1.6; Interface Types 3.2.2; null 4.1.3; Object-Orientation Java Style 5.3; *PrimitiveType* 3.1; The instanceof Operator 4.8.5

3.2.1 Class Types

The name of a class can be used to specify the type of a reference. If a variable is declared as a class type, the variable either contains null or a reference to an object of that class or a subclass of that class. It is not allowed to contain any other kinds of values. For example:

```
class Shape { ... }
class Triangle extends Shape { ... }
...
Shape s;
Triangle t;
...
s = t;
```

This example declares a class called Shape and a subclass of Shape called Triangle. The code later declares a reference variable called s that can contain a reference to a Shape object and another variable called t that can contain a reference to a Triangle object. The value of s can be assigned to the value of t because an object is not only an instance of its declared class, but also an instance of every superclass of its declared class. Since instances of the Triangle class are also instances of its superclass Shape, the Java compiler has no problem with s = t.

However, saying t = s generates an error message from the compiler. Java does not allow a reference variable declared as a class type to contain a reference to a superclass of the declared class. The assignment t = s is illegal because Shape is a superclass of Triangle. The assignment can be accomplished if s is first cast to a reference to Triangle:

```
t = (Triangle)s;
```

The cast operation ensures that the object referenced by s is a class type that is either Triangle or a descendant of Triangle. When you cast an object reference to a subclass of the reference type, you are saying that you want to treat the object being referenced as an instance of the specified subclass. If the compiler cannot determine whether the argument of a cast will be of the required type, the compiler generates runtime code that ensures that the argument really is an instance of the specified subclass. At runtime, if the class of the object being referenced is not an instance of the specified subclass, a ClassCastException is thrown.

References Casts 4.4.5; Classes 5.3.1; Class Declarations 5.4; Object Allocation Expressions 4.2.1; Runtime exceptions 9.4.1.1

3.2.1.1 *Specially supported classes*

Java provides special support for the String and StringBuffer classes. All string literals are compiled into String objects. The result of a string concatenation operation is a String object. An intermediate StringBuffer object is used to compute the result of a concatenation operation. Because operations on strings are generally based on the length of the string, Java does not automatically supply a NUL character (\u0000) at the end of a string literal. For the same reason, it is not customary for Java programs to put a NUL character at the end of a string.

Java also provides special support for the Object class. This class is the ultimate superclass of all other classes in Java. If a class is declared without its superclass being specified, the language automatically specifies Object as its superclass.

The throw statement in Java is special, in that it requires the use of a Throwable object.

References Object 10.14; String 10.20; StringBuffer 10.21; String Concatenation Operator + 4.6.3; String literals 2.2.3.5; The throw Statement 6.11; Throwable 10.25

3.2.2 Interface Types

The name of an interface can be used to specify the type of a reference. A reference variable declared using an interface name as its type can only reference instances of classes that implement that interface. For example, Java provides an interface called `Runnable`. Java also provides a class called `Thread` that implements `Runnable`. This means that the following assignment is allowed:

```
Runnable r;
r = new Thread();
```

The Java compiler does not allow a value to be assigned to a variable declared using an interface type unless the compiler can be sure that the object referenced by the value implements the specified interface. Casting a reference variable to an interface type allows the variable to be assigned to that interface type, because the cast operation provides its own guarantee that the object implements the specified interface. Unless the compiler is able to determine the actual class of the object that will be referenced at runtime, the cast produces code that verifies at runtime that the object being cast really does implement the specified interface. At runtime, if the object being cast does not implement the required interface, a `ClassCastException` is thrown.

References Casts 4.4.5; Interfaces 5.3.6; Interface Declarations 5.5; Object Allocation Expressions 4.2.1; Runtime exceptions 9.4.1.1

3.2.3 Array Types

An array is a special kind of object that contains values called *elements*. Array elements are similar to variables in that they contain values that can be used in expressions and set by assignment operations. Elements differ from variables, however, in that they do not have names. Instead, they are identified by non-negative integers. The elements in an array are identified by a contiguous range of integers from 0 to one less than the number of elements in the array. The elements of an array must all contain the same type of value; the type of the array is specified when the array is created.

An array-type variable is declared as follows:

```
int [] a;
```

This declaration specifies that the variable `a` refers to an array of `int` values. Java actually allows two styles of array declarations: the one shown above and a style that

is more like that used in C/C++. In other words, you can put the square brackets
after the variable name instead of after the type:

```
int a[];
```

Technically, all arrays in Java are one-dimensional. However, Java does allow you to
declare an array of arrays, which is a more flexible data structure than a multi-
dimensional array. The additional flexibility comes from the fact that the arrays in
an array of arrays do not have to be the same length. Because arrays of arrays are
typically used to represent multi-dimensional arrays, this book refers to them as
multi-dimensional arrays, even though that is not precisely correct.

A multi-dimensional array is declared using multiple pairs of square brackets, as in
the following examples:

```
int [][] d2;        // Refers to a 2-dimensional array
int [][][] d3;      // Refers to a 3-dimensional array
```

When you declare a variable to refer to a multi-dimensional array, the number of
dimensions in the array is determined by the number of pairs of square brackets.
Whether the brackets follow the type name or the variable name is not important.
Thus, the above variables could have been declared like this:

```
int [] d2[],        // Refers to a 2-dimensional array
       d3[][];      // Refers to a 3-dimensional array
```

The actual length of each dimension of an array object is specified when the array
object is created, not when the array variable is declared. An array object is not created at the same time that an array variable is declared. An array object is created
with the new operator. Here are some examples:

```
int j[] = new int[10];        // An array of 10 ints
int k[][] = new float[3][4];  // An array of 3 arrays of 4 floats
```

The arrays contained in an array of arrays can also be of different lengths:

```
int a[][] = new int [3][];
a[0] = new int [5];
a[1] = new int [6];
a[2] = new int [7];
```

Although the first new operator is creating a two-dimensional array, only the
length of one dimension is specified. In this case, just the array of arrays is created.
The subarrays are created by the subsequent new operators.

The expression used to specify the length of an array does not have to be a constant. Consider the following example:

```
int[] countArray(int n){
    int[] a = new int[n];
    for (int i=0; i<n; i++) {
        a[i]=i+1;
    }
    return a;
}
```

The number of elements in an array object is fixed at the time that the array object is created and cannot be changed.[*] Every array object has a public variable called length that contains the number of elements in the array. The variable length is final, which means that its value cannot be changed by assignment.

The Java notion of arrays is fundamentally different than that of C/C++. Subscripting a Java array does not imply pointer arithmetic, so there is no danger of an out-of-range index accessing memory that shouldn't be accessed. Array objects in Java detect out-of-range subscripts; when they do they throw an ArrayIndexOutOf-BoundsException. And unlike C/C++, arrays of type char are not strings in Java. Instead, Java uses the String class to support strings.

Although array objects are reference types, array objects are different from other kinds of objects. The Object class is the parent class of all array objects, but array objects do not really belong to a class of their own. An array object inherits all of the variables and methods of the Object class. Every array also defines the variable length, but there is no class declaration for an array type.

References *ArrayInitializer* 5.4.5.4; Array Allocation Expressions 4.2.2; Index Expressions 4.1.7; Object 10.14; String 10.20

---

[*] The standard class java.util.Vector implements an array-like object with a length that can be changed.

4.

Expressions

Expressions in Java are used to fetch, compute, and store values. To fetch a value, you use a type of expression called a primary expression. To compute and store values, you use the various operators described in this chapter. In Java, expressions are most often used in methods and constructors; they can also appear in field variable initializers and static initializers.

Most expressions, when they are evaluated, produce values that can be used by other expressions. The one exception is an expression that calls a method declared with the void return type. An expression that invokes a void method cannot be embedded in another expression. The evaluation of an expression can also produce side effects, such as variable assignments and increment and decrement operations.

The value produced by an expression can be either a pure value or a variable or array element. The distinction is that a *pure value* cannot be used to store a value, while a variable or array element can.* An expression that produces a variable or an array element can be used anywhere that an expression that produces a pure value can be used.

This chapter refers to values as being either pure values or variables. Saying that a value is a pure value means that it is a value such as 24 that contains information, but cannot be used as the target of an assignment expression. Saying that a value is a variable means that it is something like var or ar[i] that can be used as the target of an assignment. The generic term "value" is used to mean either a variable or a pure value.

The formal definition of an expression is:

The above diagram may seem deceptively simple; why is such a definition even necessary? Expressions in Java are defined with a number of mutually recursive railroad diagrams. You can think of the *Expression* definition as being both the lowest-level definition and the highest-level definition of these mutually recursive diagrams. In other words, a=b[i]+c[i] is an expression, as are b[i], c[i], a, b, c, and i. This first diagram defines an expression to be an *AssignmentExpression*, which is the final definition used to describe Java expressions.

References *AssignmentExpression* 4.13

4.1 Primary Expressions

A primary expression is the most elementary type of expression. Primary expressions are constructs that fetch or create values, but do not directly perform computations on them:

Terms are those primary expressions that produce values, by doing such things as accessing fields in classes, invoking methods, and accessing array elements:

---

* Note that Java's distinction between pure values and variable and array elements is similar to the distinction in C and C++ between rvalues and lvalues.

Term

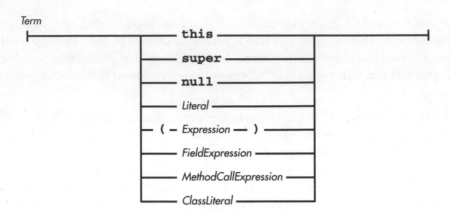

References *AllocationExpression* 4.2; *Expression* 4; *FieldExpression* 4.1.6; *Identifier* 2.2.1; *IndexExpression* 4.1.7; *Literal* 2.2.3; *MethodCallExpression* 4.1.8; *ClassLiteral* 4.1.9

4.1.1 *this*

The keyword this can be used only in the body of a constructor or an instance method (i.e., a method that is not declared static), or in the initializer for an instance variable. A static method is not associated with an object, so this makes no sense in such a method and is treated as an undefined variable. If this is used in an inappropriate place, a compile-time error occurs.

The value produced by this is a reference to the object associated with the expression that is being evaluated. The type of the primary expression this is a reference to the class in which it appears.

One common use for this is to allow access to a field variable when there is a local variable with the same name. For example:

```
int foo;
void setFoo(int foo) {
    this.foo = foo;
}
```

Another common usage is to implement a callback mechanism. Passing this to another object allows that object to call methods in the object associated with the calling code. For example, to allow an object inside of an applet to be able to access parameters passed to the applet in the HTML <applet> tag, you can use code like the following:

```
public class MyApplet extends Applet {
    ...
    Foo foo;
    public void init() {
        foo = new Foo(this);
    ...
```

```
        }
    }

    class Foo {
        Applet app;
        ...
        Foo(Applet app) {
            this.app = app;
        }
        ...
        void doIt() {
            String dir = app.getParameter("direction");
            ...
        }
        ...
    }
```

Another use for the keyword this is in a special kind of *FieldExpression* that refers to an enclosing instance of this object. A reference to an enclosing instance is written as the class name of the enclosing instance followed by a dot and the keyword this (as described in 5.3.7.2 Member classes). Consider the following code:

```
public class ImageButton extends Canvas {
    ...
    private class MyImage extends Image {
        Image fileImage;
        MyImage(String fileName) throws IOException {
            URL url = new URL(fileName);
            ImageProducer src = (ImageProducer)url.getContent();
            Image fileImage = createImage(src);
            prepareImage(this, ImageButton.this);
        }
        ...
```

The call to prepareImage() takes two arguments. The first argument is a reference to this instance of the MyImage class. The second argument is a reference to this object's enclosing instance, which is an instance of the ImageButton class.

References Constructors 5.4.7; *ExplicitConstructorCallStatement* 5.4.7.6; *FieldExpression* 4.1.6; Inner Classes 5.3.7; Methods 5.4.6

4.1.2 *super*

The keyword super can be used only in the body of a constructor or an instance method (i.e., a method that is not declared static), or in the initializer for an instance variable. In addition, super cannot appear in the class Object because Object has no superclass. If super is used in an inappropriate place, a compile-time error occurs.

In most cases, the primary expression super has a value that is equivalent to casting the value of the primary expression this to the superclass of the class in which it appears. In other words, super causes the object to be treated as an instance of its superclass. The type of the primary expression super is a reference to the superclass of the class in which it appears.

There are two situations in which super produces a result that is different than what would be produced by casting this to its superclass:

- When super is used to explicitly call a constructor in the superclass from a constructor in the class, the field variables for the class are initialized when the superclass's constructor returns.

- If a class contains a method that overrides a method declared in its superclass, calling the method by casting this to the superclass results in a call to the overriding method. However, calling the method with the special reference provided by super calls the overridden method in the superclass.

The main purpose of super is to allow the behavior of methods and constructors to be extended, rather than having to be totally replaced. Consider the following example:

```
class A {
    public int foo(int x) {
        return x*x;
    }
    public int bar(int x) {
        return x*8;
    }
}

class B extends A{
    public int foo(int x) {
        return super.foo(x)+x;
    }
    public int bar(int x){
        return x*5;
    }
}
```

The foo() method in class B extends the behavior of the foo() method in class A by calling that method and performing further computations on its result. On the other hand, the bar() method in class B totally replaces the behavior of the bar() method in class A.

References Constructors 5.4.7; *ExplicitConstructorCallStatement* 5.4.7.6; Methods 5.4.6

4.1.3 null

The primary expression null produces a special object reference value that does not refer to any object, but is assignment-compatible with all object reference types.

An operation on an object reference that does not attempt to access the referenced object works the same way for null as it does for other object reference values. For example:

```
foo == null
```

However, any operation that attempts to access an object through a null reference throws a NullPointerException. The one exception to this rule is the string concatenation operator (+), which converts a null operand to the string literal "null".

References Runtime exceptions 9.4.1.1; String Concatenation Operator + 4.6.3

4.1.4 Literal Expressions

A primary expression that consists of a literal produces a pure value. The data type of this pure value is the data type of the literal.

References Literals 2.2.3

4.1.5 Parenthetical Expressions

A primary expression that consists of a parenthesized expression produces the same pure value as the expression in parentheses. The data type of this pure value is also the same as the data type of the expression in parentheses. A parenthetical expression can only produce a pure value. Thus, the following code produces an error:

```
(x) = 5;          // Illegal
```

References *Expression* 4

4.1.6 Field Expressions

A *field expression* is a primary expression that fetches such things as local variables, formal parameters, and field variables. A field expression can evaluate to a pure value or a variable. The data type of a field expression is the data type of the pure value, variable, or array element produced by the following expression.

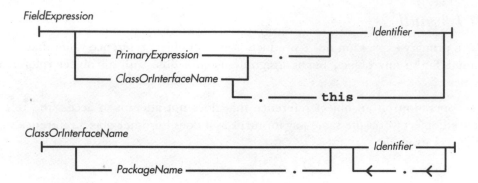

Essentially, a field expression can be a simple identifier, a primary expression followed by an identifier, or a class or interface name followed by an identifier. Here's an example of a field expression that consists of a simple *Identifier*:

    myVar

Before the Java compiler can decide what to do with a lone identifier such as this, it must first match it with a declaration. The compiler first looks in the method where the identifier appears for a local variable or formal parameter with the same name as the identifier. If the compiler finds a matching local variable or formal parameter, the field expression produces the matching variable or parameter.

If the identifier does not match a local variable or a formal parameter, it is expected to match the name of a field variable in the class in which it occurs.

If the matching variable is declared `final`, the field expression produces the pure value specified by the variable's initializer. Otherwise, the field expression produces the matching field variable. If the method that the identifier appears in is declared `static`, the matching variable must also be declared `static` or the compiler declares an error.

A lone identifier that matches the name of a field variable is equivalent to:

    this.*Identifier*

This form of a field expression can be used to access a field variable that is shadowed by a local variable or a formal parameter. For example:

```
class Shadow {
    int value;
    Shadow(int value) {
        this.value=value;
    }
}
```

In the above example, the identifier `value` is used as both the name of a field variable and the name of a formal parameter in the constructor. Within the constructor, the unqualified identifier `value` refers to the formal parameter, not to the field variable. In order to access the field variable, you have to qualify `value` with `this`.

In addition to allowing an object to refer to itself, the keyword `this` has another use in field expressions. The construct *ClassOrInterfaceName*`.this` identifies the enclosing instance of an object that is an instance of an inner class.[*] Consider the following example:

```
public class ImageButton extends Canvas {
    ...
    private class MyImage extends Image {
        Image fileImage;
        MyImage(String fileName) throws IOException {
            URL url = new URL(fileName);
            ImageProducer src = (ImageProducer)url.getContent();
            Image fileImage = createImage(src);
            prepareImage(this, ImageButton.this);
        }
    }
    ...
```

The call to `prepareImage()` takes two arguments. The first argument is a reference to `this` instance of the `MyImage` class. The second argument is a reference to this object's enclosing instance, which is an instance of the `ImageButton` class.

Here are some examples of field expressions that consist of a *PrimaryExpression* and an *Identifier*.

```
this.myVar
size().height
(new Foo()).bar
```

A primary expression that appears at the beginning of a field expression must produce a reference to an object. The identifier to the right of the dot must be the name of a field variable in the object referred to by the primary expression. If, at runtime, the primary expression in a field expression produces the value `null`, a `NullPointerException` is thrown.

Here's an example of a field expression that consists of a *ClassOrInterfaceName* and an *Identifier*.

```
Double.POSITIVE_INFINITY
```

A field expression that begins with *ClassOrInterfaceName* produces a field variable of the specified class. If the field variable is not declared `static`, the specified class must either be the same class in which the field expression appears or a superclass of that class.

---

[*] Since this construct fetches an object reference, you might expect it to be a primary expression. However, due to the way in which inner classes are implemented, this construct is actually a field expression.

Such a field expression is approximately equivalent to:

((*ClassOrInterfaceName*)this).*Identifier*

If *ClassOrInterfaceName* specifies a class or interface defined in a different package than the package in which the field expression appears, the class name must be qualified by the package in which the class is defined. For example:

```
java.awt.Event.MOUSE_UP
```

However, if an import statement imports the specified class, the package name is not necessary.

ClassOrInterfaceName can refer to an inner class or a nested top-level class or interface by qualifying the name of the class or interface with the name of the enclosing class. For example, consider the following declaration:

```
public class A {
    public class B {
    }
}
```

Based on this declaration, you can create a new instance of B as follows:

```
new A.B()
```

Most field expressions produce variables when they are evaluated. This means that the field expression can be used as the left operand of an assignment operator. A field expression produces a pure value, rather than a variable, if the identifier at the end of the field expression is a field variable that is declared `final`. Such a field expression returns a pure value because the value of a `final` variable cannot be modified. A field expression that produces a pure value cannot be the left operand of an assignment operator, or the operand of the ++ or -- operators. Here's an erroneous example:

```
final int four=4
four++
```

This is equivalent to:

```
4++
```

As such, it causes the Java compiler to issue an error message.

When the Java compiler detects an expression that uses the value of a local variable that may not have been initialized, it issues an error message. For example:

```
{
    int x;
    if (testForSomething())
        x = 4;
```

```
    System.out.println(x);    // Compiler complains
}
```

The compiler complains about the use of x in the println() method because x may not have been given an explicit value when the program reaches that statement. Even though there is an assignment to x in the preceding statement, the compiler recognizes that the assignment may not have been performed, since it is enclosed within a conditional statement. The Java language specification requires that a compiler issue an error message when it detects an uninitialized local variable.

References *Identifier* 2.2.1; Inheritance 5.3.5; Inner Classes 5.3.7; Interface Variables 5.5.5; Local Variables 6.1.1; *PackageName* 7.2; *PrimaryExpression* 4.1; Runtime exceptions 9.4.1.1; Variables 5.4.5

4.1.7 Index Expressions

An *index expression* is a primary expression that produces an array element when it is evaluated. The value produced by an index expression is a variable; it can be used as the left operand of an assignment expression. The data type of an index expression is the data type of the array element produced by the expression:

IndexExpression
├─────────── Term ─────────── [─── Expression ───] ───────────┤

When the compiler evaluates an index expression, the term to the left of the square brackets is evaluated before the expression inside of the square brackets. If the term produces the value null, a NullPointerException is thrown.

Array indexing uses an int-valued expression between the square brackets. If the type of the expression is byte, char, or short, the value is automatically converted to int. An array index cannot be of type long. The value of the array index must be in the range zero to one less than the length of the array. An array object detects an out-of-range index value and throws an ArrayIndexOutOf-BoundsException.

Because of the precedence of Java expressions, an array allocation expression can only be indexed when the expression is enclosed in parentheses. For example:

```
(new int[6])[3]
```

This expression refers to the fourth element of the newly created array. Leaving out the parentheses results in the following:

```
new int[6][3]
```

This is not an index expression, but an array allocation expression that allocates an array of 3 arrays of 6 integers.

References Array Allocation Expressions 4.2.2; Array Types 3.2.3; *Expression* 4; *Term* 4.1; Exceptions 9.4.1

4.1.8 Method Call Expression

A *method call expression* is a primary expression that invokes a method:

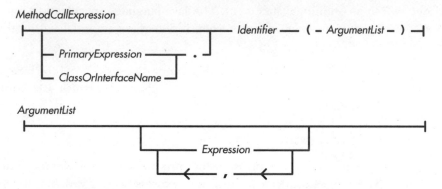

A method call expression produces the pure value returned by the method; the type of this value is specified by the return type in the method declaration. But if the method has the return type void, the expression does not produce a value.

The *PrimaryExpression*, if present, is evaluated first. Then expressions provided as method arguments are evaluated from left to right. Finally, the method is invoked.

When a method call is made to a method that is not static, the call is made through an object reference:

- If the method call expression does not contain a *PrimaryExpression* or *ClassOrInterfaceName* before the method name, the method call is made implicitly through the object referenced by the keyword this. This form of a method call expression is treated as if it were written:

    this.*Identifier*(...)

- If the method call expression contains a *PrimaryExpression* before the method name, the call is made through the object reference produced by the *PrimaryExpression.*

- If the method call expression contains a *ClassOrInterfaceName* before the method name, then the specified class must either be the same class in which the method call expression appears or a superclass of that class. In this case, the method call is made through the object referenced by the keyword this. This form of a method call expression is treated as if it were written:

    ((*ClassOrInterfaceName*)this).*Identifier*(...)

When a method call is made to a `static` method, the call is made through a class or interface type:

- If the method call expression does not contain a *PrimaryExpression* or *ClassOrInterfaceName* before the method name, the method call is made implicitly through the class that contains the call.

- If the method call expression contains a *PrimaryExpression* before the method name, the call is made through the class of the object reference produced by the *PrimaryExpression*.

- If the method call expression contains a *ClassOrInterfaceName* before the method name, the method call is made through the specified class or interface type.

The rules for supplying actual values for the formal parameters of a method are similar to the rules for assignment. A particular value can be specified as the actual value of a formal parameter if and only if it is assignment-compatible with the type of the formal parameter. You can use a type cast to make a value assignment compatible with a formal parameter.

The process that the Java compiler uses to select the actual method that will be invoked at runtime is rather involved. The compiler begins by finding any methods that have the specified name. If the method call has been made through an object reference, the compiler searches in the class of that object reference. If the call has been made through a specific class or interface name, the compiler searches in that class or interface. The compiler searches all of the methods defined in the particular class or interface, as well as any methods that are inherited from superclasses or super-interfaces. At this point, the compiler is searching for both `static` and non-static methods, since it does not know which type of method is being called.

If the compiler finds more than one method, that means the method is overloaded. Consider this example:

```
public class MyMath {
    public int square(int x) { return x*x; }
    public long square(long x) { return x*x; }
    public float square(float x) { return x*x; }
    public double square(double x) { return x*x; }

    public double hypotenuse(double x, double y) {
        return Math.sqrt(x*x + y*y);
    }
}
```

In the above example, the `square()` method is overloaded, while `hypotenuse()` is not.

If the method is overloaded, the compiler then determines which of the methods has formal parameters that are compatible with the given arguments. If more than one method is compatible with the given arguments, the method that most closely matches the given parameters is selected. If the compiler cannot select one of the methods as a better match than the others, the method selection process fails and the compiler issues an error message. Note that the return types of overloaded methods play no part in selecting which method is to be invoked.

After the compiler successfully selects the method that most closely matches the specified arguments, it knows the name and signature of the method that will be invoked at runtime. It does not, however, know for certain what class that method will come from. Although the compiler may have selected a method from `MyMath`, it is possible that a subclass of `MyMath` could define a method that has the same name and the same number and types of parameters as the selected method. In this case, the method in the subclass overrides the method in `MyMath`. The compiler cannot know about overriding methods, so it generates runtime code that dynamically selects the appropriate method.

Here are the details of the three-step method selection process:

Step One

The method definitions are searched for methods that, taken in isolation, could be called by the method call expression. If the method call expression uses an object reference, the search takes place in the class of that object reference. If the expression uses a specific class or interface name, the search takes place in that class or interface. The search includes all of the methods defined in the particular class or interface, as well as any methods inherited from superclasses or super-interfaces. The search also includes both `static` and non-`static` methods.

A method is a candidate if it meets the following criteria:

- The name of the method is the same as the name specified in the method call expression.

- The method is accessible to the method call expression, based on any access modifiers specified in the method's declaration.

- The number of formal parameters declared for the method is the same as the number of actual arguments provided in the method call expression.

- The data type of each actual parameter is assignment-compatible with the corresponding formal parameter.

Consider the following expression that calls a method defined in the preceding example:

```
MyMath m;
m.square(3.4F)
```

Here is how the Java compiler uses the above criteria to decide which method the expression actually calls:

- The name `square` matches four methods defined in the `MyMath` class, so the compiler must decide which one of those methods to invoke.

- All four methods are declared `public`, so they are all accessible to the above expression and are thus all still viable candidates.

- The method call expression provides one argument. Since the four methods under consideration each take one argument, there are still four possible choices.

- The method call expression is passing a `float` argument. Because a `float` value cannot be assigned to an `int` or a `long` variable, the compiler can eliminate the versions of `square()` that take these types of arguments. That still leaves two possible methods for the above expression: the version of `square()` that takes a `float` argument and the one that takes a `double` argument.

Step Two

If more than one method meets the criteria in Step One, the compiler tries to determine if one method is a more specific match than the others. If there is no method that matches more specifically, the selection process fails and the compiler issues an error message.

Given two methods, `A()` and `B()`, that are both candidates to be invoked by the same method call expression, `A()` is more specific than `B()` if:

- The class in which the method `A()` is declared is the same class or a subclass of the class in which the method `B()` is declared.

- Each parameter of `A()` is assignment-compatible with the corresponding parameter of `B()`.

Let's go back to our previous example. We concluded by narrowing the possible methods that the expression `m.square(3.4F)` might match to the methods in `MyMath` named `square()` that take either a `float` or a `double` argument. Using the criteria of this step, we can further narrow the possibilities. These methods are declared in the same class, but the version of `square()` that takes a `float` value is more specific than the one that takes a `double` value. It is more specific because a `float` value can be assigned to a `double` variable, but a `double` value cannot be assigned to a `float` variable without a type cast.

There are some cases in which it is not possible to choose one method that is more specific than others. When this happens, the Java compiler treats the situation as an error and issues an appropriate error message.

For example, consider a situation where the compiler needs to choose between two methods declared as follows:

```
double foo(float x, double y)
double foo(double x, float y)
```

Neither method is more specific than the other. The first method is not more specific because the type of its second parameter is `double` and `double` values cannot be assigned to `float` variables. The second method is not more specific because of a similar problem with its first parameter.

Step Three

After successfully completing the previous two steps, the Java compiler knows that the expression in our example will call a method named `square()` and that the method will take one `float` argument. However, the compiler does not know if the method called at runtime will be the one defined in the `MyMath` class. It is possible that a subclass of `MyMath` could define a method that is also called `square()` and takes a single `float` argument. This method in a subclass would override the method in `MyMath`. If the variable m in the expression `m.square(3.4F)` refers to such a subclass, the method defined in the subclass is called instead of the one defined in `MyMath`.

The Java compiler generates code to determine at runtime which method named `square()` that takes a single `float` argument it should call. The Java compiler must always generate such runtime code for method call expressions, unless it is able to determine at compile time the exact method to be invoked at runtime.

There are four cases in which the compiler can know exactly which method is to be called at runtime:

- The method is called through an object reference, and the type of the reference is a `final` class. Since the type of the reference is a `final` class, Java does not allow any subclasses of that class to be defined. Therefore, the object reference will always refer to an object of the class declared `final`. The Java compiler knows the actual class that the reference will refer to, so it can know the actual method to be called at runtime.

- The method is invoked through an object reference, and the type of the reference is a class that defines or inherits a `final` method that has the method name, number of parameters, and types of parameters determined by the preceding steps. In this case, the compiler knows the actual method to be called at runtime because `final` methods cannot be overridden.

- The method is a `static` method. When a method is declared static, it is also implicitly declared final. Thus, the compiler can be sure that the method to be called at runtime is the one defined in or inherited by the specified class that has the method name, number of parameters, and types of parameters determined by the preceding steps.

- The compiler is able to deduce that a method is invoked through an object reference that will always refer to the same class of object at runtime. One way the compiler might deduce this is through data flow analysis.

If none of the above cases applies to a method call expression, the Java compiler must generate runtime code to determine the actual method to be invoked. The runtime selection process begins by getting the class of the object through which the method is being invoked. This class is searched for a method that has the same name and the same number and types of parameters as the method selected in Step Two. If this class does not contain such a definition, its immediate superclass is searched. If the immediate superclass does not contain an appropriate definition, its superclasses are searched, and so on up the inheritance hierarchy. This search process is called *dynamic method lookup.*

Dynamic method lookup always begins with the class of the actual object being referenced. The type of the reference being used to access the object does not influence where the search for a method begins. The one exception to this rule occurs when the keyword `super` is used as part of the method call expression. The form of this type of method call expression is:

    super.*Identifier*(...)

In this case, dynamic method lookup begins by searching the superclass of the class that the calling code appears in.

Now that we've gone through the entire method selection process, let's consider an example that illustrates the process:

```
class A {}
class B extends A {}
class C extends B {}
class D extends C {}

class W {
    void foo(D d) {System.out.println("C");}
}
```

```
class X extends W {
    void foo(A a) {System.out.println("A");}
    void foo(B b) {System.out.println("X.B");}
}
class Y extends X {
    void foo(B b) {System.out.println("Y.B");}
}
class Z extends Y {
    void foo(C c) {System.out.println("D");}
}
public class CallSelection {
    public static void main(String [] argv) {
        Z z = new Z();
        ((X) z).foo(new C());
    }
}
```

In the class `CallSelection`, the method `main()` contains a call to a method named `foo()`. This method is called through an object reference. Although the object refers to an instance of the class Z, it is treated as an instance of the class X because the reference is type cast to the class X. The process of selecting which method to call proceeds as follows:

1. The compiler finds all of the methods named `foo()` that are accessible through an object of class X: `foo(A)`, `foo(B)`, and `foo(D)`. However, because a reference to an object of class C cannot be assigned to a variable of class D, `foo(D)` is not a candidate to be invoked by the method call expression.

2. Now the compiler must choose one of the two remaining `foo()` methods as more specific than the other. Both methods are defined in the same class, but `foo(B)` is more specific than `foo(A)` because a reference to an object of class B can be assigned to a variable declared with a type of class A.

3. At runtime, the dynamic method lookup process finds that it has a reference to an object of class Z. The fact that the reference is cast to class X is not significant, since dynamic lookup is concerned with the class of an object, not the type of the reference used to access the object. The definition of class Z is searched for a method named `foo()` that takes one parameter that is a reference to an object of class B. No such method is found in the definition of class Z, so its immediate superclass, class Y, is searched. Such a method is found in class Y, so that method is invoked.

Here is another example that shows some ambiguous and erroneous method call expressions:

```
class A {}
class B extends A {}
class AmbiguousCall {
    void foo(B b, double x){}
    void foo(A a, int i){}
```

```
        void doit() {
            foo(new A(), 8);    // Matches foo(A, int)
            foo(new A(), 8.0);  // Error: doesn't match anything
            foo(new B(), 8);    // Error: ambiguous, matches both
            foo(new B(), 8.0);  // Matches foo(B, double)
        }
    }
```

References Assignment Compatibility 4.13.1; *ClassOrInterfaceName* 4.1.6; Casts 4.4.5; *Expression* 4; *Identifier* 2.2.1; Inheritance 5.3.5; Interface Methods 5.5.6; Methods 5.4.6; *PrimaryExpression* 4.1

4.1.9 Class Literals

A *class literal* is an expression that produces a reference to a Class object that identifies a specified data type. Class literals are not supported prior to Java 1.1. Here's the syntax for a class literal:

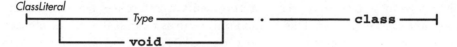

If the type in a class literal is a reference type, the class literal produces a reference to the Class object that defines the specified reference type. The following are some examples of this type of class literal:

```
String.class
java.util.Stack.class
myNewClass.class
```

Such a class literal can throw a NoClassDefFoundError if the specified class is not available.

You can also call Class.forName() with the name of a specified reference type to retrieve the Class object for that type. For example:

```
Class.forName("java.util.Stack")
```

A class literal and a call to Class.forName() for the same reference type return the same Class object. There are certain situations when it makes sense to use a class literal, while in other cases a call to Class.forName() is more appropriate. Here are the differences between the two techniques for retrieving a Class object:

● A class literal cannot contain an expression, so it always refers to the same type. However, the argument passed to Class.forName() can be an expression that produces different strings that name different classes.

- The class or interface name passed to `Class.forName()` must be fully quali-fied by its package name. The class or interface name in a class literal, how-ever, does not typically need to include a package name because the Java com-piler can use information provided in package and import directives to deduce the package name.

- The name of an inner class can be used directly with a class literal. Because of the way that inner-class names are encoded, however, when an inner-class name is passed to `Class.forName()`, the name must contain dollar signs ($) in place of dots (`.`).

- The efficiency of a class literal is comparable to a field reference; it is more efficient than the method call required by `Class.forName()`.

If the type in a class literal is `void` or a primitive type, the class literal produces a reference to a unique `Class` object that represents `void` or the specified type. The special `Class` object that represents `void` or a primitive type can be distin-guished from a `Class` object that represents a reference type by calling its `isPrimitive()` method. This method only returns `true` if the `Class` object rep-resents `void` or a primitive type. The `getName()` method of a special `Class` object returns a string that contains the name of the primitive type represented by the object. The easiest way to determine the primitive type of a special `Class` object is to compare it to the `TYPE` variables of the primitive wrapper classes. The following comparisons always produce `true`:

```
boolean.class == Boolean.TYPE
byte.class == Byte.TYPE
short.class == Short.TYPE
int.class == Integer.TYPE
long.class == Long.TYPE
char.class == Character.TYPE
float.class == Float.TYPE
double.class == Double.TYPE
void.class == Void.TYPE
```

References Boolean 10.1; Byte 10.2; Character 10.3; Class 10.4; Double 10.8; Errors 9.4.2; Float 10.9; Inner Classes 5.3.7; Integer 10.10; Long 10.11; Short 10.19; Void 10.26; *Type* 3

4.2 *Allocation Expressions*

An *allocation expression* is a primary expression that creates an object or an array. An allocation expression also produces a reference to the newly created object or array:

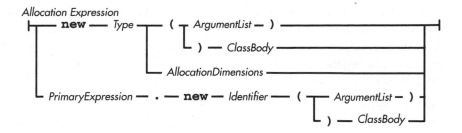

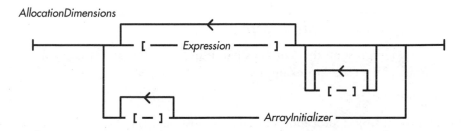

When *AllocationExpression* contains parentheses, the allocation expression creates a non-array object. When *AllocationExpression* contains square brackets, the allocation expression creates an array.

An object created by an allocation expression continues to exist until the program terminates or it is freed by the garbage collector (see 5.3.4 Object Destruction). Consider the following code:

```
class X {
    Double perm;
    void foo() {
        Double d = new Double(8.9473);
        int a[] = new int [2];
        d = new Double(3.1415926);
        a[0] = d.intValue();
        perm = d;
    }
}
```

The first line of foo() creates a Double object and uses it as the initial value of the variable d. The second line creates an array of integers and uses it as the initial value of the variable a. At this point, neither of the two objects that has been created is a candidate for garbage collection because there is a variable referencing each of them.

The third line of foo creates another Double object and assigns it to the variable d. Now there is nothing that refers to the first Double object that we created, so that object can now be garbage collected at any time.

When the block in this example finishes executing, the variables declared inside of the block, a and d, pass out of scope. Now there is nothing referring to the array object that we created; now that object can be garbage-collected at any time. However, because the variable perm now refers to the second Double object we created, that object is not a candidate for garbage collection.

References *ArgumentList* 4.1.8; *ClassBody* 5.4; *ArrayInitializer* 5.4.5.4; *Expression* 4; *Identifier* 2.2.1; Object Creation 5.3.3; Object Destruction 5.3.4; *PrimaryExpression* 4.1; *Type* 3

4.2.1 Object Allocation Expressions

An allocation expression that contains parentheses creates a non-array object; that is, an instance of a class. For example:

```
new Double(93.1872)
```

The *Type* in an object allocation expression must be a class or interface type. The argument list supplied between the parentheses provides the actual arguments to be passed to the object's constructor. However, if a *ClassBody* follows the parentheses, no arguments may appear between the parentheses, and different rules apply. (These rules are discussed in 4.2.1.1 Allocating instances of anonymous classes.)

If new is preceded by a *PrimaryExpression* and a dot, the *PrimaryExpression* must produce a reference to an object. Furthermore, the object's class must be an inner or nested top-level class that is named by the identifier that follows new. If the specified class is a non-static inner class, the object created by the allocation expression has the object referenced by the *PrimaryExpression* as its enclosing instance. For example:

```
class Z {
    class Y {
    ...
    }

    public static void main(String[] argv) {
        Z myZ = new Z();
        Z.Y myY = myZ.new Y();
    }
}
```

In the preceding example, we must supply an explicit enclosing instance of Z to create a Z.Y object because main() is a static method. A non-static method of Z could create an instance of Z.Y without supplying an explicit enclosing instance of Z because the method itself is associated with an instance of Z. However, because a static method is not associated with an instance of its class, it must supply an explicit enclosing instance when creating an instance of an inner class.

The syntax that allows new to be preceded by a *PrimaryExpression* and a dot is not supported prior to Java 1.1.

The remainder of this section applies only to allocation expressions that contain parentheses but no *ClassBody*. Allocation expressions that contain a *ClassBody* are described in 4.2.1.1 Allocating instances of anonymous classes.

An object allocation expression performs the following steps:

1.   Creates a new object with all of its instance variables set to their default values. The default values for these variables are determined by their types.

2.   Calls the constructor that matches the given argument list.

3.   Produces a reference to the initialized object.

The process of selecting the appropriate constructor to call is similar to the process used to select the method invoked by a method call expression. The compiler determines which constructors have formal parameters compatible with the given arguments. If there is more than one suitable constructor, the compiler must select the constructor that most closely matches the given arguments. If the compiler cannot select one constructor as a better match than the others, the constructor selection process fails and an error message is issued.

Here are the details of the constructor selection process:

Step One
>   The constructor definitions are searched for constructors that, taken in isolation, could be called by the allocation expression. A constructor is a candidate if it meets the following criteria:
>
>   •   The constructor is accessible to the allocation expression, based on any access modifiers specified in the constructor's declaration.
>
>   •   The number of formal parameters declared for the constructor is the same as the number of actual arguments provided in the allocation expression.
>
>   •   The data type of each actual parameter is assignment-compatible with the corresponding formal parameter.

Step Two
>   If more than one constructor meets the criteria in Step One, the Java compiler tries to determine if one constructor is a more specific match than the others. If there is no constructor that matches more specifically, the constructor selection process fails and an error message is issued.

Given two constructors that are both candidates to be invoked by the same object allocation expression, one constructor is more specific than another constructor if each parameter of the first constructor is assignment-compatible with the corresponding parameter of the second constructor.

When an object allocation expression is evaluated, the constructor selected in Step Two is invoked. This constructor returns a reference to the newly created object.

Here's an example that shows how the constructor selection process works:

```
class Consel {
    Consel() { }
    Consel(Object o, double d) {}
    Consel(String s, int i) {}
    Consel(int i, int j) {}
    public void main(String[] argv) {
        Consel c = new Consel("abc",4);
    }
}
```

The main() method in the Consel class creates a new Consel object. The process of selecting which constructor to call proceeds as follows:

1. The compiler finds all of the constructors that are accessible to the new operator. Since all of the constructors are accessible, the compiler then narrows its choices to those constructors that have the same number of formal parameters as the number of actual arguments in the allocation expression. This step eliminates the constructor with no formal parameters, so now there are three choices. The compiler again narrows its choices to those constructors with formal parameters that are assignment-compatible with the actual values. Because a String is not assignment-compatible with an int variable, the compiler eliminates the constructor that takes two int parameters.

2. Now the compiler must choose which of the two remaining constructors is more specific than the other. Because a String object reference can be assigned to an Object variable and an int value can be assigned to a double variable, the constructor Consel(String s, int i) is the more specific of the two. This constructor is the one that is invoked to create the Consel object.

References Allocating instances of anonymous classes 4.2.1.1; Assignment Compatibility 4.13.1; *ClassBody* 5.4; Class Types 3.2.1; Constructors 5.4.7; Interface Types 3.2.2; *PrimaryExpression* 4.1

4.2.1.1 Allocating instances of anonymous classes

An allocation expression that contains a *ClassBody* creates an instance of an *anonymous class*. It is called an anonymous class because it has no name of its own. The variables and methods of an anonymous class are defined in the *ClassBody*. If the type specified after new is a class, the anonymous class is a subclass of that class. If the type specified after new is an interface, the anonymous class implements that interface and is a subclass of Object. For example:

```
public class MainFrame extends Frame {
    ...
    public MainFrame(String title) {
        super(title);
        WindowAdapter listener;
        listener = new WindowAdapter() {
            public void windowClosing(WindowEvent evt) {
                exit();
            }
        };
        addWindowListener(listener);
    }
    ...
}
```

The example creates an instance of an anonymous subclass of the WindowAdapter class. If an allocation expression contains a *ClassBody*, it cannot contain any arguments between the parentheses because an anonymous class cannot declare any constructors. Instead, an anonymous class must use instance initializers to handle any complex initialization.

The body of an anonymous class cannot declare any static variables, static methods, static classes, or static initializers. Anonymous classes are not supported prior to Java 1.1.

References Anonymous classes 5.3.7.4; *ClassBody* 5.4; Constructors 5.4.7; Instance Initializers 5.4.10; Methods 5.4.6; Nested Top-Level and Member Classes 5.4.11; Static Initializers 5.4.9; Variables 5.4.5

4.2.2 Array Allocation Expressions

An allocation expression that contains square brackets creates an array, such as:

```
new int[10]
```

An array allocation expression performs the following steps:

1. Allocates storage for the array

2. Sets the length variable of the array and initializes the array elements to their default values

3. Produces a reference to the initialized array

Although Java does not support multi-dimensional arrays, it does support arrays of arrays. The most important distinction between a multi-dimensional array and an array of arrays is that in an array of arrays, each array need not be of the same length. Because arrays of arrays are most often used to represent multi-dimensional arrays, this book refers to them as multi-dimensional arrays, even though that is not precisely correct.

The type of the array created by an array allocation expression can be expressed by removing both the word new and the expressions from within the square brackets. For example, here is an allocation expression:

```
new int[3][4][5]
```

The type of the array produced by that expression is:

```
int[][][]
```

This means that the number of dimensions in the array produced by an allocation expression is the same as the number of pairs of square brackets in the allocation expression.

The expressions that appear in the square brackets must be of type int, short, char, or byte. Each of the expressions specifies the length of a single dimension of the array that is being created. For example, the allocation expression above creates an array of 3 arrays of 4 arrays of 5 int values. The length supplied for an array must not be negative. At runtime, if an expression in square brackets produces a negative array length, a NegativeArraySizeException is thrown.

The syntax of an array allocation expression specifies that the first pair of square brackets must contain an expression, while the trailing square brackets do not need to. This means that an array allocation expression can be written to build fewer dimensions of an array than there are dimensions in the array's type. For example, consider this allocation expression:

```
new char [10][]
```

The array produced by this allocation expression is an array of arrays of char. The allocation expression creates a single array of 10 elements, where each of those elements is a char array of unspecified length.

Array allocation expressions are often used to initialize array variables. Here are some examples:

```
int j[] = new int[10];        // array of 10 ints
ing k[][] = new float[3][4];  // array of 3 arrays
                              // of 4 floats
```

Here's an example that builds an array of different length arrays, or in other words a non-rectangular array of arrays:

```
int a[][] = new int [3][];
a[0] = new int [5];
a[1] = new int [6];
a[2] = new int [7];
```

None of the array allocation expressions presented so far have used array initializers. When an array allocation expression does not include an array initializer, the array is created with all of its elements set to a default value. The default value is based on the type of the array. Table 4-1 shows the default values used for the various types in Java.

Table 4–1: Default Values for Array Elements

Array Type	Default Value
byte	0
char	'\u0000'
short	0
int	0
long	0L
float	0.0F
double	0.0
Boolean	false
Object reference	null

If you want to create an array that contains elements with different initial values, you can include an *ArrayInitializer* at the end of the allocation expression. For example:

```
new int [] { 4,7,9 }
```

Notice that there is no expression between the square brackets. If an allocation expression contains square brackets and no *ArrayInitializer*, at least the first pair of square brackets must contain an expression. However, if an allocation expression does contain an *ArrayInitializer*, there cannot be any expressions between any of the square brackets. An allocation expression that contains an *ArrayInitializer* can be used to create an anonymous array: one that is created and initialized without using a variable initializer.

The syntax that allows an *ArrayInitializer* in an allocation expression is not supported prior to Java 1.1.

References Array Types 3.2.3; *ArrayInitializer* 5.4.5.4; Index Expressions 4.1.7

4.3 Increment/Decrement Operators

The ++ operator is used to increment the contents of a variable or an array element by one, while the -- operator is used to decrement such a value by one. The operand of ++ or -- must evaluate to a variable or an array element; it cannot be an expression that produces a pure value. For example, the following operations succeed because the operand of the ++ operator produces a variable:

```
int g = 0;
g++;
```

However, the following uses of ++ generate error messages:

```
final int h = 23;
h++;
5++;
```

The expression h++ produces an error because h is declared final, which means that its value cannot be changed. The expression 5++ generates an error message because 5 is a literal value, not a variable.

The increment and decrement operators can be used in both postfix expressions (e.g., i++ or i--) and in prefix expressions (e.g., ++i or --i). Although both types of expression have the same side effect of incrementing or decrementing a variable, they differ in the values that they produce. A postfix expression produces a pure value that is the value of the variable before it is incremented or decremented, while a prefix expression produces a pure value that is the value of the variable after it has been incremented or decremented. For example, consider the following code fragment:

```
int i = 3, j = 3;
System.out.println( "i++ produces " + i++);
System.out.println( "++j produces " + ++j);
```

The above code fragment produces the following output:

```
i++ produces 3
++j produces 4
```

After the code fragment has been evaluated, both i and j have the value 4.

In essence, what you need to remember is that a prefix expression performs its increment or decrement before producing a value, while a postfix expression performs its increment or decrement after producing a value.

4.3.1 Postfix Increment/Decrement Operators

A postfix increment/decrement expression is a primary expression that may be followed by either a ++ or a – –:

The postfix increment and decrement operators are equal in precedence and are effectively non-associative.

If a postfix expression includes a ++ or – –, the primary expression must produce a variable or an array element of an arithmetic type. The postfix increment operator (++) has the side effect of incrementing the contents of the variable or array element by one. The postfix decrement operator (– –) has the side effect of decrementing the contents of the variable or array element by one.

The data type of the value produced by a postfix increment/decrement operator is the same as the data type of the variable or array element produced by the primary expression. A postfix increment/decrement operator produces the original pure value stored in the variable or array element before it is incremented or decremented.

The following is an example of using a postfix decrement operator:

```
char j = '\u0100';
while (j-- > 0)        // call doit for char values
    doit(j);           // '\u00ff' through '\u0000'
```

This example works because Java treats char as an arithmetic data type.

References Arithmetic Types 3.1.1; Order of Operations 4.14; *PrimaryExpression* 4.1

4.3.2 Prefix Increment/Decrement Operators

A prefix increment/decrement expression is a primary expression that may be preceded by either a ++ or a – –:

The prefix increment and decrement operators are equal in precedence and are effectively non-associative.

If a prefix expression includes a ++ or – –, the primary expression must produce a variable or an array element of an arithmetic type. The prefix increment operator (++) has the side effect of incrementing the contents of the variable or array element by one. The prefix decrement operator (– –) has the side effect of decrementing the contents of the variable or array element by one.

The data type of the value produced by a prefix increment/decrement operator is the same as the data type of the variable or array element produced by the primary expression. A prefix increment/decrement operator produces the pure value stored in the variable or array element after it has been incremented or decremented.

Here's an example of using a prefix increment operator:

```
void foo(int a[]) {
    int j = -1;
    while (++j < a.length)      // call doit for each element
        doit(a[j]);             // of a
}
```

References Arithmetic Types 3.1.1; Order of Operations 4.14; *PrimaryExpression* 4.1

4.4 *Unary Operators*

Unary operators are operators that take exactly one argument. Unary operators may appear in a unary expression:

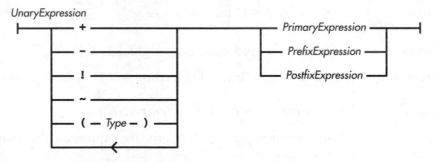

The unary plus and minus operators, a Boolean negation operator (!), a bitwise negation operator (~), and the cast construct comprise the unary operators in Java. The unary operators are equal in precedence and are evaluated from right to left.

References Order of Operations 4.14; *PostfixExpression* 4.3.1; *PrefixExpression* 4.3.2; *PrimaryExpression* 4.1; *Type* 3

4.4.1 Unary Plus Operator +

The unary plus operator (+) can appear as part of a unary expression. The operator does no explicit computation; it produces the same pure value that is produced by its operand. However, the unary + operator may perform a type conversion on its operand. The type of the operand must be an arithmetic data type, or a compile-time error occurs. If the type of the operand is byte, short, or char, the unary + operator produces an int value; otherwise the operator produces a value of the same type as its operand.

References Arithmetic Types 3.1.1

4.4.2 Unary Minus Operator −

The unary minus operator (−) can appear as part of a unary expression. The type of the operand of the unary − operator must be an arithmetic data type, or a compile-time error occurs. The operator produces a pure value that is the arithmetic negation (i.e., additive inverse) of the value of its operand.

The unary − operator may perform a type conversion. If the type of the operand is byte, short, or char, the operation converts the operand to an int before computing the value's arithmetic negation and producing an int value. Otherwise, unary − produces a value of the same type as its operand.

For integer data types, the unary − operator produces a value equivalent to subtracting its operand from zero. There are, however, negative values for which the unary − operator cannot produce a positive value; in these cases it produces the same negative value as its operand. This behavior results from the two's complement representation Java uses for integer values. The magnitude of the most negative number that can be represented using two's complement notation cannot be represented as a positive number. No exception is thrown when the unary − operator is given a value that cannot be negated. However, you can detect this situation by explicitly testing for these special values. The most negative int value is available as the predefined constant Integer.MIN_VALUE and the most negative long value is available as the predefined constant Long.MIN_VALUE.

For floating-point data types, the unary − operator changes the sign of its operand from + to − or from − to +, for both regular values, positive and negative zero, and positive and negative infinity. The only case where this is not true occurs when the operand is not-a-number (NaN). Given the value NaN, the unary − operator produces NaN.

References Arithmetic Types 3.1.1; Integer 10.10; Long 10.11

4.4.3 Boolean Negation Operator !

The Boolean negation operator (!) may appear as part of a unary expression. The type of the operand of the ! operator must be `boolean`, or a compile-time error occurs. If the value of its operand is `false`, the ! operator produces the pure `boolean` value `true`. If the value of its operand is `true`, the operator produces the pure `boolean` value `false`.

Here is an example that uses the Boolean negation operator:

```
public void paint(Graphics g) {
    if (!loaded) {
        //The next 2 lines are executed if loaded is false
        g.drawString("Loading data", 25, 25);
        return;
    }
    g.drawImage(img, 25, 25, this);
}
```

References Boolean Type 3.1.2

4.4.4 Bitwise Negation Operator ˜

The bitwise negation operator (˜) may appear as part of a unary expression. The type of the operand of the ˜ operator must be an integer data type, or a compile-time error occurs. The ˜ operator may perform a type conversion before it performs its computation. If the type of the operand is `byte`, `short`, or `char`, the operator converts its operand to `int` before producing a value. Otherwise the ˜ operator produces a value of the same type as its operand.

After type conversion, the bitwise negation operator produces a pure value that is the bitwise complement of its operand. In other words, if a bit in the converted operand contains a one, the corresponding bit in the result contains a zero. If a bit in the converted operand contains a zero, the corresponding bit in the result contains a one.

Here's an example that shows the use of the bitwise negation operator:

```
// zero low order four bits
int getNibble(int x) {
    return x & ˜0xf;
}
```

References Integer types 3.1.1.1

4.4.5 *Casts*

A *Type* enclosed in parentheses specifies a type cast operation. A cast may appear as part of a unary expression. A cast operation always produces a pure value of the specified type, by converting its operand to that type if necessary. This is different from a type cast in C/C++, which can produce garbage if it is given a pointer to a data type different than that implied by the pointer's declaration. If the actual data type of the operand of a cast cannot be guaranteed at compile-time, the Java compiler must produce code to check the type of the operand at runtime. In Java, any value that gets past all of the type-checking done on a cast is guaranteed to be compatible with the type specified by the cast.

A cast can convert between certain primitive types. A cast between object reference types never alters the type or content of the object, but may alter the type of the reference to the object.

Because it is not possible to convert between all types, some cast operations are permitted and others are not. Here are the rules governing casts:

- A value of any data type can be cast to its own type.

- A value of any arithmetic data type can be cast to any other arithmetic data type. Casting a floating-point value to an integer data type rounds toward zero.

- A value of the `boolean` data type cannot be cast to any other data type, nor can a value of any other data type be cast to `boolean`.

- A value of any primitive data type cannot be cast to a reference data type, nor can a reference be cast to any primitive data type.

- A reference to a class type can be cast to the type of the superclass of that class.

- A reference to a class type can be cast to the type of a subclass of that class if the reference actually refers to an object of the specified class or any of its subclasses. Unless the Java compiler can prove that the object actually referenced is of the specified class or any of its subclasses, the compiler must generate a runtime test to verify that the object is of an appropriate type. At runtime, if the object actually referenced is not of an appropriate type, a `ClassCast-Exception` is thrown. Consider the following example:

```
Object o = "ABC";
String s = (String)o;   // This is okay
Double d = (Double)o,   // Throws an exception
```

The cast of o to `String` is fine because o is really a reference to a `String` object. The cast of o to `Double` throws an exception at runtime because the object that o references is not an instance of `Double`.

- A reference to a class type can be cast to an interface type if the reference actually refers to an object of a class that implements the specified interface. If the class of the reference being cast is a `final` class, the compiler can determine if the reference actually refers to an object of a class that implements the specified interface, because a `final` class cannot have any subclasses. Otherwise, the compiler must generate a runtime test to determine if the reference actually refers to an object of a class that implements the specified interface. At runtime, if the object actually referenced is not of a class that implements the interface, a `ClassCastException` is thrown. Here is an example that illustrates the rules governing casts to interface types:

```
interface Weber { double flux(double x); }
class B {}
final class C {}
class D implements Weber {
    public double flux(double x) {
        return Math.PI*x*x;
    }
}
class Intercast {
    public void main(String[] argv) {
        B b = new B();
        C c = new C();
        D d = new D();
        Weber w;
        w = (Weber)b;    // Throws an exception
        w = (Weber)c;    // Compiler complains
        w = (Weber)d;    // Okay, D implements Weber
    }
}
```

    The cast of b to `Weber` is fine with the compiler because the class B might have a subclass that implements `Weber`. At runtime, however, this cast throws an exception because B does not implement `Weber`. The cast of c to `Weber` produces an error message from the compiler, as the C class does not implement `Weber`. Because C is `final`, it will not have any subclasses and therefore there is no possibility of c containing a reference to an object that implements the `Weber` interface. The cast of d to `Weber` is fine because the D class implements the `Weber` interface.

- A reference to the class `Object` can be cast to an array type if the reference actually refers to an array object of the specified type. The compiler generates a runtime test to determine if the reference actually refers to the specified type of array object. At runtime, if the object actually referenced is not the specified type of array, a `ClassCastException` is thrown.

- A reference to an interface type can be cast to a class type if the reference actually refers to an instance of the specified class or any of its subclasses. If the specified class is a `final` class that does not implement the referenced interface, the compiler can reject the cast because a `final` class cannot have any subclasses. Otherwise, the compiler generates a runtime test to determine if the reference actually refers to an object of the appropriate type. At runtime, if the object actually referenced is not of the appropriate type, a `ClassCastException` is thrown.

Here is an example to illustrate these points:

```
interface Weber { double flux(double x); }
class B {}
final class C {}
class D implements Weber {
    public double flux(double x) {
        return Math.PI*x*x;
    }
}
class Intercast {
    public void doit(Weber w) {
        B b = (B)w;    // May throw an exception
        C c = (C)w;    // Compiler complains
        D d = (D)w;    // Okay
    }
}
```

The cast of w to class B is fine with the compiler even though B does not implement Weber. The compiler lets it pass because B might have a subclass that implements Weber and w could contain a reference to that class. However, at runtime, the cast will throw an exception if the object actually referenced is not an instance of B or a subclass of B. The cast of w to class C produces an error message from the compiler. C does not implement Weber and C cannot have any subclasses because it is final; any object that implements Weber cannot be an instance of C. The cast of w to class D is fine at compile-time because D implements Weber. At runtime, if w references an object that is not an instance of D, a `ClassCastException` is thrown.

- A reference to an interface type can be cast to another interface type if the reference actually refers to an object of a class that implements the specified interface. If the referenced interface extends the specified interface, the compiler knows that the cast is legal. Otherwise, the compiler generates a runtime test to determine if the reference actually refers to an object that implements the specified interface. At runtime, if the object actually referenced does not implement the specified interface, a `ClassCastException` is thrown.

Here is an example to illustrate these points:

```
interface Weber { double flux(double x); }
interface Dyn { double squeeze(); }
interface Press extends Dyn {
    double squeeze(double theta);
}
class D implements Press {
    public double squeeze() { return Math.PI; }
    public double squeeze(double theta) {
        return Math.PI*Math.sin(theta);
    }
}
class Interinter {
    public static void doit(D d) {
        Dyn dyn = d;            // Okay
        Weber w = (Weber)d;     // May throw exception
    }
}
```

The assignment of d to dyn works because d is of class D, D implements Press, and Press extends Dyn. Therefore, d refers to an object that implements Dyn and we have assignment compatibility. The compiler lets the cast of d to Weber pass because there may be a subclass of D that implements Weber. At runtime, the cast will throw an exception if D does not implement Weber.

- A reference to an array object can be cast to the class type Object.

- A reference to an array object can be cast to another array type if either of the following is true:

  - The elements of the referenced array and the elements of the specified array type are of the same primitive type.

  - The elements of the referenced array are of a type that can be cast to the type of the elements of the specified array type.

Any cast operation not covered by the preceding rules is not allowed and the Java compiler issues an error message.

References Arithmetic Types 3.1.1; Array Types 3.2.3; Boolean Type 3.1.2; Class Types 3.2.1; Interface Types 3.2.2; Runtime exceptions 9.4.1.1

4.5 *Multiplicative Operators*

The multiplicative operators in Java are binary operators that are used for multiplication (*), division (/), and the remainder operation (%). The multiplicative operators appear in multiplicative expressions:

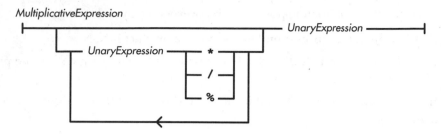

The multiplicative operators are equal in precedence and are evaluated from left to right.

References *UnaryExpression* 4.4; Order of Operations 4.14

4.5.1 Multiplication Operator *

The binary multiplication operator * produces a pure value that is the product of its operands. The * operator may appear in a multiplicative expression. The multiplication operator never throws an exception.

Here is an example that uses the multiplication operator:

```
int doubleIt(int x) {
    return x*2;
}
```

The types of both operands of the multiplication operator must be arithmetic types, or a compile-time error occurs. The * operator may perform type conversions on its operands:

- If either operand is of type double, the other operand is converted to double and the operation produces a double value.

- Otherwise, if either operand is of type float, the other operand is converted to float and the operation produces a float value.

- Otherwise, if either operand is of type long, the other operand is converted to long and the operation produces a long value.

- Otherwise, both operands are converted to int and the operation produces an int value.

If the multiplication of integer data overflows, the low order bits of the product are returned; no exception is thrown. The most significant bit of the low order bits is treated as a sign bit. When overflow occurs, the sign of the number produced may not be the same as the sign of the mathematically correct product, due to the limitations of the two's complement representation used for integer data.

The multiplication of floating-point data is governed by the following rules:

- If either operand is not-a-number (NaN), the product is NaN.

- If neither operand is NaN and if both operands have the same sign, the product is positive.

- If neither operand is NaN and if the operands have different signs, the product is negative.

- If one of the operands is positive or negative infinity and the other operand is positive or negative zero, the product is NaN.

- If one of the operands is an infinity value and the other operand is neither zero nor NaN, the product is either positive or negative infinity, as determined by the rules governing the sign of products.

- If neither operand is a zero value, an infinity value, or NaN, the product is rounded to the nearest representable value. If the magnitude of the product is too large to be represented, the operation overflows and an infinity value of the appropriate sign is produced. If the magnitude of the product is too small to be represented, the operation underflows and a zero value of the appropriate sign is produced.

References Arithmetic Types 3.1.1

4.5.2 Division Operator /

The binary division operator / produces a pure value that is the quotient of its operands. The left operand is the dividend and the right operand is the divisor. The / operator may appear in a multiplicative expression.

Here is an example that uses the division operator:

```
int halfIt(int x) {
    return x/2;
}
```

The types of both operands of the division operator must be arithmetic types, or a compile-time error occurs. The / operator may perform type conversions on its operands:

- If either operand is of type double, the other operand is converted to double and the operation produces a double value.

- Otherwise, if either operand is of type float, the other operand is converted to float and the operation produces a float value.

- Otherwise, if either operand is of type long, the other operand is converted to long and the operation produces a long value.

- Otherwise, both operands are converted to int and the operation produces an int value.

The division of integer data rounds toward zero. If the divisor of an integer division operator is zero, an ArithmeticException is thrown. If the dividend is Integer.MIN_VALUE or Long.MIN_VALUE and the divisor is -1, the quotient produced is Integer.MIN_VALUE or Long.MIN_VALUE, due to the limitations of the two's complement representation used for integer data.

The division of floating-point data is governed by the following rules:

- If either operand is not-a-number (NaN), the quotient is NaN.

- If neither operand is NaN and if both operands have the same sign, the quotient is positive.

- If neither operand is NaN and if the operands have different signs, the quotient is negative.

- If both of the operands are positive or negative infinity, the quotient is NaN.

- If the dividend is an infinity value and the divisor is a finite number, the quotient is either positive or negative infinity, as determined by the rules governing the sign of quotients.

- If the dividend is a finite number and the divisor is an infinity value, the quotient is either positive or negative zero, as determined by the rules governing the sign of quotients.

- If the divisor is positive or negative zero and the dividend is not zero or NaN, the quotient is either positive or negative infinity, as determined by the rules governing the sign of quotients.

- If both operands are zero values, the quotient is NaN.

- If the dividend is a zero value and the divisor is a non-zero finite number, the quotient is either positive or negative zero, as determined by the rules governing the sign of quotients.

- If the dividend is a non-zero finite number and the divisor is a zero value, the quotient is either positive or negative infinity, as determined by the rules governing the sign of quotients.

- If neither operand is a zero value, an infinity value, or NaN, the quotient is rounded to the nearest representable value. If the magnitude of the quotient is too large to be represented, the operation overflows and an infinity value of the appropriate sign is produced. If the magnitude of the quotient is too small to be represented, the operation underflows and a zero value of the appropriate sign is produced.

References Arithmetic Types 3.1.1; Integer 10.10; Long 10.11; Runtime exceptions 9.4.1.1

4.5.3 Remainder Operator %

The binary remainder operator % produces a pure value that is the remainder from an implied division of its operands. The left operand is the dividend and the right operand is the divisor. The % operator may appear in a multiplicative expression.

Here is an example that uses the remainder operator:

```
// format seconds into hours, minutes and seconds
String formatTime(int t) {
    int minutes, seconds;
    seconds = t%60;
    t /= 60;
    minutes = t%60;
    return t/60 + ":" + minutes + ":" + seconds;
}
```

The types of both operands of the remainder operator must be arithmetic types, or a compile-time error occurs. The % operator may perform type conversions on its operands:

- If either operand is of type double, the other operand is converted to double and the operation produces a double value.

- Otherwise, if either operand is of type float, the other operand is converted to float and the operation produces a float value.

- Otherwise, if either operand is of type long, the other operand is converted to long and the operation produces a long value.

- Otherwise, both operands are converted to int and the operation produces an int value.

When the remainder operation is performed on integer data, the following expression is guaranteed to produce the same value as a%b:

```
a-((a/b)*b)
```

The sign of the value produced by the remainder operator is always the sign of the dividend. The magnitude of the value produced by the remainder operator is always less than the absolute value of the divisor. If the divisor is zero, an ArithmeticException is thrown.

Unlike C/C++, Java provides a remainder operation for floating-point data. The remainder of floating-point data is computed in a manner similar to the remainder of integer data. The remainder operation uses a truncating division to compute its value. This is unlike the IEEE 754 remainder operation, which uses a rounding division. The IEEE remainder operation is provided by the `Math.IEEEremainder()` method.

The computation of the remainder of `double` and `float` data is governed by the following rules:

- If either operand is not-a-number (NaN), the remainder is NaN.

- If neither operand is NaN, the sign of the remainder is the same as the sign of the dividend.

- If the dividend is positive or negative infinity or the divisor is positive or negative zero, the remainder is NaN.

- If the dividend is a finite number and the divisor is an infinity value, the remainder is equal to the dividend.

- If the dividend is a zero value and the divisor is a finite number, the remainder is equal to the dividend.

- If neither operand is a zero value, an infinity value, or NaN, the remainder is computed according to the following mathematical formula:

$$p - \left\lfloor \frac{p}{d} \right\rfloor \times d$$

p is the dividend and d is the divisor. The notation $\lfloor x \rfloor$ means the greatest integer less than or equal to x; this is called the floor operation.

References Arithmetic Types 3.1.1; Math 10.12; Runtime exceptions 9.4.1.1

4.6 *Additive Operators*

The additive operators in Java are binary operators that are used for addition and string concatenation (+) and subtraction (-). The additive operators appear in additive expressions.

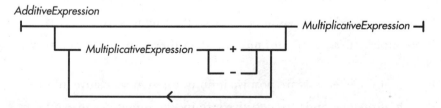

The additive operators are equal in precedence and are evaluated from left to right.

References *MultiplicativeExpression* 4.5; Order of Operations 4.14

4.6.1 Arithmetic Addition Operator +

The binary arithmetic addition operator + produces a pure value that is the sum of its operands. The arithmetic + operator may appear in an additive expression. The arithmetic addition operator never throws an exception.

Here is an example that uses the arithmetic addition operator:

```
int addThree (int x, int y, int z) {
    return x + y + z;
}
```

If the type of either operand of + is a reference to a `String` object, the operator is the string concatenation operator, not the arithmetic addition operator. The string concatenation operator is described in 4.6.3 String Concatenation Operator +.

Otherwise, the types of both operands of the arithmetic addition operator must be arithmetic types, or a compile-time error occurs. The + operator may perform type conversions on its operands:

- If either operand is of type `double`, the other operand is converted to `double` and the operation produces a `double` value.

- Otherwise, if either operand is of type `float`, the other operand is converted to `float` and the operation produces a `float` value.

- Otherwise, if either operand is of type `long`, the other operand is converted to `long` and the operation produces a `long` value.

- Otherwise, both operands are converted to `int` and the operation produces an `int` value.

If the addition of integer data overflows, the value produced by + contains the low order bits of the sum and the sign of the value is the opposite of the mathematically correct sign, due to the limitations of the two's complement representation used for integer data.

The addition of floating-point data is governed by the following rules:

- If either operand is not-a-number (NaN), the sum is NaN.

- If one operand is positive infinity and the other is negative infinity, the sum is NaN.

- If both of the operands are positive infinity, the sum is positive infinity.

- If both of the operands are negative infinity, the sum is negative infinity.

- If one of the operands is an infinity value and the other operand is a finite value, the sum is the same infinity value as the operand.

- If one operand is positive zero and the other is negative zero; the sum is positive zero.

- If both operands are positive zero, the sum is positive zero.

- If both operands are negative zero, the sum is negative zero.

- If neither operand is NaN nor an infinity value, the sum is rounded to the nearest representable value. If the magnitude of the sum is too large to be represented, the operation overflows and an infinity value of the appropriate sign is produced. If the magnitude of the sum is too small to be represented, the operation underflows and a zero value of the appropriate sign is produced.

References Arithmetic Types 3.1.1; String Concatenation Operator + 4.6.3

4.6.2 *Arithmetic Subtraction Operator* –

The binary subtraction operator – produces a pure value that is the difference between its operands; it subtracts its right operand from its left operand. The arithmetic – operator may appear in an additive expression. The arithmetic subtraction operator never throws an exception.

Here is an example that uses the arithmetic subtraction operator:

```
int subThree (int x, int y, int z) {
    return x - y - z;
}
```

The types of both operands of the arithmetic subtraction operator must be arithmetic types, or a compile-time error occurs. The – operator may perform type conversions on its operands:

- If either operand is of type `double`, the other operand is converted to `double` and the operation produces a `double` value.

- Otherwise, if either operand is of type `float`, the other operand is converted to `float` and the operation produces a `float` value.

- Otherwise, if either operand is of type `long`, the other operand is converted to `long` and the operation produces a `long` value.

- Otherwise, both operands are converted to `int` and the operation produces an `int` value.

For both integer and floating-point data, `a-b` always produces the same result as `a-(+b)`.

If the subtraction of integer data overflows, the value produced by – contains the low order bits of the difference and the sign of the value is the opposite of the mathematically correct sign, due to the limitations of the two's complement representation used for integer data.

The subtraction of floating-point data is governed by the following rules:

- If either operand is not-a-number (NaN), the difference is NaN.

- If the left operand is positive infinity and the right operand is negative infinity, the difference is positive infinity.

- If the left operand is negative infinity and the right operand is positive infinity, the difference is negative infinity.

- If both operands are positive infinity, the difference is NaN.

- If both operands are negative infinity, the difference is NaN.

- If the left operand is an infinity value and the right operand is a finite value, the difference is the same infinity value as the left operand.

- If the left operand is a finite value and the right argument is an infinity value, the difference is the opposite infinity value of the right operand.

- If both operands are either positive zero or negative zero, the difference is positive zero.

- If the left operand is positive zero and the right operand is negative zero, the difference is positive zero.

- If the left operand is negative zero and the right operand is positive zero, the difference is negative zero.

- If neither operand is NaN nor an infinity value, the difference is rounded to the nearest representable value. If the magnitude of the difference is too large to be represented, the operation overflows and an infinity value of the appropriate sign is produced. If the magnitude of the difference is too small to be represented, the operation underflows and a zero value of the appropriate sign is produced.

References Arithmetic Types 3.1.1

4.6.3 String Concatenation Operator +

The string concatenation operator + produces a pure value that is a reference to a `String` object that it creates. The `String` object contains the concatenation of the operands; the characters of the left operand precede the characters of the right operand in the newly created string. The string concatenation + operator may appear in an additive expression.

Here is an example of some code that uses the string concatenation operator:

```
// format seconds into hours, minutes, and seconds
String formatTime(int t) {
    int minutes, seconds;
    seconds = t%60;
    t /= 60;
    minutes = t%60;
    return t/60 + ":" + minutes + ":" + seconds;
}
```

If neither operand of + is a reference to a `String` object, the operator is the arithmetic addition operator, not the string concatenation operator. Note that Java does not allow a program to define overloaded operators. However, the language defines the + operator to have a meaning that is fundamentally different from arithmetic addition if at least one of its operands is a `String` object.

The way in which Java decides if + means arithmetic addition or string concatenation means that the use of parentheses can alter the meaning of the + operator. Consider the following code:

```
int x = 3, y = 4;
System.out.println("x = " + x + ", y = " + y);
System.out.println("\"??\" + x + y ==> " + "??" + x + y);
System.out.println("\"??\" + (x + y) ==> " + "??"+ (x + y));
```

In the output from this code, you can see that the addition of parentheses changes the meaning of the last + from string concatenation to arithmetic addition:

```
x = 3, y = 4
"??" + x + y ==> ??34
"??" + (x + y) ==> ??7
```

If one of the operands of + is a `String` object and the other is not, the operand that is not a `String` object is converted to one using the following rules:

- If the operand is an object reference that is `null`, it is converted to the string literal `"null"`.

- If the operand is a non-null reference to an object that is not a string, the object's `toString()` method is called. The result of the conversion is the string value returned by the object's `toString()` method, unless the return value is `null`, in which case the result of the conversion is the string literal `"null"`. Since the `Object` class defines a `toString()` method, every class in Java has such a method.

- If the type of the operand is `char`, the operand is converted to a reference to a `String` object that has a length of one and contains that character.

- If the type of the operand is an integer type other than char, the operand is converted to a base 10 string representation of its value. If the value is negative, the string value starts with a minus sign; if it is positive there is no sign character. If the value is zero, the result of the conversion is "0". Otherwise, the string representation of the integer does not have any leading zeros.

- If the type of the operand is a floating-point type, the exact string representation depends on the value being converted. If the absolute value of d is greater than or equal to 10^{-3} or less than or equal to 10^7, it is converted to a string with an optional minus sign (if the value is negative) followed by up to eight digits before the decimal point, a decimal point, and the necessary number of digits after the decimal point (but no trailing zero if there is more than one significant digit). There is always a minimum of one digit after the decimal point.

  Otherwise, the value is converted to a string with an optional minus sign (if the value is negative), followed by a single digit, a decimal point, the necessary number of digits after the decimal point (but no trailing zero if there is more than one significant digit), and the letter E followed by a plus or a minus sign and a base 10 exponent of at least one digit. Again, there is always a minimum of one digit after the decimal point.

  In addition, the values NaN, NEGATIVE_INFINITY, POSITIVE_INFINITY, -0.0, and +0.0 are represented by the strings "NaN", "-Infinity", "Infinity", "-0.0", and "0.0", respectively.

  Note that the specification for this conversion has changed as of Java 1.1. Prior to that release, the conversion provided a string representation that was equivalent to the %g format of the printf function in C. In addition, the string representations of the infinity values, the zero values, and NaN are not specified prior to Java 1.1.

- If the type of the operand is boolean, the value is converted to a reference to either the string literal "true" or the string literal "false".

Java uses the StringBuffer object to implement string concatenation. Consider the following code:

```
String s, s1,s2;
s = s1 + s2;
```

To compute the string concatenation, Java compiler generates code equivalent to:

```
s = new StringBuffer().append(s1).append(s2).toString();
```

Consider another expression:

```
s = 1 + s1 + 2
```

In this case, the Java compiler generates code equivalent to:

```
s = new StringBuffer().append(1).append(s1).append(2).toString()
```

No matter how many strings are being concatenated in an expression, the expression always produces exactly one `StringBuffer` object and one `String` object.[*] From an efficiency standpoint, if you concatenate more than two strings, it may be more efficient to do so in a single expression, rather than in multiple expressions.

References Arithmetic Addition Operator + 4.6.1; Object 10.14; String 10.20; StringBuffer 10.21

4.7 Shift Operators

The shift operators in Java are used for left shift (<<), right shift (>>), and unsigned right shift (>>>) operations. The shift operators may appear in a shift expression:

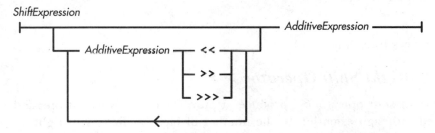

The shift operators are equal in precedence and are evaluated from left to right.

References *AdditiveExpression* 4.6; Order of Operations 4.14

4.7.1 Left Shift Operator <<

The left shift operator << produces a pure value that is its left operand left-shifted by the number of bits specified by its right operand. The << operator may appear in a shift expression. The left shift operator never throws an exception.

Here are some examples of the left shift operator:

```
(3<<2) == 12
(-3<<2) == -12
(0x01234567<<4) == 0x12345670
(0xF1234567<<4) == 0x12345670
```

---

[*] Although an optimizing compiler should be smart enough to combine multiple concatenation expressions when it is advantageous, the compiler provided with Sun's reference implementation of Java does not do this.

The type of each operand of the left shift operator must be an integer data type, or a compile-time error occurs. The << operator may perform type conversions on its operands; unlike arithmetic binary operators, each operand is converted independently. If the type of an operand is byte, short, or char, that operand is converted to an int before the value of the operator is computed. The type of the value produced by the left shift operator is the type of its left operand.

If the converted type of the left operand is int, only the five least significant bits of the value of the right operand are used as the shift distance. Therefore, the shift distance is in the range 0 through 31. In this case, the value produced by r << s is mathematically equivalent to:

$$r \times 2^{s \bmod 32}$$

If the type of the left operand is long, only the six least significant bits of the value of the right operand are used as the shift distance. Therefore, the shift distance is in the range 0 through 63. In this case, the value produced by r << s is mathematically equivalent to:

$$r \times 2^{s \bmod 64}$$

References Integer types 3.1.1.1

4.7.2 Right Shift Operator >>

The right shift operator >> produces a pure value that is its left operand right-shifted with sign extension by the number of bits specified by its right operand. Right-shifting with sign extension means that shifting a value n places to the right causes the n high order bits to contain the same value as the sign bit of the unshifted value. The >> operator may appear as part of a shift expression. The right shift operator never throws an exception. Here are some examples of the right shift operator:

```
(0x01234567>>4) == 0x00123456
(0xF1234567>>4) == 0xFF123456
```

The type of each operand of the right shift operator must be an integer data type, or a compile-time error occurs. The >> operator may perform type conversions on its operands; unlike arithmetic binary operators, each operand is converted independently. If the type of an operand is byte, short, or char, that operand is converted to an int before the value of the operator is computed. The type of the value produced by the right shift operator is the type of its left operand.

If the converted type of the left operand is int, only the five least significant bits of the value of the right operand are used as the shift distance. Therefore, the shift distance is in the range 0 through 31.

In this case, the value produced by r >> s is mathematically equivalent to:

$$\left\lfloor \frac{r}{2^{s \bmod 32}} \right\rfloor$$

The notation $\lfloor x \rfloor$ means the greatest integer less than or equal to x; this is called the floor operation.

If the type of the left operand is long, only the six least significant bits of the value of the right operand are used as the shift distance. Therefore, the shift distance is in the range 0 through 63. In this case, the value produced by r >> s is mathematically equivalent to:

$$\left\lfloor \frac{r}{2^{s \bmod 64}} \right\rfloor$$

References Integer types 3.1.1.1

4.7.3 Unsigned Right Shift Operator >>>

The unsigned right shift operator >>> produces a pure value that is its left operand right-shifted with zero extension by the number of bits specified by its right operand. Right-shifting with zero extension means that shifting a value n places to the right causes the n high order bits to contain zero. The >>> operator may appear as part of a shift expression. The unsigned right shift operator never throws an exception.

Here are some examples of the unsigned right shift operator:

```
(0x01234567>>>4)  ==  0x00123456
(0xF1234567>>>4)  ==  0x0F123456
```

The type of each operand of the unsigned right shift operator must be an integer data type, or a compile-time error occurs. The >>> operator may perform type conversions on its operands; unlike arithmetic binary operators, each operand is converted independently. If the type of an operand is byte, short, or char, that operand is converted to an int before the value of the operator is computed. The type of the value produced by the unsigned right shift operator is the type of its left operand. If the converted type of the left operand is int, only the five least significant bits of the value of the right operand are used as the shift distance. So, the shift distance is in the range 0 through 31. Here, the value produced by r >>> s is the same as:

```
s==0 ? r : (r >> s) & ~(-1<<(32-s))
```

If the type of the left operand is long, then only the six least significant bits of the value of the right operand are used as the shift distance. So, the shift distance is in the range 0 through 63. Here, the value produced by `r >>> s` is the same as the following:

```
s==0 ? r : (r >> s) & ~(-1<<(64-s))
```

References Integer types 3.1.1.1

4.8 Relational Comparison Operators

The relational comparison operators in Java are used for less than (<), less than or equal to (<=), greater than or equal to (>=), greater than (>), and `instanceof` comparison operations. They may appear in a relational expression:

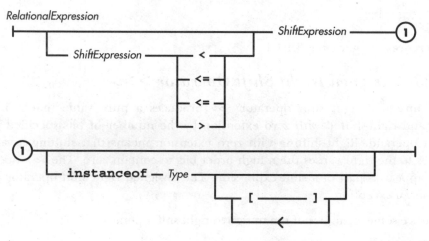

The relational comparison operators are equal in precedence and are evaluated from left to right. The <, <=, >=, and > operators are numerical comparison operators, while `instanceof` is a type comparison operator. All of these operators produce `boolean` values.

References *ShiftExpression* 4.7; Order of Operations 4.14; *Type* 3

4.8.1 Less-Than Operator <

The less-than operator < performs a comparison between its operands and returns a `boolean` value. It returns the pure value `true` if its left operand is less than its right operand; otherwise the operator returns the pure value `false`. The < operator may appear as part of a relational expression. The less-than operator never throws an exception.

The types of both operands of the less-than operator must be arithmetic types, or a compile-time error occurs. The < operator may perform type conversions on its operands:

- If either operand is of type `double`, then the other operand is converted to `double`.

- Otherwise, if either operand is of type `float`, the other operand is converted to `float`.

- Otherwise, if either operand is of type `long`, the other operand is converted to `long`.

- Otherwise, both operands are converted to `int`.

The comparison of any two arithmetic values produces `true` if the value of the left operand is less than the value of the right operand; otherwise the comparison produces `false`. The comparison of floating-point data is governed by the following additional rules:

- If either operand is not-a-number (NaN), the comparison produces `false`.

- Negative infinity is the most negative value. If the left operand is negative infinity, the comparison produces `true`, unless the right operand is also negative infinity, in which case the comparison produces `false`.

- Positive infinity is the most positive value. If the right operand is positive infinity, the comparison produces `true`, unless the left operand is also positive infinity, in which case the comparison produces `false`.

- Positive and negative zero are treated as equal, so `-0.0 < 0.0` produces `false`.

References Arithmetic Types 3.1.1

4.8.2 Less-Than-Or-Equal-To Operator `<=`

The less-than-or-equal-to operator `<=` performs a comparison between its operands and returns a `boolean` value. It returns the pure value `true` if its left operand is less than or equal to its right operand; otherwise the operator returns the pure value `false`. The `<=` operator may appear as part of a relational expression. The less-than-or-equal-to operator never throws an exception.

The types of both operands of the less-than-or-equal-to operator must be arithmetic types, or a compile-time error occurs. The `<=` operator may perform type conversions on its operands:

- If either operand is of type `double`, then the other operand is converted to `double`.

- Otherwise, if either operand is of type `float`, the other operand is converted to `float`.

- Otherwise, if either operand is of type `long`, the other operand is converted to `long`.

- Otherwise, both operands are converted to `int`.

The comparison of any two arithmetic values produces `true` if the value of the left operand is less than or equal to the value of the right operand; otherwise the comparison produces `false`. The comparison of floating-point data is governed by the following additional rules:

- If either operand is not-a-number (NaN), the comparison produces `false`.

- Negative infinity is the most negative value. If the left operand is negative infinity, the comparison always produces `true`.

- Positive infinity is the most positive value. If the right operand is positive infinity, the comparison always produces `true`.

- Positive and negative zero are treated as equal, so `0.0 <= -0.0` produces `true`.

References Arithmetic Types 3.1.1

4.8.3 Greater-Than-Or-Equal-To Operator >=

The greater-than-or-equal-to operator `>=` performs a comparison between its operands and returns a `boolean` value. It returns the pure value `true` if its left operand is greater than or equal to its right operand; otherwise the operator returns the pure value `false`. The `>=` operator may appear as part of a relational expression. The greater-than-or-equal-to operator never throws an exception.

The types of both operands of the greater-than-or-equal-to operator must be arithmetic types, or a compile-time error occurs. The `>=` operator may perform type conversions on its operands:

- If either operand is of type `double`, then the other operand is converted to `double`.

- Otherwise, if either operand is of type `float`, the other operand is converted to `float`.

- Otherwise, if either operand is of type `long`, the other operand is converted to `long`.

- Otherwise, both operands are converted to `int`.

The comparison of any two arithmetic values produces `true` if the value of the left operand is greater than or equal to the value of the right operand; otherwise the comparison produces `false`. The comparison of floating-point data is governed by the following additional rules:

- If either operand is not-a-number (NaN), the comparison produces `false`.

- Negative infinity is the most negative value. If the right operand is negative infinity, the comparison always produces `true`.

- Positive infinity is the most positive value. If the left operand is positive infinity, the comparison always produces `true`.

- Positive and negative zero are treated as equal, so `-0.0 >= 0.0` produces `true`.

References Arithmetic Types 3.1.1

4.8.4 Greater-Than Operator >

The greater-than operator > performs a comparison between its operands and returns a `boolean` value. It returns the pure value `true` if its left operand is greater than its right operand; otherwise the operator returns the pure value `false`. The > operator may appear as part of a relational expression. The greater-than operator never throws an exception.

The types of both operands of the greater-than operator must be arithmetic types, or a compile-time error occurs. The > operator may perform type conversions on its operands:

- If either operand is of type `double`, then the other operand is converted to `double`.

- Otherwise, if either operand is of type `float`, the other operand is converted to `float`.

- Otherwise, if either operand is of type `long`, the other operand is converted to `long`.

- Otherwise, both operands are converted to `int`.

The comparison of any two arithmetic values produces `true` if the value of the left operand is greater than the value of the right operand; otherwise the comparison produces `false`. The comparison of floating-point data is governed by the following additional rules:

- If either operand is not-a-number (NaN), the comparison produces `false`.

- Negative infinity is the most negative value. If the right operand is negative infinity, the comparison produces `true`, unless the left operand is also negative infinity, in which case the comparison produces `false`.

- Positive infinity is the most positive value. If the left operand is positive infinity, the comparison produces true, unless the right operand is also positive infinity, in which case the comparison produces false.

- Positive and negative zero are treated as equal, so 0.0 > -0.0 produces false.

References Arithmetic Types 3.1.1

4.8.5 *The instanceof Operator*

The instanceof operator performs a type comparison between its operands and returns a boolean value. It returns the pure value true if the object referred to by the left operand can be cast to the type specified as the right operand; otherwise the operator returns the pure value false. If the value of the left operand is null, the instanceof operator returns the pure value false. The instanceof operator may appear as part of a relational expression. The instanceof operator never throws an exception.

The type of the left operand of the instanceof operator must be a reference type, or a compile-time error occurs.

All objects inherit a method called equals() from the Object class. The equals() method defined in the Object class returns true if the two objects being compared are the same object. For some classes, it is more appropriate to override the equals() method so that it compares the contents of two objects. Before such a method can do the comparison, it should verify that the objects are instances of the same class by using instanceof. For example, let's suppose that you are defining a class to represent complex numbers. Since you want the equals() method to compare the contents of complex number objects, you define an equals method for the complex number class that looks like this:

```
boolean equals (Object o) {
    if (o instanceof complexNumber)
        return o.real == this.real
            && o.imaginary == this.imaginary;
}
```

The instanceof operator can also be used to find out if an object is an instance of a class that implements an interface. For example:

```
if (o instanceof Runnable)
    (new Thread((Runnable)o).start;
```

References Casts 4.4.5; Class Types 3.2.1; Interface Types 3.2.2

4.9 Equality Comparison Operators

The equality comparison operators in Java are used for equal-to (==) and not-equal-to (!=) comparison operations. The equality comparison operators may appear in an equality expression:

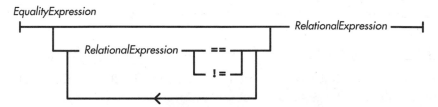

The equality comparison operators are equal in precedence and are evaluated from left to right. The == and != comparison operators can perform numerical comparisons, boolean comparisons, and reference type comparisons. Both of these operators produce boolean values.

References *RelationalExpression* 4.8; Order of Operations 4.14

4.9.1 Equal-To Operator ==

The equal-to operator == performs a comparison between its operands and returns a boolean value. It returns the pure value true if the operands are equal to each other; otherwise it returns the pure value false. The == operator may appear as part of an equality expression. The equal-to operator never throws an exception.

The operands of == may be of any type, but they must both be of the same kind of type or a compile-time error occurs. If one operand is of an arithmetic type, the other must also be of an arithmetic type. If one operand is of type boolean, the other must also be of type boolean. If one operand is a reference type, the other must also be a reference type. Note that neither operand can be an expression that invokes a void method.

If both operands are of arithmetic types, then the operator performs an arithmetic equality comparison. The operator may perform type conversions on the operands:

- If either operand is of type double, then the other operand is converted to double.

- Otherwise, if either operand is of type float, the other operand is converted to float.

- Otherwise, if either operand is of type long, the other operand is converted to long.

- Otherwise, both operands are converted to int.

The equality comparison of any two arithmetic values produces true if and only if both operands are the same value; otherwise the comparison produces false. The comparison of floating-point data is governed by the following additional rules:

- If either operand is not-a-number (NaN), the comparison produces false.

- Positive infinity is a distinct value that is equal to itself, and not equal to any other value.

- Negative infinity is a distinct value that is equal to itself, and not equal to any other value.

- Positive and negative zero are treated as equal, so -0.0==0.0 produces true.

If both operands are boolean values, the operator performs a Boolean equality comparison. The comparison produces true if both operands are true or both operands are false. Otherwise, the comparison produces false.

If both operands are reference types, the operator performs an object equality comparison. In order to perform this type of comparison, it must be possible to cast the value of one of the operands to the type of the other operand, or a compile-time error occurs. The comparison produces true if both of its operands refer to the same object or if both of its operands are null; otherwise the comparison produces false.

Because the == operator determines if two objects are the same object, it is not appropriate for comparisons that need to determine if two objects have the same contents. For example, if you need to know whether two String objects contain the same sequences of characters, the == operator is inappropriate. You should use the equals() method instead:[*]

```
string1.equals (string2)    // Compares contents of strings
string1 == string2          // Compares actual string objects
```

References Arithmetic Types 3.1.1; Boolean Type 3.1.2; Reference Types 3.2

---

[*] This is similar to the difference in C between writing string1==string2 and strcmp(string1, string2)==0.

4.9.2 Not-Equal-To-Operator !=

The not-equal-to operator != performs a comparison between its operands and returns a boolean value. It returns the pure value true if the operands are not equal to each other; otherwise it returns the pure value false. The != operator may appear as part of an equality expression. The not-equal-to operator never throws an exception.

The operands of != may be of any type, but they must both be of the same kind of type or a compile-time error occurs. If one operand is of an arithmetic type, the other must also be of an arithmetic type. If one operand is of type boolean, the other must also be of type boolean. If one operand is a reference type, the other must also be a reference type. Note that neither operand can be an expression that invokes a void method.

If both operands are of arithmetic types, the operator performs an arithmetic inequality comparison. The operator may perform type conversions on the operands:

- If either operand is of type double, then the other operand is converted to double.

- Otherwise, if either operand is of type float, the other operand is converted to float.

- Otherwise, if either operand is of type long, the other operand is converted to long.

- Otherwise, both operands are converted to int.

The inequality comparison of any two arithmetic values produces true if and only if both operands are not the same value; otherwise the comparison produces false. The comparison of floating-point data is governed by the following additional rules:

- If either operand is not-a-number (NaN), the comparison produces true. NaN is the only value that compares as not equal to itself.

- Positive infinity is a distinct value that is equal to itself, and not equal to any other value.

- Negative infinity is a distinct value that is equal to itself, and not equal to any other value.

- Positive and negative zero are treated as equal, so -0.0!=0.0 produces false.

If both operands are boolean values, the operator performs a Boolean inequality comparison. The comparison produces false if both operands are true or both operands are false. Otherwise, the comparison produces true.

If both operands are reference types, the operator performs an object equality comparison. In order to perform this type of comparison, it must be possible to cast the value of one of the operands to the type of the other operand, or a compile-time error occurs. The comparison produces `true` if both of its operands refer to different objects and if both of its operands are not `null`; otherwise the comparison produces `false`.

Because the `!=` operator determines if two objects are different objects, it is not appropriate for comparisons that need to determine if two objects have different contents. For example, if you need to know whether two `String` objects contain different sequences of characters, the `!=` operator is inappropriate. You should use the `equals()` method instead:[*]

```
!string1.equals (string2)  // Compares contents of strings
string1 != string2         // Compares actual string objects
```

References Arithmetic Types 3.1.1; Boolean Type 3.1.2; Reference Types 3.2

4.10 Bitwise/Logical Operators

The bitwise/logical operators in Java are used for bitwise and logical AND (`&`), bitwise and logical exclusive OR (`^`), and bitwise and logical inclusive OR (`|`) operations. These operators have different precedence; the `&` operator has the highest precedence of the group and the `|` operator has the lowest. All of the operators are evaluated from left to right.

The unary operator `~` provides a bitwise negation operation.

References Bitwise Negation Operator `~` 4.4.4; Order of Operations 4.14

4.10.1 Bitwise/Logical AND Operator &

The bitwise/logical AND operator `&` produces a pure value that is the AND of its operands. The `&` operator may appear in a bitwise or logical AND expression:

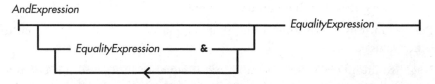

The bitwise/logical AND operator is evaluated from left to right. The operator never throws an exception.

---

[*] This is similar to the difference in C between writing `string1!=string2` and `strcmp(string1, string2)!=0`.

Here is a code example that shows the use of the bitwise AND operator:

```
boolean isOdd(int x) {
    return (x & 1) == 1;
}
```

The operands of the bitwise/logical AND operator must both be of either an integer type or the type `boolean`, or a compile-time error occurs.

If both operands are of integer types, the operator performs a bitwise AND operation. The operator may perform type conversions on the operands:

- If either operand is of type `long`, the other operand is converted to `long` and the operation produces a `long` value.

- Otherwise, both operands are converted to `int` and the operation produces an `int` value.

The bitwise AND operator produces a pure value that is the bitwise AND of its operands. If the corresponding bits in both of the converted operands are 1s, the corresponding bit in the result is a 1; otherwise the corresponding bit in the result is a 0.

If both operands are of type `boolean`, the operator performs a logical AND operation. The logical AND operation produces a pure value of type `boolean`. If both operands are `true`, the operation produces `true`; otherwise the operation produces `false`. This operator differs from the conditional AND operator (`&&`) because it always evaluates both of its operands, even if its left operand evaluates to `false`.

References Boolean AND Operator && 4.11.1; Boolean Type 3.1.2; *EqualityExpression* 4.9; Integer types 3.1.1.1; Order of Operations 4.14

4.10.2 Bitwise/Logical Exclusive OR Operator ^

The bitwise/logical exclusive OR operator ^ produces a pure value that is the exclusive OR of its operands. The ^ operator may appear in a bitwise or logical exclusive OR expression:

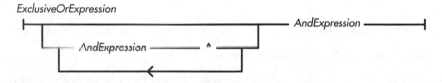

The bitwise/logical exclusive OR operator is evaluated from left to right. The operator never throws an exception.

The operands of the bitwise/logical exclusive OR operator must both be of either an integer type or the type `boolean`, or a compile-time error occurs.

If both operands are of integer types, the operator performs a bitwise exclusive OR operation. The operator may perform type conversions on the operands:

- If either operand is of type `long`, the other operand is converted to `long` and the operation produces a `long` value.

- Otherwise, both operands are converted to `int` and the operation produces an `int` value.

The bitwise exclusive OR operator produces a pure value that is the bitwise exclusive OR of its operands. If the corresponding bits in the converted operands are both 0 or both 1, the corresponding bit in the result is a 0; otherwise the corresponding bit in the result is a 1.

If both operands are of type `boolean`, the operator performs a logical exclusive OR operation. The logical exclusive OR operation produces a pure value of type `boolean`. If either, but not both, operands are `true`, the operation produces `true`; otherwise the operation produces `false`.

References *AndExpression* 4.10.1; Boolean Type 3.1.2; Integer types 3.1.1.1; Order of Operations 4.14

4.10.3 Bitwise/Logical Inclusive OR Operator |

The bitwise/logical inclusive OR operator | produces a pure value that is the inclusive OR of its operands. The | operator may appear in a bitwise or logical inclusive OR expression:

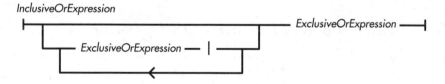

The bitwise/logical inclusive OR operator is evaluated from left to right. The operator never throws an exception.

Here is a code example that shows the use of the bitwise inclusive OR operator:

```
setFont("Helvetica", Font.BOLD | Font.ITALIC, 18);
```

The operands of the bitwise/logical inclusive OR operator must both be of either an integer type or the type `boolean`, or a compile-time error occurs.

If both operands are of integer types, the operator performs a bitwise inclusive OR operation. The operator may perform type conversions on the operands:

- If either operand is of type long, the other operand is converted to long and the operation produces a long value.

- Otherwise, both operands are converted to int and the operation produces an int value.

The bitwise inclusive OR operator produces a pure value that is the bitwise inclusive OR of its operands. If the corresponding bits in either or both of the converted operands are 1s, the corresponding bit in the result is a 1; otherwise the corresponding bit in the result is a 0.

If both operands are of type boolean, the operator performs a logical inclusive OR operation. The logical inclusive OR operation produces a pure value of type boolean. If either or both operands are true, the operation produces true; otherwise the operation produces false. This operator differs from the conditional OR operator (||) because it always evaluates both of its operands, even if its left operand evaluates to true.

References Boolean OR Operator || 4.11.2; Boolean Type 3.1.2; *ExclusiveOrExpression* 4.10.2; Integer types 3.1.1.1; Order of Operations 4.14

4.11 Boolean Operators

The Boolean operators in Java are used for conditional AND (&&) and conditional OR (||) operations. These operators have different precedence; the && operator has the higher precedence and || the lower precedence. Both of the operators are evaluated from left to right.

The unary operator ! provides a Boolean negation operation.

References Boolean Negation Operator ! 4.4.3; Order of Operations 4.14

4.11.1 Boolean AND Operator &&

The conditional AND operator && produces a pure boolean value that is the conditional AND of its operands. The && operator may appear in a conditional AND expression:

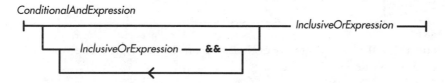

The conditional AND operator is evaluated from left to right. The operator never throws an exception.

Here is a code example that shows the use of the conditional AND operator:

```
public final short readShort() throws IOException {
    int ch1, ch2;
    if ((ch1 = in.read()) >= 0 && (ch2 = in.read()) >= 0)
        return (short)((ch1 << 8) + ch2);
    throw new EOFException();
}
```

The operands of the conditional AND operator must both be of type `boolean`, or a compile-time error occurs.

The operands of the conditional AND operator are evaluated in a different way from the operands for most other operators in Java. Most other operators evaluate all of their operands before performing their operation; the conditional AND operator does not necessarily evaluate both of its operands.

As with all binary operators, the left operand of `&&` is evaluated first. If the left operand evaluates to `true`, the conditional AND operator evaluates its right operand and produces a pure value that has the same value as its right operand. However, if the left operand evaluates to `false`, the right operand is not evaluated and the operator produces the pure value `false`.

In the above example, the expression `(ch2 = in.read())` is evaluated only if the expression `(ch1 = in.read())` produces a value that is greater than or equal to zero.

References Bitwise/Logical AND Operator & 4.10.1; Boolean Type 3.1.2; *Inclusive-OrExpression* 4.10.3; Order of Operations 4.14

4.11.2 Boolean OR Operator ||

The conditional OR operator || produces a pure `boolean` value that is the conditional OR of its operands. The || operator may appear in a conditional OR expression:

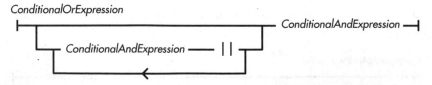

The conditional OR operator is evaluated from left to right. The operator never throws an exception.

Here is a code example that shows the use of the conditional OR operator:

```
public final short readShort() throws IOException {
    int ch1, ch2;
    if ((ch1 = in.read()) < 0 || (ch2 = in.read()) < 0)
        throw new EOFException();
    return (short)((ch1 << 8) + ch2);
}
```

The operands of the conditional OR operator must both be of type `boolean`, or a compile-time error occurs.

The operands of the conditional OR operator are evaluated in a different way from the operands for most other operators in Java. Most other operators evaluate all of their operands before performing their operation; the conditional OR operator does not necessarily evaluate both of its operands.

As with all binary operators, the left operand of || is evaluated first. If the left operand evaluates to `false`, the conditional OR operator evaluates its right operand and produces a pure value that has the same value as its right operand. However, if the left operand evaluates to `true`, the right operand is not evaluated and the operator produces the pure value `true`.

References Bitwise/Logical Inclusive OR Operator | 4.10.3; Boolean Type 3.1.2; *ConditionalAndExpression* 4.11.1; Order of Operations 4.14

4.12 Conditional Operator

The conditional operator (? :) is a ternary operator. The operator selects one of two expressions for evaluation, based on the value of its first operand. In this way, the conditional operator is similar to an `if` statement. A conditional operator may appear in a conditional expression:

ConditionalExpression

├── ConditionalOrExpression ─────────────────────────────────┤
         └─ **?** ─ Expression ─ **:** ─ ConditionalExpression ─┘

The conditional operator produces a pure value. Conditional expressions group from right to left. Consider the following expression:

```
g?f:e?d:c?b:a
```

It is equivalent to

```
g?f:(e?d:(c?b:a))
```

The first operand of the conditional operator must be of type `boolean`, or a compile-time error occurs. If the first operand evaluates to `true`, the operator evaluates the second operand (i.e., the one following the ?) and produces the pure value of that expression. Otherwise, if the first operand evaluates to `false`, the operator evaluates the third operand (i.e., the one following the :) and produces the pure value of that expression. Note that the conditional operator evaluates either its second operand or its third operand, but not both.

The second and third operands of the conditional operator may be of any type, but they must both be of the same kind of type or a compile-time error occurs. If one operand is of an arithmetic type, the other must also be of an arithmetic type. If one operand is of type `boolean`, the other must also be of type `boolean`. If one operand is a reference type, the other must also be a reference type. Note that neither the second nor the third operand can be an expression that invokes a `void` method.

The types of the second and third operands determine the type of pure value that the conditional operator produces. If the second and third operands are of different types, the operator may perform a type conversion on the operand that it evaluates. The operator does this to ensure that it always produces the same type of result for a given expression, regardless of the value of its first operand.

If the second and third operands are both of arithmetic types, the conditional operator determines the type of value it produces as follows:[*]

- If both operands are of the same type, the conditional operator produces a pure value of that type.

- If one operand is of type `short` and the other operand is of type `byte`, the conditional operator produces a `short` value.

- If one operand is of type `short`, `char`, or `byte` and the other operand is a constant expression that can be represented as a value of that type, the conditional operator produces a pure value of that type.

- Otherwise, if either operand is of type `double`, the operator produces a `double` value.

- Otherwise, if either operand is of type `float`, the operator produces a `float` value.

- Otherwise, if either operand is of type `long`, the operator produces a `long` value.

- Otherwise, if either operand is of type `int`, the operator produces an `int` value.

---

[*] Some of these rules are different from the way it is done in C/C++. In those languages, integer data of types smaller than `int` are always converted to `int` when they appear in any expression.

If the second and third operands are both of type `boolean`, the conditional operator produces a pure `boolean` value.

If the second and third operands are both reference types, the conditional operator determines the type of value it produces as follows:

- If both operands are `null`, the conditional operator produces the pure value `null`.

- Otherwise, if exactly one of the operands is `null`, the conditional operator produces a value of the type of the other operand.

- Otherwise, it must be possible to cast the value of one of the operands to the type of the other operand, or a compile-time error occurs. The conditional operator produces a value of the type that would be the target of the cast.

References Arithmetic Types 3.1.1; Boolean Type 3.1.2; *ConditionalOrExpression* 4.11.2; *Expression* 4; Order of Operations 4.14; Reference Types 3.2

4.13 *Assignment Operators*

Assignment operators set the values of variables and array elements. An assignment operator may appear in an assignment expression:

AssignmentExpression
    ConditionalExpression
    UnaryExpression — *AssignmentOperator* — *AssignmentExpression*

The actual assignment operator in an assignment expression can be the simple assignment operator = or one of the compound assignment operators shown below. All of the assignment operators are equal in precedence. Assignment operators are evaluated from right to left, so a=b=c is equivalent to a=(b=c).

The left operand of an assignment operator must be an expression that produces a variable or an array element. The left operand of an assignment operator cannot be an expression that evaluates to a pure value, or a compile-time error occurs. So, for example, the left operand cannot be a `final` variable, since a `final` variable evaluates to a pure value, not a variable.

The assignment operator itself produces a pure value, not a variable or an array element. The pure value produced by an assignment operator is the value of the variable or array element after it has been set by the assignment operation. The type of this pure value is the type of the variable or array element.

The simple assignment operator = just sets the value of a variable or array element. It does not imply any other computation. The right operand of the simple assignment operator can be of any type, as long as that type is assignment-compatible with the type of the left operand, as described in the next section. If the right operand is not assignment-compatible, a compile-time error occurs.

The compound assignment operators are:

CompoundAssignmentOperator

+=	-=	*=
/=	|=	&=
^=	%=	<<=
>>=	>>>=	

Both of the operands of a compound assignment operator must be of primitive types, or a compile-time error occurs. The one exception is if the left operand of the += operator is of type `String`; in this case the right operand can be of any type.

A compound assignment operator combines a binary operator with the simple assignment operator =. Thus, to be assignment-compatible, the right operand of a compound assignment operator must be of a type that complies with the rules for the indicated binary operation. Otherwise, a compile-time error occurs. An assignment expression of the form:

```
e1 op= e2
```

is approximately equivalent to:

```
e1 = (type) ((e1) op (e2))
```

where *type* is the type of the expression e1. The only difference is that e1 is only evaluated once in the expression that uses the compound assignment operator.

For example, consider the following code fragment:

```
j = 0;
a[0] = 3;
a[1]=6;
a[j++] += 2;
```

After this code is executed, j equals 1 and a[0] is 5. Contrast this with the following code:

```
j = 0;
a[0] = 3;
a[1]=6;
a[j++] = a[j++] + 2;
```

After this code is executed, j equals 2 and a[0] is 8 because j++ is evaluated twice.

References Array Types 3.2.3; *AssignmentOperator* 2.2.5; *ConditionalExpression* 4.12; Interface Variables 5.5.5; Local Variables 6.1.1; Order of Operations 4.14; Primitive Types 3.1; Reference Types 3.2; String 10.20; *UnaryExpression* 4.4; Variables 5.4.5

4.13.1 Assignment Compatibility

Saying that one type of value is *assignment-compatible* with another type of value means that a value of the first type can be assigned to a variable of the second type. Here are the rules for assignment compatibility in Java:

- Every type is assignment-compatible with itself.

- The boolean type is not assignment-compatible with any other type.

- A value of any integer type can be assigned to a variable of any other integer type if the variable is of a type that allows it to contain the value without any loss of information.

- A value of any integer type can be assigned to a variable of any floating-point type, but a value of any floating-point type cannot be assigned to a variable of any integer type.

- A float value can be assigned to a double variable, but a double value cannot be assigned to a float variable.

- With a type cast, a value of any arithmetic type can be assigned to a variable of any other arithmetic type.

- Any reference can be assigned to a variable that is declared of type Object.

- A reference to an object can be assigned to a class-type reference variable if the class of the variable is the same class or a superclass of the class of the object.

- A reference to an object can be assigned to an interface-type reference variable if the class of the object implements the interface.

- A reference to an array can be assigned to an array variable if either of the following conditions is true:

  - Both array types contain elements of the same type.

  - Both array types contain object references and the type of reference contained in the elements of the array reference can be assigned to the type of reference contained in the elements of the variable.

Here's an example that illustrates the rules about assignment compatibility of arrays:

```
class Triangle extends Shape {...}
...
int[] i = new int[8];
int j[];
long l[];
short s[];
Triangle[] t;
Shape[] sh;

j = i;      // Okay
s = i;      // Error
l = i;      // Error
sh = t;     // Okay
t = sh;     // Error
```

Assigning i to j is fine because both variables are declared as references to arrays that contain int values. On the other hand, assigning i to s is an error because the variables are declared as references to arrays that contain different kinds of elements and these elements are not object references. Assigning i to l is an error for the same reason. Assigning t to sh is fine because the variables are declared as references to arrays that contain object references, and sh[0]=t[0] is legal. However, assigning sh to t is an error because t[0]=sh[0] is not legal.

It is not always possible for the compiler to determine if an assignment to an array element is legal; in these cases the assignment compatibility is checked at runtime. This situation can occur when a variable contains a reference to an array whose type of elements is specified by a class or interface name. In this case, it may not be possible to determine the actual type of the array elements until runtime. Consider the following example:

```
void foo (InputStream a[]) {
    a[0] = new FileInputStream("/dev/null");
}
```

Figure 4-1 shows the InputStream class and some of its subclasses in the java.io package.

Any array with elements that contain references to objects of class InputStream or any of its subclasses can be passed to the method foo() shown in the above example. For example:

```
FileInputStream f[] = new FileInputStream[3];
foo(f);
```

Since FileInputStream is a subclass of InputStream, the call to foo() does not cause any problems at runtime.

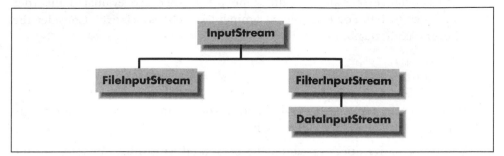

Figure 4–1: InputStream and some of its classes

However, the following call to foo() is problematic:

```
DataInputStream f[] = new DataInputStream[3];
foo(f);
```

This call causes an `ArrayStoreException` to be thrown at runtime. Although `DataInputStream` is a subclass of `InputStream`, it is not a superclass of `FileInputStream`, so the array element assignment in foo() is not assignment-compatible.

References Arithmetic Types 3.1.1; Array Types 3.2.3; Boolean Type 3.1.2; Class Types 3.2.1; Interface Types 3.2.2

4.14 Order of Operations

In an expression that contains multiple operators, Java uses a number of rules to decide the order in which the operators are evaluated. The first and most important rule is called *operator precedence*. Operators in an expression that have higher precedence are executed before operators with lower precedence. For example, multiplication has a higher precedence than addition. In the expression 2+3*4, the multiplication is done before the addition, producing a result of 14.

If consecutive operators in an expression have the same precedence, a rule called *associativity* is used to decide the order in which those operators are evaluated. An operator can be left-associative, right-associative, or non-associative:

- Left-associative operators of the same precedence are evaluated in order from left to right. For example, addition and subtraction have the same precedence and they are left-associative. In the expression 10-4+2, the subtraction is done first because it is to the left of the addition, producing a value of 8.

- Right-associative operators of the same precedence are evaluated in order from right to left. For example, assignment is right-associative. Consider the following code fragment:

```
int a = 3;
int b = 4;
a = b = 5;
```

After the code has been evaluated, both a and b contain 5 because the assignments are evaluated from right to left.

- A non-associative operator cannot be combined with other operators of the same precedence.

Table 4-2 shows the precedence and associativity of all the operators in Java.[*]

Table 4–2: Precedence and Associativity of Operators in Java

Precedence	Operator	Associativity
1	( ), [ ]	non-associative
2	new	non-associative
3	.	left-associative
4	++, - -	non-associative
5	- (unary), + (unary), !, ~, ++, - -, (*type*)	right-associative
6	*, /, %	left-associative
7	+, -	left-associative
8	<<, >>, >>>	left-associative
9	<, >, <=, >=, instanceof	non-associative
10	==, !=	left-associative
11	&	left-associative
12	^	left-associative
13	|	left-associative
14	&&	left-associative
15	||	left-associative
16	? :	right-associative
17	=, *=, /=, %=, -=, <<=, >>=, >>>=, &=, ^=, |=	right-associative

As in C/C++, the order in which operators are evaluated can be modified by the use of parentheses.

---

[*] Although the precedence of operators in Java is similar to that in C++, there are some differences. For example, new has a higher precedence in Java than it does in C++. Another difference is that the ++ and - - operators are effectively non-associative in Java.

The rest of the rules that concern order of operations have to do with the evaluation of operands or arguments in a single expression.

- The left operand of a binary operator is evaluated before its right operand.

- The operands of an operator are evaluated before the operator is evaluated. Consider the following expression:

    ```
    ((x=4) * x)
    ```

    First, the left operand of * is evaluated; it produces the value 4. Then the right operand of * is evaluated. Since evaluation of the left operand set x to 4, evaluation of the right operand produces 4. Finally, the * operator itself is evaluated, producing the value 16.

- In an index expression, the expression to the left of the square brackets is evaluated before the expression inside the square brackets.

- In an expression that calls a method through an object reference, the object reference is evaluated before the argument expressions.

- In any expression that calls a method or constructor, the expressions supplied as the actual arguments are evaluated from left to right.

- In an array allocation expression, the expressions that appear in square brackets and provide the dimensions of the array are evaluated from left to right.

The intent of all of these rules is to guarantee that every implementation of Java evaluates any given expression in the same way.[*] In order to produce optimized code, a Java compiler is allowed to deviate from the rules governing the order in which operations are performed, provided that the result is the same as if it had followed the rules.

References Array Allocation Expressions 4.2.2; Index Expressions 4.1.7; Method Call Expression 4.1.8; Object Allocation Expressions 4.2.1

4.15 Data Type of an Expression

If an expression produces a value, that value is of some particular data type. In some cases, it is possible to determine the exact type that is produced by an expression, based on the types of the literals, variables, and methods that an expression references. For those expressions that produce object references, it is typically only possible to determine the type of the referenced object when the expression is evaluated at runtime.

---

[*] This is different than C/C++, which leaves a number of details of expression evaluation up to an implementation, such as the order in which the actual parameters of a function call are evaluated.

The types of many expressions are ambiguous because of the way Java data types are defined. There is no ambiguity for variables, array elements, and method return values of primitive types, however. These expressions always produce the exact types specified in their declarations.

There can be ambiguity when a variable, array element, or method return value is declared to have a class or interface reference type. The ambiguity exists because a class reference may actually refer to an object of the intended class or a subclass of that class. For example, consider a variable that is declared to contain a reference to a Number object:

```
double square(Number n){
    return n.doubleValue()*n.doubleValue();
}
```

When the Java compiler sees the variable n used in an expression, it knows that the object that is referenced could be an Integer, Long, Float, or Double object because the java.lang package defines those subclasses of Number. It is also possible, however, that the variable refers to some other subclass of Number defined elsewhere. All that the compiler can be certain of is that at runtime n will refer to an object of a subclass of Number. The variable n cannot refer to a Number object because Number is an abstract class, so there are no Number objects.

The one exception to the ambiguity of class-type object references occurs when the class used to declare a variable, array element, or method return type is a final class. If a class is declared to be final, it cannot be subclassed, so there is no ambiguity.

Ambiguity also exists if the type of a reference is an interface type, since the reference can refer to an object of any class that implements the interface. The actual class is not usually known until runtime.

The fact that the type of value produced by an object reference expression cannot be determined until it is evaluated at runtime can affect the evaluation of other expressions in the following ways:

- If a method is called through an object reference expression, the actual method to be called may depend on the type of the object. The selection of the appropriate method in the object is made at compile-time. For example, f.read() causes the selection of a method named read() that takes no arguments.

  However, if the compiler cannot determine the actual class of the object, the actual method to be called is determined at runtime, when the class is known. The compiler generates code to handle a runtime selection process called dynamic method lookup. The process begins by searching the actual class for an appropriate method. If there is no such method, the superclass of the class is searched, followed by its superclass and on up the inheritance hierarchy, until an appropriate method is found. This process ensures that the appropriate method gets called, even if the actual class of the object is a subclass of the type used for the object reference.

Even if the compiler cannot determine the actual class of the object, there is one case in which it does not need to generate code to handle dynamic method lookup. When the compiler selects the appropriate method in the object, if it finds that the method is declared `final`, it can be sure that it is the method to be called.

- The success of a cast operation may need to be determined at runtime. When a class-type object reference is cast to another class, the operation can only succeed if the actual class of the object is the same class or a subclass of the class being cast to. If the compiler cannot determine the actual class of the object, it generates runtime code that can verify that the cast is permitted. If the actual class of the object at runtime makes the cast illegal, a `ClassCastException` is thrown.

- The value produced by the `instanceof` operator may need to be determined at runtime. If the compiler cannot determine the type of the left operand in an `instanceof` expression, it generates runtime code to decide whether the expression produces `true` or `false`.

- The legality of an assignment to an array element may need to be determined at runtime. If a variable contains a reference to an array and the type of elements in the array is specified with a class or an interface name, it may not be possible to determine the actual type of the array elements until runtime. Consider the following example:

```
void foo (InputStream a[]) {
    a[0] = new FileInputStream("/dev/null");
}
```

Any array with elements that contain references to objects of class `Input-Stream` or any of its subclasses can be passed to the method `foo()` shown above.

```
FileInputStream f[] = new FileInputStream[3];
foo(f);
```

Since `FileInputStream` is a subclass of `InputStream`, the call to `foo()` does not cause any type-related problems at runtime. However, the following call to `foo()` does cause problems:

```
DataInputStream f[] = new DataInputStream[3];
foo(f);
```

This call causes an `ArrayStoreException` to be thrown at runtime. Although `DataInputStream` is a subclass of `InputStream`, it is not a superclass of `FileInputStream`, so the assignment is not legal.

- The type of object thrown by a `throw` statement may need to be determined at runtime. If the object thrown by a `throw` statement is obtained through a reference that comes from a variable, an array element, or a method return value, the compiler generates runtime code that determines the type of the object that is thrown. In addition, this runtime code determines whether or not the object is caught.

References Array Types 3.2.3; Assignment Operators 4.13; Casts 4.4.5; Class Types 3.2.1; Interface Types 3.2.2; Method Call Expression 4.1.8; The instanceof Operator 4.8.5; The throw Statement 6.11

4.16 Constant Expressions

A constant expression is an expression that always produces the same result. More precisely, a constant expression is an expression that produces a pure value of a primitive data type and is only composed of the following:

- Literals of primitive data types
- String literals
- Variables that are declared `final` and are initialized by constant expressions
- Type casts to primitive data types or the type `String`
- The unary operators + -, ~, and !
- The binary operators *, /, %, +, -, <<, >>, >>>, <, <=, >=, >, ==, !=, &, ^, |, &&, and ||
- The ternary operator ? :

Note that expressions that use ++, --, and `instanceof` are not constant expressions. Also note that expressions that produce or contain references to objects that are not `String` objects are never constant expressions.

The compiler generally evaluates a constant expression and substitutes the result for the expression during the compilation process.

References Additive Operators 4.6; Bitwise/Logical Operators 4.10; Boolean Operators 4.11; Casts 4.4.5; Conditional Operator 4.12; Equality Comparison Operators 4.9; Interface Variables 5.5.5; Local Variables 6.1.1; Literals 2.2.3; Multiplicative Operators 4.5; Relational Comparison Operators 4.8; Shift Operators 4.7; Unary Operators 4.4; Variables 5.4.5

5

Declarations

A declaration is a construct that associates a name with storage that contains specified data or a specified type of data. More specifically, declarations associate names with classes, interfaces, methods, and variables. In addition, the declaration of a class, interface, or method defines the actual class, interface, or method that is associated with the name. Methods and variables can only be declared within classes and interfaces, so this chapter covers method and variable declarations in the context of class and interface declarations.

Every name has a *lexical scope*. The scope of a declaration determines the portions of a program in which the declaration is applicable.

A declaration can be preceded by modifiers that specify attributes of the name or of the data associated with the name. One such attribute for a name is its accessibility. The accessibility modifiers specify the other classes that can access the data associated with the name. The static modifier specifies an attribute for data; it indicates whether the data is associated with a class or with individual instances of a class.

Because Java is an object-oriented programming language, this chapter also describes the object-oriented model used by the language. An understanding of this model is necessary for a complete understanding of class and interface declarations.

5.1 Naming Conventions

The Java language has no requirements for choosing names, aside from the lexical requirements for identifiers stated in 2.2.1 Identifiers. However, there are certain conventions that you should follow when choosing names; these conventions are the ones used by Sun in much of the Java API. Following these conventions makes your programs easier to read, as many programmers are already accustomed to reading programs that use them:

- If an identifier is logically made up of multiple words, the first letter of each word other than the first is uppercase and the rest of the letters are lowercase (e.g., `aSimpleExample`). Sun is consistent about following this convention.

- The first letter of the name of a class or interface is uppercase, while the first letter of all other names is lowercase. Sun is also consistent about following this convention.

- The names of final variables that are intended to represent symbolic constants are all uppercase; logical words contained in the name are separated by underscore characters (e.g., `MAX_LEGAL_VALUE`). Sun uses this convention quite often, but is not entirely consistent.

- Some Java programmers have adopted the additional convention of beginning the names of instance variables with an underscore (e.g., `_value`).

- Avoid the use of $ in names to prevent confusion with compiler-generated names. Sun is consistent about following this convention.

References Class Name 5.4.2; Identifiers 2.2.1; Interface Name 5.5.2; Interface Variables 5.5.5; Variables 5.4.5

5.2 Lexical Scope of Declarations

The lexical scope of a declaration determines where the named entity is a valid identifier. Every declaration is associated with a lexical level that corresponds to one of the following Java constructs:

Package

> The names at this level include all of the non-nested, outer-level class and interface declarations in files that belong to the same package as the file that is being compiled. This level also includes non-nested, outer-level class and interface declarations that are declared `public` in other packages.

.java file

> The names at this level include all of the class and interface declarations in the file, as well as all of the classes and interfaces that are imported by the file. The names declared directly in a file are defined from the beginning to the end of the file. An `import` statement defines simple identifiers as synonyms for names that are only fully qualified with the name of a package. These synonyms for fully qualified names are defined from the `import` statement that defines them to the end of the file.

Class or interface declaration

> The names at this level include the names of methods, variables, and classes or interfaces that are declared directly in the class or interface declaration, as well as names inherited from superclasses or super interfaces. The names declared in a class or interface are defined throughout the class or interface.

Method declaration

> The names at this level include the formal parameters of the method. The formal parameters are defined throughout the method.

Block

> The names at this level include the local variables, local classes, and statement labels declared in the block. Statement labels are defined throughout a block, while local variables and classes are defined from their declaration to the end of the block.

A nested block or a `for` statement

> The names at this level include local variables declared in the initialization of the `for` statement or the local variables, classes, and statement labels declared in a nested block. Local variables declared in the initialization of a `for` statement are defined from their declaration to the end of the `for` statement. Statement labels are defined throughout a nested block, while local variables and classes are defined from their declaration to the end of the nested block.

These lexical levels correspond to nested constructs. When the Java compiler encounters a name in a program, it finds the declaration for that name by first looking in the lexical level where the name is encountered. If the compiler does not find the name in that lexical level, it searches progressively higher lexical levels until it finds the declaration. If all of the lexical levels are exhausted, the compiler issues an error message.

If, however, an identifier is qualified by a class or package name, the compiler only searches that lexical level for a declaration.

References Blocks 6.1; Class Declarations 5.4; Interface Declarations 5.5; Packages 7.2; Methods 5.4.6; The for Statement 6.7.3

5.3 *Object-Orientation Java Style*

Before considering class and interface declarations in Java, it is essential that you understand the object-oriented model used by the language. No useful programs can be written in Java without using objects. Java deliberately omits certain C++ features that promote a less object-oriented style of programming. Thus, all executable code in a Java program must be part of an object (or a class to be more precise).

The two main characteristics of objects in Java are:

- Objects are always dynamically allocated. The lifetime of the storage occupied by an object is determined by the program's logic, not by the lifetime of a procedure call or the boundaries of a block. The lifetime of the storage occupied by an object refers to the span of time that begins when the object is created and ends at the earliest time it can be freed by the garbage collector.

- Objects are not contained by variables. Instead, a variable contains a reference to an object. A reference is similar to what is called a pointer in some other languages. If there are two variables of the same reference type and one of the variables is assigned to the other, both variables refer to the same object. If the information in that object is changed, the change is visible through both variables.

5.3.1 Classes

An object is a collection of variables, associated methods, and other associated classes. Objects in Java are described by *classes*; a particular object is an *instance* of a particular class. A class describes the data an object can contain by defining variables to contain the data in each instance of the class. A class describes the behavior of an object by defining methods for the class and possibly other auxiliary classes. Methods are named pieces of executable code; they are similar to what other programming languages call functions or procedures. Collectively, the variables, methods, and auxiliary classes of a class are called its members.

A class can define multiple methods with the same name if the number or type of parameters for each method is different. Multiple methods with the same name are called *overloaded methods*. Like C++, Java supports overloaded methods, but unlike C++, Java does not support overloaded operators. Overloaded methods are useful when you want to describe similar operations on different types of data. For example, Java provides a class called `java.io.OutputStream` that is used to write data. The `OutputStream` class defines three different `write()` methods: one to write a single byte of data, another to write some of the bytes in an array, and another to write all of the bytes in an array.

References Class Declarations 5.4

5.3.2 Encapsulation

Encapsulation is the technique of hiding the details of the implementation of an object, while making its functionality available to other objects. When encapsulation is used properly, you can change an object's implementation without worrying that any other object can see, and therefore depend on, the implementation details.

The portion of an object that is accessible to other types of objects is called the object's *interface.*[*] For example, consider a class called Square. The interface for this class might consist of:

- Methods to get and set the size of a square.

- A method to tell a square to draw itself at a particular location on the screen.

The implementation of this Square class would include executable code that implements the various methods, as well as an internal variable that an object would use to remember its size. Variables that an object uses to remember things about itself are called *state variables*.

The point of the distinction between the interface and the implementation of a class is that it makes programs easier to maintain. The implementation of a class may change, but as long as the interface remains the same, these changes do not require changes to any other classes that may use the class.

In Java, encapsulation is implemented using the public, protected, and private access modifiers. If a field of a class is part of the interface for the class, the field should be declared with the public modifier or with no access modifier. The private and protected modifiers limit the accessibility of a field, so these modifiers should be used for state variables and other implementation-specific functionality.

Here's a partial definition of a Square class that has the interface just described:

```
class Square {
    private int sideLength;

    public void setSideLength(int len) {
        sideLength = len;
    }
    public int getSideLength() {
        return sideLength;
    }
    public void draw(int x, int y) {
        // code to draw the square
        ...
    }
}
```

References Method modifiers 5.4.6.1; Inner class modifiers 5.4.11.1; Variable modifiers 5.4.5.1

---

[*] The notion of an object's interface is a commonly accepted concept in the object-oriented community. Later in this chapter, a Java construct called an interface is described. A Java interface is not the same thing as the interface of an object, so there is some potential for confusion. Outside of this section, the term "interface" is only used to mean the Java interface construct.

5.3.3 Object Creation

An object is typically created using an allocation expression. The newInstance()
methods of the Class or java.lang.reflect.Contructor class can also be
used to create an instance of a class. In either case, the storage needed for the
object is allocated by the system.

When a class is instantiated, a special kind of method called a *constructor* is invoked.
A constructor for a class does not have its own name; instead it has the same name
as the class of which it is a part. Constructors can have parameters, just like regular
methods, and they can be overloaded, so a class can have multiple constructors. A
constructor does not have a return type. The main purpose of a constructor is to
do any initialization that is necessary for an object.

If a class declaration does not define any constructors, Java supplies a default public constructor that takes no parameters. You can prevent a class from being
instantiated by methods in other classes by defining at least one private constructor for the class without defining any public constructors.

References Class 10.4; Constructors 5.4.7; Object Allocation Expressions 4.2.1

5.3.4 Object Destruction

Java does not provide any way to explicitly destroy an object. Instead, an object is
automatically destroyed when the garbage collector detects that it is safe to do so.
The idea behind *garbage collection* is that if it is possible to prove that a piece of storage will never be accessed again, that piece of storage can be freed for reuse. This
is a more reliable way of managing storage than having a program explicitly dealло-
cate its own storage. Explicit memory allocation and deallocation is the single
largest source of programming errors in C/C++. Java eliminates this source of
errors by handling the deallocation of memory for you.

Java's garbage collector runs continuously in a low priority thread. You can cause
the garbage collector to take a single pass through allocated storage by calling
System.gc().

Garbage collection will never free storage before it is safe to do so. However,
garbage collection usually does not free storage as soon as it would be freed using
explicit deallocation. The logic of a program can sometimes help the garbage collector recognize that it is safe to free some storage sooner rather than later. Consider the following code:

```
class G {
    byte[] buf;
    String readIt(FileInputStream f) throws IOException {
        buf = new byte[20000];
```

```
        int length = f.read(buf);
        return new String(buf, 0, 0, length);
    }
}
```

The first time `readIt()` is called, it allocates an array that is referenced by the instance variable `buf`. The variable `buf` continues to refer to the array until the next time that `readIt()` is called, when `buf` is set to a new array. Since there is no longer any reference to the old array, the garbage collector will free the storage on its next pass. This situation is less than optimal. It would be better if the garbage collector could recognize that the array is no longer needed once a call to `read-It()` returns. Defining the variable `buf` as a local variable in `readIt()` solves this problem:

```
class G {
    String readIt(FileInputStream f) throws IOException {
        byte[] buf;
        buf = new byte[20000];
        int length = f.read(buf);
        return new String(buf, 0, 0, length);
    }
}
```

Now the reference to the array is in a local variable that disappears when `read-It()` returns. After `readIt()` returns, there is no longer any reference to the array, so the garbage collector will free the storage on its next pass.

Just as a constructor is called when an object is created, there is a special method that is called before an object is destroyed by the garbage collector. This method is called a *finalizer*; it has the name `finalize()`. A `finalize()` method is similar to a destructor in C++. The `finalize()` method for a class must be declared with no parameters, the `void` return type, and no modifiers. A finalizer can be used to clean up after a class, by doing such things as closing files and terminating network connections.

If an object has a `finalize()` method, it is normally called by the garbage collector before the object is destroyed. A program can also explicitly call an object's `finalize()` method, but in this case, the garbage collector does not call the method during the object destruction process. If the garbage collector does call an object's `finalize()` method, the garbage collector does not immediately destroy the object because the `finalize()` method might do something that causes a variable to refer to the object again.* Thus the garbage collector waits to destroy the object until it can again prove it is safe to do so. The next time the garbage collector decides it is safe to destroy the object, it does so without calling the finalizer

---

* A `finalize()` method should not normally do something that results in a reference to the object being destroyed, but Java does not do anything to prevent this situation from happening.

again. In any case, a `finalize()` method is never called more than once for a particular object.

The garbage collector guarantees that the thread it uses to call a `finalize()` method will not be holding any programmer-visible synchronization locks when the method is called. This means that a `finalize()` method never has to wait for the garbage collector to release a lock. If the garbage collector calls a `finalize()` method and the `finalize()` method throws any kind of exception, the garbage collector catches and ignores the exception.

References System 10.22; The finalize method 5.4.8

5.3.5 *Inheritance*

One of the most important benefits of object-oriented programming is that it promotes the reuse of code, particularly by means of inheritance. *Inheritance* is a way of organizing related classes so that they can share common code and state information. Given an existing class declaration, you can create a similar class by having it inherit all of the fields in the existing definition. Then you can add any fields that are needed in the new class. In addition, you can replace any methods that need to behave differently in the new class.

To illustrate the way that inheritance works, let's start with the following class definition:

```
class RegularPolygon {
    private int numberOfSides;
    private int sideLength;

    RegularPolygon(int n, int len) {
        numberOfSides = n;
        sideLength = len;
    }
    public void setSideLength(int len) {
        sideLength = len;
    }
    public int getSideLength() {
        return sideLength;
    }
    public void draw(int x, int y) {
        // code to draw the regular polygon
        ...
    }
}
```

The `RegularPolygon` class defines a constructor, methods to set and get the side length of the regular polygon, and a method to draw the regular polygon. Suppose that after writing this class you realize that you have been using it to draw a lot of squares. You can use inheritance to build a more specific `Square` class from the existing `RegularPolygon` class as follows:

```
class Square extends    RegularPolygon {
    Square(int len) {
        super(4,len);
    }
}
```

The `extends` clause indicates that the `Square` class is a *subclass* of the `Regular-Polygon` class, or looked at another way, `RegularPolygon` is a *superclass* of `Square`. When one class is a subclass of another class, the subclass inherits all of the fields of its superclass that are not `private`. Thus `Square` inherits `setSide-Length()`, `getSideLength()`, and `draw()` methods from `RegularPolygon`. These methods work fine without any modification, which is why the definition of `Square` is so short. All the `Square` class needs to do is define a constructor, since constructors are not inherited.

There is no limit to the depth to which you can carry subclassing. For example, you could choose to write a class called `ColoredSquare` that is a subclass of the `Square` class. The `ColoredSquare` class would inherit the public methods from both `Square` and `RegularPolygon`. However, `ColoredSquare` would need to override the `draw()` method with an implementation that handles drawing in color.

Having defined the three classes `RegularPolygon`, `Square`, and `Colored-Square`, it is correct to say that `RegularPolygon` and `Square` are superclasses of `ColoredSquare` and `ColoredSquare` and `Square` are subclasses of `Regular-Polygon`. To describe a relationship between classes that extends through exactly one level of inheritance, you can use the terms *immediate superclass* and *immediate subclass*. For example, `Square` is an immediate subclass of `RegularPolygon`, while `ColoredSquare` is an immediate subclass of `Square`. By the same token, `RegularPolygon` is the immediate superclass of `Square`, while `Square` is the immediate superclass of `ColoredSquare`.

A class can have any number of subclasses or superclasses. However, a class can only have one immediate superclass. This constraint is enforced by the syntax of the `extends` clause; it can only specify the name of one superclass. This style of inheritance is called *single inheritance*; it is different from the multiple inheritance scheme that is used in C++.

Every class in Java (except `Object`) has the class `Object` as its ultimate superclass. The class `Object` has no superclass. The subclass relationships between all of the

Java classes can be drawn as a tree that has the `Object` class as its root. Another important difference between Java and C++ is that C++ does not have a class that is the ultimate superclass of all of its classes.

References Class Inheritance 5.4.3; Interfaces 5.3.6; Object 10.14

5.3.5.1 Abstract classes

If a class is declared with the `abstract` modifier, the class cannot be instantiated. This is different than C++, which has no way of explicitly specifying that a class cannot be instantiated. An `abstract` class is typically used to declare a common set of methods for a group of classes when there are no reasonable or useful implementations of the methods at that level of abstraction.

For example, the `java.lang` package includes classes called `Byte`, `Short`, `Integer`, `Long`, `Float`, and `Double`. These classes are subclasses of the `abstract` class `Number`, which declares the following methods: `byteValue()`, `shortValue()`, `intValue()`, `longValue()`, `floatValue()`, and `doubleValue()`. The purpose of these methods is to return the value of an object converted to the type implied by the method's name. Every subclass of `Number` implements all of these methods. The advantage of the abstraction is that it allows you to write code to extract whatever type of value you need from a `Number` object, without knowing the actual type of the underlying object.

Methods defined in an `abstract` class can be declared `abstract`. An `abstract` method is declared without any implementation; it must be overridden in a subclass to provide an implementation.

References Class Modifiers 5.4.1; Inner class modifiers 5.4.11.1; Local class modifiers 6.1.2.1; Method modifiers 5.4.6.1; Number 10.13

5.3.5.2 Final classes

If a class is declared with the `final` modifier, the class cannot be subclassed. Declaring a class `final` is useful if you need to ensure the exact properties and behavior of that class. Many of the classes in the `java.lang` package are declared `final` for that reason.

Methods defined in a non-abstract class can be declared `final`. A `final` method cannot be overridden by any subclasses of the class in which it appears.

References Class Modifiers 5.4.1; Inner class modifiers 5.4.11.1; Local class modifiers 6.1.2.1; Method modifiers 5.4.6.1

5.3.6 Interfaces

Java provides a construct called an interface to support certain multiple inheritance features that are desirable in an object-oriented language. An interface is similar to a class, in that an interface declaration can define both variables and methods. But unlike a class, an interface cannot provide implementations for its methods.

A class declaration can include an `implements` clause that specifies the name of an interface. When a class declaration specifies that it implements an interface, the class inherits all of the variables and methods declared in that interface. The class declaration must then provide implementations for all of the methods declared in the interface, unless the class is declared as an `abstract` class. Unlike the `extends` clause, which can only specify one class, the `implements` clause can specify any number of interfaces. Thus a class can implement an unlimited number of interfaces.

Interfaces are most useful for declaring that an otherwise unrelated set of classes have a common set of methods, without needing to provide a common implementation. For example, if you want to store a variety of objects in a database, you might want all of the those objects to have a common set of methods for storing and fetching. Since the fetch and store methods for each object need to be different, it is appropriate to declare these methods in an interface. Then any class that needs fetch and store methods can implement the interface.

Here is a simplistic example that illustrates such an interface:

```
public interface Db {
    void dbStore(Database d, Object key);
    Object dbFetch(Database d, Object key);
}
```

The `Db` interface declaration contains two methods, `dbStore()` and `dbFetch()`. Here is a partial class definition for a class that implements the `Db` interface:

```
class DbSquare extends Square implements Db {
    public void dbStore(Database d, Object key) {
        // Perform database operation to store Square
        ...
    }
    public Square dbFetch(Database d, Object key) {
        // Perform database operation to fetch Square
        ...
    }
    ...
}
```

The `DbSquare` class defines implementations for both of the methods declared in the `Db` interface. The point of this interface is that it provides a uniform way for unrelated objects to arrange to be stored in a database. The following code shows part of a class that encapsulates database operations:

```
class Database {
    ...
    public void store(Object o, Object key) {
        if (o instanceof Db)
            ((Db)o).dbStore(this, key);
    }
    ...
}
```

When the database is asked to store an object, it does so only if the object implements the Db interface, in which case it can call the dbStore() of the object.

References Interface Declarations 5.5

5.3.7 *Inner Classes*

Java 1.1 provides a new feature that allows programmers to encapsulate even more functionality within objects. With the addition of inner classes to the Java language, classes can be defined as members of other classes, just like variables and methods. Classes can also be defined within blocks of Java code, just like local variables. The ability to declare a class inside of another class allows you to encapsulate auxiliary classes inside of a class, thereby limiting access to the auxiliary classes. A class that is declared inside of another class may have access to the instance variables of the enclosing class; a class declared within a block may have access to the local variable and/or formal parameters of that block.

5.3.7.1 *Nested top-level classes and interfaces*

A *nested top-level class* or *interface* is declared as a static member of an enclosing top-level class or interface. The declaration of a nested top-level class uses the static modifier, so you may also see these classes called *static classes.* A nested interface is implicitly static, but you can declare it to be static to make it explicit. Nested top-level classes and interfaces are typically used to group related classes in a convenient way.

A nested top-level class or interface functions like a normal top-level class or interface, except that the name of the nested entity includes the name of the class in which it is defined. For example, consider the following declaration:

```
public class Queue {
    ...
    public static class EmptyQueueException extends Exception {
    }
    ...
}
```

Code that calls a method in `Queue` that throws an `EmptyQueueException` can catch that exception with a `try` statement like this:

```
try {
    ...
} catch (Queue.EmptyQueueException e) {
    ...
}
```

A nested top-level class cannot access the instance variables of its enclosing class. It also cannot call any non-`static` methods of the enclosing class without an explicit reference to an instance of that class. However, a nested top-level class can use any of the `static` variables and methods of its enclosing class without qualification.

Only top-level classes in Java can contain nested top-level classes. In other words, a `static` class can only be declared as a direct member of a class that is declared at the top level, directly as a member of a package. In addition, a nested top-level class cannot declare any `static` variables, `static` methods, or static initializers.

References Class Declarations 5.4; Methods 5.4.6; Nested Top-Level and Member Classes 5.4.11; Variables 5.4.5

5.3.7.2 *Member classes*

A *member class* is an inner class that is declared within an enclosing class without the `static` modifier. Member classes are analogous to the other members of a class, namely the instance variables and methods. The code within a member class can refer to any of the variables and methods of its enclosing class, including `private` variables and methods.

Here is a partial definition of a `Queue` class that uses a member class:

```
public class Queue {
    private QueueNode queue;
    ...
    public Enumeration elements() {
        return new QueueEnumerator();
    }
    ...
    private class QueueEnumerator implements Enumeration {
        private QueueNode start, end;
        QueueEnumerator() {
            synchronized (Queue.this) {
                if (queue != null) {
                    start = queue.next;
                    end = queue;
                }
            }
        }
        public boolean hasMoreElements() {
            return start != null;
```

```
        }
        public synchronized Object nextElement() {
            ...
        }
    }

    private static class QueueNode {
        private Object obj;
        QueueNode next;
        QueueNode(Object obj) {
            this.obj = obj;
        }
        Object getObject() {
            return obj;
        }
    }
}
```

The QueueEnumerator class is a private member class that implements the
java.util.Enumeration interface. The advantage of this approach is that the
QueueEnumerator class can access the private instance variable queue of the
enclosing Queue class. If QueueEnumerator were declared outside of the Queue
class, this queue variable would need to be public, which would compromise the
encapsulation of the Queue class. Using a member class that implements the Enu-
meration interface provides a means to offer controlled access to the data in a
Queue without exposing the internal data structure of the class.

An instance of a member class has access to the instance variables of exactly one
instance of its enclosing class. That instance of the enclosing class is called the
enclosing instance. Thus, every QueueEnumerator object has exactly one Queue
object that is its enclosing instance. To access an enclosing instance, you use the
construct *ClassName*.this. The QueueEnumerator class uses this construct in the
synchronized statement in its constructor to synchronize on its enclosing
instance. This synchronization is necessary to ensure that the newly created
QueueEnumerator object has exclusive access to the internal data of the Queue
object.

The Queue class also contains a nested top-level, or static, class, QueueNode.
However, this class is also declared private, so it is not accessible outside of
Queue. The main difference between QueueEnumerator and QueueNode is that
QueueNode does not need access to any instance data of Queue.

A member class cannot declare any static variables, static methods, static
classes, or static initializers.

Although member classes are often declared private, they can also be public or
protected or have the default accessibility. To refer to a class declared inside of
another class from outside of that class, you prefix the class name with the names

of the enclosing classes, separated by dots. For example, consider the following declaration:

```
public class A {
    public class B {
        public class C {
            ...
        }
        ...
    }
    ...
}
```

Outside of the class named A, you can refer to the class named C as A.B.C.

References Class Declarations 5.4; Field Expressions 4.1.6; Methods 5.4.6; Nested Top-Level and Member Classes 5.4.11; Variables 5.4.5

5.3.7.3 *Local classes*

A *local class* is an inner class that is declared inside of a block of Java code. A local class is only visible within the block in which it is declared, so it is analogous to a local variable. However, a local class can access the variables and methods of any enclosing classes. In addition, a local class can access any `final` local variables or method parameters that are in the scope of the block that declares the class.

Local classes are most often used for *adapter classes*. An adapter class is a class that implements a particular interface, so that another class can call a particular method in the adapter class when a certain event occurs. In other words, an adapter class is Java's way of implementing a "callback" mechanism. Adapter classes are commonly used with the new event-handling model required by the Java 1.1 AWT and by the JavaBeans API.

Here is an example of a local class functioning as an adapter class:

```
public class Z extends Applet {
    public void init() {
        final Button b = new Button("Press Me");
        add(b);
        class ButtonNotifier implements ActionListener {
            public void actionPerformed(ActionEvent e) {
                b.setLabel("Press Me Again");
                doIt();
            }
        }
        b.addActionListener(new ButtonNotifier());
    }
    ...
}
```

The above example is from an applet that has a `Button` in its user interface. To tell a `Button` object that you want to be notified when it is pressed, you pass an instance of an adapter class that implements the `ActionListener` interface to its `addActionListener()` method. A class that implements the `ActionListener` interface is required to implement the `actionPerformed()` method. When the `Button` is pressed, it calls the adapter object's `actionPerformed()` method. The main advantage of declaring the `ButtonNotifier` class in the method that creates the `Button` is that it puts all of the code related to creating and setting up the `Button` in one place.

As the preceding example shows, a local class can access local variables of the block in which it is declared. However, any local variables that are accessed by a local class must be declared `final`. A local class can also access method parameters and the exception parameter of a `catch` statement that are accessible within the scope of its block, as long as the parameter is declared `final`. The Java compiler complains if a local class uses a non-`final` local variable or parameter. The lifetime of a parameter or local variable is extended indefinitely, as long as there is an instance of a local class that refers to it.

References Blocks 6.1; Class Declarations 5.4; Local Classes 6.1.2; Local Variables 6.1.1; Method formal parameters 5.4.6.4; Methods 5.4.6; The try Statement 6.12; Variables 5.4.5

5.3.7.4 Anonymous classes

An *anonymous class* is a kind of local class that does not have a name and is declared inside of an allocation expression. As such, an anonymous class is a more concise declaration of a local class that combines the declaration of the class with its instantiation.

Here is how you can rewrite the previous adapter class example to use an anonymous class instead of a local class:

```
public class Z extends Applet {
    public void init() {
        final Button b = new Button("Press Me");
        add(b);
        b.addActionListener(new ActionListener () {
            public void actionPerformed(ActionEvent e) {
                b.setLabel("Press Me Again");
            }
        } );
    }
    ...
}
```

As you can see, an anonymous class is declared as part of an allocation expression. If the name after new is the name of an interface, as is the case in the preceding example, the anonymous class is an immediate subclass of Object that implements the given interface. If the name after new is the name of a class, the anonymous class is an immediate subclass of the named class.

Obviously, an anonymous class doesn't have a name. The other restriction on an anonymous class is it can't have any constructors other than the default constructor. Any constructor-like initialization must be done using an instance initializer. Other than these differences, anonymous classes function just like local classes.

References Allocation Expressions 4.2; Class Declarations 5.4; Instance Initializers 5.4.10; Object 10.14

5.3.7.5 Implementation of inner classes

It is possible to use inner classes without knowing anything about how they are implemented. However, a high-level understanding can help you comprehend the filenames that the compiler produces, and also some of the restrictions associated with inner classes. The implementation of inner classes is less than transparent in a number of ways, primarily because the Java virtual machine does not know about inner classes. Instead, the Java compiler implements inner classes by rewriting them in a form that does not use inner classes. The advantage of this approach is that the Java virtual machine does not require any new features to be able to run programs that use inner classes.

Since a class declared inside another class is rewritten by the compiler as an external class, the compiler must give it a name unique outside of the class in which it is declared. The unique name is formed by prefixing the name of the inner class with the name of the class in which it is declared and a dollar sign ($). Thus, when the Queue class is compiled, the Java compiler produces four *.class* files:

- *Queue.class*
- *Queue$EmptyQueueException.class*
- *Queue$QueueEnumerator.class*
- *Queue$QueueNode.class*

Because anonymous classes do not have names, the Java compiler gives each anonymous class a number for a name; the numbers start at 1. When the version of the z applet that uses an anonymous class is compiled, the Java compiler produces two *.class* files:

- *Z.class*
- *Z$1.class*

In order to give an inner class access to the variables of its enclosing instance, the compiler adds a `private` variable to the inner class that references the enclosing instance. The compiler also inserts a formal parameter into each constructor of the inner class and passes the reference to the enclosing instance using this parameter. Therefore, the `QueueEnumerator` class is rewritten as follows:

```
class Queue$QueueEnumerator implements Enumeration {
    private Queue this$0;
    private QueueNode start, end;
    QueueEnumerator(Queue this$0) {
        this.this$0 = this$0;
        synchronized (this$0) {
            if (queue != null) {
                start = queue.next;
                end = queue;
            }
        }
    }
    ...
}
```

As you can see, the compiler rewrites all references to the enclosing instance as `this$0`. One implication of this implementation is that you cannot pass the enclosing instance as an argument to its superclass's constructor because `this$0` is not available until after the superclass's constructor returns.

5.4 Class Declarations

A class declaration creates a reference type in Java. The class declaration also specifies the implementation of the class, including its variables, constructors, and methods. The formal definition of a class declaration is:

ClassDeclaration

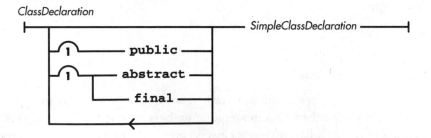

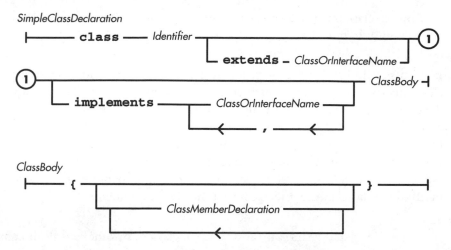

While the above diagram may seem complicated, a class declaration is really made up of six distinct things:

- Optional modifiers that specify attributes of the class

- The keyword `class`

- An identifier that names the class

- An optional `extends` clause that specifies the superclass of the declared class

- An optional `implements` clause that specifies the interfaces implemented by the declared class

- Any number of member declarations, which can include variables, methods, constructors, static initializers, instance initializers, nested top-level classes and interfaces, and member classes

References Classes 5.3.1; *ClassOrInterfaceName* 4.1.6; *ClassMemberDeclaration* 5.4.4; *Identifier* 2.2.1

5.4.1 Class Modifiers

The keywords `public`, `abstract`, and `final` can appear as modifiers at the beginning of a class declaration. In this situation, these modifiers have the following meanings:[*]

`public`
> If a class is declared `public`, it can be referenced by any other class. If the `public` modifier is not used, however, the class can only be referenced by other classes in the same package. A single source file, or compilation unit,

---

[*] Version 1.0 of Java included a `private protected` access specification; this specification has been removed as of version 1.0.2 of the language.

can only declare one `public` class or interface (see 7.1 Compilation Units for an exception to this rule).

`abstract`

If a class is declared `abstract`, no instances of the class may be created. A class declared `abstract` may contain `abstract` methods. Classes not declared `abstract` may not contain abstract methods and must override any abstract methods they inherit with methods that are not `abstract`. Furthermore, classes that implement an interface and are not declared `abstract` must contain or inherit methods that are not `abstract` that have the same name, number of parameters, and corresponding parameter types as the methods declared in the interfaces that the class implements.

`final`

If a class is declared `final`, it cannot be subclassed. In other words, it cannot appear in the `extends` clause of another class.

You want to declare a class `final` if it is important to ensure the exact properties and behavior of that class. Many of the classes in the `java.lang` package are declared `final` for that reason. In addition, the compiler can often optimize operations on `final` classes. For example, the compiler can optimize operations involving the `String` class because it can safely assume the exact logic of `String` methods. The compiler does not have to account for the possibility of methods of a `final` class being overridden in a subclass.

References Compilation Units 7.1; Inner class modifiers 5.4.11.1; Local class modifiers 6.1.2.1; Method modifiers 5.4.6.1; Variable modifiers 5.4.5.1

5.4.2 Class Name

The identifier that follows the keyword `class` is the name of the class. This identifier can be used as a reference type wherever the class is accessible.

References Class Types 3.2.1

5.4.3 Class Inheritance

The `extends` clause specifies the superclass of the class being declared. If a class is declared without an `extends` clause, the class `Object` is its implicit superclass. The class inherits all of the accessible methods and variables of its superclass.

If a class is declared `final`, it cannot appear in an `extends` clause for any other class.

The `implements` clause specifies any interfaces implemented by the class being declared. Unless it is an `abstract` class, the class (or one of its superclasses) must define implementations for all of the methods declared in the interfaces.

References Inheritance 5.3.5; Interfaces 5.3.6; Interface Declarations 5.5; Object 10.14

5.4.4 Class Members

Fields are the variables, methods, constructors, static (load-time) initializers, instance initializers, nested top-level classes and interfaces, and member classes that are declared as part of a class:

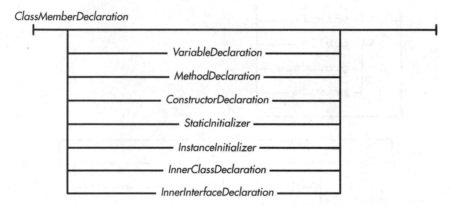

A member declaration causes the member to be defined throughout the entire class and all of its subclasses. This means that it is not a problem to have forward references to members, or in other words, you can use members in a class before you have defined them. For example:

```
class foo {
    void doIt() {
        countIt();
    }
    void countIt() {
        i++;
    }
    int i;
}
```

References *ConstructorDeclaration* 5.4.7; *InnerClassDeclaration* 5.4.11; *InnerInterfaceDeclaration* 5.5.7; *InstanceInitializer* 5.4.10; *MethodDeclaration* 5.4.6; *StaticInitializer* 5.4.9; *VariableDeclaration* 5.4.5

5.4.5 Variables

A variable that is declared as a member in a class is called a *field variable*. A field variable is different from a local variable, which is declared within a method or a block. The formal definition of a variable declaration is:

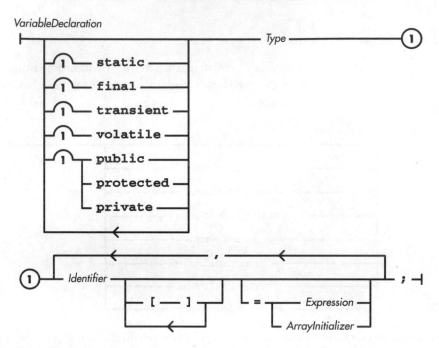

While the above diagram may seem complicated, a variable declaration is really made up of four distinct things:

- Optional modifiers that specify attributes of the variable.

- A type, which can be either a primitive type or a reference type.

- Any number of identifiers that name variables. Each name can be followed by pairs of square brackets to indicate an array variable.

- An optional initializer for each variable declared.

Here are some examples of variable declarations:

```
int x;
public static final double[] k, m[];
```

References *ArrayInitializer* 5.4.5.4; *Expression* 4; *Identifier* 2.2.1; Local Variables 6.1.1; *Type* 3

5.4.5.1 *Variable modifiers*

The modifiers `public`, `protected`, and `private` can be used in the declaration of a field variable to specify the accessibility of the variable. In this situation, the modifiers have the following meanings:[*]

public
> A field variable that is declared `public` is accessible from any class.

protected
> A field variable that is declared `protected` is accessible to any class that is part of the same package as the class in which the variable is declared. Such a field variable is also accessible to any subclass of the class in which it is declared; this occurs regardless of whether or not the subclass is part of the same package.

private
> A field variable that is declared `private` is only accessible in the class in which it is declared. Such a field variable is not accessible to other classes. In particular, a field variable that is declared `private` is not accessible in subclasses of the class in which it is declared.

If a field variable is not declared with any of the access modifiers, the variable has the default accessibility. Default access is often called "friendly" access because it is similar to `friendly` access in C++. A variable with default access is accessible in any class that is part of the same package as the class in which the variable is declared. However, a friendly variable is not accessible to classes outside of the package in which it is declared, even if the desired classes are subclasses of the class in which it is declared.

The keywords `static`, `final`, `transient`, and `volatile` can also be used in the declaration of a field variable. These modifiers have the following meanings:

static
> A field variable that is declared with the `static` modifier is called a *class variable*. There is exactly one copy of each class variable associated with the class; every instance of the class shares the single copy of the class's `static` variables. Thus, setting the value of a class variable changes the value of the variable for all objects that are instances of that class or any of its subclasses.

---

[*] Version 1.0 of Java included a `private protected` access specification; this specification has been removed as of version 1.0.2 of the language.

For example, if you want to count how many instances of a class have been instantiated, you can write:

```
class Foo {
    ...
    static int fooCount = 0;
    Foo() {
        fooCount++;
    }
    ...
}
```

A field variable that is not declared with the static modifier is called an *instance variable*. There is a distinct copy of each instance variable associated with every instance of the class. Thus, setting the value of an instance variable in one object does not affect the value of that instance variable in any other object.

final

If a field variable is declared with the final modifier, the variable is a named constant value. As such, it must be assigned an initial value. Any assignment to a final variable, other than the one that provides its initial value, is a compile-time error. The initial value for a final variable is typically provided by an initializer that is part of the variable's declaration. For example:

```
final int X = 4;
```

A final field variable that is not initialized in its declaration is called a *blank final*. Blank finals are not supported prior to Java 1.1. A blank final that is declared static must be assigned a value exactly once in a static initializer. A blank final that is not declared static must be assigned a value exactly once in an instance initializer or exactly once in each constructor. The compiler uses flow analysis that takes if statements and iteration statements into account to ensure that a blank final is assigned a value exactly once. Thus, it is possible to have multiple assignments to a blank final, so long as exactly one of them can be executed. For example, here is an instance initializer that sets the value of a blank final:

```
{
    final int DAYS_IN_YEAR;
    if (isLeapYear(new Date()))
        DAYS_IN_YEAR = 366;
    else
        DAYS_IN_YEAR = 365;
    ...
}
```

Note that the meaning of final in a variable declaration is very different from the meaning of final in a method or class declaration. In particular, if a class contains a `final` variable, you can declare a variable with the same name in a subclass of that class without causing an error.

`transient`

   The `transient` modifier is used to indicate that a field variable is not part of the persistent state of an object. The `java.io.ObjectOutputStream` class defines `write()` methods that output a representation of an object that can be read later to create a copy of the object. These `write()` methods do not include field variables that are declared `transient` in the representation of an object.

`volatile`

   The `volatile` modifier is used to tell the compiler that a field variable will be modified asynchronously by methods that are running in different threads. Each time the variable is accessed or set, it is fetched from or stored into global memory in a way that avoids the assumption that a version of the variable in a cache or a register is consistent with the version in global memory.

References Class Modifiers 5.4.1; Inner class modifiers 5.4.11.1; Local class modifiers 6.1.2.1; Method modifiers 5.4.6.1

5.4.5.2 *Variable type*

A field variable declaration must always specify the type of the variable. If the declaration of a field variable uses a primitive type, the variable contains a value of the specified primitive type. If the declaration uses a reference type, the variable contains a reference to the specified type of object.

The presence of square brackets in a variable declaration, after either the type or variable name, indicates that the variable contains a reference to an array. For example:

```
int a[];      // a is an array of int
int[] b;      // b is also an array of int
```

It is also possible to declare a variable to contain an array of arrays, or more generally, arrays nested to any level. Each pair of square brackets in the declaration corresponds to a dimension of the array; it makes no difference whether the brackets appear after the type or the variable name. For example:

```
int[][][] d3;      // Each of these is an array of
int[][] f3[];      // arrays of arrays of integers
int[] g3[][];
int h3[][][];
int[] j3, k3[];    // An array and an array of arrays
```

References Array Types 3.2.3; Primitive Types 3.1; Reference Types 3.2

5.4.5.3 Variable name

The identifier that follows the variable type is the name of the variable. This identifier can be used anywhere that the variable is accessible.

It is an error to declare two field variables with the same name in the same class. It is also an error to declare a field variable with the same name as a method declared in the same class or any of its superclasses.

If a field variable is declared with the same name as a variable declared in a superclass, the variable in the superclass is considered to be *shadowed*. If a variable is shadowed in a class, it cannot be accessed as a field of that class. However, a shadowed variable can be accessed by casting a reference to an object of that class to a reference to the appropriate superclass in which the variable is not shadowed. For example:

```
class A {
    int x = 4;
}
class B extends A {
    int x = 7;
    B () {
        int i = x;                 // i gets the value of B's x
        int h = ((A)this).x;       // h gets the value of A's x
    }
}
```

Alternatively, if a variable is shadowed in a class but not in its immediate superclass, the methods of the class can access the shadowed variable using the keyword super. In the above example, this would look as follows:

```
int h = super.x;          // h gets the value of A's x
```

If a method is declared with the same name and parameters as a method in a superclass, the method in the superclass is considered to be overridden. Note that variable shadowing is different than method overriding. The most important difference is that using a reference to an instance of an object's superclass does not provide access to overridden methods. Overriding is described in detail in 5.4.6.3 Method name.

References Field Expressions 4.1.6; Identifiers 2.2.1; Inheritance 5.3.5; Method name 5.4.6.3

5.4.5.4 Variable initializers

A variable declaration can contain an initializer. However, if a variable is declared to be final, it must either have an initializer or be initialized exactly once in a static initializer, instance initializer, or constructor. If the variable is of a non-array type, the expression in the initializer is evaluated and the variable is set to the result of the expression, as long as the result is assignment-compatible with the variable. If the variable is of an array type, the initializer must be an array initializer:

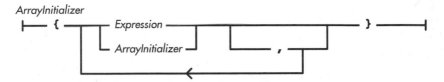

Each expression or array initializer in an array initializer is evaluated and becomes an element of the array produced by the initializer. The variable is set to the array produced by the initializer, as long as the assignment is assignment-compatible. Here are some examples of actual array initializers:

```
short a[] = {2,5,8,2,11};     // array of 5 shorts
int s[][] = { {3,45,8},       // array of 4 arrays
            {12,9,33},        // of 3 ints
            {7,22,53},
            {33,1,2} };
```

Note that a trailing comma is allowed within an array initializer. For example, the following is legal:

```
int x[] = {2,23,4,};
```

Any initializers for class variables (i.e., `static` variables) are evaluated when the class is loaded. The initializer for a class variable cannot refer to any instance variables in the class. An initializer for a `static` variable cannot refer to any `static` variables that are declared after its own declaration. The initial value of a class variable can also be set in a static initializer for the class; static initializers are described in 5.4.9 Static Initializers.

Any initializers for instance variables are evaluated when a constructor for the class is called to create an instance of the class. Every class has at least one constructor that explicitly or implicitly calls one of the constructors of its immediate superclass before it does anything else. When the superclass's constructor returns, any instance variable initializers (and instance initializers) are evaluated before the constructor does anything else. The initial value of an instance variable can also be set in an instance initializer; instance initializers are described in 5.4.10 Instance Initializers. Of course, it is also possible to set the initial values of instance variables explicitly in a constructor. Constructors are described in 5.4.7 Constructors.

If a variable declaration does not contain an initializer, the variable is set to a default value. The actual value is determined by the variable's type. Table 5-1 shows the default values used for the various types in Java.

Table 5–1: Default Values for Field Variables

Type	Default Value
byte	0
char	'\u0000'
short	0
int	0
long	0L
float	0.0F
double	0.0
boolean	false
Object reference	null

For an array, every element of the array is set to the appropriate default value, based on the type of elements in the array.

Here are some examples of variable declarations, with and without initializers:

```
int i,j;                   // initialized to zero
long k = 243L;
double d = k*1.414;
String s;                  // initialized to null
char c[] = new char[123];
float f[] = { 3.2f, 4.7f, 9.12f, 345.9f};
Double dbl = new Double(382.3748);
java.io.File fl = new File("/dev/null");
Object o = fl;
```

References Array Types 3.2.3; Assignment Operators 4.13; Constructors 5.4.7; *Expression* 4; Instance Initializers 5.4.10; Static Initializers 5.4.9; Variable modifiers 5.4.5.1

5.4.6 Methods

A method is a piece of executable code that can be called as a subroutine or a function. A method can be passed parameters by its caller; the method can also return a result to its caller. In Java, a method can only be declared as a field in a class. The formal definition of a method declaration is:

MethodDeclaration

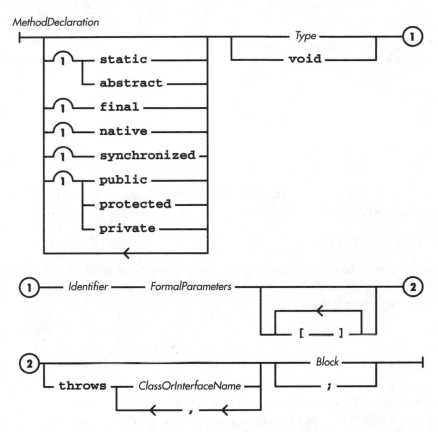

While the above diagram may seem complicated, a method declaration is really made up of six distinct things:

- Optional modifiers that specify attributes of the method
- A type that specifies the type of value returned by the method
- An identifier that names the method
- A list of formal parameters that specifies the values that are passed to the method
- An optional `throws` clause that specifies any exceptions that can be thrown by the method
- A block that defines the functionality of the method

Here are some examples of method declarations:

```
public static void main(String[] argv) {
    System.out.println( argv[0] );
}
int readSquare(DataInputStream d) throws IOException {
    int i = d.readInt();
```

```
        return i*i;
    }
int filledArray(int length, int value) [] {
    int [] array = new int [length];
    for (int i = 0; i < length; i++ ) {
        array[i] = value;
    }
    return array;
}
```

Unlike C/C++, Java only allows method declarations that fully specify the type and number of parameters that the method can be called with.

References *Block* 6.1; *ClassOrInterfaceName* 4.1.6; Exception Handling 9; *FormalParameters* 5.4.6.4; *Identifier* 2.2.1; *Type* 3

5.4.6.1 *Method modifiers*

The modifiers `public`, `protected`, and `private` can be used in the declaration of a method to specify the accessibility of the method. In this situation, the modifiers have the following meanings:

public
  A method that is declared `public` is accessible from any class.

protected
  A method that is declared `protected` is accessible in any class that is part of the same package as the class in which the method is declared. Such a method is also accessible to any subclass of the class in which it is declared, regardless of whether or not the subclass is part of the same package.

private
  A method that is declared `private` is only accessible in the class in which it is declared. Such a method is not accessible in other classes. In particular, a method that is declared `private` is not accessible in subclasses of the class in which it is declared. A method cannot be declared both `private` and `abstract`.

If a method is not declared with any of the access modifiers, it has the default accessibility. Default access is often called "friendly" access because it is similar to `friendly` access in C++. A method with default access is accessible in any class that is part of the same package as the class in which the method is declared. However, a friendly method is not accessible to classes outside of the package in which it is declared, even if the classes are subclasses of the class in which it is declared.

The keywords `static`, `final`, `abstract`, `native`, and `synchronized` can also be used in the declaration of a method. These modifiers have the following meanings:

static

A method that is declared with the static modifier is called a *class method*. Class methods are not associated with an instance of a class. This means that a class method cannot directly refer to other, non-static methods or variables in its class, unless the method or variable is accessed through an explicit object reference. In addition, the keywords this and super are treated as undefined variables within static methods. A method that is declared static is also implicitly final, or in other words, static methods cannot be overridden. A method that is declared static cannot also be declared abstract.

Because static methods are not associated with a class instance, you do not need an instance of a class to invoke such a method. For example, the Math class contains a collection of mathematical methods that can be called using the class name:

```
Math.tan(x)
```

A method that is not declared with the static modifier is called an *instance method*. Instance methods are associated with an instance of a class, so an instance method may contain direct references to any other methods or variables in its class.

final

A method that is declared with the final modifier cannot be overridden. In other words, if a method in a class is declared final, no subclass of that class can declare a method with the same name, number of parameters, and parameter types as the final method. Although final methods cannot be overridden, declaring a method to be final in no way prevents it from being overloaded.

abstract

If a method is declared with the abstract modifier, the declaration must end with a semicolon rather than a block. An abstract method declaration specifies the name, number and type of parameters, and return type of the method; it does not specify the implementation of the method. If a class contains an abstract method, the class must also be declared abstract. If a non-abstract class inherits an abstract method, the class must override the method and provide an implementation.

An abstract method cannot also be declared either private or static because neither private nor static methods can be overridden. A private method cannot be overridden because it is not inherited by its subclasses; a static method cannot be overridden because it is implicitly final.

native

> If a method is declared with the native modifier, the declaration must end with a semicolon rather than a block. A native method is implemented in a platform-specific way using a language other than Java, such as C++. Because the implementation of a native method is not done in Java, Java requires the semicolon in place of an implementation.

> Because the implementation of a native method is platform-specific, you should avoid using native methods in classes that are expected to run on different kinds of clients. Native methods also require an installation process, which is another reason to avoid them for use on clients.

synchronized

> If a method is declared with the synchronized modifier, a thread must obtain a lock before it can invoke the method. If the method is not declared static, the thread must obtain a lock associated with the object used to access the method. If the method is declared static, the thread must obtain a lock associated with the class in which the method is declared.

> A synchronized method is one of two mechanisms for providing single-threaded access to the contents of a class or object. The other mechanism is the synchronized statement. Of the two, a synchronized method is usually the preferred mechanism. If all access to instance data that is shared by multiple threads is through synchronized methods, the integrity of the instance data is guaranteed, no matter what the callers of the methods do. On the other hand, if instance data shared by multiple threads is directly accessible outside of the class that defines it or its subclasses, providing single-threaded access to the data requires the use of synchronized statements.

References Class Modifiers 5.4.1; Inner class modifiers 5.4.11.1; Local class modifiers 6.1.2.1; Variable modifiers 5.4.5.1

5.4.6.2 Method return type

A method declaration must always specify the type of value returned by the method. The return value can be of a primitive type or of a reference type. If the method does not return a value, it should be declared with its return type specified as void. The return type comes before the name of the method in the method declaration.

The presence of square brackets in a method declaration, after either the return type or the formal parameters, indicates that the method returns a reference to the specified type of array.

For example:

```
int a()[] {...};     // a returns an array of int
int[] b() {...};     // b also returns an array of int
```

It is also possible to declare that a method returns a reference to an array of arrays, or more generally, arrays nested to any level. Each pair of square brackets in the declaration corresponds to a dimension of the array; it makes no difference whether the brackets appear after the return type or the formal parameters. For example:

```
int[][][] d3() {...};     // Each of these returns an array of
int[][] f3()[] {...};     // arrays of arrays of integers
int[] g3()[][] {...};
int h3()[][][] {...};
```

If a method is declared with the void return type, any return statement that appears within the method must not contain a return value. Because a method with a void return type does not return a value, such a method can only be called from an expression statement that consists of a method call expression.

On the other hand, if a method is declared with a return type other than void, it must return through an explicit return statement that contains a return value that is assignment-compatible with the return type of the method.

References Array Types 3.2.3; Expression Statements 6.4; Primitive Types 3.1; Reference Types 3.2; The return Statement 6.10

5.4.6.3 Method name

The identifier that follows the return type is the name of the method. This identifier can be used anywhere that the method is accessible.

It is an error to declare two methods that have the same name, the same number of parameters, and the same type for each corresponding parameter in the same class. It is also an error to declare a method with the same name as a variable declared in the same class or any of its superclasses.

A method is said to be *overloaded* if there is more than one accessible method in a class with the same name, but with parameters that differ in number or type.[*] This situation can arise if two or more such methods are declared in the same class. It can also occur when at least one of the methods is defined in a superclass and the rest are in a subclass.

---

[*] Although Java supports overloaded methods, it does not allow programs to define overloaded operators. While it is true that the + operator is defined in an overloaded way, that operator is part of the language specification and it is the only overloaded operator.

Overloaded methods aren't required to have the same return type. For example:

```
int max(int x, int y){return x>y ? x : y;}
double max(double x, double y){return x>y ? x : y;}
```

A method that is inherited from a superclass is said to be *overridden* if a method in the inheriting class has the same name, number of parameters, and types of parameters as the inherited method. If the overridden method returns void, the overriding method must also return void. Otherwise, the return type of the overriding method must be the same as the type of the overridden method.

An overriding method can be more accessible than the overridden method, but it cannot be less accessible. In other words, a subclass cannot hide things that are visible in its superclass, but it can make visible things that are hidden. An object is considered to be an instance of its own class, as well as an instance of each of its superclasses. As a result, you can use an object reference to call a method in an object and not worry about whether the object is actually an instance of a subclass of the type of the reference. If a subclass were allowed to override methods of its superclass with methods that were less accessible, you would no longer be able to use a reference without regard to the actual type of the object being referenced.

For example, Object is the superclass of String. This means that a variable declared to contain a reference to an Object may actually refer to a String. The Object class defines a public method called hashCode(), so a reference to the Object class can be used to call the hashCode() method of whatever subclass of Object it refers to. Allowing a subclass of Object to declare a private hashcode() method would be inconsistent with this usage.

Table 5-2 shows the access modifiers that are permitted for an overriding method, based on the access allowed for the overridden method.

Table 5–2: Permitted Access Modifiers for Overriding Methods

| | | **Access declared for overridden method** | | |
		no modifier	protected	public
Access for overriding method	private	not allowed	not allowed	not allowed
	no modifier	allowed	not allowed	not allowed
	protected	allowed	allowed	not allowed
	public	allowed	allowed	allowed

If a method in the superclass is declared private, it is not inherited by the subclass. This means that a method in the subclass that has the same name, number of parameters, and types of parameters does not override the `private` method in the superclass. As a result, the method in the subclass can have any return type and there are no restrictions on its accessibility.

Non-`static` methods must be called through an object reference. If a non-`static` method is called with no explicit object reference, it is implicitly called using the object reference `this`. At compile-time, the type of the object reference is used to determine the combinations of method names and parameters that are accessible to the calling expression (see 4.1.8 Method Call Expression). At run-time, however, the actual type of the object determines which of the methods is called. If the actual object is an instance of a subclass of the referenced class and the subclass overrides the method being called, the overriding method in the subclass is invoked.

In other words, the actual type of the object is used to determine which method to call, not the type of the reference to that object. This means that you cannot simply cast an object reference to a superclass of the class of the actual object to call to an overridden method. Instead, you use the keyword `super` to access an overridden method in the superclass. For example:

```
class A {
    void doit() {
        ...
    }
}

class B extends A {
    void doit() {
        super.doit();        // calls overridden A.doit()
    }
    public static void main(String argv[]) {
        B b = new B();
        ((A)b).doit();       // calls B.doit()
    }
}
```

The `doit()` method in class `B` calls the overridden `doit()` method in class `A` using the `super` construct. But, in `main()`, the `doit()` method in class `B` is invoked because casting a reference does not provide access to overridden methods.

References Identifiers 2.2.1; Inheritance 5.3.5; Method Call Expression 4.1.8; Variable name 5.4.5.3

5.4.6.4 *Method formal parameters*

The formal parameters in a method declaration specify a list of variables to which values are assigned when the method is called:

FormalParameters

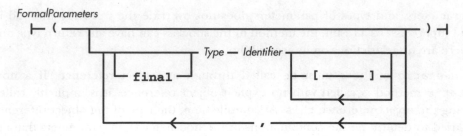

Within the block that contains the implementation of the method, the method's formal parameters are treated as local variables; the name of each formal parameter is available as an identifier in the method's implementation. Formal parameters differ from local variables only in that their declaration and value come from outside the method's block.

If a formal parameter is declared `final`, any assignment to that parameter generates an error. The syntax for declaring `final` parameters is not supported prior to Java 1.1.

If a method has no formal parameters, the parentheses must still appear in the method declaration.

Here's an example of a method declaration with formal parameters:

```
abstract int foo(DataInputStream d, Double[] values, int weights[]) ;
```

The presence of square brackets in a formal parameter declaration, either as part of a reference type or after the name of a formal parameter, indicates that the formal parameter is an array type. For example:

```
foo(int a[],     // a is an array of int
    int[] b)     // b is also an array of int
```

It is also possible to declare that a formal parameter is an array of arrays, or more generally, arrays nested to any level. Each pair of square brackets in the declaration corresponds to a dimension of the array; it makes no difference whether the brackets appear with the type or after the name of the formal parameter. For example:

```
int[][][] d3       // Each of these is an array of
int[][] f3[]       // arrays of arrays of integers
int[] g3[][]
int h3[][][]
```

References Array Types 3.2.3; Blocks 6.1; *Identifier* 2.2.1; Local Variables 6.1.1; *Type* 3

5.4.6.5 *Method throws clause*

If a method is expected to throw any exceptions, the method declaration must declare that fact in a throws clause. Java requires that most types of exceptions either be caught or declared, so bugs caused by programmers forgetting to handle particular types of exceptions are uncommon in Java programs.

If a method implementation contains a throw statement, or if the method calls another method declared with a throws clause, there is the possibility that an exception will be thrown from within the method. If the exception is not caught, it will be thrown out of the method to its caller. Any exception that can be thrown out of a method in this way must be listed in a throws clause in the method declaration, unless the exception is an instance of Error, RuntimeException, or a subclass of one of those classes. Subclasses of the Error class correspond to situations that are not easily predicted, such as the system running out of memory. Subclasses of RuntimeException correspond to many common runtime problems, such as illegal casts and array index problems. The classes listed in a throws clause must be Throwable or any of its subclasses; the Throwable class is the superclass of all objects that can be thrown in Java.

Consider the following example:

```
import java.io.IOException;

class throwsExample {
    char[] a;
    int position;
    ...
    // Method explicitly throws an exception
    int read() throws IOException {
        if (position >= a.length)
            throw new IOException();
        return a[position++];
    }

    // Method implicitly throws an exception
    String readUpTo(char terminator) throws IOException {
        StringBuffer s = new StringBuffer();
        while (true) {
            int c = read(); // Can throw IOException
            if (c == -1 || c == terminator) {
                return s.toString();
            }
            s.append((char)c);
        }
        return s.toString():
    }

    // Method catches an exception internally
    int getLength() {
```

```
        String s;
        try {
            s = readUpTo(':');
        } catch (IOException e) {
            return 0;
        }
        return s.length();
    }

    // Method can throw a RuntimeException
    int getAvgLength() {
        int count = 0;
        int total = 0;
        int len;
        while (true){
            len = getLength();
            if (len == 0)
                break;
            count++;
            total += len;
        }
        return total/count; // Can throw ArithmeticException
    }
}
```

The method read() can throw an IOException, so it declares that fact in its throws clause. Without that throws clause, the compiler would complain that the method must either declare IOException in its throws clause or catch it. Although the readUpTo() method does not explicitly throw any exceptions, it calls the read() method that does throw an IOException, so it declares that fact in its throws clause. Whether explicitly or implicitly thrown, the requirement to catch or declare an exception is the same. The getLength() method catches the IOException thrown by readUpTo(), so it does not have to declare the exception. The final method, getAvgLength(), can throw an ArithmeticException if count is zero. Because ArithmeticException is a subclass of Runtime-Exception, the fact that it can be thrown out of getAvgLength() does not need to be declared.

If a method overrides another method, the overriding method cannot throw anything that the overridden method does not throw. Specifically, if the declaration of a method contains a throws clause, any method that overrides that method cannot include any classes in its throws clause that are not declared in the overridden method. This restriction avoids surprises. When a method is called, the Java compiler requires that all of the objects listed the method's throws clause are either caught by the calling method or declared in the calling method's throws clause. The requirement that an overriding method cannot include any class in its throws clause that is not in the overridden method's throws clause ensures that the guarantee made by the compiler is respected by the runtime environment.

References Exception Handling 9; The throw Statement 6.11; The try Statement 6.12

5.4.6.6 Method implementation

A method declaration must end with either a block or a semicolon. If either the abstract or native modifier is used in the declaration, the declaration must end with a semicolon. All other method declarations must end with a block that defines the implementation of the method.

References Blocks 6.1; Method modifiers 5.4.6.1

5.4.7 Constructors

A constructor is a special kind of method that is designed to set the initial values of an object's instance variables and do anything else that is necessary to create an object. Constructors are only called as part of the object creation process. The declaration of a constructor does not include a return type. The name of a constructor is always the same as the name of the class:

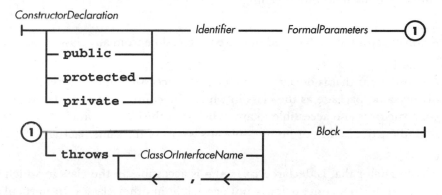

A constructor declaration is really made up of five distinct things:

- Optional modifiers that specify attributes of the constructor

- An identifier that names the constructor; this identifier must be the same as the name of the class

- A list of formal parameters that specifies the values that are passed to the constructor

- An optional throws clause that specifies any exceptions that can be thrown by the constructor

- A block that defines the functionality of the constructor

Here is an example that shows a class with some constructors:

```
class Construct {
    private Construct(Double[] values, int weights[]) {
    }
    public Construct(OutputStream o, Double[] values, int weights[])
                    throws IOException {
        this(values, weights);
        o.write(weights[0]);
    }
    public Construct() {
    }
}
```

References *Block* 6.1; *ClassOrInterfaceName* 4.1.6; Exception Handling 9; *FormalParameters* 5.4.6.4; *Identifier* 2.2.1; Object Creation 5.3.3

5.4.7.1 Constructor modifiers

The modifiers `public`, `protected`, and `private` can be used in the declaration of a constructor to specify the accessibility of the constructor. In this situation, the modifiers have the following meanings:

`public`
> A constructor that is declared `public` is accessible from any class.

`protected`
> A constructor that is declared `protected` is accessible in any class that is part of the same package as the class in which the constructor is declared. Such a constructor is also accessible to any subclass of the class in which it is declared, regardless of whether or not the subclass is part of the same package.

`private`
> A constructor that is declared `private` is accessible in the class in which it is declared. Such a constructor is not accessible in other classes. In particular, a constructor that is declared `private` is not accessible in subclasses of the class in which it is declared.

> If a class is declared with at least one constructor, to prevent Java from providing a default `public` constructor, and all of the constructors are declared `private`, no other class can create an instance of the class. It makes sense to prevent the instantiation of a class if the class exists only to provide a collection of `static` methods. An example of this type of class is `java.lang.Math`.

> `private` constructors can be used by `static` methods in the same class.

If a constructor is not declared with any of the access modifiers, the constructor has the default accessibility. Default access is often called "friendly" access because it is similar to `friendly` access in C++. A constructor with default access is accessible in any class that is part of the same package as the class in which the constructor is declared. However, a friendly constructor is not accessible in sub-classes of the class in which it is declared.

References Class Modifiers 5.4.1; Inner class modifiers 5.4.11.1; Local class modifiers 6.1.2.1

5.4.7.2 Constructor name

A constructor has no name of its own. The identifier that appears in a constructor declaration must be the same as the name of the class in which the constructor is declared. This identifier can be used anywhere that the constructor is accessible.

References Class Types 3.2.1

5.4.7.3 Constructor return type

A constructor has no declared return type; it always returns an object that is an instance of its class. A `return` statement in a constructor is treated the same as it is in a method declared to return `void`; the `return` statement must not contain a return value. Note that it is not possible to explicitly declare a constructor to have the return type `void`.

References The return Statement 6.10

5.4.7.4 Constructor formal parameters

The formal parameters in a constructor declaration specify a list of variables to which values are assigned when the constructor is called. Within the block that contains the implementation of the constructor, the constructor's formal parameters are treated as local variables; the name of each formal parameter is available as an identifier in the constructor's implementation. Formal parameters differ from local variables only in that their declaration and value come from outside the constructor's block.

If a formal parameter is declared `final`, any assignment to that parameter generates an error. The syntax for declaring `final` parameters is not supported prior to Java 1.1.

If a constructor has no formal parameters, the parentheses must still appear in the constructor declaration.

The presence of square brackets in a formal parameter declaration, either as part of a reference type or after the name of a formal parameter, indicates that the formal parameter is an array type. For example:

```
Foo(int a[],     // a is an array of int
    int[] b)     // b is also an array of int
```

It is also possible to declare that a formal parameter is an array of arrays, or more generally, arrays nested to any level. Each pair of square brackets in the declaration corresponds to a dimension of the array; it makes no difference whether the brackets appear with the type or after the name of the formal parameter. For example:

```
int[][][] d3        // Each of these is an array of
int[][] f3[]        // arrays of arrays of integers
int[] g3[][]
int h3[][][]
```

References Array Types 3.2.3; Blocks 6.1; *FormalParameters* 5.4.6.4; Local Variables 6.1.1

5.4.7.5 *Constructor throws clause*

If a constructor is expected to throw any exceptions, the constructor declaration must declare that fact in a throws clause. If a constructor implementation contains a throw statement, or if the constructor calls another constructor or method declared with a throws clause, there is the possibility that an exception will be thrown from within the constructor.

If the exception is not caught, it will be thrown out of the constructor to its caller. Any exception that can be thrown out of a constructor in this way must be listed in a throws clause in the constructor declaration, unless the exception is an instance of Error, RuntimeException, or a subclass of one of those classes.

Subclasses of the Error class correspond to situations that are not easily predicted, such as the system running out of memory. Subclasses of RuntimeException correspond to many common runtime problems, such as illegal casts and array index problems. The classes listed in a throws clause must be Throwable or any of its subclasses; the Throwable class is the superclass of all objects that can be thrown in Java.

References Exception Handling 9; The throw Statement 6.11; The try Statement 6.12

5.4.7.6 *Constructor implementation*

The block at the end of a constructor declaration contains the implementation of the constructor. The block is called the constructor body. The first statement in a constructor body is special; it is the only place that Java allows an explicit call to a constructor outside of an allocation expression. An explicit call to a constructor has a special form:

ExplicitConstructorCallStatement

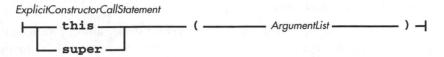

In an explicit constructor call, the keyword this can be used to specify a call to a constructor in the same class. The keyword super can be used to specify a call to a constructor in the immediate superclass.

For example:

```
class Square extends RegularPolygon {
    // Construct a square without specifying the length of the sides
    Square() {
        this(5);
    }

    // Construct a square with sides of a specified length
    Square(int len) {
        super(4,len);
    }
}
```

The first constructor simply calls the second constructor with the argument 5. The second constructor calls a constructor in the immediate superclass to create a four-sided regular polygon with sides of the given length.

Except for the constructors in the class Object, a constructor always begins by calling another constructor in the same class or in its immediate superclass. If the first statement in a constructor is not an explicit call to another constructor using this or super and the class is not Object, the compiler inserts a call to super() before the first statement in the constructor.

In other words, if a constructor does not begin with an explicit call to another constructor, it begins with an implicit call to the constructor of its immediate superclass that takes no argument. The result is constructor chaining: a constructor for each superclass of a class is called before the constructor of the class executes any of its own code. After all of the calls to the superclasses' constructors (explicit or implicit) have returned, any instance variables that have initializers are initialized, and finally the constructor executes its own code.

Constructor chaining places a restriction on the arguments that can be passed to a constructor in an explicit constructor call. The expressions provided as arguments must not refer to any instance variables of the object being created because these instance variables are not initialized until the superclass's constructor returns.

References *ArgumentList* 4.1.8; Object Allocation Expressions 4.2.1; this 4.1.1; super 4.1.2

5.4.7.7 *The default constructor*

If a class declaration does not contain any constructor declarations, Java supplies a default constructor for the class. The default constructor is `public`, it takes no arguments, and it simply calls the constructor of its class's superclass that takes no arguments. The default constructor is approximately equivalent to:

```
public MyClass() {
    super();
}
```

Because Java creates a default constructor only for a class that does not have any explicitly declared constructors, it is possible for the superclass of that class not to have a constructor that takes no arguments. If a class declaration does not contain a constructor declaration and its immediate superclass does not have a constructor that takes no arguments, the compiler issues an error message because the default constructor references a non-existent constructor in the superclass. The default constructor for the class `Object` does not contain a call to another constructor because class `Object` has no superclass.

References Object 10.14

5.4.7.8 *Constructor inheritance*

A subclass does not inherit constructors from its superclass, as it does normal methods. This is one important difference between regular methods and constructors: constructors are not inherited. However, a subclass can access a constructor in its superclass, as long as the constructor is accessible, based on any access modifiers used in its declaration.

This example illustrates the difference between inheritance and accessibility:

```
public class A {
    public A (int q) {
    }
}
public class B extends A {
    public B () {
        super(5);
    }
}
```

Although class B is a subclass of class A, B does not inherit the public constructor in A that takes a single argument. This means that if you try to create a new instance of B using an allocation expression with a single argument, you'll get an error message from the compiler. Here's an erroneous call:

```
B b1 = new B(9);
```

However, as shown in the example, the constructor in B can access the constructor in A using the keyword super.

5.4.8 The finalize method

A class declaration can include a special method that is called before an instance of the class is destroyed by the garbage collector. This method is called a *finalizer*; it has the name finalize(). The finalize() method for a class must be declared with no parameters, a void return type, and no modifiers:

```
void finalize() {...}
```

If a class has a finalize() method, it is normally called by the garbage collector before an object of that class type is destroyed. A program can also explicitly call an object's finalize() method, but in this case, the garbage collector does not call the method during the object destruction process. If the garbage collector does call an object's finalize() method, the garbage collector does not immediately destroy the object because the finalize() method might do something that results in a reference to the object. Thus the garbage collector waits to destroy the object until it can again prove it is safe to do so. The next time the garbage collector decides it is safe to destroy the object, it does so without calling the finalizer again. In any case, a finalize() method is never called more than once by the garbage collector for a particular object.

A superclass of the class may also define a finalize() method, but Java does not provide a mechanism that automatically calls the superclass's finalize() method. If a class contains a finalize() method, it is a good idea for that method to call super.finalize() as the very last thing that it does. This technique ensures that the finalize() method of the superclass gets called. The technique even works if the superclass does not explicitly define a finalize() method, since every class inherits a default finalize() method from the Object class. This default finalize method does not do anything.

References Object Destruction 5.3.4

5.4.9 Static Initializers

A *static initializer* is a piece of code that is executed when a class is loaded. A static initializer is simply a block of code in a class declaration that is preceded by the keyword static:

StaticInitializer

├──── **static** ──────────────────── *Block* ────────────┤

A class is loaded when its definition is needed by another class. You can specifically request that a class be loaded by calling the `forName()` method of the `Class` class on the class you want to load. Alternatively, you can use the `loadClass()` method of a `ClassLoader` object to load a class directly.

When a class is loaded, a `Class` object is created to represent it and storage for the class's `static` variables is allocated. When a class is initialized, its static initializers and `static` variable initializers are evaluated in the order in which they appear in the class declaration. For example, here is a class that contains both static initializers and `static` variable initializers:

```
class foo {
    static int i = 4;
    static {
        i += 2;
        j = 5 * i;
    }
    static int j = 7;
    static double d;
    static frame f = new Frame();
    static { d = Math.tan(Math.PI/j); }
}
```

When the `foo` class is loaded, here is what happens. First, the variable `i` is set to 4. Then the first static initializer is executed. It increments `i` by 2, which makes it 6, and sets `j` to `5*i`, which is 30. Next, the variable `j` is set to 7 by its initializer; this overwrites the value that was set in the static initializer. The variable `f` is then set to the new `Frame` object created by its initializer. Finally, the second static initializer is executed. It sets the variable `d` to $\tan(\frac{\pi}{j})$, which is $\tan(\frac{\pi}{7})$.

Notice that the first static initializer uses the variable `j`, even though the variable is not declared until after the static initializer. A static initializer can refer to a `static` variable that is declared after the static initializer. However, the same is not true for `static` variable initializers. A `static` variable initializer cannot refer to any variables that are declared after its own declaration, or the compiler generates an error message. The following class declaration is erroneous:

```
class foo {
    static int x = y*3;    // error because y defined after x
    static int y;
}
```

If an exception is thrown out of a static initializer, the method that caused the class to be defined throws an `ExceptionInInitializerError`. This `Exception-InInitializerError` contains a reference to the original exception that can be fetched by calling its `getException()` method.

References *Block* 6.1; Class 10.4; Errors 9.4.2; Variables 5.4.5

5.4.10 Instance Initializers

An *instance initializer* is a piece of code that is executed when an instance of a class is created. Specifically, it is executed after the object's immediate superclass constructor returns, but before the constructor of the class itself runs. An instance initializer is simply a block of code in a class that is not in any method. Here is the formal syntax:

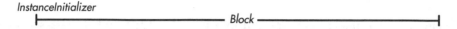

Every class has at least one constructor that explicitly or implicitly calls one of the constructors of its immediate superclass before it does anything else. When the superclass's constructor returns, any instance initializers and instance variable initializers are evaluated before the constructor does anything else. The instance initializers and instance variable initializers are evaluated in the order in which they appear in the class declaration. If an instance initializer throws an exception, the exception appears to have come from the constructor that called the superclass's constructor.

References *Block* 6.1; Constructors 5.4.7; Variable initializers 5.4.5.4

5.4.11 Nested Top-Level and Member Classes

Nested top-level classes and member classes are classes that are declared inside of another class. Just as with a top-level class declaration, the declaration of a nested top-level class or member class creates a reference type in Java. Here's the formal definition of a nested top-level or member class declaration:

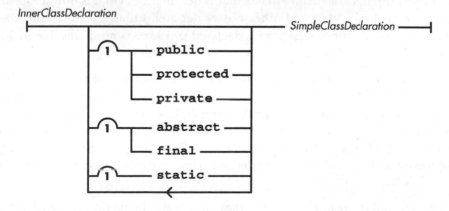

A class declared inside of another class has access to all of the variables, methods, and other inner classes of the enclosing class. If a nested top-level or member class is not `private`, it can also be accessed outside of its enclosing class by qualifying its name with the name of its enclosing class, as follows:

`EnclosingClass.InnerClass`

The syntax for declaring nested top-level classes and member classes is not supported prior to Java 1.1.

References Nested top-level classes and interfaces 5.3.7.1; Member classes 5.3.7.2; *SimpleClassDeclaration* 5.4

5.4.11.1 Inner class modifiers

The keywords `public`, `protected`, and `private` can be used in the declaration of a nested top-level or member class to specify the accessibility of the inner class. In this situation, the modifiers have the following meanings:

public
> A nested top-level or member class that is declared `public` is accessible from any class that can access the enclosing class.

protected
> A nested top-level or member class that is declared `protected` is accessible from any class that is part of the same package as the enclosing class. Such an inner class is also accessible to any subclass of the enclosing class, regardless of whether or not the subclass is part of the same package.

private
> A nested top-level or member class that is declared `private` is only accessible from its enclosing class and other classes declared within the enclosing class. In particular, an inner class that is declared `private` is not accessible in subclasses of its enclosing class.

If a nested top-level or member class is not declared with any of the access modifiers, the class has the default accessability. Default access is often called "friendly" access because it is similar to `friendly` access in C++. An inner class with default access is accessible in any class that is part of the same package as the enclosing class. However, a friendly inner class is not accessible to classes outside of the package of the enclosing class, even if the desired classes are subclasses of the enclosing class.

The keywords `abstract`, `final`, and `static` can also be used in the declaration of a nested top-level or member class. These modifiers have the following meanings:

abstract

> If a nested top-level or member class is declared abstract, no instances of the class may be created. An inner class declared abstract may contain abstract methods; classes not declared abstract may not contain abstract methods and must override any abstract methods they inherit with methods that are not abstract. Furthermore, classes that implement an interface and are not declared abstract must contain or inherit methods that are not abstract, that have the same name, have the same number of parameters, and have corresponding parameter types as the methods declared in the interfaces that the class implements.

final

> If a nested top-level or member class is declared final, it cannot be subclassed. In other words, it cannot appear in the extends clause of another class.

static

> An inner class that is declared with the static modifier is called a nested top-level class. A class can only be declared with the static modifier if its enclosing class is a top-level class (i.e., it is not declared within another class). The code within a nested top-level class cannot directly access non-static variables and methods of its enclosing class.

> An inner class that is not declared with the static modifier is called a member class. The code within a member class can access all of the variables and methods of its enclosing class, including private variables and methods.

References Class Modifiers 5.4.1; Local class modifiers 6.1.2.1

5.4.11.2 Inner class members

The body of a nested top-level or member class cannot declare any static variables, static methods, static classes, or static initializers. Beyond those restrictions, the remainder of the declaration is the same as that for a top-level class declaration, which is described in 5.4 Class Declarations.

References Class Declarations 5.4; Constructors 5.4.7; Instance Initializers 5.4.10; Methods 5.4.6; Nested Top-Level and Member Classes 5.4.11; Static Initializers 5.4.9; Variables 5.4.5

5.5 Interface Declarations

An interface declaration creates a reference type in Java. An interface declaration is similar to a class declaration, with the following two very important differences.

- All of the methods in an interface are implicitly `abstract`. Every method declaration in an interface specifies the formal parameters and return type of the method, but it does not include an implementation of the method.

- All of the variables in an interface are implicitly `static` and `final`.

Interfaces are most useful for declaring that an otherwise unrelated set of classes have a common set of methods. For example, if you want to store a variety of objects in a database, you might want all of those objects to have fetch and store methods. The fetch and store methods of each object require different implementations, so it makes sense to declare the fetch and store methods in an interface declaration. Then any class that needs fetch and store methods can implement the interface.

The formal definition for an interface declaration is:

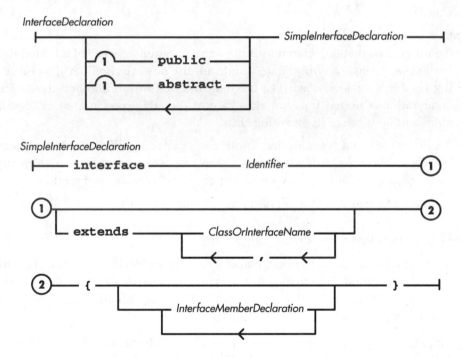

While the above diagram may seem complicated, an interface declaration is really made up of five distinct things:

- Optional modifiers that specify attributes of the class

- The keyword `interface`

- An identifier that names the interface

- An optional `extends` clause that specifies the super interfaces of the declared interface

- Any number of interface member declarations, which can include variables and methods

Here are some sample interface declarations:

```
interface Dyn {
    double squeeze();
}
interface Press extends Dyn {
    double squeeze(double theta);
}
```

Here is an example of a class that implements `Press`:

```
class Clamp implements Press {
    ...
    double squeeze() {
        return squeeze(0);
    }
    double squeeze(double theta) {
        return force*Math.cos(theta);
    }
    ...
}
```

Since the `Press` interface extends the `Dyn` interface, the `Clamp` class must implement the methods declared in both `Dyn` and `Press`.

References Class Declarations 5.4; *ClassOrInterfaceName* 4.1.6; *Identifier* 2.2.1; Interfaces 5.3.6; *InterfaceMemberDeclaration* 5.5.4

5.5.1 Interface Modifiers

The keywords `public` and `abstract` can appear as modifiers at the beginning of an interface declaration. In this situation, these modifiers have the following meanings:

`public`

If an interface is declared `public`, it can be referenced by any class or interface. If the `public` modifier is not used, however, the interface can only be referenced by classes and interfaces in the same package. A single source file, or compilation unit, can only declare one `public` class or interface (see 7.1 Compilation Units for an exception to this rule).

`abstract`
> An interface is implicitly `abstract`; so all of the methods in an interface are implicitly `abstract`. Including the `abstract` modifier in an interface declaration is permitted, but it does not change the meaning of the interface declaration.

References Compilation Units 7.1; Inner interface modifiers 5.5.7.1; Interface method modifiers 5.5.6.1; Interface variable modifiers 5.5.5.1

5.5.2 Interface Name

The identifier that follows the keyword `interface` is the name of the interface. This identifier can be used as a reference type wherever the interface is accessible.

References Interface Types 3.2.2

5.5.3 Interface Inheritance

The `extends` clause specifies any super-interfaces of the interface being declared; the `extends` keyword can be followed by the names of one or more interfaces. If an interface has an `extends` clause, the clause can only name other interfaces.

Including an interface in the `extends` clause of another interface means that the declared interface inherits the variables and methods declared in the super-interface. A class that implements the declared interface must implement all of the methods in the declared interface, as well as all of the methods inherited from the super-interface.

If an interface declaration does not include an `extends` clause, the interface does not extend any other interfaces.

5.5.4 Interface Members

The members of an interface can be variables or methods; an interface cannot have constructors, static initializers, instance initializers, nested top-level classes or interfaces, or member classes:

References *InterfaceMethodDeclaration* 5.5.6; *InterfaceVariableDeclaration* 5.5.5

5.5.5 *Interface Variables*

Any field variables declared in an interface are implicitly static and final. In other words, field variables in an interface are named constants. Every field variable declaration in an interface must contain an initializer that sets the value of the named constant:

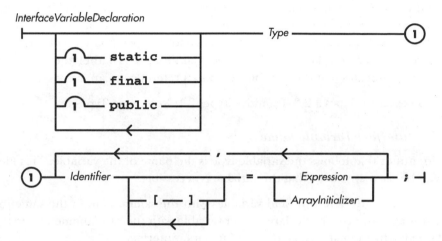

A variable declaration in an interface is made up of three distinct things:

- Optional modifiers that specify attributes of the variable.

- A type, which can be either a primitive type or a reference type.

- Any number of identifiers that name variables. Each name must be followed by an initializer that sets the value of the constant.

References *ArrayInitializer 5.4.5.4; Expression 4; Identifier 2.2.1; Type 3*

5.5.5.1 *Interface variable modifiers*

Variables in an interface are implicitly static and final. Including these modifiers in a variable declaration is permitted, but it is not necessary and it does not change the meaning of the variable declaration. Thus, by definition, all variables in an interface are named constants.

If an interface is declared public, a field variable declared in the interface is public, even if it is declared with the private or protected modifier. If an interface is not declared public, however, any field variables in the interface have the default accessibility, which means that they are only accessible in classes and interfaces in the same package.

It is an error to declare a field variable in an interface with the `transient` or `volatile` modifier.

References Interface Modifiers 5.5.1; Variable modifiers 5.4.5.1

5.5.5.2 *Interface variable type*

If the interface variable declaration uses a primitive type, the variable contains a constant value of the specified primitive type. If the declaration uses a reference type, the variable contains a constant reference to the specified type of object. The presence of square brackets in a variable declaration, after either the type or variable name, indicates that the variable contains a reference to an array.

References Array Types 3.2.3; Primitive Types 3.1; Reference Types 3.2

5.5.5.3 *Interface variable name*

The identifier that follows the variable type is the name of the variable. This identifier can be used anywhere that the variable is accessible.

It is an error to declare two field variables with the same name in the same interface. It is also an error to declare a field variable with the same name as a method declared in the same interface or any of its super-interfaces.

An interface that extends another interface inherits all of the variables in its super-interface. Any class that implements an interface has access to all of the variables defined in that interface, as well as the variables inherited from super-interfaces.

If a field variable is declared with the same name as a variable declared in a super-interface, the variable in the super-interface is considered to be shadowed. If a variable is shadowed in an interface, it cannot be accessed as a field of that interface. However, a shadowed variable can be accessed by casting a reference to an object that implements the interface to a reference to the appropriate super-interface in which the variable is not shadowed. For example:

```
interface A {
    int x = 4;
}
interface B extends A {
    int x = 7;
}
class Z implements B {
    Z() {
        int i = x;              // i gets the value of B's x
        int h = ((A)this).x;    // h gets the value of A's x
    }
}
```

The variable x in interface A is shadowed by the variable x in interface B. Class Z implements interface B, so a reference to x produces the value 7, as defined in interface B. However, it is possible to access the shadowed variable by casting this to a reference to interface A.

In some situations, an interface may inherit multiple field variables with the same name. This leads to a single, ambiguous variable name. For example:

```
interface A {
    int x = 4;
}
interface B {
    int x = 43;
}
interface C extends A, B {
    int y = 22;
}
class Z implements C {
    public static void main (String[] argv) {
        System.out.println(x);        // Ambiguous
    }
}
```

In this example, the interface C inherits two variables named x. This is fine, as long as C does not refer to the variable x by its simple name in any of its declarations. If C needs to use x, it must qualify the name with the appropriate interface name (e.g., A.x). Class Z implements interface C, so it also has access to two variables named x. As a result, the use of x in main() is ambiguous. This problem can be resolved by qualifying the variable name with the appropriate interface name (e.g., B.x).

A class that implements multiple interfaces can also inherit multiple field variables with the same name. Again, this leads to a single, ambiguous variable name:

```
interface A {
    int x - 4;
}
interface B {
    int x = 43;
}
class Z implements A, B {
    public static void main (String[] argv) {
        System.out.println(x);        // Ambiguous
    }
}
```

The class Z implements both interface A and interface B, so it inherits two variables named x. As a result, the use of x in main() is ambiguous. This problem can again be resolved by qualifying the variable name with the appropriate interface name (e.g., B.x).

References Field Expressions 4.1.6; Identifiers 2.2.1; Interface method name 5.5.6.3

5.5.5.4 *Interface variable initializers*

Every variable declaration in an interface must include an initializer that sets the value of the constant. The initializer does not, however, have to be a constant expression. If the variable is of a non-array type, the expression in the initializer is evaluated and the variable is set to the result of the expression, as long as the result is assignment-compatible with the variable. If the variable is of an array type, the initializer must be an array initializer.

The initializer for a variable in an interface cannot refer to any variables that are declared after its own declaration.

References *ArrayInitializer* 5.4.5.4; Array Types 3.2.3; Assignment Operators 4.13; Constant Expressions 4.16; *Expression* 4

5.5.6 *Interface Methods*

Any methods declared in an interface are implicitly `abstract`. In other words, methods in an interface do not have a specified implementation:

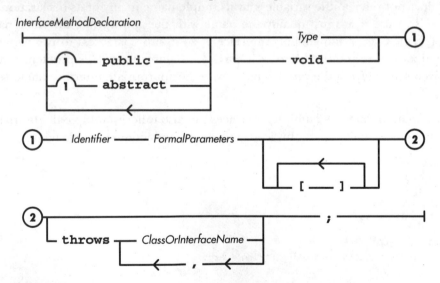

A method declaration in an interface is made up of six distinct things:

- Optional modifiers that specify attributes of the method
- A type that specifies the type of value returned by the method

- An identifier that names the method

- A list of formal parameters that specifies the values that are passed to the method

- An optional throws clause that specifies any exceptions that can be thrown by the method

- A semicolon, since the method declaration does not include an implementation

References *ClassOrInterfaceName* 4.1.6; Exception Handling 9; *FormalParameters* 5.4.6.4; *Identifier* 2.2.1; *Type* 3

5.5.6.1 Interface method modifiers

Methods in an interface are implicitly abstract. Including this modifier in a method declaration is permitted, but it is not necessary and it does not change the meaning of the method declaration. Thus, by definition, none of the methods in an interface has a specified implementation.

If an interface is declared public, a method declared in the interface is public, even if it is declared with the private or protected modifier. If the interface is not declared public, however, any methods in the interface have the default accessibility, which means that they are only accessible in classes and interfaces in the same package.

It is an error to declare a method in an interface with the static, final, native, or synchronized modifier. These modifiers are not allowed because defining a method in an interface is not meant to imply anything about the nature of the implementation, other than the return type of the method and the types of the formal parameters. A class that implements the interface has control over the implementation of the methods and can use any of these modifiers when they are appropriate for the implementation.

References Interface Modifiers 5.5.1; Method modifiers 5.4.6.1

5.5.6.2 Interface method return type

A method declaration in an interface must specify the type of value returned by the method. The return value can be of a primitive type or of a reference type. The presence of square brackets in a method declaration, after either the return type or the formal parameters, indicates that the method returns a reference to the specified type of array. If the method does not return a value, the declaration uses void to indicate that. The return type comes before the name of the method in the method declaration.

References Array Types 3.2.3; Method return type 5.4.6.2; Primitive Types 3.1; Reference Types 3.2

5.5.6.3 Interface method name

The identifier that follows the return type is the name of the method. This identifier can be used anywhere that the method is accessible.

It is an error to declare two methods that have the same name, the same number of parameters, and the same type for each corresponding parameter in the same interface. It is also an error to declare a method with the same name as a variable declared in the same interface or any of its super-interfaces.

An interface that extends another interface inherits all of the methods in its super-interface. Any class that implements an interface must provide an implementation for each of the methods defined in that interface, as well as each of the methods inherited from super-interfaces.

If an interface inherits methods from multiple super-interfaces that have the same name, formal parameters, and return type, there is no problem. The various super-interfaces are in agreement about the method. The interface can also override the inherited methods by declaring a method with the same name, formal parameters, and return type. In any case, a class that implements the interface has to provide a single implementation for the method.

However, if an interface inherits methods from multiple super-interfaces that have the same name and same formal parameters, but different return types, a compile-time error results. By the same token, if the interface attempts to override an inherited method with a method that has the same name and same formal parameters, but a different return type, a compile-time error results.

If an interface inherits methods from multiple super-interfaces that have the same name but different formal parameters, there is no problem. The methods are simply considered overloaded in the interface. The interface can even declare additional methods that have the same name but different formal parameters. A class that implements the interface simply has to provide an implementation for each of the overloaded methods.

References Identifiers 2.2.1; Interface variable name 5.5.5.3; Method Call Expression 4.1.8

5.5.6.4 Interface method formal parameters

The formal parameters in a method declaration specify a list of variables to which values are assigned when the method is called. If a method has no formal parameters, the parentheses must still appear in the method declaration. The presence of square brackets in a formal parameter declaration, either as part of a reference type or after the name of a formal parameter, indicates that the formal parameter is an array type.

References Array Types 3.2.3; *FormalParameters* 5.4.6.4; Method formal parameters 5.4.6.4; *Type* 3

5.5.6.5 Interface method throws clause

If a method is expected to throw any exceptions, the method declaration must declare that fact in a `throws` clause. If the declaration of a method in an interface contains a `throws` clause, any method in a sub-interface that overrides that method cannot include any classes in its `throws` clause that are not declared in the overridden method.

References Exception Handling 9; Method throws clause 5.4.6.5

5.5.7 Nested Top-Level Interfaces

Nested top-level interfaces are interfaces that are declared inside of another class. Just as with a top-level interface declaration, the declaration of a nested top-level interface creates a reference type in Java. Here's the formal definition of a nested top-level interface:

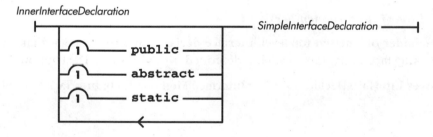

A nested top-level interface can be accessed outside of its enclosing class by qualifying its name with the name of its enclosing class, as follows:

```
EnclosingClass.InnerInterface
```

The syntax for declaring nested top-level interfaces is not supported prior to Java 1.1.

References Nested top-level classes and interfaces 5.3.7.1; *SimpleInterfaceDeclaration* 5.5

5.5.7.1 Inner interface modifiers

The keywords `public`, `abstract`, and `static` can be used in the declaration of a nested top-level interface. In this situation, these modifiers have the following meanings:

`public`
> If a nested top-level interface is declared `public`, it is accessible from any class or interface that can access the enclosing class. If the `public` modifier is not used, however, the nested top-level interface can only be referenced by classes and interfaces in the same package as the enclosing class.

`abstract`
> A nested top-level interface is implicitly `abstract`; thus, all of the methods in the interface are implicitly `abstract`. Including the `abstract` modifier in a nested top-level interface declaration is permitted, but it does not change the meaning of the interface declaration.

`static`
> A nested top-level interface is implicitly `static`. Including the `static` modifier in a nested top-level interface declaration is permitted, but it does not change the meaning of the interface declaration.

References Interface Modifiers 5.5.1

5.5.7.2 Inner interface members

The remainder of a nested top-level interface declaration is the same as that for a top-level interface declaration, which is described in 5.5 Interface Declarations.

References Interface Declarations 5.5; Interface Methods 5.5.6; Interface Variables 5.5.5

6

Statements and Control Structures

A statement is the construct used to control the flow of program execution in Java:

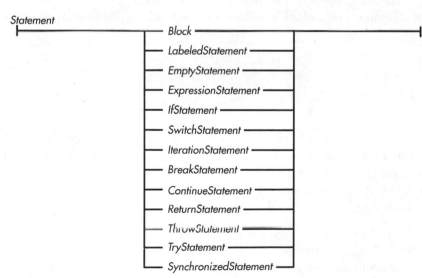

Statements are executed in sequence, unless a statement alters the flow of control. Statements usually correspond to executable code.

References *Block* 6.1; *BreakStatement* 6.8; *ContinueStatement* 6.9; *EmptyStatement* 6.3; *ExpressionStatement* 6.4; *IfStatement* 6.5; *IterationStatement* 6.7; *LabeledStatement* 6.2; *ReturnStatement* 6.10; *SwitchStatement* 6.6; *SynchronizedStatement* 6.13; *ThrowStatement* 6.11; *TryStatement* 6.12

6.1 Blocks

A block is a sequence of zero or more statements, local variable declarations, or local class declarations enclosed in curly braces:

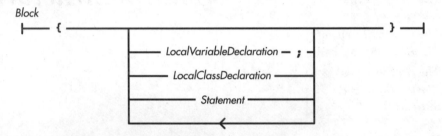

The bodies of methods, constructors, static initializers, and instance initializers are blocks. A variable declaration in a block causes a local variable to be defined, while a class declaration in a block causes a local class to be defined. A block is itself a kind of statement, so a block can contain other blocks. Here is an example of a block:

```
{
    int tmp = x;
    x = y;
    y = tmp;
}
```

The statements in a block are executed in the sequence in which they occur, unless a statement that alters the sequence of execution is executed. If, as a result of such a statement, the Java compiler can determine that a statement will never be executed, the compiler is required to produce an error message about the unreachable statement.

The one exception to this rule allows `if` statements that have constant Boolean expressions. The compiler recognizes `if` statements that have constant Boolean expressions and does not generate code for the portion of the statement that can never be executed. This mechanism can be used for conditional compilation; it is similar to the C/C++ preprocessor features that are used for this purpose.

References Constant Expressions 4.16; Constructors 5.4.7; Instance Initializers 5.4.10; *LocalClassDeclaration* 6.1.2; *LocalVariableDeclaration* 6.1.1; Methods 5.4.6; *Statement* 6; Static Initializers 5.4.9; The switch Statement 6.6

6.1.1 Local Variables

Local variables declared in a block exist only from their declaration to the end of the block. A local variable declaration cannot include any modifiers except the final modifier. In other words, a variable declaration in a block cannot include any of the following keywords: public, protected, private, static, transient, or volatile. The syntax that permits the use of the final modifier with local variables is new as of Java 1.1; the usage is not permitted with earlier versions of the language.

The syntax of a local variable declaration is:

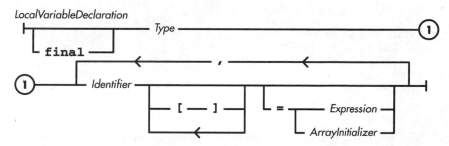

A local variable declaration is really made up of two distinct things:

- A type, which can be either a primitive type or a reference type.

- Any number of identifiers that name variables. Each name can be followed by pairs of square brackets to indicate an array variable, as well as an optional initializer for the variable.

A local variable declared within a block that has an initializer is initialized when its declaration is executed. Within the body of a method or constructor, its formal parameters are treated as local variables. Formal parameters are initialized when a method is called. A local variable can also be declared in the header of a for statement.

The following are some examples of local variable declarations:

```
int x;
double[] k, m[];
```

References *ArrayInitializer* 5.4.5.4; *Expression* 4; *Identifier* 2.2.1; Interface Variables 5.5.5; *Type* 3; The for Statement 6.7.3; Variables 5.4.5

6.1.1.1 *Final local variables*

If a local variable is declared with the `final` modifier, the variable is a named constant value. As such, it must be assigned an initial value. Any assignment to a `final` local variable, other than the one that provides its initial value, is a compile-time error. The initial value for a `final` local variable is typically provided by an initializer that is part of the variable's declaration. For example:

```
final int X = 4;
```

A `final` local variable that is not initialized in its declaration is called a *blank final*. A blank final must be assigned a value exactly once. The compiler uses flow analysis that takes `if` statements and iteration statements into account to ensure that a blank final is assigned a value exactly once. Thus, it is possible to have multiple assignments to a blank final, so long as exactly one of them can be executed. For example, here is an instance initializer that sets the value of a blank final:

```
{
    final int DAYS_IN_YEAR;
    if (isLeapYear(new Date()))
        DAYS_IN_YEAR = 366;
    else
        DAYS_IN_YEAR = 365;
    ...
}
```

Local variables that are declared `final` are not supported prior to Java 1.1.

References Instance Initializers 5.4.10; The do Statement 6.7.2; The for Statement 6.7.3; The if Statement 6.5; The while Statement 6.7.1; Variable modifiers 5.4.5.1

6.1.1.2 *Local variable type*

A local variable declaration must always specify the type of the variable. If the declaration of a local variable uses a primitive type, the variable contains a value of the specified primitive type. If the declaration uses a reference type, the variable contains a reference to the specified type of object.

The presence of square brackets in a variable declaration, after either the type or the variable name, indicates that the variable contains a reference to an array. For example:

```
int a[];        // a is an array of int
int[] b;        // b is also an array of int
```

It is also possible to declare a variable to contain an array of arrays, or more generally, arrays nested to any level. Each pair of square brackets in the declaration corresponds to a dimension of the array; it makes no difference whether the brackets appear after the type or the variable name. For example:

```
int[][][] d3;        // Each of these is an array of
int[][] f3[];        // arrays of arrays of integers
int[] g3[][];
int h3[][][];
int[] j3, k3[];      // An array and an array of arrays
```

References Array Types 3.2.3; Primitive Types 3.1; Reference Types 3.2

6.1.1.3 Local variable name

The identifier that follows the variable type is the name of the local variable. When
a local variable definition is in effect, all occurrences of that name are taken to
mean the local variable. If a local variable is declared with the same name as a
class, an interface, or a field of the class in which the local variable is declared, the
definition of the class, interface, or field is hidden. Fields that are hidden by a
local variable can be referenced using the keyword this. For example:

```
class myClass {
    int value;
    void doit(int x) {
        int value;
        value = x*4;             // Set local variable
        this.value = value + 1;  // Set field variable
}
```

A block cannot have multiple local variables with the same name. This means that
a local variable cannot be declared at a point in a block where a local variable with
the same name is already defined. For example, consider the following code:

```
myMethod(char c){
    int j;       // Okay
    char c;      // Error
    int j;       // Error
    {
        int j;   // Error
    }
    {
        int x;   // Okay
    }
    {
        int x;   // Okay
    }
    int x;       // Okay
}
```

In the above example, the declaration of c as a local variable is an error because it
occurs in a method that has a formal parameter with that name. The second declaration of j is an error because there is already a local variable defined with that
name. The third declaration of j as a local variable is also an error for the same
reason; the nested block sees all of the declarations that are visible in the enclosing
block, including the declaration of j in the outer block.

The first declaration of x is fine because there is no previous declaration of x for it to conflict with. The second declaration of x is also fine because there is no previous declaration of x in the enclosing block for it to conflict with. The first declaration of x occurs in a nested block, so it is not visible in the enclosing block. The third declaration of x is also fine because the preceding declarations occurred in nested blocks; they are not visible in the enclosing block.

References Identifiers 2.2.1; this 4.1.1

6.1.1.4 *Local variable initializers*

A local variable declaration can contain an initializer. If the variable is of a non-array type, the expression in the initializer is evaluated and the variable is set to the result of the expression, as long as the result is assignment-compatible with the variable. If the variable is of an array type, the initializer must be an array initializer, as described in 5.4.5.4 Variable initializers. If the variable is declared final, the initializer sets the value of the named constant.

A local variable declaration with an initializer is similar in effect to a local variable declaration without an initializer immediately followed by an assignment statement that sets the declared variable. Take the following example:

```
int a = 4;
```

This is equivalent to:

```
int a;
a = 4;
```

If a local variable has an initializer, the value of the variable is set to the value of the initializer when the declaration is executed.

Any attempt to access the value of a local variable before its value is set by an assignment statement or an initializer is treated as an error by the Java compiler. For example:

```
int foo(int x) {
    int a = x + 1;
    int b, c;
    if (a > 4)
        b = 3;

    a = a * c;        // Error: c not initialized

    a = b * 8 + a;    // Error: b might not be initialized
```

This example contains two errors. First, the compiler complains about the expression a*c because c is not initialized. The compiler also complains about the expression b* 8+a because the preceding assignment to b may not executed, depending on the value of a. If the compiler cannot guarantee that a local variable will be initialized, it generates an error message when the variable is used.

References *ArrayInitializer* 5.4.5.4; Assignment Operators 4.13

6.1.2 Local Classes

Local classes declared in a block exist only in the scope of that block. Local classes are not supported prior to Java 1.1 Here's the syntax of a local class declaration:

LocalClassDeclaration

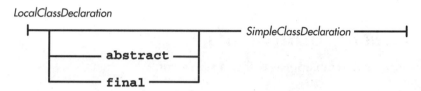

A local class can access local variables in the enclosing block that are declared `final`. A local class can also access instance variables of the enclosing class if they are not declared inside of a `static` method or static initializer.

There is an alternate syntax for a local class that allows an anonymous local class to be defined. This syntax is available as part of an allocation expression.

References Allocation Expressions 4.2; Anonymous classes 5.3.7.4; Local classes 5.3.7.3; Local Variables 6.1.1; *SimpleClassDeclaration* 5.4; Variables 5.4.5

6.1.2.1 Local class modifiers

The keywords `abstract` and `final` can be used in the declaration of a local class. These modifiers have the following meanings:

`abstract`
> If a local class is declared `abstract`, no instances of the class may be created. A local class declared `abstract` may contain `abstract` methods. Classes not declared `abstract` may not contain `abstract` methods and must override any `abstract` methods they inherit with methods that are not `abstract`. Classes that implement an interface and are not declared `abstract` must contain or inherit methods that are not `abstract` that have the same name, have the same number of parameters, and have corresponding parameter types as the methods declared in the interfaces that the class implements.

`final`
> If a local class is declared `final`, it cannot be subclassed. In other words, it cannot appear in the `extends` clause of another class.

References Class Modifiers 5.4.1; Inner class modifiers 5.4.11.1

6.1.2.2 *Local class members*

The body of a local class cannot declare any `static` variables, `static` methods, `static` classes, or static initializers. Beyond those restrictions, the remainder of the declaration is the same as that for a top-level class declaration, which is described in 5.4 Class Declarations.

References Class Declarations 5.4; Constructors 5.4.7; Instance Initializers 5.4.10; Methods 5.4.6; Nested Top-Level and Member Classes 5.4.11; Static Initializers 5.4.9; Variables 5.4.5

6.2 Labeled Statements

Zero or more labels can appear before a statement:

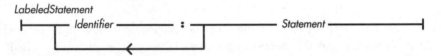

LabeledStatement

A label is defined throughout the block in which it occurs. The names of labels are independent of all other kinds of names. In other words, if a label has the same name as a local variable, formal parameter, class, interface, field variable, or method, there is never any confusion or interaction between those names.[*] For example, the following code works even though it contains a label and formal parameter with the same name:

```
public static void main (String[] argv) {
  argv:
    while (true) {
        System.out.println(argv[0]);
        if ( Math.random() >.4)
            break argv;
        System.out.println("Again");
    }
}
```

Labels are used to mark statements, but a labeled statement does not affect the order of execution when it is defined. The statement following the label is executed as if the label were not present. However, a label can be used in a `break` or `continue` statement to transfer control to a labeled statement. Unlike C/C++, Java does not have a `goto` statement.

References *Identifier* 2.2.1; *Statement* 6; The break Statement 6.8; The continue Statement 6.9

---

[*] Prior to version 1.0.2, Java required labels to have names that did not conflict with the names of local variables or formal parameters.

6.3 The Empty Statement

The empty statement does nothing:

EmptyStatement

```
├──────────────────────────── ; ────────────────────────────┤
```

The empty statement can be useful as a place holder. For example, if a `for` statement contains all of the necessary functionality in its header, the body of the `for` statement can be the empty statement. Here's an example:

```
// Find the first element of array nx that equals 5
int x;
for (x = 0; x < nx.length && nx[x] != 5; x++)
// for requires a statement here: use an empty statement
   ;

if (x < nx.length) {
// The for statement found a 5 at nx[x]
}
```

6.4 Expression Statements

Expression statements are the most common statements in Java. An expression statement consists of an expression that is executed for its side effects. Only certain kinds of expressions can be used in an expression statement:

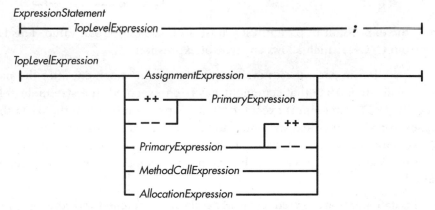

Here are some examples of expression statements.

```
x = 3*y;
foo(x);
x++;
--y;
new zombie();
```

Notice that a top-level expression is an expression that has a side effect or calls a method. An assignment expression has the side effect of altering the value of a variable or array element. A statement expression that consists of an increment or decrement operator has the side effect of incrementing or decrementing the contents of a variable or an array element. A method call expression has the side effect of calling a method. If the method returns a result, the result is discarded. A special variant of *MethodCallExpression*, called *ExplicitConstructorCallStatement*, allows a constructor to be called explicitly as the first statement of another constructor. An allocation expression creates an object and has the side effect of calling its constructor.

An expression statement is evaluated fully, including its side effects, before the next statement is executed.[*]

References *AllocationExpression* 4.2; *AssignmentExpression* 4.13; *ExplicitConstructorCallStatement* 5.4.7.6; *MethodCallExpression* 4.1.8; *PrimaryExpression* 4.1

6.5 The if Statement

An `if` statement determines which of two statements is executed, based on the value of a Boolean expression:

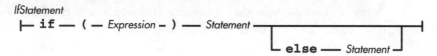

In Java, the expression in parentheses must produce a `boolean` value. This is different from C/C++, which allows any type of expression.

If the expression in parentheses evaluates to `true`, the statement after the parentheses is executed. After that statement has been executed, the statement following the entire `if` statement is executed. If the expression between the parentheses evaluates to `false`, the next statement to be executed depends on whether or not the `if` statement has an `else` clause. If there is an `else` clause, the statement after the `else` is executed. Otherwise, the statement after the entire `if` statement is executed.

When `if` statements are nested, each `else` clause is matched with the last preceding `if` statement in the same block that has not yet been matched with an `if` statement.

---

* A Java compiler can produce code that follows a different order of evaluation, provided that the code produces the same result as code that does follow the specified order of evaluation.

Here is an example of an `if` statement:

```
if (j == 4) {
    if (x > 0 ) {
        x *= 7;
    } else {
        x *= -7;
    }
}
return;
```

The outer `if` statement has no `else` clause. If `j` is not 4, the `return` statement is executed. Otherwise, the inner `if` statement is executed. This `if` statement does have an `else` clause. If `x` is greater than zero, the value of `x` is multiplied by 7. Otherwise, the value of `x` is multiplied by –7. Regardless of the value of `x`, the `return` statement is executed.

References Boolean Type 3.1.2; *Expression* 4; *Statement* 6

6.6 *The switch Statement*

A `switch` statement selects a specially labeled statement in its block as the next statement to be executed, based on the value of an expression:

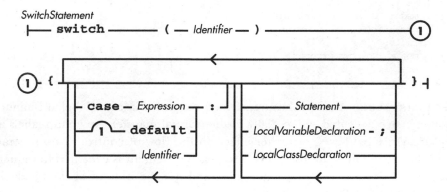

In Java, the type of the expression in parentheses must be `byte`, `char`, `short`, or `int`. This is unlike C/C++, which allows the type of a `switch` statement to be any integer type, including `long`.

The body of a `switch` statement must be a block. The top-level statements inside a `switch` may contain `case` labels. The expression following a `case` label must be a constant expression that is assignable to the type of the `switch` expression. No two `case` labels in a `switch` can contain the same value. At most one of the top-level statements in a `switch` can contain a `default` label.

A `switch` statement does the following:

- Evaluates the expression in parentheses. If the type of the expression is not `int`, the value produced by the expression is converted to `int`.

- Compares the value produced by the expression to the values in the `case` labels. Prior to comparison, the value in the `case` label is converted to `int` if it is not already `int`.

- If a `case` label is found that has the same value as the expression, that label's statement is the next statement to be executed.

- If no `case` label is found with the same value as the expression, and a statement in the block has a `default` label, that statement is the next one to be executed.

- If there is no statement in the block that has a `default` label, the statement after the `switch` statement is the next statement to be executed.

Here's an example of a `switch` statement:

```
switch (rc) {
  case 1:
    msg = "Syntax error";
    break;
  case 2:
    msg = "Undefined variable";
    break;
  default:
    msg = "Unknown error";
    break;
}
```

After the `switch` statement has transferred control to a case-labeled statement, statements are executed sequentially in the normal manner. Any `case` labels and the `default` label have no further effect on the flow of control. If no statement inside the block alters the flow of control, each statement is executed in sequence with control flowing past each `case` label and out the bottom of the block. The following example illustrates this behavior:

```
void doInNTimes(int n){
    switch (n > 5 ? 5 : n) {
      case 5:
        doIt();
      case 4:
        doIt();
      case 3:
        doIt();
      case 2:
```

```
        doIt();
     case 1:
        doIt();
     }
   }
```

The above method calls the `doIt()` method up to 5 times.

To prevent control from flowing through `case` labels, it is common to end each `case` with a flow-altering statement such as a `break` statement. Other statements used for this purpose include the `continue` statement and the `return` statement.

References Constant Expressions 4.16; *Expression* 4; *Identifier* 2.2.1; Integer types 3.1.1.1; *LocalClassDeclaration* 6.1.2; *LocalVariableDeclaration* 6.1.1; *Statement* 6; The break Statement 6.8; The continue Statement 6.9; The return Statement 6.10

6.7 *Iteration Statements*

Iteration statements are used to specify the logic of a loop. Java has three varieties of iteration statement: `while`, `do`, and `for`.

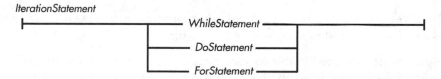

References *DoStatement* 6.7.2; *ForStatement* 6.7.3; *WhileStatement* 6.7.1

6.7.1 *The while Statement*

A `while` statement evaluates a Boolean expression. If the expression is `true`, a given statement is repeatedly executed for as long as the expression continues to evaluate to `true`.

In Java, the expression in parentheses must produce a `boolean` value. This is different from C/C++, which allows any type of expression.

If the expression in parentheses evaluates to `true`, the statement contained in the `while` statement is executed and the expression in parentheses is evaluated again. This process continues until the expression evaluates to `false`.

If the expression in parentheses evaluates to `false`, the statement following the `while` statement is the next statement to be executed. The expression in parentheses is evaluated before the contained statement is executed, so it is possible for the contained statement not to be executed even once.

Here is an example of a `while` statement:

```
while ( (c = in.read()) >= 0) {
    out.write(c);
}
```

References Boolean Type 3.1.2; *Expression* 4; *Statement* 6

6.7.2 The do Statement

A do statement executes a given statement and then evaluates a Boolean expression. If the expression evaluates to `true`, the statement is executed repeatedly as long as the expression continues to evaluate to `true`:

DoStatement

├─── **do** ─── *Statement* ─── **while** ─── (─── *Expression* ───) ─── ; ───┤

In Java, the expression in parentheses must produce a `boolean` value. This is unlike C/C++, which allows any type of expression.

The statement contained in the do statement is executed and then the expression in parentheses is evaluated. If the expression evaluates to `true`, the process is repeated.

If the expression evaluates to false, the statement following the do statement is the next statement to be executed. Because the expression is evaluated after the contained statement is executed, the statement is always executed at least once.

Here's an example of a do statement:

```
do {
    c = in.read();
    out.write(c);
} while (c != ';');
```

References Boolean Type 3.1.2; *Expression* 4; *Statement* 6

6.7.3 The for Statement

A `for` statement is a more structured form of a `while` statement. A `for` statement performs an initialization step and then evaluates a Boolean expression. If the expression evaluates to `true`, a given statement is executed and an increment expression is evaluated repeatedly as long as the expression continues to evaluate to `true`:

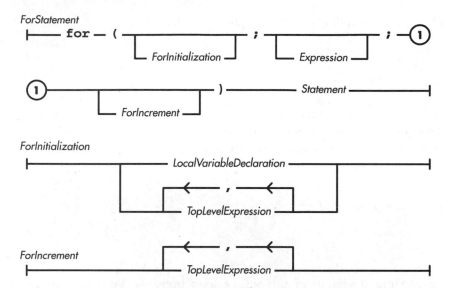

ForStatement

ForInitialization

Expression

ForIncrement

Statement

ForInitialization

LocalVariableDeclaration

TopLevelExpression

ForIncrement

TopLevelExpression

Here is an example of a `for` statement:

```
for (i = 0; i < a.length; i++) {
    a[i] = i;
}
```

The initialization part of the `for` statement is executed first. If the initialization part contains nothing, no initialization is performed. The expression that follows must produce a `boolean` value. Before the body of the `for` statement is executed, the expression is evaluated. If the expression portion of the `for` statement is omitted, the default expression `true` is used. If the expression evaluates to `true`, the body of the `for` statement is executed and then the increment portion of the `for` statement is evaluated. Finally, the expression is evaluated again to determine if there should be another iteration. This process continues until the expression evaluates to `false`, at which point the statement following the `for` statement is the next statement to be executed. The `for` statement in the above example can be rewritten as a `while` statement as follows:

```
i = 0;
while (i < a.length) {
    a[i] = i;
    i++;
}
```

One difference between comparable `for` and `while` loops is that a `continue` statement in the body of a `for` statement causes the increment portion of the statement to be evaluated. However, this may not be the case in a comparable `while` statement.

Here's a new version of our `for` example:

```
for (i = 0; i < a.length; i++) {
    a[i] = i;
    continue;
}
```

The added `continue` statement at the end of the `for` loop does not change the behavior of the loop. In particular, `i++` is still evaluated after each iteration through the body of the loop. Now let's add a `continue` statement at the equivalent place in our `while` example:

```
i = 0;
while (i < a.length) {
    a[i] = i;
    continue;
    i++;
}
```

The `continue` statement in this `while` loop prevents the statement `i++` from being executed. The `continue` statement would have to be moved after the increment operation to match the logic of the `for` statement.

If the expression portion of a `for` statement is omitted, the default expression `true` is supplied. Take, for example, the following `for` statement:

```
for ( FileInputStream in = new FileInputStream(fname);;) {
    c = in.read();
    if (c < 0)
        return;
    System.out.print((char)c);
}
```

This example uses a local variable declaration in the initialization portion of the `for` statement. Local variable declarations in a `for` statement are subject to the same restrictions as local variable declarations in a block. In particular, a `for` statement cannot declare a local variable with the same name as a local variable or formal parameter that is defined in an enclosing block.

The above `for` statement is equivalent to the following `while` statement:

```
{
    FileInputStream in = new FileInputStream(fname);
    while (true) {
        c = in.read();
        if (c < 0)
            return;
        System.out.print((char)c);
    }
}
```

The enclosing block in the above example is provided to limit the scope of the local variable in to just the while statement.

The initialization portion of a for statement can also be empty. The following statement is a legal way of specifying an infinite loop:

```
for (;;) {...}
```

This is equivalent to the following while statement:

```
while (true) {...}
```

Unlike C/C++, there is no comma operator in Java. However, commas are explicitly allowed in the initialization portion of a for statement. For example, a for initialization can consist of multiple expressions separated by commas:

```
i=2, j=5, k=44
```

When the initialization portion of a for statement contains local variable declarations, commas are also allowed because the syntax for declarations allows multiple variables, separated by commas, to be declared in one declaration. For example:

```
int i=2, j=5, k=44
```

References Boolean Type 3.1.2; *Expression* 4; *Statement* 6; *LocalVariableDeclaration* 6.1.1; *TopLevelExpression* 6.4; The continue Statement 6.9; The while Statement 6.7.1

6.8 The break Statement

A break statement transfers control out of an enclosing statement:

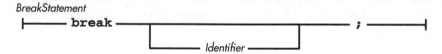

BreakStatement

If a break statement does not contain an identifier, the statement attempts to transfer control to the statement that follows the innermost enclosing while, for, do, or switch statement. The Java compiler issues an error message if a break statement without an identifier occurs without an enclosing while, for, do, or switch statement. Here is an example of a break statement that contains no identifier:

```
while (true) {
    c = in.read();
    if (Character.isSpace(c)
        break;
    s += (char)c;
}
```

In this example, the break statement is used to exit from the while loop.

The innermost while, for, do, or switch statement that encloses the break statement must be in the immediately enclosing method or initializer block. In other words, a break statement cannot be used to leave a method or initializer block. The break statement in the following example is used incorrectly and generates an error:

```
while (true) {
    class X {
        void doIt() {
            break;
        }
    }
    new X().doIt();
}
```

If a break statement contains an identifier, the identifier must be defined as the label of an enclosing statement. A break statement that contains an identifier attempts to transfer control to the statement that immediately follows the statement labeled with that identifier. Here's an example of a break statement that contains an identifier:

```
foo:{
    doIt();
    if (n > 4) break foo;
    doIt();
}
```

In this example, the break statement transfers control to the statement following the block labeled foo.

The label used in a break statement must be in the immediately enclosing method or initializer block. The break statement in the following example is used incorrectly and generates an error:

```
foo: {
    class X {
        void doIt() {
            break foo;
        }
    }
    new X().doIt();
}
```

The statement to which a break statement attempts to transfer control is called the *target statement*. If a break statement occurs inside a try statement, control may not immediately transfer to the target statement. If a try statement has a finally clause, the `finally` block is executed before control leaves the `try` statement for any reason. This means that if a break statement occurs inside a `try` statement (but not in its `finally` block) and the target statement is outside of the `try` statement, the `finally` block is executed first, before the control transfer can take place.

If the `finally` block contains a `break`, `continue`, `return`, or `throw` statement, the pending control transfer for the previously executed `break` statement is forgotten. Instead, control is transferred to the target of the `break`, `continue`, `return`, or `throw` statement in the `finally` block.

If the `finally` block does not contain a `break`, `continue`, `return`, or `throw` statement, the pending control transfer happens after the `finally` block is done executing, unless the target statement is enclosed by another `try` statement. If there is another enclosing `try` statement and it has a `finally` clause, that `finally` block is also executed before the control transfer can take place. Execution proceeds in this manner until the target statement of the `break` is executed.

Here is an example that illustrates a simple scenario:

```
ll:{
    try {
        f = new FileInputStream(fname);
        i = f.read();
        if (i != ' ')
            break ll;
        i = f.read();
    } catch (IOException e) {
        System.out.println("Got an IO Exception!");
        break ll;
    } finally {
        f.close();            // Always executed
    }
    // Only reached if we don't break out of the try
    System.out.println("No breaks");
}
```

In this example, a `break` statement is executed if one of two things happens. First, if an `IOException` is thrown, the `catch` clause prints a message and then executes a `break` statement. Otherwise, if the first call to `read()` does not return a space, a `break` statement is executed. In either case, the `finally` clause is executed before control is transferred to the statement following the statement labeled with `ll`.

References *Identifier* 2.2.1; Labeled Statements 6.2; The continue Statement 6.9; The do Statement 6.7.2; The for Statement 6.7.3; The return Statement 6.10; The throw Statement 6.11; The try Statement 6.12; The while Statement 6.7.1

6.9 *The continue Statement*

A continue statement stops the current iteration of an iteration statement and transfers control to the start of the next iteration:

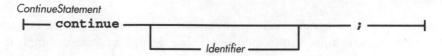

ContinueStatement

A continue statement must occur within a while, for, or do statement or the compiler issues an error message.

If a continue statement does not contain an identifier, the statement stops the current iteration in the innermost enclosing while, for, or do statement and attempts to transfer control to the start of the next iteration. This means that in a while or do statement, the continue statement transfers control to just after the contained statement of the while or do statement. In a for statement, the continue statement transfers control to the increment portion of the for statement. Here is an example of a continue statement that contains no identifier:

```
public static void main (String[] argv) {
    for (int i=0; i<=15; i++) {
        System.out.println(i);
        if ( (i&1) == 0 )
            continue;
        System.out.println("That's odd");
    }
}
```

The above example outputs the numbers 0 through 15, printing "That's odd" after each odd number.

The innermost while, for, do, or switch statement that encloses the continue statement must be in the immediately enclosing method or initializer block. The continue statement in the following example is used incorrectly and generates an error:

```
while (true) {
    class X {
        void doIt() {
            continue;
        }
    }
    new X().doIt();
}
```

If a continue statement contains an identifier, the identifier must be defined as the label of an enclosing while, for, or do statement. A continue statement that contains an identifier stops the current iteration of the labeled iteration statement and attempts to transfer control to the start of the next iteration of that loop. Here is an example of a `continue` statement that contains an identifier:

```
public boolean search(int x, int a[][]) {
    int count = 0;

  top:
    for (int i=0; i<a.length; i++) {
        int b[] = a[i];
        for (int j=0; j < b.length; j++) {
            if (x == b[j])
                return true;
            if ( x < b[j])
                continue top;
        } // for j
        count++;
        if (count > 100)
            return false;
    } // for i
    return false;
} // search()
```

The above method searches an array of arrays of integers for a specified value. The method assumes that the values in the sub-arrays are in descending order. The method gives up after checking 100 values.

The label used in a `continue` statement must be in the immediately enclosing method or initializer block.

The statement to which a `continue` statement attempts to transfer control is called the target statement. If a `continue` statement occurs inside a `try` statement, control may not immediately transfer to the target statement. If a `try` statement has a `finally` clause, the `finally` block is executed before control leaves the `try` statement for any reason. This means that if a `continue` statement occurs inside a `try` statement (but not in its `finally` block) and the target statement is outside of the `try` statement, the `finally` block is executed first, before the control transfer can take place.

If the `finally` block contains a `break`, `continue`, `return`, or `throw` statement, the pending control transfer for the previously executed `continue` statement is forgotten. Instead, control is transferred to the target of the `break`, `continue`, `return`, or `throw` statement in the `finally` block.

If the `finally` block does not contain a `break`, `continue`, `return`, or `throw` statement, the pending control transfer happens after the `finally` block is done executing, unless the target statement is enclosed by another `try` statement. If there is another enclosing `try` statement and it has a `finally` clause, that `finally` block is also executed before the control transfer can take place. Execution proceeds in this manner until the target statement of the `continue` is executed.

References *Identifier* 2.2.1; Labeled Statements 6.2; The break Statement 6.8; The do Statement 6.7.2; The for Statement 6.7.3; The return Statement 6.10; The throw Statement 6.11; The try Statement 6.12; The while Statement 6.7.1

6.10 The return Statement

A `return` statement returns control of the current method or constructor to the caller:

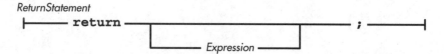

If a `return` statement does not contain an expression, the statement must be in a method declared with the `void` return type or in a constructor. Otherwise, the compiler issues an error message. When a `return` statement does not contain an expression, the statement simply attempts to transfer control back to the method or constructor that invoked the current method or constructor.

If a `return` statement contains an expression, it must be in a method that returns a value or the compiler issues an error message. The type of the expression must be assignment-compatible with the declared return type of the method. The `return` statement attempts to transfer control back to the method or constructor that invoked the current method. The value produced by the expression is the return value of the current method.

Here's an example of a `return` statement:

```
int doubleIt (int k) {
    return k*2;
}
```

If a `return` statement occurs inside a `try` statement, control may not immediately transfer to the invoking method or constructor. If a `try` statement has a `finally` clause, the `finally` block is executed before control leaves the `try` statement for any reason. This means that if a `return` statement occurs inside a `try` statement (but not in its `finally` block), the `finally` block is executed first, before the control transfer can take place.

If the `finally` block contains a `break`, `continue`, `return`, or `throw` statement, the pending control transfer for the previously executed `return` statement is forgotten. Instead, control is transferred to the target of the `break`, `continue`, `return`, or `throw` statement in the `finally` block.

If the `finally` block does not contain a `break`, `continue`, `return`, or `throw` statement, the pending control transfer happens after the `finally` block is done executing, unless there is another enclosing `try` statement. If there is such a `try` statement and it has a `finally` clause, that `finally` block is also executed before the control transfer can take place. Execution proceeds in this manner until control is transferred to the invoking method or constructor.

References Constructors 5.4.7; *Expression* 4; *Identifier* 2.2.1; Methods 5.4.6; The break Statement 6.8; The continue Statement 6.9; The throw Statement 6.11; The try Statement 6.12

6.11 The throw Statement

A `throw` statement is used to cause an exception to be thrown:

ThrowStatement

```
|——— throw ——————— Expression ——————— ; ———|
```

The expression in a `throw` statement must produce a reference to an object that is an instance of the `Throwable` class or one of its subclasses. Otherwise, the compiler issues an error message. You typically want the expression in a `throw` statement to produce an object that is an instance of a subclass of the `Exception` class.

Here is an example of a `throw` statement:

```
throw new ProtocolException();
```

A `throw` statement causes normal program execution to stop. Control is immediately transferred to the innermost enclosing `try` statement in the search for a `catch` clause that can handle the exception. If the innermost `try` statement cannot handle the exception, the exception propagates up through enclosing statements in the current method. If the current method does not contain a `try` statement that can handle the exception, the exception propagates up to the invoking method. If this method does not contain an appropriate `try` statement, the exception propagates up again, and so on. Finally, if no `try` statement is found to handle the exception, the currently running thread terminates. The termination of a thread is described in 8.1.2.1 Stopping a thread.

As an exception propagates through enclosing try statements, any finally blocks associated with those try statements are executed until the exception is caught. If a finally block contains a break, continue, return, or throw statement, the pending control transfer initiated by the throw statement is forgotten. Instead, control is transferred to the target of the break, continue, return, or throw statement in the finally block.

References Exception Handling 9; *Expression* 4; The break Statement 6.8; The continue Statement 6.9; The return Statement 6.10; The try Statement 6.12; Throwable 10.25

6.12 *The try Statement*

A try statement provides a way to catch exceptions and execute clean-up code for a block:

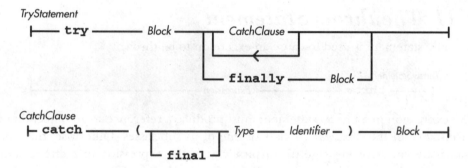

A try statement contains a block of code to be executed. A try statement can have any number of optional catch clauses; these clauses act as exception handlers for the try block. A try statement can also have a finally clause. If present, the finally block is always executed before control leaves the try statement, so it is a good place to supply clean-up code for the try block. Note that a try statement must have either a catch clause or a finally clause.

Here is an example of a try statement that includes a catch clause and a finally clause:

```
try {
    out.write(b);
} catch (IOException e) {
    System.out.println("Output Error");
} finally {
    out.close();
}
```

If out.write() throws an IOException, the exception is caught by the catch clause. Regardless of whether out.write() returns normally or throws an exception, the finally block is executed, which ensures that out.close() is always called.

A try statement begins by executing the block that follows the keyword try. If an exception is thrown from within the try block and the try statement has any catch clauses, those clauses are searched in order for one that can handle the exception. A catch clause can handle an exception if the *ClassOrInterfaceName* specified in the clause is the same class as or a superclass of the object specified in the throw statement that caused the exception. The *ClassOrInterfaceName* specified in a catch clause must be Throwable or be one of its subclasses. If a catch clause handles an exception, that catch block is executed.

If an exception is thrown from within the try block and the try statement does not have any catch clauses that can handle the exception, the exception propagates up to the next enclosing try statement. An exception also propagates up if it is thrown from within a catchblock in a try statement.

The identifier specified in parentheses for the catch clause is defined as a local variable within the catch block. The local variable is initialized to refer to the thrown object, in a manner that is similar to the way it which formal parameters for a method are handled. This means that an identifier in a catch clause cannot have the same name as a local variable or formal parameter that is defined in an enclosing block. If the catch parameter is declared as final, any assignment to that parameter in the catch block generates an error. The syntax for specifying final catch parameters is not supported prior to Java 1.1.

Any catch clauses in a try statement are checked in sequence to see if they can handle a given exception. Thus, the order in which catch clauses appear is important. In essence, more specific catch clauses should appear before more general catch clauses. Figure 6-1 shows the inheritance hierarchy for a few of the classes of objects that can be thrown in Java.

Based on the classes shown in Figure 6-1, consider the following example:

```
try {
    System.out.write(b);
} catch (InterruptedIOException e) { ...
} catch (IOException e) { ...
} catch (Exception e) { ...
}
```

The catch clauses in this example appear in order from most specific to least specific. That means that if an InterruptedIOException were thrown, it would be

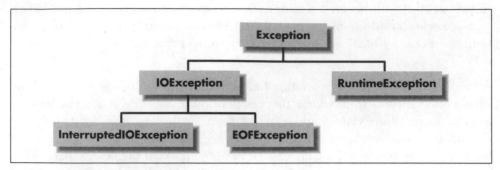

Figure 6–1: Some exception classes in Java

caught by the first catch clause. Similarly, an IOException would be caught by the second catch clause and an Exception would be caught by the third clause. If, however, the catch clause for Exception appeared first, neither of the other catch clauses would ever be executed because the catch clause for Exception would catch all of the exceptions.

If a try statement includes a finally clause, the finally block is always executed before control leaves the try statement. There are two different ways that control can leave a try statement:

• The try statement completes normally. Normal completion occurs when all of the statements in the try block have been executed, so that control falls out of the bottom of the try block. Normal completion can also occur when an exception is thrown in the try block, as long as the exception is handled by a catch clause in the try statement.

• The try statement completes abruptly, due to an attempted control transfer out of the try block. A break, continue, or return statement in the try block causes an abrupt completion. In addition, abrupt completion can occur when an exception occurs and is not handled by a catch clause in the try statement, since the exception propagates out of the try block.

If a try statement completes normally and it does not have a finally clause, the statement following the try statement is the next statement to be executed. However, if the try statement does have a finally clause, the finally block is executed first, before control can be transferred to the statement following the try statement. If the finally block contains a break, continue, return, or throw statement, the pending control transfer is forgotten and control is instead transferred to the target of the break, continue, return, or throw statement in the finally block.

If a `try` statement completes abruptly and it does not have a `finally` clause, the control transfer out of the `try` block takes place immediately. However, if the `try` statement does have a `finally` clause, the `finally` block is executed first, before the control transfer can take place. If the `finally` block contains a `break`, continue, `return`, or `throw` statement, the pending control transfer is forgotten and control is instead transferred to the target of the `break`, `continue`, `return`, or `throw` statement in the `finally` block.

References *Block* 6.1; Exception Handling 9; *Expression* 4; *Identifier* 2.2.1; The break Statement 6.8; The continue Statement 6.9; The return Statement 6.10; The throw Statement 6.11; Throwable 10.25 *Type* 3;

6.13 The synchronized Statement

A synchronized statement provides a way of synchronizing the execution of a block, so that only one thread can be executing the block at a time:

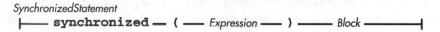

SynchronizedStatement

The expression in parentheses must produce a reference type, or the compiler issues an error message. If the expression evaluates to `null`, a `NullPointer-Exception` is thrown.

Before executing the block in a synchronized statement, the current thread obtains a lock for the object referenced by the expression. While the block is being executed, no other thread can obtain the lock for that object. When the thread is done executing the block, it releases the lock, so it is available for other threads. See Chapter 8 for a complete discussion of threads in Java.

References *Block* 6.1; *Expression* 4; Runtime exceptions 9.4.1.1; Threads 8

7

In this chapter:
- *Compilation Units*
- *Packages*
- *The import Directive*
- *Documentation Comments*
- *Applications*
- *Applets*

Program Structure

This chapter discusses the higher levels of program structure for Java programs. The two levels of organization discussed in this chapter are compilation units and packages. A *compilation unit* contains the source code for one or more classes or interfaces. A *package* is a collection of related compilation units.

This chapter also discusses the two most common top-level Java program architectures: applications and applets. An *application* is a stand-alone Java program that can be run directly from the command line (or other operating system environment). An *applet* is a Java program that must be run from within another program, such as a Web browser. In the future, applets will even be hosted by other environments, such as cellular phones and personal digital assistants.

7.1 Compilation Units

A compilation unit is the highest-level syntactic structure that Java recognizes:

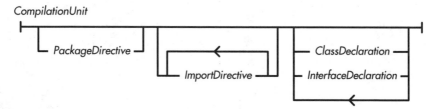

Only one of the classes or interfaces declared in a compilation unit can be declared `public`.

A compilation unit usually corresponds to a single source code file. However, the Java language specification allows compilation units to be stored in a database. If compilation units are stored in a database, the limit of one `public` class or interface per compilation unit does not apply, as long as there is a way to extract the compilation units from the database and place them in individual files that contain no more than one `public` class or interface per file. This exception to the one `public` class or interface per compilation unit rule is useful if you are implementing a Java development environment.

Every compilation unit is part of exactly one package. That package is specified by the `package` directive that appears at the beginning of the compilation unit. If there is no `package` directive, the compilation unit is part of the default package.

References *ClassDeclaration* 5.4; Class Modifiers 5.4.1; *ImportDirective* 7.3; *InterfaceDeclaration* 5.5; Interface Modifiers 5.5.1; *PackageDirective* 7.2

7.2 *Packages*

A package is a group of classes. If a class is not declared as `public`, it can only be referenced by other classes in the same package. A class is specified as being part of a particular package by a `package` directive at the beginning of its compilation unit:

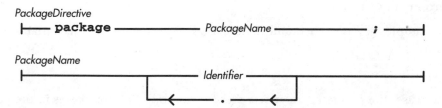

A package directive can only occur at the beginning of a compilation unit (ignoring comments and white space). If there is no `package` directive in a compilation unit, the compilation unit is part of the default package. A package is identified by its name. However, the default package has no name. Here are some examples of package directives:

```
package tools.text;
package COM.geomaker;
```

A class or interface definition can refer to class and interface definitions in a different package by qualifying the class or interface name with the package name and a period. For example, you can refer to the `Socket` class as follows:

```
java.net.Socket
```

However, if you attempt to use a non-public class or interface defined in another package, the Java compiler issues an error message.

An import directive, described in the next section, makes the class and interface definitions in another package available by their simple names. In other words, if you use an import directive, you do not have to qualify the names of the classes and interfaces in the package with the package name.

In Sun's implementation of Java, the name of the package for a given compilation unit is used to determine the directories that the Java interpreter searches to find the compiled Java code (i.e., the .class file) for the compilation unit. The Java interpreter uses a two-step process to find the compiled code for a class in a named package:

- The name of the package is converted into a relative path. Each identifier in the package name becomes the name of a directory in this relative path. (This scheme assumes that the Java interpreter is operating in an environment that supports a hierarchical file system.)

- The relative path is appended to the directories specified in the CLASSPATH environment variable and the resulting paths are searched for the .class file.

If the Java interpreter is searching for the compiled code for a class that is in the default package, it simply searches the directories specified in the CLASSPATH environment variable.

For example, say that the value of the CLASSPATH environment variable is as follows:[*]

```
\java\classes;.\;
```

In this case, the Java interpreter searches for the .class files for classes in the package named COM.geomaker in the following directories:

```
\java\classes\COM\geomaker
.\COM\geomaker
```

If a package name contains a Unicode character that cannot directly appear in a directory name, the character is represented in the directory name by an "at" sign (@) followed by one to four hexadecimal digits. For example, the package name:

```
COM.geomaker.hg\u00f8
```

---

[*] This example uses Windows syntax for directory names. The syntax for directory names is different in other environments. In particular, the character used to separate directory names varies in other environments.

becomes the relative path:

```
\COM\geomaker\hg@f8
```

Java classes can also be retrieved out of a *.zip* file if the file is specified as part of the CLASSPATH. For instance, the value of CLASSPATH could be set as follows:

```
\java\classes;\java\classes.zip;.\;
```

When the Java interpreter finds a *.zip* file in the CLASSPATH, it searches the *.zip* file for the appropriate *.class* file. The core classes in the Java API are supplied in a file that is typically named something like *jdk1.1/lib/classes.zip*. As of Java 1.1, you do not normally need to put that *.zip* file in CLASSPATH because the Java interpreter automatically puts *startDir/../classes.zip* on the end of CLASSPATH (where *startDir* is the directory that contains the interpreter's executable file).

The Java language specification defines a scheme for creating package names that should be globally unique. Since Internet domain names are globally unique, the idea is to incorporate them into package names. This is done by reversing the order of the components of the domain name, capitalizing the top-level component of the domain name, and using the result as a prefix for the descriptive portion of a package name. For example, if different organizations were to create packages that they all wanted to call opinion_poll, they could use this scheme to ensure global uniqueness. The resulting package names might be:

```
COM.cnn.opinion_poll
GOV.whitehouse.opinion_poll
EDU.syracuse.newhouse.opinion_poll
```

Package names that begin with an identifier that does not contain all uppercase letters are reserved for use as local package names. The one exception is package names that begin with the identifier java, which are reserved for packages that are part of the standard Java distribution.

References Class Declarations 5.4; *Identifier* 2.2.1; Interface Declarations 5.5; The import Directive 7.3

7.3   *The import Directive*

You can refer to classes and interfaces defined in a particular package by qualifying their names with the package name and a period. For example, you can refer to the Socket class as java.net.Socket. Using this notation, you could write a declaration like the following:

```
java.net.Socket s = new java.net.Socket();
```

This declaration is rather verbose. As you can imagine, it would quickly become cumbersome to refer to classes this way in all of your programs.

The `import` directive provides an alternative to prefixing the names of classes and interfaces defined in particular packages with their package names. An `import` directive makes definitions from another package available by their simple names:

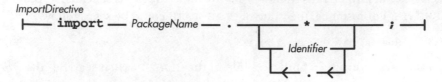

An `import` directive can only occur after the `package` directive in a compilation unit (if there is one) and before any class or interface declarations.

An `import` directive with an identifier after the package name defines that identifier to have the same meaning as the fully qualified class or interface name. When an identifier is defined using an `import` directive, the definition exists only from the `import` directive that defines it to the end of the compilation unit.

For example, you could use the following `import` directive:

```
import java.net.Socket;
```

Now the identifier `Socket` is defined to mean `java.net.Socket`. With the above `import` directive at the beginning of a compilation unit, you can rewrite the previous declaration as follows:

```
Socket s = new Socket();
```

If more than one `import` directive provides a definition for the same identifier, the compiler issues an error message.

An `import` directive can also be used to define an identifier as a synonym for the fully qualified name of a class that is declared inside of another class. For example, consider the following class declaration:

```
package COM.geomaker;
...
public class z {
    ...
    class zz {
        ...
    }
}
```

A class in another file can refer to the class `COM.geomaker.z.zz` as just `zz` if the file contains the following `import` directive:

```
import COM.geomaker.z.zz;
```

An import directive with an asterisk (*) after the package name tells the compiler to search the specified package when it cannot find a definition for an identifier. In other words, this type of import directive makes all of the classes and interfaces in the package available by their simple names. Here's an example of such an import directive:

```
import java.awt.*;
```

When the compiler is searching packages specified by this type of import directive, it issues an error message if it finds the same name defined in two different packages.

Every package in Java is considered separate and distinct, even if the name of a package begins with the name of another package. For example, the package java.awt is separate and distinct from the package java.awt.image. Even though the names imply a parent-child relationship, Java recognizes no such relationship between packages. Consider the following directive:

```
import java.awt.*;
```

This tells the Java compiler to search the java.awt package for class and interface names; it docs not, however, tell the compiler to search java.awt.image for such names. For that to happen, a compilation unit must also include the following directive:

```
import Java.awt.image.*;
```

It is important to understand that an import directive does not cause the Java compiler to read any class or interface definitions. An import directive simply defines an identifier as a synonym for a fully qualified class or interface name or directs the compiler to search a package when it needs to find a definition. The compiler only reads a class or interface definition when its finds an actual reference to the class or interface.

References Compilation Units 7.1; *Identifier* 2.2.1; *PackageName* 7.2

7.4 *Documentation Comments*

Documentation comments are used to create stand-alone documentation for classes. Documentation comments are processed into Web pages by the *javadoc* program that is part of Sun's Java Development Kit (JDK). The *javadoc* program and the way that it processes *.java* files into Web pages is fully described in the documentation for *javadoc* provided by Sun. The remainder of this section describes the special formatting information that can be embedded in documentation comments.

Documentation comments are comments that begin with /**. If a documentation comment immediately precedes the declaration of a class, interface, method, or field variable, it is assumed to describe that class, interface, method, or field variable.

HTML tags can be included in a documentation comment; they are passed directly to the generated Web page. In addition to passing HTML tags, *javadoc* recognizes special tags that start with an "at" sign (@). These tags must appear as the first word on a line in order to be recognized. Here is an example of a documentation comment that includes these special *javadoc* tags:

```
/**
 * RomanNumeral is a class similar to Integer, except that
 * it uses roman numerals for its string based
 * representation.  It only represents positive numbers.
 *
 * @see      Integer
 * @see      Number
 * @see      Float
 * @see      Double
 * @version  1.1, 9/27/96
 * @author   Mark Grand
 */
```

Here are the special documentation comment tags recognized by *javadoc*:

@author author-name

    Formats the given author name. This tag can only be used in a class or interface documentation comment.

@exception name description

    Formats the given exception name and its description in the throws section of a method description. The name should be the fully qualified class name of the exception. This tag can only be used in a method documentation comment.

@param name description

    Formats the given parameter name and its description in the parameters section of a method description. This tag can only be used in a method documentation comment.

@return description

    Formats the given description in the returns section of a method description. This tag can only be used in a method documentation comment.

@see classname

    Generates a hypertext link to the specified class. The class name may be qualified by its package name.

`@see classname#method-name`
> Generates a hypertext link to the specified method in the specified class. The class name may be qualified by its package name.

`@version text`
> Formats the given text as version information. This tag can only be used in a class or interface documentation comment.

`@deprecated`
> Indicates that a class, method, or variable is deprecated, which means that it has been superceded by a newer, preferred class, method, or variable. Deprecated features should not be used in new Java programs. In addition, you should try to update existing code so that it does not rely on deprecated features. While the deprecated features in Java 1.1 are still supported, there is no guarantee that they will be supported in future releases. The `@deprecated` tag is new as of Java 1.1.

The documentation comment that immediately precedes a declaration is associated with the declaration. If two comments precede a declaration, only the one immediately preceding the declaration is processed by *javadoc*. The first comment is not considered to be associated with a declaration, so it is ignored. If there is anything but white space between a documentation comment and a declaration, the documentation comment is not considered to be associated with the declaration.

References Comments 2.2.6

7.5 *Applications*

For a Java program to run as an application, it must have at least one `public` class that contains a `public static` method called `main()` that takes exactly one parameter, an array of `String` objects.

Here is a very simple sample application that outputs "Hello World!" and then exits:

```
class DoIt {
    public static void main  (String argv[]){
        System.out.println ("Hello World!");
    }
}
```

The `main()` method must be `public` so that the Java virtual machine can find it. If the method is not `public`, its name is not included in the compiler's output. The system does not create any objects prior to the start of the application's `main()` method, so the `main()` method must be `static` because it cannot be associated with an object.

If an application has a graphical user interface, then it typically creates a `java.awt.Frame` object in `main()`. The `Frame` object acts as the top-level window for the application.

In Sun's implementation of Java, you run a Java application by running the Java interpreter with a command-line argument that specifies the name of the class that contains the `main()`. The name of the Java interpreter is *java*. Here's the command-line for our sample application:

```
C:\> java DoIt
```

The capitalization of the class name on the command line must match the capitalization of the class name within the program. If the class is part of a named package, the name of the class must be qualified with the package name. For example, if you have a package called `COM.geomaker` and it contains the class called `DoIt`, you would use the following command to run the application:

```
C:\> java COM.geomaker.DoIt
```

Any additional information that you provide on the command line is passed to the application as command line arguments. These arguments are passed to the application using the `String` array passed to `main()`. The number of elements in the array is equal to the number of arguments passed to the application. If there are no arguments to the application, the length of the array passed to `main()` is zero.

References Methods 5.4.6; Packages 7.2

7.6 *Applets*

A Java applet must be run from within another program, called a host application. At this point, most host applications are Web browsers. The interaction between an applet and its host application is rather involved.

From the viewpoint of an applet, the interaction involves defining a subclass of the `java.applet.Applet` class. The `Applet` class defines a number of methods that control the applet. A subclass of `Applet` overrides one or more of the methods:

`init()`
> The `init()` method is called to initialize the applet. Most initialization of an applet is done here instead of in a constructor because the constructor may be called before the hosting program is ready to provide all of the services needed for initialization.

`start()`
> The `start()` method is called in a separate thread to tell the applet to start doing whatever it is supposed to do.

`paint()`

The `paint()` method is called at unpredictable times to draw the applet onto the screen.

`stop()`

The `stop()` method is called to tell the applet to stop doing whatever it does.

`destroy()`

The `destroy()` method is called to tell the applet to release any resources that it holds.

From the viewpoint of the host application, the interaction typically follows a standard sequence of events. The host application usually does the following:

1. Installs a `SecurityManager` object to implement a security policy.

2. Creates a `ClassLoader` object to load the applet.

3. Loads the applet and calls its default constructor.

4. Passes an `AppletStub` object to the applet's `setStub()` method.

5. Calls the applet's `init()` method in a separate thread.

6. Marks the applet as active.

7. Starts a new thread to run the applet's `start()` method.

8. Calls the applet's `show()` method, which makes the applet visible and causes the applet's `paint()` method to be called for the first time.

9. Calls the applet's `paint()` method whenever the applet needs to be refreshed.

10. Calls the applet's `start()` and `stop()` methods when the host wants the applet to start or stop. These methods are typically called when the applet is exposed or hidden.

11. Calls the applet's `hide()` method followed by its `destroy()` method when the host wants to shut down the applet.

7.6.1 Embedding an Applet in a Web Page

Web pages are written in a language called HTML. This explanation of how to embed an applet in a Web page assumes that you have some knowledge of basic HTML. An applet is embedded in a Web page using an `<applet>` tag. A minimal `<applet>` tag looks as follows:

```
<applet code=Clock height=300 width=350>
</applet>
```

The code attribute of this sample <applet> tag specifies that the applet to be run is a class named Clock. The width and height attributes specify that the applet should be given a screen area that is 300 pixels high and 350 pixels wide.

The following list shows all of the attributes that can be specified in an <applet> tag. The attributes should be specified in the order in which they are listed. The code, height, and width attributes are required in an <applet> tag; the other attributes are optional:

codebase

> The codebase attribute should specify a URL that identifies the directory used to find the .*class* files needed for the applet. Files for classes that belong to the default package should be in this directory. Files for classes that belong to named packages should be in subdirectories of this directory, where the relative path is specified by individual identifiers in the package name. If codebase is not specified, the <applet> tag uses the directory that contains the HTML file as a default.

code

> The code attribute specifies the name of the class that implements the applet. If the applet is part of a named package, you must specify the fully qualified class name. So, if the name of the class is DataPlot and it is part of a package called COM.geomaker.graph, the value of the code attribute should be:

```
code=COM.geomaker.graph.DataPlot.class
```

> The browser locates the compiled code for the class by appending .*class* to the filename and searching the directory specified by the base URL for the document.

object

> The object attribute specifies the name of a file that contains a serialized representation of an applet. If this attribute is specified, the applet is created by deserialization, rather than by calling its default constructor. The serialization is assumed to have occurred after the applet's init() method has been invoked, so the start() method is called instead of the init() method. Any attributes specified when the applet was serialized are not restored; the applet sees the attributes specified for this invocation.

> The object attribute is new as of Java 1.1. An <applet> tag must include either the code attribute or the object attribute, but it cannot include both.

archive

> The archive attribute specifies a list of one or more archives that contain classes or other resources for an applet. Archives can be JAR or ZIP files. If this attribute is specified, the resources in the archives are loaded before the

applet is run. If multiple archives are listed, they should be separated by commas. The `archive` attribute is new for Java 1.1.

`alt`

> The `alt` attribute specifies the text that should be displayed by Web browsers that understand the `<applet>` tag but cannot run Java applets. If the text contains space characters, it should be enclosed in quotation marks.

`name`

> The `name` attribute specifies a name for a particular instance of an applet. An applet can get a reference to another applet on the same Web page using the `getApplet()` method.

`width`

> The `width` attribute specifies the width of the applet in pixels.

`height`

> The `height` attribute specifies the height of the applet in pixels.

`align`

> The `align` attribute specifies the positioning of the applet. The possible values are: `left`, `right`, `top`, `texttop`, `middle`, `absmiddle`, `baseline`, `bottom`, or `absbottom`.

`vspace`

> The `vspace` attribute specifies the amount of vertical space above and below the applet in pixels.

`hspace`

> The `hspace` attribute specifies the amount of horizontal space to the left and right of the applet in pixels.

Applet-specific parameters can be provided to an applet using `<param>` tags inside the `<applet>` tag. A `<param>` tag must specify `name` and `value` attributes. For example:

```
<param name=speed value=65>
```

If a Web browser does not support the `<applet>` tag, it ignores the tag and simply displays any HTML content provided inside the tag. However, if the browser understands the `<applet>` tag, this HTML content is ignored. This means that you can provide HTML content inside an `<applet>` tag to inform users of non-Java-enabled browsers about what they are missing.

Here is an example that combines all of these elements:

```
<applet code=Compass height=400 width=300>
<param name=direction value=north>
<param name=speed value=65>
```

```
<p>
<i>If you can see this message, your Web browser is not Java enabled.
There is a Java applet on this Web page that you are not seeing.</i>
<p>
</applet>
```

If a non-Java-enabled browser is used to view this HTML file, the following text is displayed:

> If you can see this message, your Web browser is not Java-enabled. There is a Java applet on this Web page that you are not seeing.

Threads

Threads provide a way for a Java program to do multiple tasks concurrently. A thread is essentially a flow of control in a program and is similar to the more familiar concept of a process. An operating system that can run more than one program at the same time uses processes to keep track of the various programs that it is running. However, processes generally do not share any state, while multiple threads within the same application share much of the same state. In particular, all of the threads in an application run in the same address space, sharing all resources except the stack. In concrete terms, this means that threads share field variables, but not local variables.

When multiple processes share a single processor, there are times when the operating system must stop the processor from running one process and start it running another process. The operating system must execute a sequence of events called a *context switch* to transfer control from one process to another. When a context switch occurs, the operating system has to save a lot of information for the process that is being paused and load the comparable information for the process being resumed. A context switch between two processes can require the execution of thousands of machine instructions. The Java virtual machine is responsible for handling context switches between threads in a Java program. Because threads share much of the same state, a context switch between two threads typically requires the execution of less than 100 machine instructions.

There are a number of situations where it makes sense to use threads in a Java program. Some programs must be able to engage in multiple activities and still be able to respond to additional input from the user. For example, a web browser should be able to respond to user input while fetching an image or playing a sound. Because threads can be suspended and resumed, they can make it easier to control multiple activities, even if the activities do not need to be concurrent. If a program models real world objects that display independent, autonomous behavior, it makes sense to use a separate thread for each object. Threads can also implement asynchronous methods, so that a calling method does not have to wait for the method it calls to complete before continuing with its own activity.

Java applets make considerable use of threads. For example, an animation is generally implemented with a separate thread. If an applet has to download extensive information, such as an image or a sound, to initialize itself, the initialization can take a long time. This initialization can be done in a separate thread to prevent the initialization from interfering with the display of the applet. If an applet needs to process messages from the network, that work generally is done in a separate thread so that the applet can continue painting itself on the screen and responding to mouse and keyboard events. In addition, if each message is processed separately, the applet uses a separate thread for each message.

For all of the reasons there are to use threads, there are also some compelling reasons not to use them. If a program uses inherently sequential logic, where one operation starts another operation and then must wait for the other operation to complete before continuing, one thread can implement the entire sequence. Using multiple threads in such a case results in a more complex program with no accompanying benefits. There is considerable overhead in creating and starting a thread, so if an operation involves only a few primitive statements, it is faster to handle it with a single thread. This can even be true when the operation is conceptually asynchronous. When multiple threads share objects, the objects must use synchronization mechanisms to coordinate thread access and maintain consistent state. Synchronization mechanisms add complexity to a program, can be difficult to tune for optimal performance, and can be a source of bugs.

8.1 Using Thread Objects

The `Thread` class in the `java.lang` package creates and controls threads in Java programs. The execution of Java code is always under the control of a `Thread` object. The `Thread` class provides a `static` method called `currentThread()` that provides a reference to the `Thread` object that controls the current thread of execution.

References Thread 10.23

8.1.1 Associating a Method with a Thread

The first thing you need to do to make a `Thread` object useful is to associate it with a method you want it to run. Java provides two ways of associating a method with a `Thread`:

- Declare a subclass of `Thread` that defines a `run()` method.

- Pass a reference to an object that implements the `Runnable` interface to a `Thread` constructor.

For example, if you need to load the contents of a URL as part of an applet's initialization, but the applet can provide other functionality before the content is loaded, you might want to load the content in a separate thread. Here is a class that does just that:

```java
import java.net.URL;

class UrlData extends Thread   {
    private Object data;
    private URL url

    public UrlData(String urlName) throws MalformedURLException {
        url = new URL(urlName);
        start();
    }

    public void run(){
        try {
            data = url.getContent();
        } catch (java.io.IOException  e) {
        }
    }

    public Object getUrlData(){
        return data;
    }
}
```

The `UrlData` class is declared as a subclass of `Thread` so that it can get the contents of the URL in a separate thread. The constructor creates a `java.net.URL` object to fetch the contents of the URL, and then calls the `start()` method to start the thread. Once the thread is started, the constructor returns; it does not wait for the contents of the URL to be fetched. The `run()` method is executed after the thread is started; it does the real work of fetching the data. The `getUrl-Data()` method is an access method that returns the value of the `data` variable. The value of this variable is `null` until the contents of the URL have been fetched, at which time it contains a reference to the actual data.

Subclassing the Thread class is convenient when the method you want to run in a separate thread does not need to belong to a particular class. Sometimes, however, you need the method to be part of a particular class that is a subclass of a class other than Thread. Say, for example, you want a graphical object that is displayed in a window to alternate its background color between red and blue once a second. The object that implements this behavior needs to be a subclass of the java.awt.Canvas class. However, at the same time, you need a separate thread to alternate the color of the object once a second.

In this situation, you want to tell a Thread object to run code in another object that is not a subclass of the Thread class. You can accomplish this by passing a reference to an object that implements the Runnable interface to the constructor of the Thread class. The Runnable interface requires that an object has a public method called run() that takes no arguments. When a Runnable object is passed to the constructor of the Thread class, it creates a Thread object that calls the Runnable object's run() method when the thread is started. The following example shows part of the code that implements an object that alternates its background color between red and blue once a second:

```
class AutoColorChange extends java.awt.Canvas implements Runnable {
    private Thread myThread;

    AutoColorChange () {
        myThread = new Thread(this);
        myThread.start();
        ...
    }

    public void run() {
        while (true) {
            setBackground(java.awt.Color.red);
            repaint();
            try {
                myThread.sleep(1000);
            } catch (InterruptedException e) {}
            setBackground(java.awt.Color.blue);
            repaint();
            try {
                myThread.sleep(1000);
            } catch (InterruptedException e) {}
        }
    }
}
```

The AutoChangeColor class extends java.awt.Canvas, alternating the background color between red and blue once a second. The constructor creates a new Thread by passing the current object to the Thread constructor, which tells the Thread to call the run() method in the AutoChangeColor class. The constructor then starts the new thread by calling its start() method, so that the color change happens asynchronously of whatever else is going on. The class has an instance variable called myThread that contains a reference to the Thread object, so that can control the thread. The run() method takes care of changing the background color, using the sleep() method of the Thread class to temporarily suspend the thread and calling repaint() to redisplay the object after each color change.

References Runnable 10.16; Thread 10.23

8.1.2 Controlling a Thread

As shown in the previous section, you start a Thread by calling its start() method. Before the start() method is called, the isAlive() method of the Thread object always returns false. When the start() method is called, the Thread object becomes associated with a scheduled thread in the underlying environment. After the start() method has returned, the isAlive() method always returns true. The Thread is now scheduled to run until it dies, unless it is suspended or in another unrunnable state.

It is actually possible for isAlive() to return true before start() returns, but not before start() is called. This can happen because the start() method can return either before the started Thread begins to run or after it begins to run. In other words, the method that called start() and the new thread are now running concurrently. On a multiprocessor system, the start() method can even return at the same time the started Thread begins to run.

Thread objects have a parent-child relationship. The first thread created in a Java environment does not have a parent Thread. However, after the first Thread object is created, the Thread object that controls the thread used to create another Thread object is considered to be the parent of the newly created Thread. This parent-child relationship is used to supply some default values when a Thread object is created, but it has no further significance after a Thread has been created.

References Thread 10.23

8.1.2.1 Stopping a thread

A thread dies when one of the following things happens:

- The run() method called by the Thread returns.

- An exception is thrown that causes the run() method to be exited.

- The stop() method of the Thread is called.

The stop() method of the Thread class works by throwing a ThreadDeath object in the run() method of the thread. Normally, you should not catch

ThreadDeath objects in a try statement. If you need to catch ThreadDeath objects to detect that a Thread is about to die, the try statement that catches ThreadDeath objects should rethrow them.

When an object (ThreadDeath or otherwise) is thrown out of the run() method for the Thread, the uncaughtException() method of the ThreadGroup for that Thread is called. If the thrown object is an instance of the ThreadDeath class, the thread dies, and the thrown object is ignored. Otherwise, if the thrown object is of any other class, uncaughtException() calls the thrown object's printStackTrace() method, the thread dies, and the thrown object is ignored. In either case, if there are other nondaemon threads running in the system, the current program continues to run.

References Errors 9.4.2; The try Statement 6.12; Thread 10.23; ThreadGroup 10.24

8.1.2.2 Interrupting a thread

In some situations, you need to kill a thread in a way that allows it to complete what it is currently doing before dying. For example, if a thread is in the middle of processing a transaction, you might want the transaction to complete before the thread dies. The Thread class provides support for this in the form of the interrupt() method.

There are a number of methods in the Java API, such as wait() and join(), that are declared as throwing an InterruptedException. Both of these methods temporarily suspend the execution of a thread. In Java 1.1, if a thread is waiting for one of these methods to return and another thread calls interrupt() on the waiting thread, the method that is waiting throws an InterruptedException.

The interrupt() method sets an internal flag in a Thread object. Before the interrupt() method is called, the isInterrupted() method of the Thread object always returns false. After the interrupt() method is called, isInterrupted() returns true.

Prior to version 1.1, the methods in the Java API that are declared as throwing an InterruptedException do not actually do so. However, the isInterrupted() method does return True if the thread has been interrupted. Thus, if the code in the run() method for a thread periodically calls isInterrupted(), the thread can respond to a call to interrupt() by shutting down in an orderly fashion.

References Other exceptions 9.4.1.2; Thread 10.23

8.1.2.3 Thread priority

One of the attributes that controls the behavior of a thread is its priority. Although Java does not guarantee much about how threads are scheduled, it does guarantee that a thread with a priority that is higher than that of another thread will be scheduled to run at least as often, and possibly more often, than the thread with the lower priority. The priority of a thread is set when the `Thread` object is created, by passing an argument to the constructor that creates the `Thread` object. If an explicit priority is not specified, the `Thread` inherits the priority of its parent `Thread` object.

You can query the priority of a `Thread` object by calling its `getPriority()` method. Similarly, you can set the priority of a `Thread` using its `setPriority()` method. The priority you specify must be greater than or equal to `Thread.MIN_PRIORITY` and less than or equal to `Thread.MAX_PRIORITY`.

Before actually setting the priority of a `Thread` object, the `setPriority()` method checks the maximum allowable priority for the `ThreadGroup` that contains the `Thread` by calling `getMaxPriority()` on the `ThreadGroup`. If the call to `setPriority()` tries to set the priority to a value that is higher than the maximum allowable priority for the `ThreadGroup`, the priority is instead set to the maximum priority. It is possible for the current priority of a `Thread` to be greater than the maximum allowable priority for the `ThreadGroup`. In this case, an attempt to raise the priority of the `Thread` results in its priority being lowered to the maximum priority.

References Thread 10.23; ThreadGroup 10.24

8.1.2.4 Daemon threads

A daemon thread is a thread that runs continuously to perform a service, without having any connection with the overall state of the program. For example, the thread that runs the garbage collector in Java is a daemon thread. The thread that processes mouse events for a Java program is also a daemon thread. In general, threads that run application code are not daemon threads, and threads that run system code are daemon threads. If a thread dies and there are no other threads except daemon threads alive, the Java virtual machine stops.

A `Thread` object has a `boolean` attribute that specifies whether or not a thread is a daemon thread. The daemon attribute of a thread is set when the `Thread` object is created, by passing an argument to the constructor that creates the `Thread` object. If the daemon attribute is not explicitly specified, the `Thread` inherits the daemon attribute of its parent `Thread` object.

The daemon attribute is queried using the `isDaemon()` method; it is set using the `setDaemon()` method.

References Thread 10.23

8.1.2.5 Yielding

When a thread has nothing to do, it can call the `yield()` method of its `Thread` object. This method tells the scheduler to run a different thread. The value of calling `yield()` depends largely on whether the scheduling mechanism for the platform on which the program is running is preemptive or nonpreemptive.

By choosing a maximum length of time a thread can continuously, a *preemptive* scheduling mechanism guarantees that no single thread uses more than its fair share of the processor. If a thread runs for that amount of time without yielding control to another thread, the scheduler preempts the thread and causes it to stop running so that another thread can run.

A *nonpreemptive* scheduling mechanism cannot preempt threads. A nonpreemptive scheduler relies on the individual threads to yield control of the processor frequently, so that it can provide reasonable performance. A thread explicitly yields control by calling the `Thread` object's `yield()` method. More often, however, a thread implicitly yields control when it is forced to wait for something to happen elsewhere.

Calling a `Thread` object's `yield()` method during a lengthy computation can be quite valuable on a platform that uses a nonpreemptive scheduling mechanism, as it allows other threads to run. Otherwise, the lengthy computation can prevent other threads from running. On a platform that uses a preemptive scheduling mechanism, calling `yield()` does not usually make any noticeable difference in the responsiveness of threads.

Regardless of the scheduling algorithm that is being used, you should not make any assumptions about when a thread will be scheduled to run again after it has called `yield()`. If you want to prevent a thread from being scheduled to run until a specified amount of time has elapsed, you should call the `sleep()` method of the `Thread` object. The `sleep()` method takes an argument that specifies a minimum number of milliseconds that must elapse before the thread can be scheduled to run again.

References Thread 10.23

8.1.2.6 Controlling groups of threads

Sometimes it is necessary to control multiple threads at the same time. Java provides the `ThreadGroup` class for this purpose. Every `Thread` object belongs to a

ThreadGroup object. By passing an argument to the constructor that creates the Thread object, the ThreadGroup of a thread can be set when the Thread object is created. If an explicit ThreadGroup is not specified, the Thread belongs to the same ThreadGroup as its parent Thread object.

References Thread 10.23; ThreadGroup 10.24

8.2 Synchronizing Multiple Threads

The correct behavior of a multithreaded program generally depends on multiple threads cooperating with each other. This often involves threads not doing certain things at the same time or waiting for each other to perform certain tasks. This type of cooperation is called *synchronization*. This section discusses some common strategies for synchronization and how they can be implemented in Java.

The simplest strategy for ensuring that threads are correctly synchronized is to write code that works correctly when executed concurrently by any number of threads. However, this is more easily said than done. Most useful computations involve doing some activity, such as updating an instance variable or updating a display, that must be synchronized in order to happen correctly.

If a method only updates its local variables and calls other methods that only modify their local variables, the method can be invoked by multiple threads without any need for synchronization. Math.sqrt() and the length() method of the String class are examples of such methods.

A method that creates objects and meets the above criterion may not require synchronization. If the constructors invoked by the method do not modify anything but their own local variables and instance variables of the object they are constructing, and they only call methods that do not need to be synchronized, the method itself does not need to be synchronized. An example of such a method is the substring() in the String class.

Beyond these two simple cases, it is impossible to give an exhaustive list of rules that can tell you whether or not a method needs to be synchronized. You need to consider what the method is doing and think about any ill effects of concurrent execution in order to decide if synchronization is necessary.

8.2.1 Single-Threaded Execution

When more than one thread is trying to update the same data at the same time, the result may be wrong or inconsistent. Consider the following example:

```
class CountIt {
    int i = 0;
```

```
    void count() {
        i = i + 1;
    }
}
```

The method `count()` is supposed to increment the variable `i` by one. However, suppose that there are two threads, A and B, that call `count()` at the same time. In this case, it is possible that `i` could be incremented only once, instead of twice. Say the value of `i` is 7. Thread A calls the `count()` method and computes `i+1` as 8. Then thread B calls the `count()` method and computes `i+1` as 8 because thread A has not yet assigned the new value to `i`. Next, thread A assigns the value 8 to the variable `i`. Finally, thread B assigns the value 8 to the variable `i`. Thus, even though the `count()` method is called twice, the variable has only been incremented once when the sequence is finished.

Clearly, this code can fail to produce its intended result when it is executed concurrently by more than one thread. A piece of code that can fail to produce its intended result when executed concurrently is called a *critical section*. However, a critical section does behave correctly when it is executed by only one thread at a time. The strategy of single-threaded execution is to allow only one thread to execute a critical section of code at a time. If a thread wants to execute a critical section that another thread is already executing, the thread has to wait until the first thread is done and no other thread is executing that code before it can proceed.

Java provides the `synchronized` statement and the `synchronized` method modifier for implementing single-threaded execution. Before executing the block in a `synchronized` statement, the current thread must obtain a lock for the object referenced by the expression. If a method is declared with the `synchronized` modifer, the current thread must obtain a lock before it can invoke the method. If the method is not declared `static`, the thread must obtain a lock associated with the object used to access the method. If the method is declared `static`, the thread must obtain a lock associated with the class in which the method is declared. Because a thread must obtain a lock before executing a `synchronized` method, Java guarantees that `synchronized` methods are executed by only one thread at a time.

Modifying the `count()` method to make it a `synchronized` method ensures that it works as intended.

```
    class CountIt {
        int i = 0;

        synchronized void count() {
            i = i + 1;
        }
    }
```

The strategy of single-threaded execution can also be used when multiple methods update the same data. Consider the following example:

```
class CountIt2 {
    int i = 0;

    void count() {
        i = i + 1;
    }
    void count2() {
        i = i + 2;
    }
}
```

By the same logic used above, if the count() and count2() methods are executed concurrently, the result could be to increment i by 1, 2, or 3. Both the count() and count2() methods can be declared as synchronized to ensure that they are not executed concurrently with themselves or each other:

```
class CountIt2 {
    int i = 0;

    synchronized void count() {
        i = i + 1;
    }
    synchronized void count2() {
        i = i + 2;
    }
}
```

Sometimes it's necessary for a thread to make multiple method calls to manipulate an object without another thread calling that object's methods at the same time. Consider the following example:

```
System.out.print(new Date());
System.out.print(" : ");
System.out.println(foo());
```

If the code in the example is executed concurrently by multiple threads, the output from the two threads will be interleaved. The synchronized keyword provides a way to ensure that only one thread at a time can execute a block of code. Before executing the block in a synchronized statement, the current thread must obtain a lock for the object referenced by the expression. The above code can be modified to give a thread exclusive access to the OutputStream object referenced by System.out:

```
synchronized (System.out) {
    System.out.print(new Date());
    System.out.print(" : ");
    System.out.println(foo());
}
```

Note that this approach only works if other code that wants to call methods in the same object also uses similar `synchronized` statements, or if the methods in question are all `synchronized` methods. In this case, the `print()` and `println()` methods are `synchronized`, so other pieces of code that need to use these methods do not need to use a `synchronized` statement.

When an inner class is updating fields in its enclosing instance, simply making a method `synchronized` does not provide the needed single-threaded execution. Consider the following code:

```
public class Z extends Frame {
    int pressCount = 0;
    ...
    private class CountButton extends Button
                            implements ActionListener {
        public void actionPerformed(ActionEvent evt) {
            pressCount ++;
        }
    }
    ...
}
```

If a `Z` object instantiates more than one instance of `CountButton`, you need to use single-threaded execution to ensure that updates to `pressCount` are done correctly. Unfortunately, declaring the `actionPerformed()` method of `CountButton` to be `synchronized` does not accomplish that goal because it only forces the method to acquire a lock on the instance of `CountButton` it is associated with before it executes. The object you need to acquire a lock for is the enclosing instance of `Z`.

One way to have a `CountButton` object capture a lock on its enclosing instance of `Z` is to update `pressCount` inside of a `synchronized` statement. For example:

```
synchronized (Z.this) {
    pressCount ++;
}
```

The drawback to this approach is that every piece of code that accesses `pressCount` in any inner class of `Z` must be in a similar `synchronized` statement. Otherwise, it is possible for `pressCount` to be updated incorrectly. The more pieces of code that need to be inside of `synchronized` statements, the more places there are to introduce bugs in your program.

A more robust approach is to have the inner class update a field in its enclosing instance by calling a `synchronized` method in the enclosing instance. For example:

```
public class Z extends Frame {
    int pressCount = 0;
    synchronized incrementPressCount() {
        pressCount++;
    }
    ...
    private class CountButton extends Button
                            implements ActionListener {
        public void actionPerformed(ActionEvent evt) {
            incrementPressCount();
        }
    }
    ...
}
```

References Inner Classes 5.3.7; Method modifiers 5.4.6.1; The synchronized Statement 6.13

8.2.2 *Optimistic Single-Threaded Execution*

When multiple threads are updating a data structure, single-threaded execution is the obvious strategy to use to ensure correctness of the operations on the data structure. However, single-threaded execution can cause some problems of its own. Consider the following example:

```
public class Queue extends java.util.Vector {
    synchronized public void put(Object obj) {
        addElement(obj);
    }

    synchronized public Object get() throws EmptyQueueException {
        if (size() == 0)
            throw new EmptyQueueException();
        Object obj = elementAt(0);
        removeElementAt(0);
        return obj;
    }
}
```

This example implements a first-in, first-out (FIFO) queue. If the get() method of a Queue object is called when the queue is empty, the method throws an exception. Now suppose that you want to write the get() method so that when the queue is empty, the method waits for an item to be put in the queue, rather than throwing an exception. In order for an item to be put in the queue, the put() method of the queue must be invoked. But using the single-threaded execution strategy, the put() method will never be able to run while the get() method is waiting for the queue to receive an item. A good way to solve this dilemma is to use a strategy called *optimistic single-threaded execution*.

The optimistic single-threaded execution strategy is similar to the single-threaded execution strategy. They both begin by getting a lock on an object to ensure that the currently executing thread is the only thread that can execute a piece of code, and they both end by releasing that lock. The difference is what happens in between. Using the optimistic single-threaded execution strategy, if a piece of code discovers that conditions are not right to proceed, the code releases the lock it has on the object that enforces single-threaded execution and waits. When another piece of code changes things in such a way that might allow the first piece of code to proceed, it notifies the first piece of code that it should try to regain the lock and proceed.

To implement this strategy, the Object class provides methods called wait(), notify(), and notifyAll(). These methods are inherited by every other class in Java. The following example shows how to implement a queue that uses the optimistic single-threaded execution strategy, so that when the queue is empty, its get() method waits for the queue to have an item put in it:

```
public class Queue extends java.util.Vector {
    synchronized public void put(Object obj) {
        addElement(obj);
        notify();
    }

    synchronized public Object get() throws EmptyQueueException {
        while (size() == 0)
            wait();
        Object obj = elementAt(0);
        removeElementAt(0);
        return obj;
    }
}
```

In the above implementation of the Queue class, the get() method calls wait() when the queue is empty. The wait() method releases the lock that excludes other threads from executing methods in the Queue object, and then waits until another thread calls the put() method. When put() is called, it adds an item to the queue and calls notify(). The notify() method tells a thread that is waiting to return from a wait() method that it should attempt to regain its lock and proceed. If there is more than one thread waiting to regain the lock on the object, notify() chooses one of the threads arbitrarily. The notifyAll() method is similar to notify(), but instead of choosing one thread to notify, it notifies all of the threads that are waiting to regain the lock on the object.

Notice that the get() method calls wait() inside a while loop. Between the time that wait() is notified that it should try to regain its lock and the time it actually does regain the lock, another thread may have called the get() method and emptied the queue. The while loop guards against this situation.

References Method modifiers 5.4.6.1; Object 10.14; The synchronized Statement 6.13

8.2.3 Rendezvous

Sometimes it is necessary to have a thread wait to continue until another thread has completed its work and died. This type of synchronization uses the rendezvous strategy. The `Thread` class provides the `join()` method for implementing this strategy. When the `join()` method is called on a `Thread` object, the method returns immediately if the thread is dead. Otherwise, the method waits until the thread dies and then returns.

References Thread 10.23

8.2.4 Balking

Some methods should not be executed concurrently, and have a time-sensitive nature that makes postponing calls to them a bad idea. This is a common situation when software is controlling real-world devices. Suppose you have a Java program that is embedded in an electronic control for a toilet. There is a method called `flush()` that is responsible for flushing a toilet, and `flush()` can be called from more than one thread. If a thread calls `flush()` while another thread is already executing `flush()`, the second call should do nothing. A toilet is capable of only one flush at a time, and having a concurrent call to the `flush()` method result in a second flush would only waste water.

This scenario suggests the use of the balking strategy. The balking strategy allows no more than one thread to execute a method at a time. If another thread attempts to execute the method, the method simply returns without doing anything. Here is an example that shows what such a `flush()` method might look like:

```
boolean busy;
void flush() {
    synchronized (this) {
        if (busy)
            return;
        busy = true;
    }
    // code to make flush happen goes here
    busy = false;
}
```

8.2.5 *Explicit Synchronization*

When the synchronization needs of a thread are not known in advance, you can use a strategy called explicit synchronization. The explicit synchronization strategy allows you to explicitly tell a thread when it can and cannot run. For example, you may want an animation to start and stop in response to external events that happen at unpredictable times, so you need to be able to tell the animation when it can run.

To implement this strategy, the `Thread` class provides methods called `suspend()` and `resume()`. You can suspend the execution of a thread by calling the `suspend()` method of the `Thread` object that controls the thread. You can later resume execution of the thread by calling the `resume()` method on the `Thread` object.

References Thread 10.23

Exception Handling

Exception handling is a mechanism that allows Java programs to handle various exceptional conditions, such as semantic violations of the language and program-defined errors, in a robust way. When an exceptional condition occurs, an *exception* is thrown. If the Java virtual machine or run-time environment detects a semantic violation, the virtual machine or run-time environment implicitly throws an exception. Alternately, a program can throw an exception explicitly using the `throw` statement. After an exception is thrown, control is transferred from the current point of execution to an appropriate `catch` clause of an enclosing `try` statement. The `catch` clause is called an exception handler because it handles the exception by taking whatever actions are necessary to recover from it.

9.1 Handling Exceptions

The `try` statement provides Java's exception-handling mechanism. A `try` statement contains a block of code to be executed. Putting a block in a `try` statement indicates that any exceptions or other abnormal exits in the block are going to be handled appropriately. A `try` statement can have any number of optional `catch` clauses that act as exception handlers for the `try` block. A `try` statement can also have a `finally` clause. The `finally` block is always executed before control leaves the `try` statement; it cleans up after the `try` block. Note that a `try` statement must have either a `catch` clause or a `finally` clause.

Here is an example of a `try` statement that includes a `catch` clause and a `finally` clause:

```
try {
    out.write(b);
} catch (IOException e) {
    System.out.println("Output Error");
```

```
    } finally {
        out.close();
    }
```

If out.write() throws an IOException, the exception is caught by the catch clause. Regardless of whether out.write() returns normally or throws an exception, the finally block is executed, which ensures that out.close() is always called.

A try statement executes the block that follows the keyword try. If an exception is thrown from within the try block and the try statement has any catch clauses, those clauses are searched, in order, for one that can handle the exception. If a catch clause handles an exception, that catch block is executed.

However, if the try statement does not have any catch clauses that can handle the exception (or does not have any catch clauses at all), the exception propagates up through enclosing statements in the current method. If the current method does not contain a try statement that can handle the exception, the exception propagates up to the invoking method. If this method does not contain an appropriate try statement, the exception propagates up again, and so on. Finally, if no try statement is found to handle the exception, the currently running thread terminates.

A catch clause is declared with a parameter that specifies the type of exception it can handle. The parameter in a catch clause must be of type Throwable or one of its subclasses. When an exception occurs, the catch clauses are searched for the first one with a parameter that matches the type of the exception thrown or is a superclass of the thrown exception. When the appropriate catch block is executed, the actual exception object is passed as an argument to the catch block. The code within a catch block should do whatever is necessary to handle the exceptional condition.

The finally clause of a try statement is always executed, no matter how control leaves the try statement. Thus it is a good place to handle clean-up operations, such as closing files, freeing resources, and closing network connections.

References The throw Statement 6.11; The try Statement 6.12; Throwable 10.25

9.2 Declaring Exceptions

If a method is expected to throw any exceptions, the method declaration must declare that fact in a throws clause. If a method implementation contains a throw statement, it is possible that an exception will be thrown from within the method. In addition, if a method calls another method declared with a throws clause, there is the possibility that an exception will be thrown from within the method. If the exception is not caught inside the method with a `try` statement, it will be thrown out of the method to its caller. Any exception that can be thrown out of a method in this way must be listed in a `throws` clause in the method declaration. The classes listed in a `throws` clause must be `Throwable` or any of its subclasses; the `Throwable` class is the superclass of all objects that can be thrown in Java.

However, there are certain types of exceptions that do not have to be listed in a `throws` clause. Specifically, if the exception is an instance of `Error`, `RuntimeException`, or a subclass of one of those classes, it does not have to be listed in a `throws` clause. Subclasses of the `Error` class correspond to situations that are not easily predicted, such as the system running out of memory. Subclasses of `RuntimeException` correspond to many common run-time problems, such as illegal casts and array index problems. The reason that these types of exceptions are treated specially is that they can be thrown from such a large number of places that essentially every method would have to declare them.

Consider the following example:

```
import java.io.IOException;

class throwsExample {
    char[] a;
    int position;
    ...
    // Method explicitly throws an exception
    int read() throws IOException {
        if (position >= a.length)
            throw new IOException();
        return a[position++];
    }

    // Method implicitly throws an exception
    String readUpTo(char terminator) throws IOException {
        StringBuffer s = new StringBuffer();
        while (true) {
            int c = read(); // Can throw IOException
            if (c == -1 || c == terminator) {
                return s.toString();
            }
            s.append((char)c);
        }
        return s.toString();
    }

    // Method catches an exception internally
    int getLength() {
        String s;
        try {
```

```
            s = readUpTo(':');
        } catch (IOException e) {
            return 0;
        }
        return s.length();
    }

    // Method can throw a RuntimeException
    int getAvgLength() {
        int count = 0;
        int total = 0;
        int len;
        while (true){
            len = getLength();
            if (len == 0)
                break;
            count++;
            total += len;
        }
        return total/count; // Can throw ArithmeticException
    }
}
```

The method read() can throw an IOException, so it declares that fact in its throws clause. Without that throws clause, the compiler would complain that the method must either declare IOException in its throws clause or catch it. Although the readUpTo() method does not explicitly throw any exceptions, it calls the read() method that does throw an IOException, so it declares that fact in its throws clause. Whether explicitly or implicitly thrown, the requirement to catch or declare an exception is the same. The getLength() method catches the IOException thrown by readUpTo(), so it does not have to declare the exception. The final method, getAvgLength(), can throw an ArithmeticException if count is zero. Because ArithmeticException is a subclass of Runtime-Exception, the fact that it can be thrown out of getAvgLength() does not need to be declared in a throws clause.

References Constructors 5.4.7; Errors 9.4.2; Methods 5.4.6; Runtime exceptions 9.4.1.1; The throw Statement 6.11; The try Statement 6.12; Throwable 10.25

9.3 Generating Exceptions

A Java program can use the exception-handling mechanism to deal with program-specific errors in a clean manner. A program simply uses the throw statement to signal an exception. The throw statement must be followed by an object that is of type Throwable or one of its subclasses. For program-defined exceptions, you typically want an exception object to be an instance of a subclass of the Exception class. In most cases, it makes sense to define a new subclass of Exception that is specific to your program.

Consider the following example:

```
class WrongDayException extends Exception {
    public WrongDayException () {}
    public WrongDayException(String msg) {
        super(msg);
    }
}

public class ThrowExample {
    void doIt() throws WrongDayException{
        int dayOfWeek =(new java.util.Date()).getDay();
        if (dayOfWeek != 2  && dayOfWeek != 4)
            throw new WrongDayException("Tue. or Thur.");
        // The rest of doIt's logic goes here
        System.out.println("Did it");
    }
    public static void main (String [] argv) {
        try {
            (new ThrowExample()).doIt();
        } catch (WrongDayException e) {
            System.out.println("Sorry, can do it only on "
                            + e.getMessage());
        }
    }
}
```

The code in this example defines a class called WrongDayException to represent
the specific type of exception thrown by the example. The Throwable class, and
most subclasses of Throwable, have at least two constructors. One constructor
takes a string argument that is used as a textual message that explains the exception, while the other constructor takes no arguments. Thus, the WrongDayException class defines two constructors.

In the class ThrowExample, if the current day of the week is neither Tuesday nor
Thursday, the doIt() method throws a WrongDayException. Note that the
WrongDayException object is created at the same time it is thrown. It is common
practice to provide some information about an exception when it is thrown, so a
string argument is used in the allocation statement for the WrongDayException.
The method declaration for the doIt() method contains a throws clause, to
indicate the fact that it can throw a WrongDayException.

The main() method in ThrowExample encloses its call to the doIt() method in
a try statement, so that it can catch any WrongDayException thrown by doIt().
The catch block prints an error message, using the getMessage() method of
the exception object. This method retrieves the string that was passed to the constructor when the exception object was created.

References Constructors 5.4.7; Exceptions 9.4.1; Methods 5.4.6; The throw Statement 6.11; The try Statement 6.12; Throwable 10.25

9.3.1 Printing Stack Traces

When an exception is caught, it can be useful to print a stack trace to figure out where the exception came from. A stack trace looks like the following:

```
java.lang.ArithmeticException: / by zero
        at t.cap(t.java:16)
        at t.doit(t.java:8)
        at t.main(t.java:3)
```

You can print a stack trace by calling the `printStackTrace()` method that all `Throwable` objects inherit from the `Throwable` class. For example:

```
int cap (x) {return 100/x}

try {
    cap(0);
} catch(ArithmeticException e) {
    e.printStackTrace();
}
```

You can also print a stack trace anywhere in an application, without actually throwing an exception. For example:

```
new Throwable().printStackTrace();
```

References Throwable 10.25

9.3.2 Rethrowing Exceptions

After an exception is caught, it can be rethrown if is appropriate. The one choice that you have to make when rethrowing an exception concerns the location from where the stack trace says the object was thrown. You can make the rethrown exception appear to have been thrown from the location of the original exception throw, or from the location of the current rethrow.

To rethrow an exception and have the stack trace indicate the original location, all you have to do is rethrow the exception:

```
try {
    cap(0);
} catch(ArithmeticException e) {
    throw e;
}
```

To arrange for the stack trace to show the actual location from which the exception is being rethrown, you have to call the exception's `fillInStackTrace()` method. This method sets the stack trace information in the exception based on the current execution context. Here's an example using the `fillInStackTrace()` method:

```
try {
    cap(0);
} catch(ArithmeticException e) {
    throw (ArithmeticException)e.fillInStackTrace();
}
```

It is important to call `fillInStackTrace()` on the same line as the `throw` statement, so that the line number specified in the stack trace matches the line on which the `throw` statement appears. The `fillInStackTrace()` method returns a reference to the `Throwable` class, so you need to cast the reference to the actual type of the exception.

References Throwable 10.25

9.4 The Exception Hierarchy

The possible exceptions in a Java program are organized in a hierarchy of exception classes. The `Throwable` class, which is an immediate subclass of `Object`, is at the root of the exception hierarchy. `Throwable` has two immediate subclasses: `Exception` and `Error`. Figure 9-1 shows the standard exception classes defined in the `java.lang` package, while Figure 9-2 shows the standard error classes defined in `java.lang`.

9.4.1 Exceptions

All of the subclasses of `Exception` represent exceptional conditions that a normal Java program may want to handle. Many of the standard exceptions are also subclasses of `RuntimeException`. Runtime exceptions represent runtime conditions that can generally occur in any Java method, so a method is not required to declare that it throws any of the runtime exceptions. However, if a method can throw any of the other standard exceptions, it must declare them in its `throws` clause.

A Java program should try to handle all of the standard exception classes, since they represent routine abnormal conditions that should be anticipated and caught to prevent program termination.

9.4.1.1 Runtime exceptions

The `java.lang` package defines the following standard runtime exception classes:

`ArithmeticException`
> This exception is thrown to indicate an exceptional arithmetic condition, such as integer division by zero.

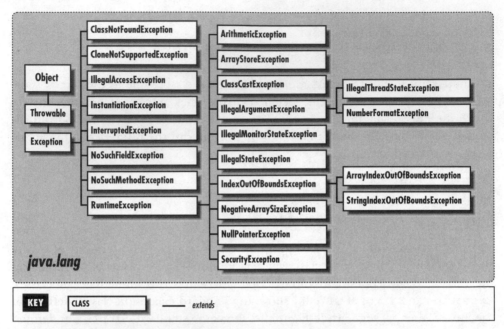

Figure 9–1: Standard Java exception classes

ArrayIndexOutOfBoundsException

This exception is thrown when an out-of-range index is detected by an array object. An out-of-range index occurs when the index is less than zero or greater than or equal to the size of the array.

ArrayStoreException

This exception is thrown when there is an attempt to store a value in an array element that is incompatible with the type of the array.

ClassCastException

This exception is thrown when there is an attempt to cast a reference to an object to an inappropriate type.

IllegalArgumentException

This exception is thrown to indicate that an illegal argument has been passed to a method.

IllegalMonitorStateException

This exception is thrown when an object's `wait()`, `notify()`, or `notify-All()` method is called from a thread that does not own the object's monitor.

IllegalStateException

This exception is thrown to indicate that a method has been invoked when the run-time environment is in an inappropriate state for the requested operation. This exception is new in Java 1.1.

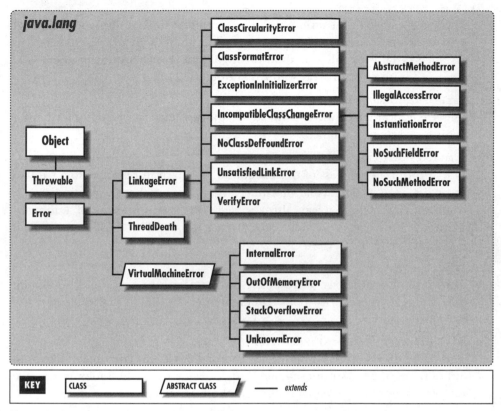

Figure 9–2: Standard Java error classes

`IllegalThreadStateException`
> This exception is thrown to indicate an attempt to perform an operation on a thread that is not legal for the thread's current state, such as attempting to resume a dead thread.

`IndexOutOfBoundsException`
> The appropriate subclass of this exception (i.e., `ArrayIndexOutOf-BoundsException` or `StringIndexOutOfBoundsException`) is thrown when an array or string index is out of bounds.

`NegativeArraySizeException`
> This exception is thrown in response to an attempt to create an array with a negative size.

NullPointerException

This exception is thrown when there is an attempt to access an object through a null object reference. This can occur when there is an attempt to access an instance variable or call a method through a null object or when there is an attempt to subscript an array with a null object.

NumberFormatException

This exception is thrown to indicate that an attempt to parse numeric information in a string has failed.

RuntimeException

The appropriate subclass of this exception is thrown in response to a runtime error detected at the virtual machine level. Because these exceptions are so common, methods that can throw objects that are instances of Runtime-Exception or one of its subclasses are not required to declare that fact in their throws clauses.

SecurityException

This exception is thrown in response to an attempt to perform an operation that violates the security policy implemented by the installed Security-Manager object.

StringIndexOutOfBoundsException

This exception is thrown when a String or StringBuffer object detects an out-of-range index. An out-of-range index occurs when the index is less than zero or greater than or equal to the length of the string.

9.4.1.2 Other exceptions

The java.lang package defines the following standard exception classes that are not runtime exceptions:

ClassNotFoundException

This exception is thrown to indicate that a class that is to be loaded cannot be found.

CloneNotSupportedException

This exception is thrown when the clone() method has been called for an object that does not implement the Cloneable interface and thus cannot be cloned.

Exception

The appropriate subclass of this exception is thrown in response to an error detected at the virtual machine level. If a program defines its own exception classes, they should be subclasses of the Exception class.

`IllegalAccessException`

> This exception is thrown when a program tries to dynamically load a class (i.e., uses the `forName()` method of the `Class` class, or the `findSystemClass()` or the `loadClass()` method of the `ClassLoader` class) and the currently executing method does not have access to the specified class because it is in another package and not `public`. This exception is also thrown when a program tries to create an instance of a class (i.e., uses the `newInstance()` method of the `Class` class) that does not have a zero-argument constructor accessible to the caller.

`InstantiationException`

> This exception is thrown in response to an attempt to instantiate an `abstract` class or an interface using the `newInstance()` method of the `Class` class.

`InterruptedException`

> This exception is thrown to signal that a thread that is sleeping, waiting, or otherwise paused has been interrupted by another thread.

`NoSuchFieldException`

> This exception is thrown when a specified variable cannot be found. This exception is new in Java 1.1.

`NoSuchMethodException`

> This exception is thrown when a specified method cannot be found.

9.4.2 Errors

The subclasses of `Error` represent errors that are normally thrown by the class loader, the virtual machine, or other support code. Application-specific code should not normally throw any of these standard error classes. If a method does throw an `Error` class or any of its subclasses, the method is not required to declare that fact in its `throws` clause.

A Java program should not try to handle the standard error classes. Most of these error classes represent non-recoverable errors and as such, they cause the Java run-time system to print an error message and terminate program execution.

The `java.lang` package defines the following standard error classes:

`AbstractMethodError`

> This error is thrown in response to an attempt to invoke an `abstract` method.

`ClassCircularityError`

> This error is thrown when a circular reference among classes is detected during class initialization.

ClassFormatError

> This error is thrown when an error is detected in the format of a file that contains a class definition.

Error

> The appropriate subclass of this error is thrown when an unpredictable error, such as running out of memory, occurs. Because of the unpredictable nature of these errors, methods that can throw objects that are instances of Error or one of its subclasses are not required to declare that fact in their throws clauses.

ExceptionInInitializerError

> This error is thrown when an unexpected exception is thrown in a static initializer. This error is new in Java 1.1.

IllegalAccessError

> This error is thrown when a class attempts to access a field or call a method it does not have access to. Usually this error is caught by the compiler; this error can occur at run-time if the definition of a class changes after the class that references it was last compiled.

IncompatibleClassChangeError

> This error or one of its subclasses is thrown when a class refers to another class in an incompatible way. This situation occurs when the current definition of the referenced class is incompatible with the definition of the class that was found when the referring class was compiled. For example, say class A refers to a method in class B. Then, after class A is compiled, the method is removed from class B. When class A is loaded, the run-time system discovers that the method in class B no longer exists and throws an error.

InstantiationError

> This error is thrown in response to an attempt to instantiate an abstract class or an interface. Usually this error is caught by the compiler; this error can occur at run-time if the definition of a class is changed after the class that references it was last compiled.

InternalError

> This error is thrown to signal an internal error within the virtual machine.

LinkageError

> The appropriate subclass of this error is thrown when there is a problem resolving a reference to a class. Reasons for this may include a difficulty in finding the definition of the class or an incompatibility between the current definition and the expected definition of the class.

NoClassDefFoundError

This error is thrown when the definition of a class cannot be found.

NoSuchFieldError

This error is thrown in response to an attempt to reference an instance or class variable that is not defined in the current definition of a class. Usually this error is caught by the compiler; this error can occur at run-time if the definition of a class is changed after the class that references it was last compiled.

NoSuchMethodError

This error is thrown in response to an attempt to reference a method that is not defined in the current definition of a class. Usually this error is caught by the compiler; this error can occur at run-time if the definition of a class is changed after the class that references it was last compiled.

OutOfMemoryError

This error is thrown when an attempt to allocate memory fails.

StackOverflowError

This error is thrown when a stack overflow error occurs within the virtual machine.

ThreadDeath

This error is thrown by the stop() method of a Thread object to kill the thread. Catching ThreadDeath objects is not recommended. If it is necessary to catch a ThreadDeath object, it is important to re-throw the object so that it is possible to cleanly stop the catching thread.

UnknownError

This error is thrown when an error of unknown origins is detected in the run-time system.

UnsatisfiedLinkError

This error is thrown when the implementation of a native method cannot be found.

VerifyError

This error is thrown when the byte-code verifier detects that a class file, though well-formed, contains some sort of internal inconsistency or security problem.

VirtualMachineError

The appropriate subclass of this error is thrown to indicate that the Java virtual machine has encountered an error.

10

The java.lang Package

The package `java.lang` contains classes and interfaces that are essential to the Java language. These include:

- `Object`, the ultimate superclass of all classes in Java
- `Thread`, the class that controls each thread in a multithreaded program
- `Throwable`, the superclass of all error and exception classes in Java
- Classes that encapsulate the primitive data types in Java
- Classes for accessing system resources and other low-level entities
- `Math`, a class that provides standard mathematical methods
- `String`, the class that is used to represent strings

Because the classes in the `java.lang` package are so essential, the `java.lang` package is implicitly imported by every Java source file. In other words, you can refer to all of the classes and interfaces in `java.lang` using their simple names.

Figure 10-1 shows the class hierarchy for the `java.lang` package.

10.1   Boolean

Synopsis

Class Name:	`java.lang.Boolean`
Superclass:	`java.lang.Object`
Immediate Subclasses:	None
Interfaces Implemented:	`java.io.Serializable`
Availability:	JDK 1.0 or later

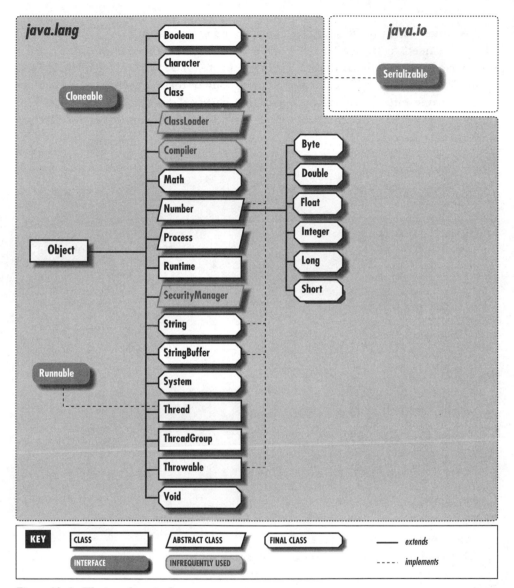

Figure 10–1: The java.lang package

Description

The Boolean class provides an object wrapper for a boolean value. This is useful when you need to treat a boolean value as an object. For example, there are a number of utility methods that take a reference to an Object as one of their arguments. You cannot specify a boolean value for one of these arguments, but you can provide a reference to a Boolean object that encapsulates the boolean value. Furthermore, as of JDK 1.1, the Boolean class is necessary to support the Reflection API and class literals.

Class Summary

```
public final class java.lang.Boolean {
    // Constants
    public final static Boolean FALSE;
    public final static Boolean TRUE;
    public final static Class TYPE;                    // New in 1.1

    // Constructors
    public Boolean(boolean value);
    public Boolean(String s);

    // Class Methods
    public static boolean getBoolean(String name);
    public static Boolean valueOf(String s);

    // Instance Methods
    public boolean booleanValue();
    public boolean equals(Object obj);
    public int hashCode();
    public String toString();
}
```

Constants

TRUE

```
public static final Boolean TRUE
```
    Description   A constant Boolean object that has the value true.

FALSE

```
public static final Boolean FALSE
```
    Description   A constant Boolean object that has the value false.

TYPE

public static final Class TYPE

    Availability   New as of JDK 1.1

    Description   The Class object that represents the type boolean. It is always true that Boolean.TYPE == boolean.class.

Constructors

Boolean

public Boolean(boolean value)

    Parameters   value   The boolean value to be made into a Boolean object.

    Description   Constructs a Boolean object with the given value.

public Boolean(String s)

    Parameters   s   The string to be made into a Boolean object.

    Description   Constructs a Boolean object with the value specified by the given string. If the string equals "true" (ignoring case), the value of the object is true; otherwise it is false.

Class Methods

getBoolean

public static boolean getBoolean(String name)

    Parameters   name   The name of a system property.

    Returns   The boolean value of the system property.

    Description   This methods retrieves the boolean value of a named system property.

valueOf

public static Boolean valueOf(String s)

    Parameters   s   The string to be made into a Boolean object.

    Returns   A Boolean object with the value specified by the given string.

    Description   This method returns a Boolean object with the value true if the string equals "true" (ignoring case); otherwise the value of the object is false.

Instance Methods

booleanValue

public boolean booleanValue()

    Returns   The boolean value contained by the object.

equals

public boolean equals(Object obj)

Parameters	obj	The object to be compared with this object.
Returns		true if the objects are equal; false if they are not.
Overrides		Object.equals()
Description		This method returns true if obj is an instance of Boolean, and it contains the same value as the object this method is associated with.

hashCode

public int hashCode()

Returns	A hashcode based on the boolean value of the object.
Overrides	Object.hashCode()

toString

public String toString()

Returns	"true" if the value of the object is true; "false" otherwise.
Overrides	Object.toString()
Description	This returns a string representation of the Boolean object.

Inherited Methods

Method	Inherited From	Method	Inherited From
clone()	Object	finalize()	Object
getClass()	Object	notify()	Object
notifyAll()	Object	wait()	Object
wait(long)	Object	wait(long, int)	Object

See Also

Boolean Type 3.1.2; Boolean literals 2.2.3.3; Class 10.4; Object 10.14; System 10.22

10.2 Byte

Synopsis

Class Name:	java.lang.Byte
Superclass:	java.lang.Number

Immediate Subclasses: None
Interfaces Implemented: None
Availability: New as of JDK 1.1

Description

The Byte class provides an object wrapper for a byte value. This is useful when you need to treat a byte value as an object. For example, there are a number of utility methods that take a reference to an Object as one of their arguments. You cannot specify a byte value for one of these arguments, but you can provide a reference to a Byte object that encapsulates the byte value. Furthermore, the Byte class is necessary as of JDK 1.1 to support the Reflection API and class literals.

The Byte class also provides a number of utility methods for converting byte values to other primitive types and for converting byte values to strings and vice versa.

Class Summary

```
public final class java.lang.Byte extends java.lang.Number {
  // Constants
  public static final byte MAX_VALUE;
  public static final byte MIN_VALUE;
  public static final Class TYPE;

  // Constructors
  public Byte(byte value);
  public Byte(String s);

  // Class Methods
  public static Byte decode(String nm);
  public static byte parseByte(String s);
  public static byte parseByte(String s, int radix);
  public static String toString(byte b);
  public static Byte valueOf(String s, int radix);
  public static Byte valueOf(String s);

  // Instance Methods
  public byte byteValue();
  public double doubleValue;
  public boolean equals(Object obj);
  public float floatValue
  public int hashCode();
  public int intValue();
  public long longValue();
  public short shortValue();
  public String toString();
}
```

Constants

MAX_VALUE

`public static final byte MAX_VALUE = 127`

The largest value that can be represented by a byte.

MIN_VALUE

`public static final byte MIN_VALUE = -128`

The smallest value that can be represented by a byte.

TYPE

`public static final Class TYPE`

The Class object that represents the primitive type byte. It is always true that Byte.TYPE == byte.class.

Constructors

Byte

`public Byte(byte value)`

Parameters	value	The byte value to be encapsulated by this object.
Description		Creates a Byte object with the specified byte value.

`public Byte(String s) throws NumberFormatException`

Parameters	s	The string to be made into a Byte object.
Throws	NumberFormatException	
		If the sequence of characters in the given String does not form a valid byte literal.
Description		Constructs a Byte object with the value specified by the given string. The string should consist of one or more digit characters. The digit characters can be preceded by a single '-' character. If the string contains any other characters, the constructor throws a NumberFormatException.

Class Methods

decode

`public static Byte decode(String nm) throws NumberFormatException`

Parameters	nm	A String representation of the value to be encapsulated by a Byte object. If the string begins with # or 0x, it is a radix 16 representation of the value. If the string begins with 0, it is a radix 8 representation of the value. Otherwise, it is assumed to be a radix 10 representation of the value.

Returns   A Byte object that encapsulates the given value.

Throws   NumberFormatException

                   If the String contains any non-digit characters other than a leading minus sign, or if the value represented by the String is less than Byte.MIN_VALUE or if it is greater than Byte.MAX_VALUE.

Description   This method returns a Byte object that encapsulates the given value.

parseByte

public static byte parseByte(String s) throws NumberFormatException

Parameters   s   The String to be converted to a byte value.

Returns   The numeric value of the byte represented by the String object.

Throws   NumberFormatException

                   If the String does not contain a valid representation of a byte or the value represented by the String is less than Byte.MIN_VALUE or greater than Byte.MAX_VALUE.

Description   This method returns the numeric value of the byte represented by the contents of the given String object. The String must contain only decimal digits, except that the first character may be a minus sign.

public static byte parseByte(String s, int radix)
              throws NumberFormatException

Parameters   s   The String to be converted to a byte value.

              radix   The radix that is used in interpreting the characters in the String as digits. This value must be in the range Character.MIN_RADIX through Character.MAX_RADIX. If radix is in the range 2 through 10, only characters for which the Character.isDigit() method returns true are considered to be valid digits. If radix is in the range 11 through 36, characters in the ranges 'A' through 'Z' and 'a' through 'z' may be considered valid digits.

Returns   The numeric value of the byte represented by the String object in the specified radix.

Throws   NumberFormatException

If the String does not contain a valid representation of a byte, radix is not in the appropriate
range, or the value represented by the String is
less than Byte.MIN_VALUE or greater than
Byte.MAX_VALUE.

Description   This method returns the numeric value of the byte represented
by the contents of the given String object in the specified
radix. The String must contain only valid digits of the specified
radix, except that the first character may be a minus sign. The
digits are parsed in the specified radix to produce the numeric
value.

toString

```
public String toString(byte b)
```

Parameters   b   The byte value to be converted to a string.

Returns   The string representation of the given value.

Description   This method returns a String object that contains the decimal
representation of the given value.

This method returns a string that begins with '-' if the given
value is negative. The rest of the string is a sequence of one or
more of the characters '0', '1', '2', '3', '4', '5', '6', '7', '8', and
'9'. This method returns "0" if its argument is 0. Otherwise, the
string returned by this method does not begin with "0" or "-0".

valueOf

```
public static Byte valueOf(String s) throws NumberFormatException
```

Parameters   s   The string to be made into a Byte object.

Returns   The Byte object constructed from the string.

Throws   NumberFormatException

If the String does not contain a valid representation of a byte or the value represented by the
String is less than Byte.MIN_VALUE or greater
than Byte.MAX_VALUE.

Description   Constructs a Byte object with the value specified by the given
string. The string should consist of one or more digit characters. The digit characters can be preceded by a single '-' character. If the string contains any other characters, the method
throws a NumberFormatException.

```
public static Byte valueOf(String s, int radix)
            throws NumberFormatException
```

| Parameters | s | The string to be made into a Byte object. |
| | radix | The radix used in converting the string to a value. This value must be in the range Character.MIN_RADIX through Character.MAX_RADIX. |

Returns The Byte object constructed from the string.

Throws NumberFormatException

If the String does not contain a valid representation of a byte, radix is not in the appropriate range, or the value represented by the String is less than Byte.MIN_VALUE or greater than Byte.MAX_VALUE.

Description Constructs a Byte object with the value specified by the given string in the specified radix. The string should consist of one or more digit characters or characters in the range 'A' to 'Z' or 'a' to 'z' that are considered digits in the given radix. The digit characters can be preceded by a single '-' character. If the string contains any other characters, the method throws a NumberFormatException.

Instance Methods

byteValue

```
public byte byteValue()
```

Returns The value of this object as a byte.

Overrides Number.byteValue()

Description This method returns the value of this object as a byte.

doubleValue

```
public double doubleValue()
```

Returns The value of this object as a double.

Overrides Number.doubleValue()

Description This method returns the value of this object as a double.

equals

```
public boolean equals(Object obj)
```

Parameters obj The object to be compared with this object.

Returns true if the objects are equal; false if they are not.

Overrides Object.equals()

Description   This method returns true if obj is an instance of Byte and it contains the same value as the object this method is associated with.

floatValue

public float floatValue()

Returns   The value of this object as a float.

Overrides   Number.floatValue()

Description   This method returns the value of this object as a float.

hashCode

public int hashCode()

Returns   A hashcode based on the byte value of the object.

Overrides   Object.hashCode()

Description   This method returns a hashcode computed from the value of this object.

intValue

public int intValue()

Returns   The value of this object as an int.

Overrides   Number.intValue()

Description   This method returns the value of this object as an int.

longValue

public long longValue()

Returns   The value of this object as a long.

Overrides   Number.longValue()

Description   This method returns the value of this object as a long.

shortValue

public short shortValue()

Returns   The value of this object as a short.

Overrides   Number.shortValue()

Description   This method returns the value of this object as a short.

toString

public String toString()

Returns   The string representation of the value of this object.

Overrides   Object.toString()

Description   This method returns a String object that contains the decimal
                  representation of the value of this object.

                  This method returns a string that begins with '-' if the given
                  value is negative. The rest of the string is a sequence of one or
                  more of the characters '0', '1', '2', '3', '4', '5', '6', '7', '8', and
                  '9'. This method returns "0" if its argument is 0. Otherwise, the
                  string returned by this method does not begin with "0" or "-0".

Inherited Methods

Method	Inherited From	Method	Inherited From
clone()	Object	finalize()	Object
getClass()	Object	notify()	Object
notifyAll()	Object	wait()	Object
wait(long)	Object	wait(long, int)	Object

See Also

Character 10.3; Class 10.4; Double 10.8; Exceptions 9.4.1; Float 10.9; Integer literals 2.2.3.1; Integer types 3.1.1.1; Integer 10.10; Long 10.11; Number 10.13; Short 10.19; String 10.20

10.3   Character

Synopsis

Class Name:	java.lang.Character
Superclass:	java.lang.Object
Immediate Subclasses:	None
Interfaces Implemented:	java.io.Serializable
Availability:	JDK 1.0 or later

Description

The Character class provides an object wrapper for a char value. This is useful when you need to treat a char value as an object. For example, there are a number of utility methods that take a reference to an Object as one of their arguments. You cannot specify a char value for one of these arguments, but you can provide a reference to a Character object that encapsulates the char value. Furthermore, as of JDK 1.1, the Character class is necessary to support the Reflection API and class literals.

In Java, Character objects represent values defined by the Unicode standard. Unicode is defined by an organization called the Unicode Consortium. The defining document for Unicode is *The Unicode Standard, Version 2.0* (ISBN 0-201-48345-9). More recent information about Unicode is available at *http://unicode.org*. Appendix A, *The Unicode 2.0 Character Set*, contains a table that lists the characters defined by the Unicode 2.0 standard.

The Character class provides some utility methods, such as methods for determining the type (e.g., uppercase or lowercase, digit or letter) of a character and for converting from uppercase to lowercase. The logic for these utility methods is based on a Unicode attribute table that is part of the Unicode standard. That table is available at *ftp://unicode.org/pub/2.0-Update/UnicodeData-2.0.14.txt*.

Some of the methods in the Character class are concerned with characters that are digits; these characters are used by a number of other classes to convert strings that contain numbers into actual numeric values. The digit-related methods all use a radix value to interpret characters. The *radix* is the numeric base used to represent numbers as characters or strings. Octal is a radix 8 representation, while hexadecimal is a radix 16 representation. The methods that require a radix parameter use it to determine which characters should be treated as valid digits. In radix 2, only the characters '0' and '1' are valid digits. In radix 16, the characters '0' through '9', 'a' through 'z', and 'A' through 'Z' are considered valid digits.

Class Summary

```
public final class java.lang.Character extends java.lang.Object
                                implements java.io.Serializable {
    // Constants
    public final static byte COMBINING_SPACING_MARK;      // New in 1.1
    public final static byte CONNECTOR_PUNCTUATION;       // New in 1.1
    public final static byte CONTROL;                     // New in 1.1
    public final static byte CURRENCY_SYMBOL;             // New in 1.1
    public final static byte DASH_PUNCTUATION;            // New in 1.1
    public final static byte DECIMAL_DIGIT_NUMBER;        // New in 1.1
    public final static byte ENCLOSING_MARK;             // New in 1.1
    public final static byte END_PUNCTUATION;             // New in 1.1
    public final static byte FORMAT;                      // New in 1.1
    public final static byte LETTER_NUMBER;               // New in 1.1
    public final static byte LINE_SEPARATOR;              // New in 1.1
    public final static byte LOWERCASE_LETTER;            // New in 1.1
    public final static byte MATH_SYMBOL;                 // New in 1.1
    public final static int MAX_RADIX;
    public final static char MAX_VALUE;
    public final static int MIN_RADIX;
    public final static char MIN_VALUE;
    public final static byte MODIFIER_LETTER;             // New in 1.1
    public final static byte MODIFIER_SYMBOL;             // New in 1.1
    public final static byte NON_SPACING_MARK;            // New in 1.1
```

```
public final static byte OTHER_LETTER;              // New in 1.1
public final static byte OTHER_NUMBER;              // New in 1.1
public final static byte OTHER_PUNCTUATION;         // New in 1.1
public final static byte OTHER_SYMBOL;              // New in 1.1
public final static byte PARAGRAPH_SEPARATOR;       // New in 1.1
public final static byte PRIVATE_USE;               // New in 1.1
public final static byte SPACE_SEPARATOR;           // New in 1.1
public final static byte START_PUNCTUATION;         // New in 1.1
public final static byte SURROGATE;                 // New in 1.1
public final static byte TITLECASE_LETTER;          // New in 1.1
public final static Class TYPE;                     // New in 1.1
public final static byte UNASSIGNED;                // New in 1.1
public final static byte UPPERCASE_LETTER;          // New in 1.1


// Constructors
public Character(char value);

// Class Methods
public static int digit(char ch, int radix);
public static char forDigit(int digit, int radix);
public static int getNumericValue(char ch);         // New in 1.1
public static int getType(char ch);                 // New in 1.1
public static boolean isDefined(char ch);
public static boolean isDigit(char ch);
public static boolean isIdentifierIgnorable(char ch);   // New in 1.1
public static boolean isISOControl(char ch);        // New in 1.1
public static boolean isJavaIdentifierPart(char ch);    // New in 1.1
public static boolean isJavaIdentifierStart(char ch);   // New in 1.1
public static boolean isJavaLetter(char ch);            // Deprecated in 1.1
public static boolean isJavaLetterOrDigit(char ch); // Deprecated in 1.1
public static boolean isLetter(char ch);
public static boolean isLetterOrDigit(char ch);
public static boolean isLowerCase(char ch);
public static boolean isSpace(char ch);             // Deprecated in 1.1
public static boolean isSpaceChar(char ch);         // New in 1.1
public static boolean isTitleCase(char ch);
public static boolean isUnicodeIdentifierPart(char ch); // New in 1.1
public static boolean isUnicodeIdentifierStart(char ch);// New in 1.1
public static boolean isUpperCase(char ch);
public static boolean isWhitespace(char ch);        // New in 1.1
public static char toLowerCase(char ch);
public static char toTitleCase(char ch);
public static char toUpperCase(char ch);

// Instance Methods
public char charValue();
public boolean equals(Object obj);
```

```
    public int hashCode();
    public String toString();
}
```

Constants

COMBINING_SPACING_MARK

public final static byte COMBINING_SPACING_MARK

Availability   New as of JDK 1.1

Description   This constant can be returned by the getType() method as the
general category of a Unicode character.

CONNECTOR_PUNCTUATION

public final static byte CONNECTOR_PUNCTUATION

Availability   New as of JDK 1.1

Description   This constant can be returned by the getType() method as the
general category of a Unicode character.

CONTROL

public final static byte CONTROL

Availability   New as of JDK 1.1

Description   This constant can be returned by the getType() method as the
general category of a Unicode character.

CURRENCY_SYMBOL

public final static byte CURRENCY_SYMBOL

Availability   New as of JDK 1.1

Description   This constant can be returned by the getType() method as the
general category of a Unicode character.

DASH_PUNCTUATION

public final static byte DASH_PUNCTUATION

Availability   New as of JDK 1.1

Description   This constant can be returned by the getType() method as the
general category of a Unicode character.

DECIMAL_DIGIT_NUMBER

public final static byte DECIMAL_DIGIT_NUMBER

Availability   New as of JDK 1.1

Description   This constant can be returned by the getType() method as the
general category of a Unicode character.

ENCLOSING_MARK

```
public final static byte ENCLOSING_MARK
```
Availability   New as of JDK 1.1

Description   This constant can be returned by the getType() method as the
general category of a Unicode character.

END_PUNCTUATION

```
public final static byte END_PUNCTUATION
```
Availability   New as of JDK 1.1

Description   This constant can be returned by the getType() method as the
general category of a Unicode character.

FORMAT

```
public final static byte FORMAT
```
Availability   New as of JDK 1.1

Description   This constant can be returned by the getType() method as the
general category of a Unicode character.

LETTER_NUMBER

```
public final static byte LETTER_NUMBER
```
Availability   New as of JDK 1.1

Description   This constant can be returned by the getType() method as the
general category of a Unicode character.

LINE_SEPARATOR

```
public final static byte LINE_SEPARATOR
```
Availability   New as of JDK 1.1

Description   This constant can be returned by the getType() method as the
general category of a Unicode character.

LOWERCASE_LETTER

```
public final static byte LOWERCASE_LETTER
```
Availability   New as of JDK 1.1

Description   This constant can be returned by the getType() method as the
general category of a Unicode character.

MATH_SYMBOL

```
public final static byte MATH_SYMBOL
```
Availability   New as of JDK 1.1

Description   This constant can be returned by the getType() method as the general category of a Unicode character.

MAX_RADIX

```
public static final int MAX_RADIX = 36
```
Description   The maximum value that can be specified for a radix.

MAX_VALUE

```
public final static char MAX_VALUE = '\ufff'f
```
Description   The largest value that can be represented by a char.

MIN_RADIX

```
public static final int MIN_RADIX = 2
```
Description   The minimum value that can be specified for a radix.

MIN_VALUE

```
public final static char MIN_VALUE = '\u0000'
```
Description   The smallest value that can be represented by a char.

MODIFIER_LETTER

```
public final static byte MODIFIER_LETTER
```
Availability   New as of JDK 1.1
Description   This constant can be returned by the getType() method as the general category of a Unicode character.

MODIFIER_SYMBOL

```
public final static byte MODIFIER_SYMBOL
```
Availability   New as of JDK 1.1
Description   This constant can be returned by the getType() method as the general category of a Unicode character.

NON_SPACING_MARK

```
public final static byte NON_SPACING_MARK
```
Availability   New as of JDK 1.1
Description   This constant can be returned by the getType() method as the general category of a Unicode character.

OTHER_LETTER

public final static byte OTHER_LETTER

Availability   New as of JDK 1.1

Description   This constant can be returned by the getType() method as the general category of a Unicode character.

OTHER_NUMBER

public final static byte OTHER_NUMBER

Availability   New as of JDK 1.1

Description   This constant can be returned by the getType() method as the general category of a Unicode character.

OTHER_PUNCTUATION

public final static byte OTHER_PUNCTUATION

Availability   New as of JDK 1.1

Description   This constant can be returned by the getType() method as the general category of a Unicode character.

OTHER_SYMBOL

public final static byte OTHER_SYMBOL

Availability   New as of JDK 1.1

Description   This constant can be returned by the getType() method as the general category of a Unicode character.

PARAGRAPH_SEPARATOR

public final static byte PARAGRAPH_SEPARATOR

Availability   New as of JDK 1.1

Description   This constant can be returned by the getType() method as the general category of a Unicode character.

PRIVATE_USE

public final static byte PRIVATE_USE

Availability   New as of JDK 1.1

Description   This constant can be returned by the getType() method as the general category of a Unicode character.

SPACE_SEPARATOR

public final static byte SPACE_SEPARATOR

Availability   New as of JDK 1.1

Description   This constant can be returned by the getType() method as the general category of a Unicode character.

START_PUNCTUATION

```
public final static byte START_PUNCTUATION
```
Availability   New as of JDK 1.1

Description   This constant can be returned by the getType() method as the general category of a Unicode character.

SURROGATE

```
public final static byte SURROGATE
```
Availability   New as of JDK 1.1

Description   This constant can be returned by the getType() method as the general category of a Unicode character.

TITLECASE_LETTER

```
public final static byte TITLECASE_LETTER
```
Availability   New as of JDK 1.1

Description   This constant can be returned by the getType() method as the general category of a Unicode character.

TYPE

```
public static final Class TYPE
```
Availability   New as of JDK 1.1

Description   The Class object that represents the type char. It is always true that Character.TYPE == char.class.

UNASSIGNED

```
public final static byte UNASSIGNED
```
Availability   New as of JDK 1.1

Description   This constant can be returned by the getType() method as the general category of a Unicode character.

UPPERCASE_LETTER

```
public final static byte UPPERCASE_LETTER
```
Availability   New as of JDK 1.1

Description   This constant can be returned by the getType() method as the general category of a Unicode character.

Constructors

Character

```
public Character(char value)
```

Parameters	value	The char value to be encapsulated by this object.
Description		Creates a Character object with the given char value.

Class Methods

digit

```
public static int digit(char ch, int radix)
```

Parameters   ch   A char value that is a legal digit in the given radix.

                      radix   The radix used in interpreting the specified character as a digit. If radix is in the range 2 through 10, only characters for which the isDigit() method returns true are considered to be valid digits. If radix is in the range 11 through 36, characters in ranges 'A' through 'Z' and 'a' through 'z' are considered valid digits.

Returns   The numeric value of the digit. This method returns –1 if the value of ch is not considered a valid digit, if radix is less than MIN_RADIX, or if radix is greater than MAX_RADIX.

Description   Returns the numeric value represented by a digit character. For example, digit('7',10) returns 7. If the value of ch is not a valid digit, the method returns –1. So, digit('7',2) returns –1 because '7' is not a valid digit in radix 2. A number of methods in other classes use this method to convert strings that contain numbers to actual numeric values. The forDigit() method is an approximate inverse of this method.

                         If radix is greater than 10, characters in the range 'A' to 'A'+radix-11 are treated as valid digits. Such a character has the numeric value ch-'A'+10. If radix is greater than 10, characters in the range 'a' to 'a'+radix-11 are treated as valid digits. Such a character has the numeric value ch- 'a'+10.

forDigit

```
public static char forDigit(int digit, int radix)
```

Parameters	digit	Numeric value represented as a digit character.
	radix	The radix used to represent the specified value.

Returns   The character that represents the digit corresponding to the specified numeric value. The method returns '\0' if digit is less than 0, if digit is equal to or greater than radix, if radix is less than MIN_RADIX, or if radix is greater than MAX_RADIX.

Description   This method returns the character that represents the digit corresponding to the specified numeric value. If digit is in the range 0 through 9, the method returns '0'+digit. If digit is in the range 10 through MAX_RADIX-1, the method returns 'a'+digit-10. The method returns '\0' if digit is less than 0, if digit is equal to or greater than radix, if radix is less than MIN_RADIX, or if radix is greater than MAX_RADIX.

getNumericValue

```
public static int getNumericValue(char ch)
```

Availability   New as of JDK 1.1

Parameters   ch   A char value.

Returns   The Unicode numeric value of the character as a non-negative integer. This method returns −1 if the character has no numeric value; it returns −2 if the character has a numeric value that is not a non-negative integer, such as $1/2$.

Description   This method returns the Unicode numeric value of the specified character as a non-negative integer.

getType

```
public static int getType(char ch)
```

Availability   New as of JDK 1.1

Parameters   ch   A char value.

Returns   An int value that represents the Unicode general category type of the character.

Description   This method returns the Unicode general category type of the specified character. The value corresponds to one of the general category constants defined by Character.

isDefined

```
public static boolean isDefined(char ch)
```

Parameters   ch   A char value to be tested.

Returns   true if the specified character has an assigned meaning in the Unicode character set; otherwise false.

Description   This method returns true if the specified character value has an assigned meaning in the Unicode character set.

isDigit

```
public static boolean isDigit(char ch)
```

Parameters   ch   A char value to be tested.

Returns   true if the specified character is defined as a digit in the Unicode character set; otherwise false.

Description   This method determines whether or not the specified character is a digit, based on the definition of the character in Unicode.

isIdentifierIgnorable

```
public static boolean isIdentifierIgnorable(char ch)
```

Availability   New as of JDK 1.1

Parameters   ch   A char value to be tested.

Returns   true if the specified character is ignorable in a Java or Unicode identifier; otherwise false.

Description   This method determines whether or not the specified character is ignorable in a Java or Unicode identifier.

The following characters are ignorable in a Java or Unicode identifier:

\u0000 - \u0008 \u000E - \u001B \u007F - \u009F	ISO control characters that aren't whitespace
\u200C - \u200F	Join controls
\u200A - \u200E	Bidirectional controls
\u206A - \u206F	Format controls
\uFEFF	Zero-width no-break space

isISOControl

```
public static boolean isISOControl(char ch)
```

Availability   New as of JDK 1.1

Parameters   ch   A char value to be tested.

Returns   true if the specified character is an ISO control character; otherwise false.

Description   This method determines whether or not the specified character is an ISO control character. A character is an ISO control character if it falls in the range \u0000 through \u001F or \u007F through \u009F.

isJavaIdentifierPart

```
public static boolean isJavaIdentifierPart(char ch)
```

Availability	New as of JDK 1.1
Parameters	ch A char value to be tested.
Returns	true if the specified character can appear after the first character in a Java identifier; otherwise false.
Description	This method returns true if the specified character can appear in a Java identifier after the first character. A character is considered part of a Java identifier if and only if it is a letter, a digit, a currency symbol (e.g., $), a connecting punctuation character (e.g., _), a numeric letter (e.g., a Roman numeral), a combining mark, a nonspacing mark, or an ignorable control character.

isJavaIdentifierStart

```
public static boolean isJavaIdentifierStart(char ch)
```

Availability	New as of JDK 1.1
Parameters	ch A char value to be tested.
Returns	true if the specified character can appear as the first character in a Java identifier; otherwise false.
Description	This method returns true if the specified character can appear in a Java identifier as the first character. A character is considered a start of a Java identifier if and only if it is a letter, a currency symbol (e.g., $), or a connecting punctuation character (e.g., _).

isJavaLetter

```
public static boolean isJavaLetter(char ch)
```

Availability	Deprecated as of JDK 1.1
Parameters	ch A char value to be tested.
Returns	true if the specified character can appear as the first character in a Java identifier; otherwise false.
Description	This method returns true if the specified character can appear as the first character in a Java identifier. A character is considered a Java letter if and only if it is a letter, the character $, or the character _. This method returns false for digits because digits are not allowed as the first character of an identifier.
	This method is deprecated as of JDK 1.1. You should use isJavaIdentifierStart() instead.

isJavaLetterOrDigit

`public static boolean isJavaLetterOrDigit(char ch)`

Availability	Deprecated as of JDK 1.1
Parameters	ch A char value to be tested.
Returns	true if the specified character can appear after the first character in a Java identifier; otherwise false.
Description	This method returns true if the specified character can appear in a Java identifier after the first character. A character is considered a Java letter or digit if and only if it is a letter, a digit, the character $, or the character _.

This method is deprecated as of JDK 1.1. You should use isJavaIdentifierPart() instead.

isLetter

`public static boolean isLetter(char ch)`

Parameters	ch A char value to be tested.
Returns	true if the specified character is defined as a letter in the Unicode character set; otherwise false.
Description	This method determines whether or not the specified character is a letter, based on the definition of the character in Unicode. This method does not consider character values in ranges that have not been assigned meanings by Unicode to be letters.

isLetterOrDigit

`public static boolean isLetterOrDigit(char ch)`

Parameters	ch A char value to be tested.
Returns	true if the specified character is defined as a letter in the Unicode character set; otherwise false.
Description	This method determines whether or not the specified character is a letter or a digit, based on the definition of the character in Unicode. Some ranges have not been assigned meanings by Unicode. If a character value is in one of these ranges, this method does not consider the character to be a letter.

isLowerCase

`public static boolean isLowerCase (char ch)`

Parameters	ch A char value to be tested.
Returns	true if the specified character is defined as lowercase in the Unicode character set; otherwise false.

Description   This method determines whether or not the specified character is lowercase. Unicode defines a number of characters that do not have case mappings; if the specified character is one of these characters, the method returns false.

isSpace

```
public static boolean isSpace(char ch)
```

Availability   Deprecated as of JDK 1.1

Parameters   ch   A char value to be tested.

Returns   true if the specified character is defined as whitespace in the ISO-Latin-1 character set; otherwise false.

Description   This method determines whether or not the specified character is whitespace. This method recognizes the whitespace characters shown in the following table.

\u0009	Horizontal tab
\u000A	Newline
\u000C	Formfeed
\u000D	Carriage return
\u0020 ' '	Space

This method is deprecated as of JDK 1.1. You should use isWhitespace() instead.

isSpaceChar

```
public static boolean isSpaceChar(char ch)
```

Availability   New as of JDK 1.1

Parameters   ch   A char value to be tested.

Returns   true if the specified character is a Unicode 2.0 space characters; otherwise false.

Description   This method determines if the specified character is a space character according to the Unicode 2.0 specification. A character is considered to be a Unicode space character if and only if it has the general category "Zs", "Zl", or "Zp" in the Unicode specification.

isTitleCase

```
public static boolean isTitleCase(char ch)
```

Parameters   ch   A char value to be tested.

Returns   true if the specified character is defined as titlecase in the Unicode character set; otherwise false.

Description   This method determines whether or not the specified character is a titlecase character. Unicode defines a number of characters that do not have case mappings; if the specified character is one of these characters, the method returns false.

Many characters are defined by the Unicode standard as having upper- and lowercase forms. There are some characters defined by the Unicode standard that also have a titlecase form. The glyphs for these characters look like a combination of two Latin letters. The titlecase form of these characters has a glyph that looks like a combination of an uppercase Latin character and a lowercase Latin character; this case should be used when the character appears as the first character of a word in a title. For example, one of the Unicode characters that has a titlecase form looks like the letter 'D' followed by the letter 'Z'. Here is what the three forms of this letter look like:

Uppercase	'DZ'
Titlecase	'Dz'
Lowercase	'dz'

isUnicodeIdentifierPart

`public static boolean isUnicodeIdentifierPart(char ch)`

Availability   New as of JDK 1.1

Parameters   ch   A char value to be tested.

Returns   true if the specified character can appear after the first character in a Unicode identifier; otherwise false.

Description   This method returns true if the specified character can appear in a Unicode identifier after the first character. A character is considered part of a Unicode identifier if and only if it is a letter, a digit, a connecting punctuation character (e.g., _), a numeric letter (e.g., a Roman numeral), a combining mark, a nonspacing mark, or an ignorable control character.

isUnicodeIdentifierStart

`public static boolean isUnicodeIdentifierStart(char ch)`

Availability   New as of JDK 1.1

Parameters   ch   A char value to be tested.

Returns   true if the specified character can appear as the first character in a Unicode identifier; otherwise false.

Description   This method returns true if the specified character can appear in a Unicode identifier as the first character. A character is considered a start of a Unicode identifier if and only if it is a letter.

isUpperCase

```
public static boolean isUpperCase(char ch)
```

Parameters   ch   A char value to be tested.

Returns   true if the specified character is defined as uppercase in the Unicode character set; otherwise false.

Description   This method determines whether or not the specified character is uppercase. Unicode defines a number of characters that do not have case mappings; if the specified character is one of these characters, the method returns false.

isWhitespace

```
public static boolean isWhitespace(char ch)
```

Availability New as of JDK 1.1

Parameters   ch   A char value to be tested.

Returns   true if the specified character is defined as whitespace according to Java; otherwise false.

Description   This method determines whether or not the specified character is whitespace. This method recognizes the following as whitespace:

Unicode category "Zs" except \u00A0 and \uFEFF	Unicode space separators except no-break spaces
Unicode category "Zl"	Unicode line separators
Unicode category "Zp"	Unicode paragraph separators
\u0009	Horizontal tab
\u000A	Linefeed
\u000B	Vertical tab
\u000C	Formfeed
\u000D	Carriage return
\u001C	File separator
\u001D	Group separator
\u001E	Record separator
\u001F	Unit separator

toLowerCase

`public static char toLowerCase(char ch)`

Parameters   ch   A char value to be converted to lowercase.

Returns   The lowercase equivalent of the specified character, or the character itself if it cannot be converted to lowercase.

Description   This method returns the lowercase equivalent of the specified character value. If the specified character is not uppercase or if it has no lowercase equivalent, the character is returned unmodified. The Unicode attribute table determines if a character has a mapping to a lowercase equivalent.

Some Unicode characters in the range \u2000 through \u2FFF have lowercase mappings. For example, \u2160 (Roman numeral one) has a lowercase mapping to \u2170 (small Roman numeral one). The toLowerCase() method maps such characters to their lowercase equivalents even though the method isUpperCase() does not return true for such characters.

toTitleCase

`public static char toTitleCase(char ch)`

Parameters   ch   A char value to be converted to titlecase.

Returns   The titlecase equivalent of the specified character, or the character itself if it cannot be converted to titlecase.

Description   This method returns the titlecase equivalent of the specified character value. If the specified character has no titlecase equivalent, the character is returned unmodified. The Unicode attribute table is used to determine the character's titlecase equivalent.

Many characters are defined by the Unicode standard as having upper- and lowercase forms. There are some characters defined by the Unicode standard that also have a titlecase form. The glyphs for these characters look like a combination of two Latin letters. The titlecase form of these characters has a glyph that looks like a combination of an uppercase Latin character and a lowercase Latin character; this case should be used when the character appears as the first character of a word in a title. For example, one of the Unicode characters that has a titlecase form looks like the letter 'D' followed by the letter 'Z'.

Here is what the three forms of this letter look like:

Uppercase	'DZ'
Titlecase	'Dz'
Lowercase	'dz'

toUpperCase

```
public static char toUpperCase(char ch)
```

Parameters   ch   A char value to be converted to lowercase.

Returns   The uppercase equivalent of the specified character, or the character itself if it cannot be converted to uppercase.

Description   This method returns the uppercase equivalent of the specified character value. If the specified character is not lowercase or if it has no uppercase equivalent, the character is returned unmodified. The Unicode attribute table determines if a character has a mapping to an uppercase equivalent.

Some Unicode characters in the range \u2000 through \u2FFF have uppercase mappings. For example, \u2170 (small Roman numeral one) has a lowercase mapping to \u2160 (Roman numeral one). The toUpperCase() method maps such characters to their uppercase equivalents even though the method isLowerCase() does not return true for such characters.

Instance Methods

charValue

```
public char charValue()
```

Returns   The char value contained by the object.

equals

```
public boolean equals(Object obj)
```

Parameters   The object to be compared with this object.

Returns   true if the objects are equal; false if they are not.

Overrides   Object.equals()

Description   This method returns true if obj is an instance of Character, and it contains the same value as the object this method is associated with.

hashCode

```
public int hashCode()
```
    Returns   A hashcode based on the char value of the object.
    Overrides   Object.hashCode()

toString

```
public String toString()
```
    Returns   A String of length one that contains the character value of the object.
    Overrides   Object.toString()
    Description   This method returns a string representation of the Character object.

Inherited Methods

Method	Inherited From	Method	Inherited From
clone()	Object	finalize()	Object
getClass()	Object	notify()	Object
notifyAll()	Object	wait()	Object
wait(long)	Object	wait(long, int)	Object

See Also

Character literals 2.2.3.4; Class 10.4; Integer types 3.1.1.1; Object 10.14

10.4   Class

Synopsis

Class Name: java.lang.Class
Superclass: java.lang.Object
Immediate Subclasses: None
Interfaces Implemented: java.io.Seriablizable
Availability: JDK 1.0 or later

Description

As of Java 1.1, instances of the Class class are used as run-time descriptions of all Java data types, both reference types and primitive types. The Class class has also been greatly expanded in 1.1 to provide support for the Reflection API. Prior to 1.1, Class just provided run-time descriptions of reference types.

A Class object provides considerable information about the data type. You can use the isPrimitive() method to find out if a Class object describes a primitive type, while isArray() indicates if the object describes an array type. If a Class object describes a class or interface type, there are numerous methods that return information about the fields, methods, and constructors of the type. This information is returned as java.lang.reflect.Field, java.lang.reflect.Method, and java.lang.reflect.Constructor objects.

There are a number of ways that you can get a Class object for a particular data type:

- If you have an object, you can get the Class object that describes the class of that object by calling the object's getClass() method. Every class inherits this method from the Object class.

- As of Java 1.1, you can get the Class object that describes any Java type using the new class literal syntax. A class literal is simply the name of a type (a class name or a primitive type name) followed by a period and the class keyword. For example:

  ```
  Class s = String.class;
  Class i = int.class;
  Class v = java.util.Vector.class;
  ```

- In Java 1.0, you can get the Class object from the name of a data type using the forName() class method of Class. For example:

  ```
  Class v = Class.forName("java.util.Vector");
  ```

  This technique still works in Java 1.1, but it is more cumbersome (and less efficient) than using a class literal.

You can create an instance of a class using the newInstance() method of a Class object, if the class has a constructor that takes no arguments.

The Class class has no public constructors; it cannot be explicitly instantiated. Class objects are normally created by the ClassLoader class or a ClassLoader object.

Class Summary

```
public final class java.lang.Class extends java.lang.Object
                                implements java.io.Serializable {
    // Class Methods
    public static native Class forName(String className);

    // Instance Methods
    public Class[] getClasses();                        // New in 1.1
    public native ClassLoader getClassLoader();
    public native Class getComponentType();             // New in 1.1
```

```
    public Constructor
            getConstructor(Class[] parameterTypes);        // New in 1.1
    public Constructor[] getConstructors();                // New in 1.1
    public Class[] getDeclaredClasses();                   // New in 1.1
    public Constructor
            getDeclaredConstructor(Class[] parameterTypes); // New in 1.1
    public Constructor[] getDeclaredConstructors();        // New in 1.1
    public Field getDeclaredField(String name);            // New in 1.1
    public Field[] getDeclaredFields();                    // New in 1.1
    public Method getDeclaredMethod(String name,
                Class[] parameterTypes)                     // New in 1.1
    public Method[] getDeclaredMethods()                   // New in 1.1
    public Class getDeclaringClass();                      // New in 1.1
    public Field getField(String name);                    // New in 1.1
    public Field[] getFields();                            // New in 1.1
    public native Class[] getInterfaces();
    public Method getMethod(String name,
                Class[] parameterTypes);                    // New in 1.1
    public Method[] getMethods();                          // New in 1.1
    public native int getModifiers();                      // New in 1.1
    public native String getName();
    public URL getResource(String name);                   // New in 1.1
    public InputStream getResourceAsStream(String name);   // New in 1.1
    public native Object[] getSigners();                   // New in 1.1
    public native Class getSuperclass();
    public native boolean isArray();                       // New in 1.1
    public native boolean isAssignableFrom(Class cls);     // New in 1.1
    public native boolean isInstance(Object obj);          // New in 1.1
    public native boolean isInterface();
    public native boolean isPrimitive();                   // New in 1.1
    public native Object newInstance();
    public String toString();
}
```

Class Methods

forName

```
public static Class forName(String className)
                throws ClassNotFoundException
```

Parameters   className   Name of a class qualified by the name of its package. If the class is defined inside of another class, all dots (.) that separate the top-level class name from the class to load must be changed to dollar signs ($) for the name to be recognized.

Returns   A Class object that describes the named class.

Throws   ClassNotFoundException

> If the class cannot be loaded because it cannot be found.

Description   This method dynamically loads a class if it has not already been loaded. The method returns a Class object that describes the named class.

The most common use of forName() is for loading classes on the fly when an application wants to use classes it wasn't built with. For example, a web browser uses this technique. When a browser needs to load an applet, the browser calls Class.forName() for the applet. The method loads the class if it has not already been loaded and returns the Class object that encapsulates the class. The browser then creates an instance of the applet by calling the Class object's newInstance() method.

When a class is loaded using a ClassLoader object, any classes loaded at the instigation of that class are also loaded using the same ClassLoader object. This method implements that security policy by trying to find a ClassLoader object to load the named class. The method searches the stack for the most recently invoked method associated with a class that was loaded using a ClassLoader object. If such a class is found, the ClassLoader object associated with that class is used.

Instance Methods

getClasses

```
public Class[] getClasses()
```

Availability   New as of JDK 1.1

Returns   An array of Class objects that contains the public classes and interfaces that are members of this class.

Description   If this Class object represents a reference type, this method returns an array of Class objects that lists all of the public classes and interfaces that are members of this class or interface. The list includes public classes and interfaces that are inherited from superclasses and that are defined by this class or interface. If there are no public member classes or interfaces, or if this Class represents a primitive type, the method returns an array of length 0.

As of Java 1.1.3, this method always returns an array of length 0, no matter how many public member classes this class or interface actually declares.

getClassLoader

    public native ClassLoader getClassLoader()

Returns   The ClassLoader object used to load this class, or null if this
               class was not loaded with a ClassLoader.

Description   This method returns the ClassLoader object that was used to
               load this class. If this class was not loaded with a ClassLoader,
               null is returned.

               This method is useful for making sure that a class gets loaded
               with the same class loader as was used for loading this Class
               object.

getComponentType

    public native Class getComponentType()

Availability   New as of JDK 1.1

Returns   A Class object that describes the component type of this class if
               it is an array type.

Description   If this Class object represents an array type, this method
               returns a Class object that describes the component type of the
               array. If this Class does not represent an array type, the
               method returns null.

getConstructor

    public Constructor getConstructor(Class[] parameterTypes)
                throws NoSuchMethodException, SecurityException

Availability   New as of JDK 1.1

Parameters   parameterTypes

                              An array of Class objects that describes the
                              parameter types, in declared order, of the con-
                              structor.

Returns   A Constructor object that reflects the specified public con-
               structor of this class.

Throws   NoSuchMethodException

                              If the specified constructor does not exist.

               SecurityException

                              If the checkMemberAccess() method of the
                              SecurityManager throws a SecurityException.

Description   If this Class object represents a class, this method returns a
               Constructor object that reflects the specified public construc-
               tor of this class. The constructor is located by searching all of
               the constructors of the class for a public constructor that has
               exactly the same formal parameters as specified. If this Class
               does not represent a class, the method returns null.

getConstructors

```
public Constructor[] getConstructors()
                throws SecurityException
```

Availability   New as of JDK 1.1

Returns   An array of Constructor objects that reflect the public constructors of this class.

Throws   SecurityException

                If the checkMemberAccess() method of the SecurityManager throws a SecurityException.

Description   If this Class object represents a class, this method returns an array of Constructor objects that reflect the public constructors of this class. If there are no public constructors, or if this Class does not represent a class, the method returns an array of length 0.

getDeclaredClasses

```
public Class[] getDeclaredClasses() throws SecurityException
```

Availability   New as of JDK 1.1

Returns   An array of Class objects that contains all of the declared classes and interfaces that are members of this class.

Throws   SecurityException

                If the checkMemberAccess() method of the SecurityManager throws a SecurityException.

Description   If this Class object represents a reference type, this method returns an array of Class objects that lists all of the classes and interfaces that are members of this class or interface. The list includes public, protected, default access, and private classes and interfaces that are defined by this class or interface, but it excludes classes and interfaces inherited from superclasses. If there are no such member classes or interfaces, or if this Class represents a primitive type, the method returns an array of length 0.

                As of Java 1.1.3, this method always returns an array of length 0, no matter how many member classes this class or interface declares.

getDeclaredConstructor

```
public Constructor getDeclaredConstructor(Class[] parameterTypes)
                throws NoSuchMethodException, SecurityException
```

Availability	New as of JDK 1.1
Parameters	parameterTypes

An array of Class objects that describes the parameter types, in declared order, of the constructor.

Returns	A Constructor object that reflects the specified declared constructor of this class.
Throws	NoSuchMethodException

If the specified constructor does not exist.

SecurityException

If the checkMemberAccess() method of the SecurityManager throws a SecurityException.

Description   If this Class object represents a class, this method returns a Constructor object that reflects the specified declared constructor of this class. The constructor is located by searching all of the constructors of the class for a public, protected, default access, or private constructor that has exactly the same formal parameters as specified. If this Class does not represent a class, the method returns null.

getDeclaredConstructors

```
public Constructor[] getDeclaredConstructors()
                throws SecurityException
```

Availability	New as of JDK 1.1
Returns	An array of Constructor objects that reflect the declared constructors of this class.
Throws	SecurityException

If the checkMemberAccess() method of the SecurityManager throws a SecurityException.

Description   If this Class object represents a class, this method returns an array of Constructor objects that reflect the public, protected, default access, and private constructors of this class. If there are no declared constructors, or if this Class does not represent a class, the method returns an array of length 0.

getDeclaredField

```
public Field getDeclaredField(String name)
                throws NoSuchFieldException, SecurityException
```

Availability	New as of JDK 1.1

Parameters   name   The simple name of the field.

Returns   A Field object that reflects the specified declared field of this class.

Throws   NoSuchFieldException
                    If the specified field does not exist.

              SecurityException
                    If the checkMemberAccess() method of the SecurityManager throws a SecurityException.

Description   If this Class object represents a class or interface, this method returns a Field object that reflects the specified declared field of this class. The field is located by searching all of the fields of the class (but not inherited fields) for a public, protected, default access, or private field that has the specified simple name. If this Class does not represent a class or interface, the method returns null.

getDeclaredFields

public Field[] getDeclaredFields() throws SecurityException

Availability New as of JDK 1.1

Returns   An array of Field objects that reflect the declared fields of this class.

Throws   SecurityException
                    If the checkMemberAccess() method of the SecurityManager throws a SecurityException.

Description   If this Class object represents a class or interface, this method returns an array of Field objects that reflect the public, protected, default access, and private fields declared by this class, but excludes inherited fields. If there are no declared fields, or if this Class does not represent a class or interface, the method returns an array of length 0.

              This method does not reflect the implicit length field for array types. The methods of the class Array should be used to manipulate array types.

getDeclaredMethod

public Method getDeclaredMethod(String name, Class[] parameterTypes)
              throws NoSuchMethodException, SecurityException

Availability New as of JDK 1.1

Parameters   name   The simple name of the method.

parameterTypes

> An array of Class objects that describes the parameter types, in declared order, of the method.

Returns   A Method object that reflects the specified declared method of this class.

Throws   NoSuchMethodException

> If the specified method does not exist.

SecurityException

> If the checkMemberAccess() method of the SecurityManager throws a SecurityException.

Description   If this Class object represents a class or interface, this method returns a Method object that reflects the specified declared method of this class. The method is located by searching all of the methods of the class (but not inherited methods) for a public, protected, default access, or private method that has the specified simple name and exactly the same formal parameters as specified. If this Class does not represent a class or interface, the method returns null.

getDeclaredMethods

public Method[] getDeclaredMethods() throws SecurityException

Availability   New as of JDK 1.1

Returns   An array of Method objects that reflect the declared methods of this class.

Throws   SecurityException

> If the checkMemberAccess() method of the SecurityManager throws a SecurityException.

Description   If this Class object represents a class or interface, this method returns an array of Method objects that reflect the public, protected, default access, and private methods declared by this class, but excludes inherited methods. If there are no declared methods, or if this Class does not represent a class or interface, the method returns an array of length 0.

getDeclaringClass

public Class getDeclaringClass()

Availability   New as of JDK 1.1

Returns   A Class object that represents the declaring class if this class is a member of another class.

Description   If this Class object represents a class or interface that is a member of another class or interface, this method returns a Class object that describes the declaring class or interface. If this class or interface is not a member of another class or interface, or if it represents a primitive type, the method returns null.

getField

```
public Field getField(String name)
          throws NoSuchFieldException, SecurityException
```

Availability   New as of JDK 1.1

Parameters   name   The simple name of the field.

Returns   A Field object that reflects the specified public field of this class.

Throws   NoSuchFieldException
                    If the specified field does not exist.

         SecurityException
                    If the checkMemberAccess() method of the SecurityManager throws a SecurityException.

Description   If this Class object represents a class or interface, this method returns a Field object that reflects the specified public field of this class. The field is located by searching all of the fields of the class, including any inherited fields, for a public field that has the specified simple name. If this Class does not represent a class or interface, the method returns null.

getFields

```
public Field[] getFields() throws SecurityException
```

Availability   New as of JDK 1.1

Returns   An array of Field objects that reflect the public fields of this class.

Throws   SecurityException
                    If the checkMemberAccess() method of the SecurityManager throws a SecurityException.

Description   If this Class object represents a class or interface, this method returns an array of Field objects that reflect the public fields declared by this class and any inherited public fields. If there are no public fields, or if this Class does not represent a class or interface, the method returns an array of length 0.

This method does not reflect the implicit length field for array types. The methods of the class Array should be used to manipulate array types.

getInterfaces

public native Class[] getInterfaces()

Returns	An array of the interfaces implemented by this class or extended by this interface.
Description	If the Class object represents a class, this method returns an array that refers to all of the interfaces that the class implements. The order of the interfaces referred to in the array is the same as the order in the class declaration's implements clause. If the class does not implement any interfaces, the length of the returned array is 0.

If the object represents an interface, this method returns an array that refers to all of the interfaces that this interface extends. The interfaces occur in the order they appear in the interface declaration's extends clause. If the interface does not extend any interfaces, the length of the returned array is 0.

If the object represents a primitive or array type, the method returns an array of length 0.

getMethod

public Method getMethod(String name, Class[] parameterTypes)
                throws NoSuchMethodException, SecurityException

Availability	New as of JDK 1.1	
Parameters	name	The simple name of the method.
	parameterTypes	
		An array of Class objects that describes the parameter types, in declared order, of the method.
Returns	A Method object that reflects the specified public method of this class.	
Throws	NoSuchMethodException	
		If the specified method does not exist.
	SecurityException	
		If the checkMemberAccess() method of the SecurityManager throws a SecurityException.
Description	If this Class object represents a class or interface, this method returns a Method object that reflects the specified public method of this class. The method is located by searching all methods of the class, including any inherited methods, for a public method that has the specified simple name and exactly the same formal parameters as specified. If this Class does not represent a class or interface, the method returns null.	

getMethods

`public Method[] getMethods() throws SecurityException`

Availability	New as of JDK 1.1
Returns	An array of `Method` objects that reflect the public methods of this class.
Throws	`SecurityException`
	If the `checkMemberAccess()` method of the `SecurityManager` throws a `SecurityException`.
Description	If this `Class` object represents a class or interface, this method returns an array of `Method` objects that reflect the public methods declared by this class and any inherited public methods. If there are no public methods or if this `Class` doesn't represent a class or interface, the method returns an array of length 0.

getModifiers

`public native int getModifiers()`

Availability	New as of JDK 1.1
Returns	An integer that represents the modifier keywords used to declare this class.
Description	If this `Class` object represents a class or interface, this method returns an integer value that represents the modifiers used to declare the class or interface. The `Modifier` class should be used to decode the returned value.

getName

`public native String getName()`

Returns	The fully qualified name of this class or interface.
Description	This method returns the fully qualified name of the type represented by this `Class` object.

If the object represents the class of an array, the method returns a `String` that contains as many left square brackets as there are dimensions in the array, followed by a code that indicates the type of element contained in the base array. Consider the following:

```
(new int [3][4][5]).getClass().getName()
```

This code returns "[[[I". The codes used to indicate the element type are as follows:

Code	Type
[	array
B	byte
C	char
d	double
F	float
I	int
J	long
L *fully_qualified_class_name*	class or interface
S	short
Z	boolean

getResource

`public URL getResource(String name)`

Availability	New as of JDK 1.1
Parameters	name A resource name.
Returns	A URL object that is connected to the specified resource, or null if the resource cannot be found.
Description	This method finds a resource with the given name for this Class object and returns a URL object that is connected to the resource. The rules for searching for a resource associated with a class are implemented by the ClassLoader for the class; this method simply calls the getResource() method of the Class-Loader. If this class does not have a ClassLoader (i.e., it is a system class), then the method calls the ClassLoader.get-SystemResource() method.

getResourceAsStream

`public InputStream getResourceAsStream(String name)`

Availability	New as of JDK 1.1
Parameters	name A resource name.
Returns	An InputStream object that is connected to the specified resource, or null if the resource cannot be found.
Description	This method finds a resource with the given name for this Class object and returns an InputStream object that is connected to the resource. The rules for searching for a resource associated with a class are implemented by the ClassLoader for the class; this method simply calls the getResourceAsStream() method of the ClassLoader. If this class does not have a Class-Loader (i.e., it is a system class), the method calls the Class-Loader.getSystemResourceAsStream() method.

getSigners

`public native Object[] getSigners()`

Availability	New as of JDK 1.1
Returns	An array of `Object`s that represents the signers of this class.
Description	This method returns an array of objects that represents the digital signatures for this class.

getSuperclass

`public native Class getSuperclass()`

Returns	The superclass of this class, or `null` if there is no superclass.
Description	If the `Class` object represents a class other than `Object`, this method returns the `Class` object that represents its superclass. If the object represents an interface, the `Object` class, or a primitive type, the method returns `null`.

isArray

`public native boolean isArray()`

Availability	New as of JDK 1.1
Returns	`true` if this object describes an array type; otherwise `false`.

isAssignableFrom

`public native boolean isAssignableFrom(Class cls)`

Availability	New as of JDK 1.1
Parameters	`cls`　　　　A `Class` object to be tested.
Returns	`true` if the type represented by `cls` is assignable to the type of this class: otherwise `false`.
Throws	`NullPointerException` 　　　　If `cls` is `null`.
Description	This method determines whether or not the type represented by `cls` is assignable to the type of this class. If this class represents a class, this class must be the same as `cls` or a superclass of `cls`. If this class represents an interface, this class must be the same as `cls` or a superinterface of `cls`. If this class represents a primitive type, this class must be the same as `cls`.

isInstance

`public native boolean isInstance(Object obj)`

Availability	New as of JDK 1.1
Parameters	`obj`　　　　An `Object` to be tested.

Returns	true if obj can be cast to the reference type specified by this class; otherwise false.
Throws	NullPointerException
	If obj is null.
Description	This method determines whether or not the object represented by obj can be cast to the type of this class object without causing a ClassCastException. This method is the dynamic equivalent of the instanceof operator.

isInterface

```
public native boolean isInterface()
```

Returns	true if this object describes an interface; otherwise false.

isPrimitive

```
public native boolean isPrimitive()
```

Availability	New as of JDK 1.1
Returns	true if this object describes a primitive type; otherwise false.

newInstance

```
public native Object newInstance () throws InstantiationException,
            IllegalAccessException
```

Returns	A reference to a new instance of this class.
Throws	InstantiationException
	If the Class object represents an interface or an abstract class.
	IllegalAccessException
	If the class or an initializer is not accessible.
Description	This method creates a new instance of this class by performing these steps:

1. It creates a new object of the class represented by the Class object.
2. It calls the constructor for the class that takes no arguments.
3. It returns a reference to the initialized object.

The newInstance() method is useful for creating an instance of a class that has been dynamically loaded using the forName() method.

The reference returned by this method is usually cast to the type of object that is instantiated.

The newInstance() method can throw objects that are not instances of the classes it is declared to throw. If the constructor invoked by newInstance() throws an exception, the exception is thrown by newInstance() regardless of the class of the object.

toString

```
public String toString()
```

Returns   A String that contains the name of the class with either "class" or "interface" prepended as appropriate.

Overrides   Object.toString()

Description This method returns a string representation of the Class object.

Inherited Methods

Method	Inherited From	Method	Inherited From
clone()	Object	equals()	Object
finalize()	Object	getClass()	Object
hashCode()	Object	notify()	Object
notifyAll()	Object	wait()	Object
wait(long)	Object	wait(long, int)	Object

See Also

ClassLoader 10.5; Class Declarations 5.4; Constructors 5.4.7; Exceptions 9.4.1; Interface Declarations 5.5; Methods 5.4.6; Nested Top-level and Member Classes 5.4.11; Object 10.14; Object Creation 5.3.3; Reference Types 3.2; SecurityManager 10.18; Variables 5.4.5

10.5 ClassLoader

Synopsis

Class Name: java.lang.ClassLoader
Superclass: java.lang.Object
Immediate Subclasses: None
Interfaces Implemented: None
Availability: JDK 1.0 or later

Description

The ClassLoader class provides a mechanism for Java to load classes over a network or from any source other than the local filesystem. The default class-loading mechanism loads classes from files found relative to directories specified by the CLASSPATH environment variable. This default mechanism does not use an instance of the ClassLoader class.

An application can implement another mechanism for loading classes by declaring a subclass of the abstract ClassLoader class. A subclass of ClassLoader must override the loadClass() to define a class-loading policy. This method implements any sort of security that is necessary for the class-loading mechanism. The other methods of ClassLoader are final, so they cannot be overridden.

A ClassLoader object is typically used by calling its loadClass() method to explicitly load a top-level class, such as a subclass of Applet. The ClassLoader that loads the class becomes associated with the class; it can be obtained by calling the getClassLoader() method of the Class object that represents the class.

Once a class is loaded, it must be resolved before it can be used. Resolving a class means ensuring that all of the other classes it references are loaded. In addition, all of the classes that they reference must be loaded, and so on, until all of the needed classes have been loaded. Classes are resolved using the resolveClass() method of the ClassLoader object that loaded the initial class. This means that when a ClassLoader object is explicitly used to load a class, the same ClassLoader is used to load all of the classes that it references, directly or indirectly.

Classes loaded using a ClassLoader object may attempt to load additional classes without explicitly using a ClassLoader object. They can do this by calling the Class class's forName() method. However, in such a situation, a ClassLoader object is implicitly used. See the description of Class.forName() for more information.

Java identifies a class by a combination of its fully qualified name and the class loader that was used to load the class. If you write a subclass of ClassLoader, it should not attempt to directly load local classes. Instead, it should call findSystemClass(). A local class that is loaded directly by a ClassLoader is considered to be a different class than the same class loaded by findSystemClass(). This can lead to having two copies of the same class loaded, which can cause a number of inconsistencies. For example, the class's equals() method may decide that the same object is not equal to itself.

Class Summary

```
public abstract class java.lang.ClassLoader extends java.lang.Object {
    // Constructors
    protected ClassLoader();
    // Class Methods
    public static final URL
        getSystemResource(String name);                // New in 1.1
    public static final InputStream
        getSystemResourceAsStream(String name);        // New in 1.1

    // Public Instance Methods
    public URL getResource(String name);               // New in 1.1
    public InputStream getResourceAsStream(String name);   // New in 1.1
    public Class loadClass(String name);               // New in 1.1

    // Protected Instance Methods
    protected final Class defineClass(byte data[],
            int offset, int length);                   // Deprecated in 1.1
    protected final Class defineClass(String name,
            byte[] data, int offset, int length);      // New in 1.1
    protected final Class findLoadedClass(String name);    // New in 1.1
    protected final Class findSystemClass(String name);
    protected abstract Class loadClass(String name, boolean resolve);
    protected final void resolveClass(Class c);
    protected final void setSigners(Class cl,
            Object[] signers);                         // New in 1.1
}
```

Constructors

ClassLoader

protected ClassLoader()

Throws   SecurityException

If there is a SecurityManager object installed
and its checkCreateClassLoader() method
throws a SecurityException when called by this
constructor.

Description   Initializes a ClassLoader object. Because ClassLoader is an
abstract class, only subclasses of the class can access this constructor.

Class Methods

getSystemResource

```
public static final URL getSystemResource(String name)
```

Availability	New as of JDK 1.1
Parameters	name A system resource name.
Returns	A URL object that is connected to the specified system resource, or null if the resource cannot be found.
Description	This method finds a system resource with the given name and returns a URL object that is connected to the resource. The resource name can be any system resource.

getSystemResourceAsStream

```
public static final InputStream getSystemResourceAsStream(String name)
```

Availability	New as of JDK 1.1
Parameters	name A system resource name.
Returns	An InputStream object that is connected to the specified system resource, or null if the resource cannot be found.
Description	This method finds a system resource with the given name and returns an InputStream object that is connected to the resource. The resource name can be any system resource.

Public Instance Methods

getResource

```
public URL getResource(String name)
```

Availability	New as of JDK 1.1
Parameters	name A resource name.
Returns	A URL object that is connected to the specified resource, or null if the resource cannot be found.
Description	This method finds a resource with the given name and returns a URL object that is connected to the resource.

A resource is a file that contains data (e.g., sound, images, text) and it can be part of a package. The name of a resource is a sequence of identifiers separated by "/". For example, a resource might have the name *help/american/logon.html*. System resources are found on the host machine using the conventions of the host implementation.

For example, the "/" in the resource name may be treated as a path separator, with the entire resource name treated as a relative path to be found under a directory in CLASSPATH.

The implementation of getResource() in ClassLoader simply returns null. A subclass can override this method to provide more useful functionality.

getResourceAsStream

```
public InputStream getResourceAsStream(String name)
```
Availability	New as of JDK 1.1
Parameters	name A resource name.
Returns	An InputStream object that is connected to the specified resource, or null if the resource cannot be found.
Description	This method finds a resource with the given name and returns an InputStream object that is connected to the resource.

A resource is a file that contains data (e.g., sound, images, text) and it can be part of a package. The name of a resource is a sequence of identifiers separated by '/'. For example, a resource might have the name *help/american/logon.html*. System resources are found on the host machine using the conventions of the host implementation. For example, the '/' in the resource name may be treated as a path separator, with the entire resource name treated as a relative path to be found under a directory in CLASSPATH.

The implementation of getResourceAsStream() in Class-Loader simply returns null. A subclass can override this method to provide more useful functionality.

loadClass

```
public Class loadClass(String name) throws ClassNotFoundException
```
Availability	New as of JDK 1.1
Parameters	name The name of the class to be returned. The class name should be qualified by its package name. The lack of an explicit package name specifies that the class is part of the default package.
Returns	The Class object for the specified class.
Throws	ClassNotFoundException If it cannot find a definition for the named class.
Description	This method loads the named class by calling loadClass(name, true).

Protected Instance Methods

defineClass

```
protected final Class defineClass(byte data[], int offset,
                                  int length)
```

Availability   Deprecated as of JDK 1.1

Parameters   data   An array that contains the byte codes that define a class.

               offset   The offset in the array of byte codes.

               length   The number of byte codes in the array.

Returns   The newly created Class object.

Throws   ClassFormatError

                     If the data array does not constitute a valid class definition.

Description   This method creates a Class object from the byte codes that define the class. Before the class can be used, it must be resolved. The method is intended to be called from an implementation of the loadClass() method.

               Note that this method is deprecated as of Java 1.1. You should use the version of defineClass() that takes a name parameter and is therefore more secure.

```
protected final Class defineClass(String name, byte data[],
                                  int offset, int length)
```

Availability   New as of JDK 1.1

Parameters   name   The expected name of the class to be defined or null if it is not known. The class name should be qualified by its package name. The lack of an explicit package name specifies that the class is part of the default package.

               data   An array that contains the byte codes that define a class.

               offset   The offset in the array of byte codes.

               length   The number of byte codes in the array.

Returns   The newly created Class object.

Throws   ClassFormatError

                     If the data array does not constitute a valid class definition.

Description   This method creates a Class object from the byte codes that define the class. Before the class can be used, it must be resolved. The method is intended to be called from an implementation of the loadClass() method.

findLoadedClass

```
protected final Class findLoadedClass(String name)
```

Availability	New as of JDK 1.1
Parameters	name The name of the class to be returned. The class name should be qualified by its package name. The lack of an explicit package name specifies that the class is part of the default package.
Returns	The Class object for the specified loaded class or null if the class cannot be found.
Description	This method finds the specified class that has already been loaded.

findSystemClass

```
protected final Class findSystemClass(String name)
                    throws ClassNotFoundException
```

Parameters	name The name of the class to be returned. The class name should be qualified by its package name. The lack of an explicit package name specifies that the class is part of the default package.
Returns	The Class object for the specified system class.
Throws	ClassNotFoundException
	If the default class-loading mechanism cannot find a definition for the class.
	NoClassDefFoundError
	If the default class-loading mechanism cannot find the class.
Description	This method finds and loads a system class if it has not already been loaded. A *system class* is a class that is loaded by the default class-loading mechanism from the local filesystem. An implementation of the loadClass() method typically calls this method to attempt to load a class from the locations specified by the CLASSPATH environment variable.

loadClass

```
protected abstract Class loadClass(String name,
                    boolean resolve)
                    throws ClassNotFoundException
```

Parameters	name The name of the class to be returned. The class name should be qualified by its package name. The lack of an explicit package name specifies that the class is part of the default package.

	resolve	Specifies whether or not the class should be resolved by calling the resolveClass() method.

Returns   The Class object for the specified class.

Throws   ClassNotFoundException

　　　　　　　　If it cannot find a definition for the named class.

Description   An implementation of this abstract method loads the named class and returns its Class object. It is permitted and encouraged for an implementation to cache the classes it loads, rather than load one each time the method is called. An implementation of this method should do at least the following:

1. Load the byte codes that comprise the class definition into a byte[].
2. Call the defineClass() method to create a Class object to represent the class definition.
3. If the resolve parameter is true, call the resolveClass() method to resolve the class.

If an implementation of this method caches the classes that it loads, it is recommended that it use an instance of the java.util.Hashtable to implement the cache.

resolveClass

```
protected final void resolveClass(Class c)
```

Parameters   c   The Class object for the class to be resolved.

Description   This method resolves the given Class object. Resolving a class means ensuring that all of the other classes that the Class object references are loaded. In addition, all of the classes that they reference must be loaded, and so on, until all of the needed classes have been loaded.

The resolveClass() method should be called by an implementation of the loadClass() method when the value of the loadClass() method's resolve parameter is true.

setSigners

```
protected final void setSigners(Class cl, Object[] signers)
```

Availability   New as of JDK 1.1

Parameters   cl   The Class object for the class to be signed.

              signers   An array of Objects that represents the signers of this class.

Description   This method specifies the objects that represent the digital signatures for this class.

Inherited Methods

Method	Inherited From	Method	Inherited From
clone()	Object	equals(Object)	Object
finalize()	Object	getClass()	Object
hashCode()	Object	notify()	Object
notifyAll()	Object	toString()	Object
wait()	Object	wait(long)	Object
wait(long, int)	Object		

See Also

Class 10.4; Errors 9.4.2; Exceptions 9.4.1; Object 10.14; SecurityManager 10.18

10.6   Cloneable

Synopsis

Interface Name:	java.lang.Cloneable
Super-interface:	None
Immediate Sub-interfaces:	
	java.text.CharacterIterator
Implemented by:	java.awt.GridBagConstraints, java.awt.Insets,
	java.awt.image.ImageFilter,
	java.text.BreakIterator,
	java.text.Collator, java.text.DateFormat,
	java.text.DateFormatSymbols,
	java.text.DecimalFormatSymbols,
	java.text.Format, java.text.NumberFormat,
	java.util.BitSet, java.util.Calendar,
	java.util.Date, java.util.Hashtable,
	java.util.Locale, java.util.TimeZone,
	java.util.Vector
Availability:	JDK 1.0 or later

Description

The Cloneable interface provides no functionality; it declares no methods or variables. This interface is simply provided as a way of indicating that an object can be cloned (that is, copied). A class that is declared as implementing this interface is assumed to have overridden the Object class's implementation of clone() with an implementation that can successfully clone instances of the class. The implementation of clone() that is provided by the Object class simply throws a CloneNotSupportedException.

Interface Declaration

```
public interface java.lang.Cloneable {
}
```

See Also

Exceptions 9.4.1; Object 10.14

10.7   Compiler

Synopsis

Class Name:	java.lang.Compiler
Superclass:	java.lang.Object
Immediate Subclasses:	None
Interfaces Implemented:	None
Availability:	JDK 1.0 or later

Description

The Compiler class encapsulates a facility for compiling Java classes to native code. As provided by Sun, the methods of this class do not actually do anything. However, if the system property java.compiler has been defined and if the method System.loadLibrary() is able to load the library named by the property, the methods of this class use the implementations provided in the library.

The Compiler class has no public constructors, so it cannot be instantiated.

Class Summary

```
public final class java.lang.Compiler extends java.lang.Object {
    // Class Methods
    public static native Object command(Object any);
    public static native boolean compileClass(Class clazz);
    public static native boolean compileClasses(String string);
```

```
    public static native void disable();
    public static native void enable();
}
```

Class Methods

command

```
public static native Object command(Object any)
```

Parameters   any   The permissible value and its meaning is determined by the compiler library.

Returns   A value determined by the compiler library, or null if no compiler library is loaded.

Description   This method directs the compiler to perform an operation
specified by the given argument. The available operations, if
any, are determined by the compiler library.

compileClass

```
public static native boolean compileClass(Class clazz)
```

Parameters   clazz   The class to be compiled to native code.

Returns   true if the compilation succeeds, or false if the compilation
fails or no compiler library is loaded.

Description   This method requests the compiler to compile the specified
class to native code.

compileClasses

```
public static native boolean compileClasses(String string)
```

Parameters   string   A string that specifies the names of the classes to
be compiled.

Returns   true if the compilation succeeds, or false if the compilation
fails or no compiler library is loaded.

Description   This method requests the compiler to compile all of the classes
named in the string.

disable

```
public static native void disable()
```

Description   This method disables the compiler if one is loaded.

enable

```
public static native void enable()
```

Description   This method enables the compiler if one is loaded.

Inherited Methods

Method	Inherited From	Method	Inherited From
clone()	Object	equals(Object)	Object
finalize()	Object	getClass()	Object
hashCode()	Object	notify()	Object
notifyAll()	Object	toString()	Object
wait()	Object	wait(long)	Object
wait(long, int)	Object		

See Also

Object 10.14; System 10.22

10.8   Double

Synopsis

Class Name:	java.lang.Double
Superclass:	java.lang.Number
Immediate Subclasses:	None
Interfaces Implemented:	None
Availability:	JDK 1.0 or later

Description

The Double class provides an object wrapper for a double value. This is useful when you need to treat a double value as an object. For example, there are a number of utility methods that take a reference to an Object as one of their arguments. You cannot specify a double value for one of these arguments, but you can provide a reference to a Double object that encapsulates the double value. Furthermore, as of JDK 1.1, the Double class is necessary to support the Reflection API and class literals.

In Java, double values are represented using the IEEE 754 format. The Double class provides constants for the three special values that are mandated by this format: POSITIVE_INFINITY, NEGATIVE_INFINITY, and NaN (not-a-number).

The Double class also provides some utility methods, such as methods for determining whether a double value is an infinity value or NaN, for converting double values to other primitive types, and for converting a double to a String and vice versa.

Class Summary

```
public final class java.lang.Double extends java.lang.Number {
    // Constants
    public final static double MAX_VALUE;
    public final static double MIN_VALUE;
    public final static double NaN;
    public final static double NEGATIVE_INFINITY;
    public final static double POSITIVE_INFINITY;
    public final static Class TYPE;                    // New in 1.1

    // Constructors
    public Double(double value);
    public Double(String s);

    // Class Methods
    public static native long doubleToLongBits(double value);
    public static boolean isInfinite(double v);
    public static boolean isNaN(double v);
    public static native double longBitsToDouble(long bits);
    public static String toString(double d);
    public static Double valueOf(String s);

    // Instance Methods
    public byte byteValue();                           // New in 1.1
    public double doubleValue();
    public boolean equals(Object obj);
    public float floatValue();
    public int hashCode();
    public int intValue();
    public boolean isInfinite();
    public boolean isNaN();
    public long longValue();
    public short shortValue();                         // New in 1.1
    public String toString();
}
```

Constants

MAX_VALUE

```
public static final double MAX_VALUE =
                    1.79769313486231570e+308
```

Description   The largest value that can be represented by a double.

MIN_VALUE

```
public static final double MIN_VALUE =
                4.94065645841246544e-324
```
Description   The smallest value that can be represented by a double.

NaN

```
public static final double NaN = 0.0 / 0.0
```
Description   This variable represents the value not-a-number (NaN), which is a special value produced by double operations such as division of zero by zero. When NaN is one of the operands, most arithmetic operations return NaN as the result.

Most comparison operators (<, <=, ==, >=, >) return false when one of their arguments is NaN. The exception is !=, which returns true when one of its arguments is NaN.

NEGATIVE_INFINITY

```
public static final double NEGATIVE_INFINITY = -1.0 / 0.0
```
Description   This variable represents the value negative infinity, which is produced when a double operation underflows or a negative double value is divided by zero. Negative infinity is by definition less than any other double value.

POSITIVE_INFINITY

```
public static final double POSITIVE_INFINITY = 1.0 / 0.0
```
Description   This variable represents the value positive infinity, which is produced when a double operation overflows or a positive double value is divided by zero. Positive infinity is by definition greater than any other double value.

TYPE

```
public static final Class TYPE
```
Availability   New as of JDK 1.1
Description   The Class object that represents the type double. It is always true that Double.TYPE == double.class.

Constructors

Double

```
public Double(double value)
```
Parameters   value   The double value to be encapsulated by this object.

Description   Creates a Double object with the specified double value.

public Double(String s) throws NumberFormatException

Parameters   s   The string to be made into a Double object.

Throws   NumberFormatException

If the sequence of characters in the given String does not form a valid double literal.

Description   Constructs a Double object with the value specified by the given string. The string must contain a sequence of characters that forms a legal double literal.

Class Methods

doubleToLongBits

public static native long doubleToLongBits(double value)

Parameters   value   The double value to be converted.

Returns   The long value that contains the same sequence of bits as the representation of the given double value.

Description   This method returns the long value that contains the same sequence of bits as the representation of the given double value. The meaning of the bits in the result is defined by the IEEE 754 floating-point format: bit 63 is the sign bit, bits 62-52 are the exponent, and bits 51-0 are the mantissa.

An argument of POSITIVE_INFINITY produces the result 0x7ff0000000000000L, an argument of NEGATIVE_INFINITY produces the result 0xfff0000000000000L, and an argument of NaN produces the result 0x7ff8000000000000L.

The value returned by this method can be converted back to the original double value by the longBitsToDouble() method.

isInfinite

static public boolean isInfinite(double v)

Parameters   v   The double value to be tested.

Returns   true if the specified value is equal to POSITIVE_INFINITY or NEGATIVE_INFINITY; otherwise false.

Description   This method determines whether or not the specified value is an infinity value.

isNaN

public static boolean isNaN(double v)

Parameters	v	The double value to be tested.
Returns		true if the specified value is equal to NaN; otherwise false.
Description		This method determines whether or not the specified value is NaN.

longBitsToDouble

public static native double longBitsToDouble(long bits)

Parameters	bits	The long value to be converted.
Returns		The double value whose representation is the same as the bits in the given long value.
Description		This method returns the double value whose representation is the same as the bits in the given double value. The meaning of the bits in the long value is defined by the IEEE 754 floating-point format: bit 63 is the sign bit, bits 62-52 are the exponent, and bits 51-0 are the mantissa. The argument 0x7f80000000000000L produces the result POSITIVE_INFINITY and the argument 0xff80000000000000L produces the result NEGATIVE_INFINITY. Arguments that are in the ranges 0x7ff0000000000001L through 0x7fffffffffffffffL and 0xfff0000000000001L through 0xffffffffffffffffL all produce the result NaN.

Except for NaN values not normally used by Java, this method is the inverse of the doubleToLongBits() method.

toString

public static String toString(double d)

Parameters	d	The double value to be converted.
Returns		A string representation of the given value.
Description		This method returns a String object that contains a representation of the given double value.

The values NaN, NEGATIVE_INFINITY, POSITIVE_INFINITY, -0.0, and +0.0 are represented by the strings "NaN", "-Infinity", "Infinity", "-0.0", and "0.0", respectively.

For other values, the exact string representation depends on the value being converted. If the absolute value of d is greater than or equal to 10^{-3} or less than or equal to 10^7, it is converted to a string with an optional minus sign (if the value is negative) followed by up to eight digits before the decimal point, a decimal point, and the necessary number of digits after the decimal point (but no trailing zero if there is more than one significant digit). There is always a minimum of one digit after the decimal point.

Otherwise, the value is converted to a string with an optional minus sign (if the value is negative), followed by a single digit, a decimal point, the necessary number of digits after the decimal point (but no trailing zero if there is more than one significant digit), and the letter E followed by a plus or a minus sign and a base 10 exponent of at least one digit. Again, there is always a minimum of one digit after the decimal point.

Note that the definition of this method has changed as of JDK 1.1. Prior to that release, the method provided a string representation that was equivalent to the %g format of the printf function in C.

valueOf

```
public static Double valueOf(String s)
                         throws NumberFormatException
```

Parameters	s	The string to be made into a Double object.
Returns		The Double object constructed from the string.
Throws	NumberFormatException	
		If the sequence of characters in the given String does not form a valid double literal.
Description		Constructs a Double object with the value specified by the given string. The string must contain a sequence of characters that forms a legal double literal. This method ignores leading and trailing white space in the string.

Instance Methods

byteValue

```
public byte byteValue()
```

Availability	New as of JDK 1.1
Returns	The value of this object as a byte.
Overrides	Number.byteValue()
Description	This method returns the truncated value of this object as a byte. More specifically, if the value of the object is NaN, the method returns 0. If the value is POSITIVE_INFINITY, or any other value that is too large to be represented by an byte, the method returns Byte.MAX_VALUE. If the value is NEGA-TIVE_INFINITY, or any other value that is too small to be repre-

sented by an byte, the method returns Byte.MIN_VALUE. Otherwise, the value is rounded toward zero and returned.

doubleValue

```
public double doubleValue()
```

Returns | The value of this object as a double.
Overrides | Number.doubleValue()
Description | This method returns the value of this object as a double.

equals

```
public boolean equals(Object obj)
```

Parameters | obj | The object to be compared with this object.
Returns | true if the objects are equal; false if they are not.
Overrides | Object.equals()
Description | This method returns true if obj is an instance of Double and it contains the same value as the object this method is associated with. More specifically, the method returns true if the double-ToLongBits() method returns the same result for the values of both objects.

This method produces a different result than the == operator when both values are NaN. In this case, the == operator produces false, while this method returns true. By the same token, the method also produces a different result when the two values are +0.0 and -0.0. In this case, the == operator produces true, while this method returns false.

floatValue

```
public float floatValue()
```

Returns | The value of this object as a float.
Overrides | Number.floatValue()
Description | This method returns this object value as a float. Rounding may occur.

hashCode

```
public int hashCode()
```

Returns | A hashcode based on the double value of the object.
Overrides | Object.hashCode()
Description | This method returns a hashcode computed from the value of this object.

More specifically, if d is the value of the object, and bitValue is defined as:

```
long bitValue = Double.doubleToLongBits(d)
```

then the hashcode returned by this method is computed as follows:

```
(int)(bitValue ^ (bitValue>>>32))
```

intValue

public int intValue()

Returns	The value of this object as an int.
Overrides	Number.intValue()
Description	This method returns the truncated value of this object as an int. More specifically, if the value of the object is NaN, the method returns 0. If the value is POSITIVE_INFINITY, or any other value that is too large to be represented by an int, the method returns Integer.MAX_VALUE. If the value is NEGATIVE_INFINITY, or any other value that is too small to be represented by an int, the method returns Integer.MIN_VALUE. Otherwise, the value is rounded toward zero and returned.

isInfinite

public boolean isInfinite()

Returns	true if the value of this object is equal to POSITIVE_INFINITY or NEGATIVE_INFINITY; otherwise false.
Description	This method determines whether or not the value of this object is an infinity value.

isNaN

public boolean isNaN()

Returns	true if the value of this object is equal to NaN; otherwise false.
Description	This method determines whether or not the value of this object is NaN.

longValue

public long longValue()

Returns	The value of this object as a long.
Overrides	Number.longValue()
Description	This method returns the truncated value of this object as a long. More specifically, if the value of the object is NaN, the method returns 0. If the value is POSITIVE_INFINITY, or any other value too large to be represented by a long, the method

returns `Long.MAX_VALUE`. If the value is `NEGATIVE_INFINITY`, or any other value too small to be represented by a `long`, the method returns `Long.MIN_VALUE`. Otherwise, the value is rounded toward zero and returned.

shortValue

`public short shortValue()`

Availability	New as of JDK 1.1
Returns	The value of this object as a `short`.
Overrides	`Number.shortValue()`
Description	This method returns the truncated value of this object as a `short`. More specifically, if the value of the object is `NaN`, the method returns 0. If the value is `POSITIVE_INFINITY`, or any other value that is too large to be represented by an `short`, the method returns `Short.MAX_VALUE`. If the value is `NEGA-TIVE_INFINITY`, or any other value that is too small to be represented by an `short`, the method returns `Short.MIN_VALUE`. Otherwise, the value is rounded toward zero and returned.

toString

`public String toString()`

Returns	A string representation of the value of this object.
Overrides	`Object.toString()`
Description	This method returns a `String` object that contains a representation of the value of this object.

The values `NaN`, `NEGATIVE_INFINITY`, `POSITIVE_INFINITY`, `-0.0`, and `+0.0` are represented by the strings `"NaN"`, `"-Infinity"`, `"Infinity"`, `"-0.0"`, and `"0.0"`, respectively.

For other values, the exact string representation depends on the value being converted. If the absolute value of this object is greater than or equal to 10^{-3} or less than or equal to 10^{7}, it is converted to a string with an optional minus sign (if the value is negative) followed by up to eight digits before the decimal point, a decimal point, and the necessary number of digits after the decimal point (but no trailing zero if there is more than one significant digit). There is always a minimum of one digit after the decimal point.

Otherwise, the value is converted to a string with an optional minus sign (if the value is negative), followed by a single digit, a decimal point, the necessary number of digits after the decimal point (but no trailing zero if there is more than one significant digit), and the letter E followed by a plus or a minus sign and a base 10 exponent of at least one digit. Again, there is always a minimum of one digit after the decimal point.

Note that the definition of this method has changed as of JDK 1.1. Prior to that release, the method provided a string representation that was equivalent to the %g format of the printf function in C.

Inherited Methods

Method	Inherited From	Method	Inherited From
clone()	Object	finalize()	Object
getClass()	Object	notify()	Object
notifyAll()	Object	wait()	Object
wait(long)	Object	wait(long, int)	Object

See Also

Class 10.4; Exceptions 9.4.1; Float 10.9; Floating-point literals 2.2.3.2; Floating-point types 3.1.1.2; Number 10.13; String 10.20

10.9 Float

Synopsis

Class Name:	java.lang.Float
Superclass:	java.lang.Number
Immediate Subclasses:	None
Interfaces Implemented:	None
Availability:	JDK 1.0 or later

Description

The Float class provides an object wrapper for a float value. This is useful when you need to treat a float value as an object. For example, there are a number of utility methods that take a reference to an Object as one of their arguments. You cannot specify a float value for one of these arguments, but you can provide a reference to a Float object that encapsulates the float value. Furthermore, as of JDK 1.1, the Float class is necessary to support the Reflection API and class literals.

In Java, float values are represented using the IEEE 754 format. The Float class provides constants for the three special values that are mandated by this format: POSITIVE_INFINITY, NEGATIVE_INFINITY, and NaN (not-a-number).

The Float class also provides some utility methods, such as methods for determining whether a floatx value is an infinity value or NaN, for converting float values to other primitive types, and for converting a float to a String and vice versa.

Class Summary

```java
public final class java.lang.Float extends java.lang.Number {
    // Constants
    public static final float MIN_VALUE;
    public static final float MAX_VALUE;
    public static final float NaN;
    public static final float NEGATIVE_INFINITY;
    public static final float POSITIVE_INFINITY;
    public final static Class TYPE;                    // New in 1.1

    // Constructors
    public Float(double value);
    public Float(float value);
    public Float(String s);

    // Class Methods
    public static native int floatToIntBits(float value);
    public static native float intBitsToFloat(int bits);
    public static boolean isInfinite(float v);
    public static boolean isNaN(float v);
    public static String toString(float f);
    public static Float valueOf(String s);
    // Instance Methods
    public byte byteValue();                           // New in 1.1
    public double doubleValue();
    public boolean equals(Object obj);
    public float floatValue();
    public int hashCode();
    public int intValue();
    public boolean isInfinite();
    public boolean isNaN();
    public long longValue();
    public short shortValue();                         // New in 1.1
    public String toString();
}
```

Constants

MAX_VALUE

> `public static final float MAX_VALUE = 3.40282346638528860e+38f`
>
> Description   The largest value that can be represented by a `float`.

MIN_VALUE

> `public static final float MIN_VALUE = 1.40129846432481707e-45f`
>
> Description   The smallest value that can be represented by a `float`.

NaN

> `public static final float NaN = 0.0f / 0.0f`
>
> Description   This variable represents the value NaN, a special value produced by `float` operations such as division of zero by zero. When NaN is one of the operands, most arithmetic operations return NaN as the result. Most comparison operators (<, <=, ==, >=, >) return `false` when one of their arguments is NaN. The exception is !=, which returns `true` when one of its arguments is NaN.

NEGATIVE_INFINITY

> `public static final float NEGATIVE_INFINITY = -1.0f / 0.0f`
>
> Description   This variable represents the value negative infinity, which is produced when a `float` operation underflows or a negative `float` value is divided by zero. Negative infinity is by definition less than any other `float` value.

POSITIVE_INFINITY

> `public static final float POSITIVE_INFINITY = 1.0f / 0.0f`
>
> Description   This variable represents the value positive infinity, which is produced when a `float` operation overflows or a positive `float` value is divided by zero. Positive infinity is by definition greater than any other `float` value.

TYPE

> `public static final Class TYPE`
>
> Availability   New as of JDK 1.1
>
> Description   The `Class` object that represents the type `float`. It is always true that `Float.TYPE == float.class`.

Constructors

Float

public Float(double value)

    Parameters   value   The double value to be encapsulated by this object.

    Description   Creates a Float object with the specified double value. The value is rounded to float precision.

public Float(float value)

    Parameters   value   The float value to be encapsulated by this object.

    Description   Creates a Float object with the specified float value.

public Float(String s) throws NumberFormatException

    Parameters   s   The string to be made into a Float object.

    Throws   NumberFormatException

                              If the sequence of characters in the given String does not form a valid float literal.

    Description   Constructs a Float object with the value specified by the given string. The string must contain a sequence of characters that forms a legal float literal.

Class Methods

floatToIntBits

public static native int floatToIntBits(float value)

    Parameters   value   The float value to be converted.

    Returns   The int value that contains the same sequence of bits as the representation of the given float value.

    Description   This method returns the int value that contains the same sequence of bits as the representation of the given float value. The meaning of the bits in the result is defined by the IEEE 754 floating-point format: bit 31 is the sign bit, bits 30-23 are the exponent, and bits 22-0 are the mantissa. An argument of POSITIVE_INFINITY produces the result 0x7f800000, an argument of NEGATIVE_INFINITY produces the result 0xff800000, and an argument of NaN produces the result 0x7fc00000.

                    The value returned by this method can be converted back to the original float value by the intBitsToFloat() method.

intBitsToFloat

`public static native float intBitsToFloat(int bits)`

Parameters	bits	The int value to be converted.
Returns		The float value whose representation is the same as the bits in the given int value.
Description		This method returns the float value whose representation is the same as the bits in the given int value. The meaning of the bits in the int value is defined by the IEEE 754 floating-point format: bit 31 is the sign bit, bits 30-23 are the exponent, and bits 22-0 are the mantissa. The argument 0x7f800000 produces the result POSITIVE_INFINITY, and the argument 0xff800000 produces the result NEGATIVE_INFINITY. Arguments in the ranges 0x7f800001 through 0x7f8fffff and 0xff800001 through 0xff8fffffL all produce the result NaN.

Except for NaN values not normally used by Java, this method is the inverse of the floatToIntBits() method.

isInfinite

`public static boolean isInfinite(float v)`

Parameters	v	The float value to be tested.
Returns		true if the specified value is equal to POSITIVE_INFINITY or NEGATIVE_INFINITY; otherwise false.
Description		This method determines whether or not the specified value is an infinity value.

isNaN

`public static boolean isNaN(float v)`

Parameters	v	The float value to be tested.
Returns		true if the specified value is equal to NaN; otherwise false.
Description		This method determines whether or not the specified value is NaN.

toString

`public static String toString(float f)`

Parameters	f	The float value to be converted.
Returns		A string representation of the given value.
Description		This method returns a String object that contains a representation of the given float value.

The values NaN, NEGATIVE_INFINITY, POSITIVE_INFINITY, -0.0, and +0.0 are represented by the strings "NaN", "-Infinity", "Infinity", "-0.0", and "0.0", respectively.

For other values, the exact string representation depends on the value being converted. If the absolute value of f is greater than or equal to 10^{-3} or less than or equal to 10^7, it is converted to a string with an optional minus sign (if the value is negative) followed by up to eight digits before the decimal point, a decimal point, and the necessary number of digits after the decimal point (but no trailing zero if there is more than one significant digit). There is always a minimum of one digit after the decimal point.

Otherwise, the value is converted to a string with an optional minus sign (if the value is negative), followed by a single digit, a decimal point, the necessary number of digits after the decimal point (but no trailing zero if there is more than one significant digit), and the letter E followed by a plus or a minus sign and a base 10 exponent of at least one digit. Again, there is always a minimum of one digit after the decimal point.

Note that the definition of this method has changed as of JDK 1.1. Prior to that release, the method provided a string representation that was equivalent to the %g format of the printf function in C.

valueOf

```
public static Float valueOf(String s)
                    throws NumberFormatException
```

Parameters	s	The string to be made into a Float object.
Returns		The Float object constructed from the string.
Throws	NumberFormatException	
		If the sequence of characters in the given String does not form a valid float literal.
Description		Constructs a Float object with the value specified by the given string. The string must contain a sequence of characters that forms a legal float literal. This method ignores leading and trailing whitespace in the string.

Instance Methods

byteValue

```
public byte byteValue()
```

Availability	New as of JDK 1.1

Returns   The value of this object as a byte.

Overrides   Number.byteValue()

Description   This method returns the truncated value of this object as a
byte. More specifically, if the value of the object is NaN, the
method returns 0. If the value is POSITIVE_INFINITY, or any
other value that is too large to be represented by an byte, the
method returns Byte.MAX_VALUE. If the value is NEGA-
TIVE_INFINITY, or any other value that is too small to be represented by an byte, the method returns Byte.MIN_VALUE. Otherwise, the value is rounded toward zero and returned.

doubleValue

```
public double doubleValue()
```

Returns   The value of this object as a double.

Overrides   Number.doubleValue()

Description   This method returns the value of this object as a double.

equals

```
public boolean equals(Object obj)
```

Parameters   obj   The object to be compared with this object.

Returns   true if the objects are equal; false if they are not.

Overrides   Object.equals()

Description   This method returns true if obj is an instance of Float and it
contains the same value as the object this method is associated
with. More specifically, the method returns true if the float-
ToIntBits() method returns the same result for the values of
both objects.

This method produces a different result than the == operator
when both values are NaN. In this case, the == operator produces false, while this method returns true. By the same
token, the method also produces a different result when the
two values are +0.0 and -0.0. In this case, the == operator produces true, while this method returns false.

floatValue

```
public float floatValue()
```

Returns   The value of this object as a float.

Overrides   Number.floatValue()

Description   This method returns the value of this object as a float.

hashCode

`public int hashCode()`

Returns	A hashcode based on the `float` value of the object.
Overrides	`Object.hashCode()`
Description	This method returns a hashcode computed from the value of this object. More specifically, if `f` is the value of the object, this method returns `Float.floatToIntBits(f)`.

intValue

`public int intValue()`

Returns	The value of this object as an `int`.
Overrides	`Number.intValue()`
Description	This method returns the truncated value of this object as an `int`. More specifically, if the value of the object is `NaN`, the method returns 0. If the value is `POSITIVE_INFINITY`, or any other value that is too large to be represented by an `int`, the method returns `Integer.MAX_VALUE`. If the value is `NEGATIVE_INFINITY`, or any other value that is too small to be represented by an `int`, the method returns `Integer.MIN_VALUE`. Otherwise, the value is rounded toward zero and returned.

isInfinite

`public boolean isInfinite(float v)`

Returns	`true` if the value of this object is equal to `POSITIVE_INFINITY` or `NEGATIVE_INFINITY`; otherwise `false`.
Description	This method determines whether or not the value of this object is an infinity value.

isNaN

`public boolean isNaN()`

Returns	`true` if the value of this object is equal to `NaN`; otherwise `false`.
Description	This method determines whether or not the value of this object is NaN.

longValue

`public long longValue()`

Returns	The value of this object as a `long`.
Overrides	`Number.longValue()`
Description	This method returns the truncated value of this object as a `long`. More specifically, if the value of the object is `NaN`, the method returns 0. If the value is `POSITIVE_INFINITY`, or any other value that is too large to be represented by a `long`, the

method returns `Long.MAX_VALUE`. If the value is `NEGA-TIVE_INFINITY`, or any other value that is too small to be represented by a `long`, the method returns `Long.MIN_VALUE`. Otherwise, the value is rounded toward zero and returned.

shortValue

`public short shortValue()`

Availability	New as of JDK 1.1
Returns	The value of this object as a `short`.
Overrides	`Number.shortValue()`
Description	This method returns the truncated value of this object as a `short`. More specifically, if the value of the object is `NaN`, the method returns 0. If the value is `POSITIVE_INFINITY`, or any other value that is too large to be represented by a `short`, the method returns `Short.MAX_VALUE`. If the value is `NEGA-TIVE_INFINITY`, or any other value that is too small to be represented by a `short`, the method returns `Short.MIN_VALUE`. Otherwise, the value is rounded toward zero and returned.

toString

`public String toString()`

Returns	A string representation of the value of this object.
Overrides	`Object.toString()`
Description	This method returns a `String` object that contains a representation of the value of this object.

The values `NaN`, `NEGATIVE_INFINITY`, `POSITIVE_INFINITY`, `-0.0`, and `+0.0` are represented by the strings `"NaN"`, `"-Infinity"`, `"Infinity"`, `"-0.0"`, and `"0.0"`, respectively.

For other values, the exact string representation depends on the value being converted. If the absolute value of this object is greater than or equal to 10^{-3} or less than or equal to 10^7, it is converted to a string with an optional minus sign (if the value is negative) followed by up to eight digits before the decimal point, a decimal point, and the necessary number of digits after the decimal point (but no trailing zero if there is more than one significant digit). There is always a minimum of one digit after the decimal point.

Otherwise, the value is converted to a string with an optional minus sign (if the value is negative), followed by a single digit, a decimal point, the necessary number of digits after the decimal point (but no trailing zero if there is more than one significant digit), and the letter E followed by a plus or a minus sign and a base 10 exponent of at least one digit. Again, there is always a minimum of one digit after the decimal point.

Note that the definition of this method has changed as of JDK 1.1. Prior to that release, the method provided a string representation that was equivalent to the %g format of the printf function in C.

Inherited Methods

Method	Inherited From	Method	Inherited From
clone()	Object	finalize()	Object
getClass()	Object	notify()	Object
notifyAll()	Object	wait()	Object
wait(long)	Object	wait(long, int)	Object

See Also

Class 10.4; Double 10.8; Exceptions 9.4.1; Floating-point literals 2.2.3.2; Floating-point types 3.1.1.2; Number 10.13; String 10.20

10.10   Integer

Synopsis

Class Name:	java.lang.Integer
Superclass:	java.lang.Number
Immediate Subclasses:	None
Interfaces Implemented:	None
Availability:	JDK 1.0 or later

Description

The Integer class provides an object wrapper for an int value. This is useful when you need to treat an int value as an object. For example, there are a number of utility methods that take a reference to an Object as one of their arguments. You cannot specify an int value for one of these arguments, but you can provide a reference to an Integer object that encapsulates the int value. Also, as of JDK 1.1, the Integer class is necessary to support the Reflection API and class literals.

The Integer class also provides a number of utility methods for converting int values to other primitive types and for converting int values to strings and vice versa.

Class Summary

```
public final class java.lang.Integer extends java.lang.Number {
    // Constants
    public static final int MAX_VALUE;
    public static final int MIN_VALUE;
    public final static Class TYPE;                    // New in 1.1

    // Constructors
    public Integer(int value);
    public Integer(String s);

    // Class Methods
    public static Integer decode(String nm)            // New in 1.1
    public static Integer getInteger(String nm);
    public static Integer getInteger(String nm, int val);
    public static Integer getInteger(String nm, Integer val);
    public static int parseInt(String s);
    public static int parseInt(String s, int radix;
    public static String toBinaryString(long i);
    public static String toHexString(long i);
    public static String toOctalString(long i);
    public static String toString(int i);
    public static String toString(int i, int radix);
    public static Integer valueOf(String s);
    public static Integer valueOf(String s, int radix);

    // Instance Methods
    public byte byteValue();                           // New in 1.1
    public double doubleValue();
    public boolean equals(Object obj);
    public float floatValue();
    public int hashCode();
    public int intValue();
    public long longValue();
    public short shortValue();                         // New in 1.1
    public String toString();
}
```

Constants

MAX_VALUE

```
public static final int MAX_VALUE = 0x7fffffff // 2147483647
```
    Description   The largest value that can be represented by an int.

MIN_VALUE

    `public static final int MIN_VALUE = 0x80000000 // -2147483648`

      Description   The smallest value that can be represented by an `int`.

TYPE

    `public static final Class TYPE`

      Availability   New as of JDK 1.1

      Description   The `Class` object that represents the type `int`. It is always true that `Integer.TYPE == int.class`.

Constructors

Integer

    `public Integer(int value)`

      Parameters   `value`   The `int` value to be encapsulated by this object.

      Description   Creates an `Integer` object with the specified `int` value.

    `public Integer(String s) throws NumberFormatException`

      Parameters   `s`   The string to be made into an `Integer` object.

      Throws   `NumberFormatException`

                If the sequence of characters in the given `String` does not form a valid `int` literal.

      Description   Constructs an `Integer` object with the value specified by the given string. The string should consist of one or more digit characters. The digit characters can be preceded by a single '–' character. If the string contains any other characters, the constructor throws a `NumberFormatException`.

Class Methods

decode

    `public static Integer decode(String nm)`

      Availability   New as of JDK 1.1

      Parameters   `nm`   A `String` representation of the value to be encapsulated by an `Integer` object. If the string begins with # or 0x, it is a radix 16 representation of the value. If the string begins with 0, it is a radix 8 representation of the value. Otherwise, it is assumed to be a radix 10 representation of the value.

      Returns   An `Integer` object that encapsulates the given value.

Throws   NumberFormatException

If the String contains any nondigit characters other than a leading minus sign or the value represented by the String is less than Integer.MIN_VALUE or greater than Integer.MAX_VALUE.

Description   This method returns an Integer object that encapsulates the given value.

getInteger

public static Integer getInteger(String nm)

Parameters   nm   The name of a system property.

Returns   The value of the system property as an Integer object, or an Integer object with the value 0 if the named property does not exist or cannot be parsed.

Description   This method retrieves the value of the named system property and returns it as an Integer object. The method obtains the value of the system property as a String using System.getProperty().

If the value of the property begins with 0x or # and is not followed by a minus sign, the rest of the value is parsed as a hexadecimal integer. If the value begins with 0, it's parsed as an octal integer; otherwise it's parsed as a decimal integer.

public static Integer getInteger(String nm, int val)

Parameters   nm   The name of a system property.

                val   A default int value for the property.

Returns   The value of the system property as an Integer object, or an Integer object with the value val if the named property does not exist or cannot be parsed.

Description   This method retrieves the value of the named system property and returns it as an Integer object. The method obtains the value of the system property as a String using System.getProperty().

If the value of the property begins with 0x or # and is not followed by a minus sign, the rest of the value is parsed as a hexadecimal integer. If the value begins with 0, it's parsed as an octal integer; otherwise it's parsed as a decimal integer.

public static Integer getInteger(String nm, Integer val)

Parameters	nm	The name of a system property.
	val	A default Integer value for the property.
Returns		The value of the system property as an Integer object, or the Integer object val if the named property does not exist or cannot be parsed.
Description		This method retrieves the value of the named system property and returns it as an Integer object. The method obtains the value of the system property as a String using System.getProperty().

If the value of the property begins with 0x or # and is not followed by a minus sign, the rest of the value is parsed as a hexadecimal integer. If the value begins with 0, it's parsed as an octal integer; otherwise it's as a decimal integer.

parseInt

public static int parseInt(String s)
                              throws NumberFormatException

Parameters	s	The String to be converted to an int value.
Returns		The numeric value of the integer represented by the String object.
Throws		NumberFormatException
		If the String does not contain a valid representation of an integer.
Description		This method returns the numeric value of the integer represented by the contents of the given String object. The String must contain only decimal digits, except that the first character may be a minus sign.

public static int parseInt(String s, int radix)
                              throws NumberFormatException

Parameters	s	The String to be converted to an int value.
	radix	The radix used in interpreting the characters in the String as digits. This value must be in the range Character.MIN_RADIX to Character.MAX_RADIX. If radix is in the range 2 through 10, only characters for which the Character.isDigit() method returns true are considered to be valid digits. If radix is in the range 11 through 36, characters in the ranges 'A' through 'Z' and 'a' through 'z' may be considered valid digits.

Returns   The numeric value of the integer represented by the String object in the specified radix.

Throws   NumberFormatException

> If the String does not contain a valid representation of an integer, or radix is not in the appropriate range.

Description   This method returns the numeric value of the integer represented by the contents of the given String object in the specified radix. The String must contain only valid digits of the specified radix, except that the first character may be a minus sign. The digits are parsed in the specified radix to produce the numeric value.

toBinaryString

public static String toBinaryString(int value)

Parameters   value   The int value to be converted to a string.

Returns   A string that contains the binary representation of the given value.

Description   This method returns a String object that contains the representation of the given value as an unsigned binary number. To convert the given value to an unsigned quantity, the method simply uses the value as if it were not negative. In other words, if the given value is negative, the method adds 2^{32} to it. Otherwise the value is used as it is.

> The string returned by this method contains a sequence of one or more '0' and '1' characters. The method returns "0" if its argument is 0. Otherwise, the string returned by this method begins with '1'.

toHexString

public static String toHexString(int value)

Parameters   value   The int value to be converted to a string.

Returns   A string that contains the hexadecimal representation of the given value.

Description   This method returns a String object that contains the representation of the given value as an unsigned hexadecimal number. To convert the given value to an unsigned quantity, the method simply uses the value as if it were not negative. In other words, if the given value is negative, the method adds 2^{32} to it. Otherwise the value is used as it is.

The string returned by this method contains a sequence of one or more of the characters '0', '1', '2', '3', '4', '5', '6', '7', '8', '9', 'a', 'b', 'c', 'd', 'e', and 'f'. The method returns "0" if its argument is 0. Otherwise, the string returned by this method does not begin with '0'.

To produce a string that contains upper- instead of lowercase letters, use the String.toUpperCase() method.

toOctalString

public static String toOctalString(int value)

Parameters	value	The int value to be converted to a string.
Returns		A string that contains the octal representation of the given value.
Description		This method returns a String object that contains a representation of the given value as an unsigned octal number. To convert the given value to an unsigned quantity, the method simply uses the value as if it were not negative. In other words, if the given value is negative, the method adds 2^{32} to it. Otherwise the value is used as it is.

The string returned by this method contains a sequence of one or more of the characters '0', '1', '2', '3', '4', '5', '6', and '7'. The method returns "0" if its argument is 0. Otherwise, the string returned by this method does not begin with '0'.

toString

public static String toString(int i)

Parameters	i	The int value to be converted to a string.
Returns		The string representation of the given value.
Description		This method returns a String object that contains the decimal representation of the given value.

This method returns a string that begins with '−' if the given value is negative. The rest of the string is a sequence of one or more of the characters '0', '1', '2', '3', '4', '5', '6', '7', '8', and '9'. This method returns "0" if its argument is 0. Otherwise, the string returned by this method does not begin with "0" or "−0".

public static String toString(int i, int radix)

Parameters	i	The int value to be converted to a string.
	radix	The radix used in converting the value to a string. This value must be in the range Character.MIN_RADIX to Character.MAX_RADIX.

Returns   The string representation of the given value in the specified radix.

Description   This method returns a `String` object that contains the representation of the given value in the specified radix.

This method returns a string that begins with '-' if the given value is negative. The rest of the string is a sequence of one or more characters that represent the magnitude of the given value. The characters that can appear in the sequence are determined by the value of `radix`. If *N* is the value of `radix`, the first *N* characters on the following line can appear in the sequence:

0123456789abcdefghijklmnopqrstuvwxyz

The method does not verify that `radix` is in the proper range. If `radix` is less than `Character.MIN_RADIX` or greater than `Character.MAX_RADIX`, the value 10 is used instead of the given value.

This method returns "0" if its argument is 0. Otherwise, the string returned by this method does not begin with "0" or "-0".

valueOf

```
public static Integer valueOf(String s)
            throws NumberFormatException
```

Parameters   s   The string to be made into an `Integer` object.
Returns   The `Integer` object constructed from the string.
Throws   NumberFormatException
               If the `String` does not contain a valid representation of an integer.

Description   Constructs an `Integer` object with the value specified by the given string. The string should consist of one or more digit characters. The digit characters can be preceded by a single '-' character. If the string contains any other characters, the method throws a `NumberFormatException`.

```
public static Integer valueOf(String s, int radix)
            throws NumberFormatException
```

Parameters   s   The string to be made into an `Integer` object.
               radix   The radix used in converting the string to a value. This value must be in the range `Character.MIN_RADIX` to `Character.MAX_RADIX`.

Returns   The Integer object constructed from the string.

Throws   NumberFormatException

                If the String does not contain a valid representation of an integer or radix is not in the appropriate range.

Description   Constructs an Integer object with the value specified by the given string in the specified radix. The string should consist of one or more digit characters or characters in the range 'A' to 'Z' or 'a' to 'z' that are considered digits in the given radix. The digit characters can be preceded by a single '–' character. If the string contains any other characters, the method throws a NumberFormatException.

Instance Methods

byteValue

```
public byte byteValue()
```

Availability   New as of JDK 1.1

Returns   The value of this object as a byte.

Overrides   Number.byteValue()

Description   This method returns the value of this object as a byte. The high order bits of the value are discarded.

doubleValue

```
public double doubleValue()
```

Returns   The value of this object as a double.

Overrides   Number.doubleValue()

Description   This method returns the value of this object as a double.

equals

```
public boolean equals(Object obj)
```

Parameters   obj   The object to be compared with this object.

Returns   true if the objects are equal; false if they are not.

Overrides   Object.equals()

Description   This returns true if obj is an instance of Integer and contains the same value as the object this method is associated with.

floatValue

```
public float floatValue()
```

Returns   The value of this object as a float.

Overrides   `Number.floatValue()`

Description   This method returns the value of this object as a `float`. Rounding may occur.

hashCode

`public int hashCode()`

Returns   A hashcode based on the `int` value of the object.

Overrides   `Object.hashCode()`

Description   This method returns a hashcode computed from the value of this object.

intValue

`public int intValue()`

Returns   The value of this object as an `int`.

Overrides   `Number.intValue()`

Description   This method returns the value of this object as an `int`.

longValue

`public long longValue()`

Returns   The value of this object as a `long`.

Overrides   `Number.longValue()`

Description   This method returns the value of this object as a `long`.

shortValue

`public short shortValue()`

Availability   New as of JDK 1.1

Returns   The value of this object as a `short`.

Overrides   `Number.shortValue()`

Description   This method returns the value of this object as a `short`. The high order bits of the value are discarded.

toString

`public String toString()`

Returns   The string representation of the value of this object.

Overrides   `Object.toString()`

Description   This method returns a `String` object that contains the decimal representation of the value of this object.

This returns a string that begins with '–' if the value is negative. The rest of the string is a sequence of one or more of the characters '0', '1', '2', '3', '4', '5', '6', '7', '8', and '9'. This method returns "0" if the value of the object is 0. Otherwise, the string returned by this method does not begin with "0" or "–0".

Inherited Methods

Method	Inherited From	Method	Inherited From
clone()	Object	finalize()	Object
getClass()	Object	notify()	Object
notifyAll()	Object	wait()	Object
wait(long)	Object	wait(long, int)	Object

See Also

Character 10.3; Class 10.4; Exceptions 9.4.1; Integer literals 2.2.3.1; Integer types 3.1.1.1; Long 10.11; Number 10.13; String 10.20; System 10.22

10.11   Long

Synopsis

Class Name: java.lang.Long
Superclass: java.lang.Number
Immediate Subclasses: None
Interfaces Implemented: None
Availability: JDK 1.0 or later

Description

The Long class provides an object wrapper for a long value. This is useful when you need to treat a long value as an object. For example, there are a number of utility methods that take a reference to an Object as one of their arguments. You cannot specify a long value for one of these arguments, but you can provide a reference to a Long object that encapsulates the long value. Furthermore, as of JDK 1.1, the Long class is necessary to support the Reflection API and class literals.

The Long class also provides a number of utility methods for converting long values to other primitive types and for converting long values to strings and vice versa.

Class Summary

```
public final class java.lang.Long extends java.lang.Number {
    // Constants
    public static final long MIN_VALUE;
    public static final long MAX_VALUE;
    public final static Class TYPE;                    // New in 1.1
```

```
// Constructors
public Long(long value);
public Long(String s);

// Class Methods
public static Long getLong(String nm);
public static Long getLong(String nm, long val);
public static Long getLong(String nm, Long val);
public static long parseLong(String s);
public static long parseLong(String s, int radix);
public static String toBinaryString(long i);
public static String toHexString(long i);
public static String toOctalString(long i);
public static String toString(long i);
public static String toString(long i, int radix);
public static Long valueOf(String s);
public static Long valueOf(String s, int radix);

// Instance Methods
public byte byteValue();                          // New in 1.1
public double doubleValue();
public boolean equals(Object obj);
public float floatValue();
public int hashCode();
public int intValue();
public long longValue();
public short shortValue();                        // New in 1.1
public String toString();
}
```

Constants

MAX_VALUE

public static final long MAX_VALUE = 0x7fffffffffffffffL

    Description   The largest value that can be represented by a long.

MIN_VALUE

public static final long MIN_VALUE = 0x8000000000000000L

    Description   The smallest value that can be represented by a long.

TYPE

public static final Class TYPE

    Availability   New as of JDK 1.1

    Description   The Class object that represents the type long. It is always true that Long.TYPE == long.class.

Constructors

Long

```
public Long(long value)
```
> Parameters   value   The long value to be encapsulated by this object.
>
> Description   Creates a Long object with the specified long value.

```
public Long(String s) throws NumberFormatException
```
> Parameters   s   The string to be made into a Long object.
>
> Throws   NumberFormatException
>
>   If the sequence of characters in the given String does not form a valid long literal.
>
> Description   Constructs a Long object with the value specified by the given string. The string should consist of one or more digit characters. The digit characters can be preceded by a single '-' character. If the string contains any other characters, the constructor throws a NumberFormatException.

Class Methods

getLong

```
public static Integer getLong(String nm)
```
> Parameters   nm   The name of a system property.
>
> Returns   The value of the system property as a Long object or a Long object with the value 0 if the named property does not exist or cannot be parsed.
>
> Description   This method retrieves the value of the named system property and returns it as a Long object. The method obtains the value of the system property as a String using System.getProperty().
>
>   If the value of the property begins with 0x or # and is not followed by a minus sign, the rest of the value is parsed as a hexadecimal integer. If the value begins with 0, it's parsed as an octal integer; otherwise it's parsed as a decimal integer.

```
public static Long getLong(String nm, long val)
```
> Parameters   nm   The name of a system property.
>
>   val   A default value for the property.
>
> Returns   The value of the system property as a Long object or a Long object with the value val if the named property does not exist or cannot be parsed.
>
> Description   This method retrieves the value of the named system property and returns it as a Long object. The method obtains the value of the system property as a String using System.getProperty().

If the value of the property begins with 0x or # and is not followed by a minus sign, the rest of the value is parsed as a hexadecimal integer. If the value begins with 0, it's parsed as an octal integer; otherwise it's parsed as a decimal integer.

```
public static Long getLong(String nm, Long val)
```

Parameters | nm | The name of a system property.
| val | A default value for the property.

Returns | The value of the system property as a Long object, or the Long object val if the named property does not exist or cannot be parsed.

Description | This method retrieves the value of the named system property and returns it as a Long object. The method obtains the value of the system property as a String using System.getProperty().

If the value of the property begins with 0x or # and is not followed by a minus sign, the rest of the value is parsed as a hexadecimal integer. If the value begins with 0, it's parsed as an octal integer; otherwise it's parsed as a decimal integer.

parseLong

```
public static long parseLong(String s)
                  throws NumberFormatException
```

Parameters | s | The String to be converted to a long value.
Returns | The numeric value of the long represented by the String object.
Throws | NumberFormatException
| | If the String does not contain a valid representation of a long value.
Description | This method returns the numeric value of the long represented by the contents of the given String object. The String must contain only decimal digits, except that the first character may be a minus sign.

```
public static long parseLong(String s, int radix)
                  throws NumberFormatException
```

Parameters | s | The String to be converted to a long value.
| radix | The radix used in interpreting the characters in the String as digits. It must be in the range Character.MIN_RADIX to Character.MAX_RADIX. If radix is in the range 2 through 10, only characters for which the Character.isDigit() method returns true are considered valid digits. If radix is in the range 11 through 36,

characters in the ranges 'A' through 'Z' and 'a' through 'z' may be considered valid digits.

Returns	The numeric value of the `long` represented by the `String` object in the specified radix.
Throws	`NumberFormatException`
	If the `String` does not contain a valid representation of a `long` or `radix` is not in the appropriate range.
Description	This method returns the numeric value of the `long` represented by the contents of the given `String` object in the specified radix. The `String` must contain only valid digits of the specified radix, except that the first character may be a minus sign. The digits are parsed in the specified radix to produce the numeric value.

toBinaryString

`public static String toBinaryString(long value)`

Parameters	`value` The `long` value to be converted to a string.
Returns	A string that contains the binary representation of the given value.
Description	This method returns a `String` object that contains the representation of the given value as an unsigned binary number. To convert the given value to an unsigned quantity, the method simply uses the value as if it were not negative. In other words, if the given value is negative, the method adds 2^{64} to it. Otherwise the value is used as it is.

The string returned by this method contains a sequence of one or more '0' and '1' characters. The method returns "0" if its argument is 0. Otherwise, the string returned by this method begins with '1'.

toHexString

`public static String toHexString(long value)`

Parameters	`value` The `long` value to be converted to a string.
Returns	A string that contains the hexadecimal representation of the given value.
Description	This method returns a `String` object that contains the representation of the given value as an unsigned hexadecimal number. To convert the given value to an unsigned quantity, the method simply uses the value as if it were not negative. In other words, if the given value is negative, the method adds 2^{64} to it. Otherwise the value is used as it is.

The string returned by this method contains a sequence of one or more of the characters '0', '1', '2', '3', '4', '5', '6', '7', '8', '9', 'a', 'b', 'c', 'd', 'e', and 'f'. The method returns "0" if its argument is 0. Otherwise, the string returned by this method does not begin with '0'.

To produce a string that contains upper- instead of lowercase letters, use the `String.toUpperCase()` method.

toOctalString

```
public static String toOctalString(long value)
```

Parameters   value   The long value to be converted to a string.

Returns   A string that contains the octal representation of the given value.

Description   This method returns a String object that contains a representation of the given value as an unsigned octal number. To convert the given value to an unsigned quantity, the method simply uses the value as if it were not negative. In other words, if the given value is negative, the method adds 2^{64} to it. Otherwise the value is used as it is.

The string returned by this method contains a sequence of one or more of the characters '0', '1', '2', '3', '4', '5', '6', and '7'. The method returns "0" if its argument is 0. Otherwise, the string returned by this method does not begin with '0'.

toString

```
public static String toString(long i)
```

Parameters   i   The long value to be converted to a string.

Returns   The string representation of the given value.

Description   This method returns a String object that contains the decimal representation of the given value.

This method returns a string that begins with – if the given value is negative. The rest of the string is a sequence of one or more of the characters '0', '1', '2', '3', '4', '5', '6', '7', '8', and '9'. This method returns "0" if its argument is 0. Otherwise, the string returned by this method does not begin with "0" or "-0".

```
public static String toString(long i, int radix)
```

Parameters   i   The long value to be converted to a string.

              radix   The radix used in converting the value to a string. This value must be in the range Character.MIN_RADIX to Character.MAX_RADIX.

Returns   The string representation of the given value in the specified radix.

Description   This method returns a `String` object that contains the representation of the given value in the specified radix.

This method returns a string that begins with '-' if the given value is negative. The rest of the string is a sequence of one or more characters that represent the magnitude of the given value. The characters that can appear in the sequence are determined by the value of `radix`. If *N* is the value of `radix`, the first *N* characters on the following line can appear in the sequence:

`0123456789abcdefghijklmnopqrstuvwxyz`

The method does not verify that `radix` is in the proper range. If `radix` is less than `Character.MIN_RADIX` or greater than `Character.MAX_RADIX`, the value 10 is used instead of the given value.

This method returns "0" if its argument is 0. Otherwise, the string returned by this method does not begin with "0" or "-0".

valueOf

```
public static Long valueOf(String s)
                    throws NumberFormatException
```

Parameters   s   The string to be made into a `Long` object.

Returns   The `Long` object constructed from the string.

Throws   `NumberFormatException`
                                If the `String` does not contain a valid representation of a `long`.

Description   Constructs a `Long` object with the value specified by the given string. The string should consist of one or more digit characters. The digit characters can be preceded by a single '-' character. If the string contains any other characters, the method throws a `NumberFormatException`.

```
public static Long valueOf(String s, int radix)
                    throws NumberFormatException
```

Parameters   s   The string to be made into a `Long` object.

                 radix   The radix used in converting the string to a value. This value must be in the range `Character.MIN_RADIX` to `Character.MAX_RADIX`.

Returns	The Long object constructed from the string.
Throws	NumberFormatException
	If the String does not contain a valid representation of a long.
Description	Constructs a Long object with the value specified by the given string in the specified radix. The string should consist of one or more digit characters or characters in the range 'A' to 'Z' or 'a' to 'z' that are considered digits in the given radix. The digit characters can be preceded by a single '–' character. If the string contains any other characters, the method throws a NumberFormatException.

The method does not verify that radix is in the proper range. If radix is less than Character.MIN_RADIX or greater than Character.MAX_RADIX, the value 10 is used instead of the given value.

Instance Methods

byteValue

```
public byte byteValue()
```

Availability	New as of JDK 1.1
Returns	The value of this object as a byte.
Overrides	Number.byteValue()
Description	This method returns the value of this object as a byte. The high order bits of the value are discarded.

doubleValue

```
public double doubleValue()
```

Returns	The value of this object as a double.
Overrides	Number.doubleValue()
Description	This method returns the value of this object as a double. Rounding may occur.

equals

```
public boolean equals(Object obj)
```

Parameters	obj	The object to be compared with this object.
Returns	true if the objects are equal; false if they are not.	
Overrides	Object.equals()	
Description	This method returns true if obj is an instance of Long and it contains the same value as the object this method is associated with.	

floatValue

public float floatValue()

Returns	The value of this object as a `float`.
Overrides	`Number.floatValue()`
Description	This method returns the value of this object as a `float`. Rounding may occur.

hashCode

public int hashCode()

Returns	A hashcode based on the `long` value of the object.
Overrides	`Object.hashCode()`
Description	This method returns a hashcode computed from the value of this object. More specifically, the result is the exclusive OR of the two halves of the `long` value represented by the object. If value is the value of the object, the method returns a result equivalent to the following expression:

```
(int)(value^(value>>>32))
```

intValue

public int intValue()

Returns	The value of this object as an `int`.
Overrides	`Number.intValue()`
Description	This method returns the value of this object as an `int`. The high-order bits of the value are discarded.

longValue

public long longValue()

Returns	The value of this object as a `long`.
Overrides	`Number.longValue()`
Description	This method returns the value of this object as a `long`.

shortValue

public short shortValue()

Availability	New as of JDK 1.1
Returns	The value of this object as a `short`.
Overrides	`Number.shortValue()`
Description	This method returns the value of this object as a `short`. The high-order bits of the value are discarded.

toString

```
public String toString()
```

Returns	The string representation of the value of this object.
Overrides	Object.toString()
Description	This method returns a String object that contains the decimal representation of the value of this object.

This method returns a string that begins with '-' if the value is negative. The rest of the string is a sequence of one or more of the characters '0', '1', '2', '3', '4', '5', '6', '7', '8', and '9'. This method returns "0" if the value of the object is 0. Otherwise, the string returned by this method does not begin with "0" or "-0".

Inherited Methods

Method	Inherited From	Method	Inherited From
clone()	Object	finalize()	Object
getClass()	Object	notify()	Object
notifyAll()	Object	wait()	Object
wait(long)	Object	wait(long, int)	Object

See Also

Character 10.3; Class 10.4; Exceptions 9.4.1; Integer 10.10; Integer literals 2.2.3.1; Integer types 3.1.1.1; Number 10.13; String 10.20; System 10.22

10.12 Math

Synopsis

Class Name:	java.lang.Math
Superclass:	java.lang.Object
Immediate Subclasses:	None
Interfaces Implemented:	None
Availability:	JDK 1.0 or later

Description

The Math class contains constants for the mathematical values π and e. The class also defines methods that compute various mathematical functions, such as trigonometric and exponential functions. All of these constants and methods are static. In other words, it is not necessary to create an instance of the Math class in order to use its constants and methods. In fact, the Math class does not define any public constructors, so it cannot be instantiated.

To ensure that the methods in this class return consistent results under different implementations of Java, all of the methods use the algorithms from the well-known Freely-Distributable Math Library package, *fdlibm*. This package is part of the network library *netlib*. The library can be obtained through the URL *http://netlib.att.com*. The algorithms used in this class are from the version of *fdlibm* dated January 4, 1995. *fdlibm* provides more than one definition for some functions. In those cases, the "IEEE 754 core function" version is used.

Class Summary

```
public final class java.lang.Math extends java.lang.Object {
    // Constants
    public static final double E;
    public static final double PI;

    // Class Methods
    public static int abs(int a);
    public static long abs(long a);
    public static float abs(float a);
    public static double abs(double a);
    public static native double acos(double a);
    public static native double asin(double a);
    public static native double atan(double a);
    public static native double atan2(double a, double b);
    public static native double ceil(double a);
    public static native double cos(double a);
    public static native double exp(double a);
    public static native double floor(double a);
    public static native double IEEEremainder(double f1, double f2);
    public static native double log(double a);
    public static int max(int a, int b);
    public static long max(long a, long b);
    public static float max(float a, float b);
    public static double max(double a, double b);
    public static int min(int a, int b);
    public static long min(long a, long b);
    public static float min(float a, float b);
    public static double min(double a, double b);
    public static native double pow(double a, double b);
    public static synchronized double random();
```

```
    public static native double rint(double a);
    public static int round(float a);
    public static long round(double a);
    public static native double sin(double a);
    public static native double sqrt(double a);
    public static native double tan(double a);
}
```

Constants

E

```
public static final double E = 2.7182818284590452354
```
    Description   The value of this constant is *e*, the base for natural logarithms.

PI

```
public static final double PI = 3.14159265358979323846
```
    Description   The value for this constant is π.

Class Methods

abs

```
public static double abs(double a)
```
    Parameters   a   A double value.

    Returns   The absolute value of its argument.

    Description   This method returns the absolute value of its argument.

    If the argument to this method is negative or positive zero, the method should return positive zero. If the argument is positive or negative infinity, the method returns positive infinity. If the argument is NaN, the method returns NaN.

```
public static float abs(float a)
```
    Parameters   a   A float value.

    Returns   The absolute value of its argument.

    Description   This method returns the absolute value of its argument.

    If the argument to this method is negative or positive zero, the method should return positive zero. If the argument is positive or negative infinity, the method returns positive infinity. If the argument is NaN, the method returns NaN.

```
public static int abs(int a)
```
    Parameters   a   An int value.

    Returns   The absolute value of its argument.

    Description   This method returns the absolute value of its argument.

    If the argument is Integer.MIN_VALUE, the method actually returns Integer.MIN_VALUE because the true absolute value of

Integer.MIN_VALUE is one greater than the largest positive value that can be represented by an int.

public static long abs(long a)

Parameters	a	A long value.
Returns		The absolute value of its argument.
Description		This method returns the absolute value of its argument.

If the argument is Long.MIN_VALUE, the method actually returns Long.MIN_VALUE because the true absolute value of Long.MIN_VALUE is one greater than the largest positive value represented by a long.

acos

public static native double acos(double a)

Parameters	a	A double value greater than or equal to -1.0 and less than or equal to 1.0.
Returns		The arc cosine measured in radians; the result is greater than or equal to 0.0 and less than or equal to π.
Description		This method returns the arc cosine of the given value.

If the value is NaN or its absolute value is greater than 1.0, the method returns NaN.

asin

public static native double asin(double a)

Parameters	a	A double value greater than or equal to -1.0 and less than or equal to 1.0.
Returns		The arc sine measured in radians; the result is greater than or equal to $-\pi/2$ and less than or equal to $\pi/2$.
Description		This method returns the arc sine of the given value.

If the value is NaN or its absolute value is greater than 1.0, the method returns NaN. If the value is positive zero, the method returns positive zero. If the value is negative zero, the method returns negative zero.

atan

public static native double atan(double a)

Parameters	a	A double value greater than or equal to -1.0 and less than or equal to 1.0.
Returns		The arc tangent measured in radians; the result is greater than or equal to $-\pi/2$ and less than or equal to $\pi/2$.

Description   This method returns the principle value of the arc tangent of the given value.

If the value is NaN, the method returns NaN. If the value is positive zero, the method returns positive zero. If the value is negative zero, the method returns negative zero.

atan2

```
public static native double atan2(double a, double b)
```

Parameters   a   A double value.

b   A double value.

Returns   The θ component of the polar coordinate (r, θ) that corresponds to the cartesian coordinate (a,b); the result is measured in radians and is greater than or equal to $-\pi$ and less than or equal to π.

Description   This method returns the θ component of the polar coordinate (r, θ) that corresponds to the cartesian coordinate (a,b). It computes θ as the principle value of the arc tangent of b/a, using the signs of both arguments to determine the quadrant (and sign) of the return value.

If either argument is NaN, the method returns NaN.

If the first argument is positive zero and the second argument is positive, then the method returns positive zero. If the first argument is positive zero and the second argument is negative, then the method returns the double value closest to π.

If the first argument is negative zero and the second argument is positive, the method returns negative zero. If the first argument is negative zero and the second argument is negative, the method returns the double value closest to $-\pi$.

If the first argument is positive and finite and the second argument is positive infinity, the method returns positive zero. If the first argument is positive and finite and the second argument is negative infinity, the method returns the double value closest to π.

If the first argument is negative and finite and the second argument is positive infinity, the method returns negative zero. If the first argument is negative and finite and the second argument is negative infinity, the method returns the double value closest to $-\pi$.

If the first argument is positive and the second argument is positive zero or negative zero, the method returns the double value closest to $\pi/2$. If the first argument is negative and the second argument is positive or negative zero, the method returns the double value closest to $-\pi/2$.

If the first argument is positive infinity and the second argument is finite, the method returns the double value closest to $\pi/2$. If the first argument is negative infinity and the second argument is finite, the method returns the double value closest to $-\pi/2$.

If both arguments are positive infinity, the method returns the double value closest to $\pi/4$. If the first argument is positive infinity and the second argument is negative infinity, the method returns the double value closest to $3\pi/4$. If the first argument is negative infinity and the second argument is positive infinity, the method returns the double value closest to $-\pi/4$. If both arguments are negative infinity, the method returns the double value closest to $-3\pi/4$.

ceil

```
public static native double ceil(double a)
```
Parameters	a	A double value.
Returns		The smallest integer greater than or equal to the given value.
Description		This method performs the ceiling operation. It returns the smallest integer that is greater than or equal to its argument.

If the argument is NaN, an infinity value, or a zero value, the method returns that same value. If the argument is less than zero but greater than -1.0, the method returns negative zero.

cos

```
public static native double cos(double a)
```
Parameters	a	A double value that's an angle measured in radians.
Returns		The cosine of the given angle.
Description		This method returns the cosine of the given angle measured in radians.

If the angle is NaN or an infinity value, the method returns NaN.

exp

```
public static native double exp(double a)
```
    Parameters   a   A double value.

    Returns e^a

    Description   This method returns the exponential function of a. In other words, e is raised to the value specified by the parameter a, where e is the base of the natural logarithms.

                  If the value is NaN, the method returns NaN. If the value is positive infinity, the method returns positive infinity. If the value is negative infinity, the method returns positive zero.

floor

```
public static native double floor(double a)
```
    Parameters   a   A double value.

    Returns   The greatest integer less than or equal to the given value.

    Description   This method performs the floor operation. It returns the largest integer that is less than or equal to its argument.

                  If the argument is NaN, an infinity value, or a zero value, the method returns that same value.

IEEEremainder

```
public static native double IEEEremainder(double a, double b)
```
    Parameters   a   A double value.

                   b   A double value.

    Returns   The remainder of a divided by b as defined by the IEEE 754 standard.

    Description   This method returns the remainder of a divided by b as defined by the IEEE 754 standard. This operation involves first determining the mathematical quotient of a/b rounded to the nearest integer. If the quotient is equally close to two integers, it is rounded to the even integer. The method then returns $a-(b \times Q)$, where Q is the rounded quotient.

                  If either argument is NaN, the method returns NaN. If the first argument is positive or negative infinity and the second argument is positive or negative zero, the method also returns NaN. If the first argument is a finite value and the second argument is positive or negative infinity, the method returns its first argument.

log

```
public static native double log(double a)
```
Parameters   a   A double value that is greater than 0.0.

Returns   The natural logarithm of a.

Description   This method returns the natural logarithm (base *e*) of its argument.

In particular, if the argument is positive infinity, the method returns positive infinity. If the argument is positive or negative zero, the method returns negative infinity. If the argument is less than zero, the method returns NaN. If the argument is NaN, the method returns NaN.

max

```
public static double max(double a, double b)
```
Parameters   a   A double value.

              b   A double value.

Returns   The greater of a and b.

Description   This method returns the greater of its two arguments. In other words, it returns the one that is closer to positive infinity.

If one argument is positive zero and the other is negative zero, the method returns positive zero. If either argument is NaN, the method returns NaN.

```
public static float max(float a, float b)
```
Parameters   a   A float value.

              b   A float value.

Returns   The greater of a and b.

Description   This method returns the greater of its two arguments. In other words, it returns the one that is closer to positive infinity.

If one argument is positive zero and the other is negative zero, the method returns positive zero. If either argument is NaN, the method returns NaN.

```
public static int max(int a, int b)
```
Parameters   a   An int value.

              b   An int value.

Returns   The greater of a and b.

Description   This method returns the greater of its two arguments. In other words, it returns the one that is closer to Integer.MAX_VALUE.

```
public static long max(long a, long b)
```
Parameters   a   A long value.
                b   A long value.
Returns   The greater of a and b.
Description   This method returns the greater of its two arguments. In other
                words, it returns the one that is closer to `Long.MAX_VALUE`.

min

```
public static double min(double a, double b)
```
Parameters   a   A double value.
                b   A double value.
Returns   The lesser of a and b.
Description   This method returns the lesser of its two arguments. In other
                words, it returns the one that is closer to negative infinity.

                If one argument is positive zero and the other is negative zero,
                the method returns negative zero. If either argument is NaN,
                the method returns NaN.

```
public static float min(float a, float b)
```
Parameters   a   A float value.
                b   A float value.
Returns   The lesser of a and b.
Description   This method returns the lesser of its two arguments. In other
                words, it returns the one that is closer to negative infinity.

                If one argument is positive zero and the other is negative zero,
                the method returns negative zero. If either argument is NaN,
                the method returns NaN.

```
public static int min(int a, int b)
```
Parameters   a   An int value.
                b   An int value.
Returns   The lesser of a and b.
Description   This method returns the lesser of its two arguments. In other
                words, it returns the one that is closer to `Integer.MIN_VALUE`.

```
public static long min(long a, long b)
```
Parameters   a   A long value.
                b   A long value.
Returns   The lesser of a and b.
Description   This method returns the lesser of its two arguments. In other
                words, it returns the one that is closer to `Long.MIN_VALUE`.

pow

```
public static native double pow(double a, double b)
```
Parameters   a   A double value.
                    b   A double value.
Returns a^b
Description   This method computes the value of raising a to the power of b.

If the second argument is positive or negative zero, the method returns 1.0. If the second argument is 1.0, the method returns its first argument. If the second argument is NaN, the method returns NaN. If the first argument is NaN and the second argument is nonzero, the method returns NaN.

If the first argument is positive zero and the second argument is greater than zero, the method returns positive zero. If the first argument is positive zero and the second argument is less than zero, the method returns positive infinity.

If the first argument is positive infinity and the second argument is less than zero, the method returns positive zero. If the first argument is positive infinity and the second argument is greater than zero, the method returns positive infinity.

If the absolute value of the first argument is greater than 1 and the second argument is positive infinity, the method returns positive infinity. If the absolute value of the first argument is greater than 1 and the second argument is negative infinity, the method returns positive zero. If the absolute value of the first argument is less than 1 and the second argument is negative infinity, the method returns positive infinity. If the absolute value of the first argument is less than 1 and the second argument is positive infinity, the method returns positive zero. If the absolute value of the first argument is 1 and the second argument is positive or negative infinity, the method returns NaN.

If the first argument is negative zero and the second argument is greater than zero but not a finite odd integer, the method returns positive zero. If the first argument is negative zero and the second argument is a positive finite odd integer, the method returns negative zero. If the first argument is negative zero and the second argument is less than zero but not a finite odd integer, the method returns positive infinity. If the first argument is negative zero and the second argument is a negative finite odd integer, the method returns negative infinity.

If the first argument is negative infinity and the second argument is less than zero but not a finite odd integer, the method returns positive zero. If the first argument is negative infinity and the second argument is a negative finite odd integer, the method returns negative zero. If the first argument is negative infinity and the second argument is greater than zero but not a finite odd integer, the method returns positive infinity. If the first argument is negative infinity and the second argument is a positive finite odd integer, the method returns negative infinity.

If the first argument is less than zero and the second argument is a finite even integer, the method returns the result of the absolute value of the first argument raised to the power of the second argument. If the first argument is less than zero and the second argument is a finite odd integer, the method returns the negative of the result of the absolute value of the first argument raised to the power of the second argument. If the first argument is finite and less than zero and the second argument is finite and not an integer, the method returns NaN.

If both arguments are integer values, the method returns the first argument raised to the power of the second argument.

random

`public static synchronized double random()`

Returns   A random number between `0.0` and `1.0`.

Description   This method returns a random number greater than or equal to `0.0` and less than `1.0`. The implementation of this method uses the `java.util.Random` class. You may prefer to use the `Random` class directly, in order to gain more control over the distribution, type, and repeatability of the random numbers you are generating.

rint

`public static native double rint(double a)`

Parameters   a   A `double` value.

Returns   The value of its argument rounded to the nearest integer.

Description   This method returns its argument rounded to the nearest integer; the result is returned as a `double` value. If the argument is equidistant from two integers (e.g., `1.5`), the method returns the even integer.

If the argument is an infinity value, a zero value, or NaN, the method returns that same value.

round

```
public static long round(double a)
```

Parameters   a   A double value.

Returns   The value of its argument rounded to the nearest `long`.

Description   This method returns its `double` argument rounded to the near-est integral value and converted to a `long`. If the argument is equidistant from two integers, the method returns the greater of the two integers.

If the argument is positive infinity or any other value greater than `Long.MAX_VALUE`, the method returns `Long.MAX_VALUE`. If the argument is negative infinity or any other value less than `Long.MIN_VALUE`, the method returns `Long.MIN_VALUE`. If the argument is NaN, the method returns 0.

```
public static int round(float a)
```

Parameters   a   A float value.

Returns   The value of its argument rounded to the nearest `int`.

Description   This method returns its `float` argument rounded to the near-est integral value and converted to an `int`. If the argument is equidistant from two integers, the method returns the greater of the two integers.

If the argument is positive infinity or any other value greater than the `Integer.MAX_VALUE`, the method returns `Integer.MAX_VALUE`. If the argument is negative infinity or any other value less than `Integer.MIN_VALUE`, the method returns `Integer.MIN_VALUE`. If the argument is NaN, the method returns 0.

sin

```
public static native double sin(double a)
```

Parameters   a   A double value that's an angle measured in radi-ans.

Returns   The sine of the given angle.

Description   This method returns the sine of the given angle measured in radians.

If the angle is NaN or an infinity value, the method returns NaN. If the angle is positive zero, the method returns positive zero. If the angle is negative zero, the method returns negative zero.

sqrt

```
public static native double sqrt(double a)
```

Parameters	a	A double value.
Returns		The square root of its argument.
Description		This method returns the square root of its argument.

If the argument is negative or NaN, the method returns NaN. If the argument is positive infinity, the method returns positive infinity. If the argument is positive or negative zero, the method returns that same value.

tan

```
public static native double tan(double a)
```

Parameters	a	A double value that is an angle measured in radians.
Returns		The tangent of the given angle.
Description		This method returns the tangent of the given angle measured in radians.

If the angle is NaN or an infinity value, the method returns NaN. If the angle is positive zero, the method returns positive zero. If the angle is negative zero, the method returns negative zero.

Inherited Methods

Method	Inherited From	Method	Inherited From
clone()	Object	equals(Object)	Object
finalize()	Object	getClass()	Object
hashCode()	Object	notify()	Object
notifyAll()	Object	toString()	Object
wait()	Object	wait(long)	Object
wait(long, int)	Object		

See Also

Double 10.8; Float 10.9; Floating-point literals 2.2.3.2; Floating-point types 3.1.1.2; Integer 10.10; Integer literals 2.2.3.1; Integer types 3.1.1.1; Long 10.11; Object 10.14

10.13 Number

Synopsis

Class Name:	java.lang.Number
Superclass:	java.lang.Object
Immediate Subclasses:	java.lang.Byte, java.lang.Double,
	java.lang.Float, java.lang.Integer,
	java.lang.Long, java.lang.Short,
	java.math.BigDecimal,
	java.math.BigInteger
Interfaces Implemented:	java.io.Serializable
Availability:	JDK 1.0 or later

Description

The Number class is an abstract class that serves as the superclass for all of the classes that provide object wrappers for primitive numeric values: byte, short, int, long, float, and double. Wrapping a primitive value is useful when you need to treat such a value as an object. For example, there are a number of utility methods that take a reference to an Object as one of their arguments. You cannot specify a primitive value for one of these arguments, but you can provide a reference to an object that encapsulates the primitive value. Furthermore, as of JDK 1.1, these wrapper classes are necessary to support the Reflection API and class literals.

The Number class defines six methods that must be implemented by its subclasses: byteValue(), shortValue(), intValue(), longValue(), floatValue(), and doubleValue(). This means that a Number object can be fetched as an byte, short, int, long, float, or double value, without regard for its actual class.

Class Summary

```
public abstract class java.lang.Number extends java.lang.Number
                                implements java.io.Serializable {
    // Instance Methods
    public abstract byte byteValue();                  // New in 1.1
    public abstract double doubleValue();
    public abstract float floatValue();
    public abstract int intValue();
    public abstract long longValue();
    public abstract short shortValue();                // New in 1.1
}
```

Instance Methods

byteValue

```
public abstract byte byteValue()
```

Availability	New as of JDK 1.1
Returns	The value of this object as a byte.
Description	This method returns the value of this object as a byte. If the data type of the value is not byte, rounding may occur.

doubleValue

```
public abstract double doubleValue()
```

Returns	The value of this object as a double.
Description	This method returns the value of this object as a double. If the data type of the value is not double, rounding may occur.

floatValue

```
public abstract float floatValue()
```

Returns	The value of this object as a float.
Description	This method returns the value of this object as a float. If the data type of the value is not float, rounding may occur.

intValue

```
public abstract int intValue()
```

Returns	The value of this object as an int.
Description	This method returns the value of this object as an int. If the type of value is not an int, rounding may occur.

longValue

```
public abstract long longValue()
```

Returns	The value of this object as a long.
Description	This method returns the value of this object as a long. If the type of value is not a long, rounding may occur.

shortValue

```
public abstract short shortValue()
```

Availability	New as of JDK 1.1
Returns	The value of this object as a short.
Description	This method returns the value of this object as a short. If the type of value is not a short, rounding may occur.

Inherited Methods

Method	Inherited From	Method	Inherited From
clone()	Object	equals(Object)	Object
finalize()	Object	getClass()	Object
hashCode()	Object	notify()	Object
notifyAll()	Object	toString()	Object
wait()	Object	wait(long)	Object
wait(long, int)	Object		

See Also

Byte 10.2; Double 10.8; Float 10.9; Integer 10.10; Long 10.11; Object 10.14; Short 10.19

10.14 Object

Synopsis

Class Name: java.lang.Object
Superclass: None
Immediate Subclasses: Too many to be listed here
Interfaces Implemented: None
Availability: JDK 1.0 or later

Description

The Object class is the ultimate superclass of all other classes in Java. Because every other class is a subclass of Object, all of the methods accessible from Object are inherited by every other class. In other words, all objects in Java, including arrays, have access to implementations of the methods in Object.

The methods of Object provide some basic object functionality. The equals() method compares two objects for equality, while the hashCode() method returns a hashcode for an object. The getClass() method returns the Class object associated with an object. The wait(), notify(), and notifyAll() methods support thread synchronization for an object. The toString() method provides a string representation of an object.

Some of these methods should be overridden by subclasses of Object. For example, every class should provide its own implementation of the toString() method, so that it can provide an appropriate string representation.

Although it is possible to create an instance of the Object class, this is rarely done because it is more useful to create specialized objects. However, it is often useful to declare a variable that contains a reference to an Object because such a variable can contain a reference to an object of any other class.

Class Summary

```
public class java.lang.Object {
    // Constructors
    public Object();

    // Public Instance Methods
    public boolean equals(Object obj);
    public final native Class getClass();
    public native int hashCode();
    public final native void notify();
    public final native void notifyAll();
    public String toString();
    public final native void wait();
    public final native void wait(long millis);
    public final native void wait(long millis, int nanos);

    // Protected Instance Methods
    protected native Object clone();
    protected void finalize() throws Throwable;
}
```

Constructors

Object

```
public Object()
```
Description   Creates an instance of the Object class.

Public Instance Methods

equals

```
public boolean equals(Object obj)
```
Parameters   obj   The object to be compared with this object.
Returns   true if the objects are equal; false if they are not.
Description   The equals() method of Object returns true if the obj parameter refers to the same object as the object this method is associated with. This is equivalent to using the == operator to compare two objects.

Some classes, such as String, override the equals() method to provide a comparison based on the contents of the two objects, rather than on the strict equality of the references. Any subclass can override the equals() method to implement an appropriate comparison, as long as the overriding method satisfies the following rules for an equivalence relation:

- The method is *reflexive*: given a reference x, x.equals(x) returns true.
- The method is *symmetric*: given references x and y, x.equals(y) returns true if and only if y.equals(x) returns true.
- The method is *transitive*: given references x, y, and z, if x.equals(y) returns true and y.equals(z) returns true, then x.equals(z) returns true.
- The method is *consistent*: given references x and y, multiple invocations of x.equals(y) consistently return true or consistently return false, provided that no information contained by the objects referenced by x or y changes.
- A comparison with null returns false: given a reference x that is non-null, x.equals(null) returns false.

getClass

public final native Class getClass()

Returns   A reference to the Class object that describes the class of this object.

Description   The getClass() method of Object returns the Class object that describes the class of this object. This method is final, so it cannot be overridden by subclasses.

hashCode

public native int hashCode()

Returns   A relatively unique value that should be the same for all objects that are considered equal.

Description   The hashCode() method of Object calculates a hashcode value for this object. The method returns an integer value that should be relatively unique to the object. If the equals() method for the object bases its result on the contents of the object, the hashcode() method should also base its result on the contents. The hashCode() method is provided for the benefit of hashtables, which store and retrieve elements using key values called *hashcodes*. The internal placement of a particular piece of data is determined by its hashcode; hashtables are designed to use hashcodes to provide efficient retrieval.

The java.util.Hashtable class provides an implementation of a hashtable that stores values of type Object. Each object is stored in the hashtable based on the hash code of its key object. It is important that each object have the most unique hash code possible. If two objects have the same hash code but they are not equal (as determined by equals()), a Hashtable that stores these two objects may need to spend additional time searching when it is trying to retrieve objects. The implementation of hashCode() in Object tries to make sure that every object has a distinct hash code by basing its result on the internal representation of a reference to the object.

Some classes, such as String, override the hashCode() method to produce values based on the contents of individual objects, instead of the objects themselves. In other words, two String objects that contain the exact same strings have the same hash code. If String did not override the hashCode() method inherited from Object, these two String objects would have different hash code values and it would be impossible to use String objects as keys for hashtables.

Any subclass can override the hashCode() method to implement an appropriate way of producing hash code values, as long as the overriding method satisfies the following rules:

- If the hashCode() method is called on the same object more than once during the execution of a Java application, it must consistently return the same integer value. The integer does not, however, need to be consistent between Java applications, or from one execution of an application to another execution of the same application.
- If two objects compare as equal according to their equals() methods, calls to the hashCode() methods for the objects must produce the same result.
- If two objects compare as not equal according to their equals() methods, calls to the hashCode() methods for the two objects are not required to produce distinct results. However, implementations of hashCode() that produce distinct results for unequal objects may improve the performance of hashtables.

In general, if a subclass overrides the equals() method of Object, it should also override the hashCode() method.

notify

`public final native void notify()`

Throws   `IllegalMonitorStateException`

If the method is called from a thread that does not hold this object's lock.

Description   The `notify()` method wakes up a thread that is waiting to return from a call to this object's `wait()` method. The awakened thread can resume executing as soon as it regains this object's lock. If more than one thread is waiting, the `notify()` method arbitrarily awakens just one of the threads.

The `notify()` method can be called only by a thread that is the current owner of this object's lock. A thread holds the lock on this object while it is executing a `synchronized` instance method of the object or executing the body of a `synchronized` statement that synchronizes on the object. A thread can also hold the lock for a `Class` object if it is executing a `synchronized` static method of that class.

This method is `final`, so it cannot be overridden by subclasses.

notifyAll

`public final native void notifyAll()`

Throws   `IllegalMonitorStateException`

If the method is called from a thread that does not hold this object's lock.

Description   The `notifyAll()` method wakes up all the threads that are waiting to return from a call to this object's `wait()` method. Each awakened thread can resume executing as soon as it regains this object's lock.

The `notifyAll()` method can be called only by a thread that is the current owner of this object's lock. A thread holds the lock on this object while it is executing a `synchronized` instance method of the object or executing the body of a `synchronized` statement that synchronizes on the object. A thread can also hold the lock for a `Class` object if it is executing a `synchronized` static method of that class.

This method is `final`, so it cannot be overridden by subclasses.

toString

```
public String toString()
```

Returns   The string representation of this object.

Description The toString() method of Object returns a generic string representation of this object. The method returns a String that consists of the object's class name, an "at" sign, and the unsigned hexadecimal representation of the value returned by the object's hashCode() method.

       Many classes override the toString() method to provide a string representation that is specific to that type of object. Any subclass can override the toString() method; the overriding method should simply return a String that represents the contents of the object with which it is associated.

wait

```
public final native void wait() throws InterruptedException
```

Throws   IllegalMonitorStateException

        If the method is called from a thread that does not hold this object's lock.

       InterruptedException

        If another thread interrupted this thread.

Description The wait() method causes a thread to wait until it is notified by another thread to stop waiting. When wait() is called, the thread releases its lock on this object and waits until another thread notifies it to wake up through a call to either notify() or notifyAll(). After the thread is awakened, it has to regain the lock on this object before it can resume executing.

       The wait() method can be called only by a thread that is the current owner of this object's lock. A thread holds the lock on this object while it is executing a synchronized instance method of the object or executing the body of a synchronized statement that synchronizes on the object. A thread can also hold the lock for a Class object if it is executing a synchronized static method of that class.

       This method is final, so it cannot be overridden by subclasses.

```
public final native void wait(long timeout)
                         throws InterruptedException
```

Parameters timeout The maximum number of milliseconds to wait.

| Throws | IllegalMonitorStateException |
| | If the method is called from a thread that does not hold this object's lock. |

InterruptedException
    If another thread interrupted this thread.

Description The wait() method causes a thread to wait until it is notified by another thread to stop waiting or until the specified amount of time has elapsed, whichever comes first. When wait() is called, the thread releases its lock on this object and waits until another thread notifies it to wake up through a call to either notify() or notifyAll(). If the thread is not notified within the specified timeout period, it is automatically awakened when that amount of time has elapsed. If timeout is zero, the thread waits indefinitely, just as if wait() had been called without a timeout argument. After the thread is awakened, it has to regain the lock on this object before it can resume executing.

The wait() method can be called only by a thread that is the current owner of this object's lock. A thread holds the lock on this object while it is executing a synchronized instance method of the object or executing the body of a synchronized statement that synchronizes on the object. A thread can also hold the lock for a Class object if it is executing a synchronized static method of that class.

This method is final, so it cannot be overridden by subclasses.

public final native void wait(long timeout, int nanos)
                throws InterruptedException

Parameters	timeout	The maximum number of milliseconds to wait.
	nanos	An additional number of nanoseconds to wait.
Throws	IllegalMonitorStateException
	If the method is called from a thread that does not hold this object's lock.

InterruptedException
    If another thread interrupted this thread.

Description The wait() method causes a thread to wait until it is notified by another thread to stop waiting or until the specified amount of time has elapsed, whichever comes first. When wait() is called, the thread releases its lock on this object and waits until another thread notifies it to wake up through a call to either notify() or notifyAll(). If the thread is not notified within the specified time period, it is automatically awakened when that amount of time has elapsed. If timeout and nanos are zero, the thread waits indefinitely, just as if wait() had been called without any arguments. After the thread is awakened, it has to regain the lock on this object before it can resume executing.

The wait() method can be called only by a thread that is the current owner of this object's lock. A thread holds the lock on this object while it is executing a synchronized instance method of the object or executing the body of a synchronized statement that synchronizes on the object. A thread can also hold the lock for a Class object if it is executing a synchronized static method of that class.

Note that Sun's reference implementation of Java does not attempt to implement the precision implied by this method. Instead, it rounds to the nearest millisecond (unless timeout is 0, in which case it rounds up to 1 millisecond) and calls wait(long).

This method is final, so it cannot be overridden by subclasses.

Protected Instance Methods

clone

protected native Object clone() throws CloneNotSupportedException

Returns   A clone of this object.

Throws   OutOfMemoryError

                If there is not enough memory to create the new object.

                CloneNotSupportedException

                If the object is of a class that does not support clone().

Description   A *clone* of an object is another object of the same type that has all of its instance variables set to the same values as the object being cloned. In other words, a clone is an exact copy of the original object.

The clone() method of Object creates a new object that is a clone of this object. No constructor is used in creating the clone. The clone() method only clones an object if the class of that object indicates that its instances can be cloned. A class indicates that its objects can be cloned by implementing the Cloneable interface.

Although array objects do not implement the Cloneable interface, the clone() method works for arrays. The clone of an array is an array that has the same number of elements as the original array, and each element in the clone array has the same value as the corresponding element in the original array. Note that if an array element contains an object reference, the clone array contains a reference to the same object, not a copy of the object.

A subclass of Object can override the clone() method in Object to provide any additional functionality that is needed. For example, if an object contains references to other objects, the clone() method should recursively call the clone() methods of all the referenced objects. An overriding clone() method can throw a CloneNotSupportedException to indicate that particular objects cannot be cloned.

finalize

protected void finalize() throws Throwable

Throws   Throwable   For any reason that suits an overriding imple-
                          mentation of this method.

Description   The finalize() method is called by the garbage collector
              when it decides that an object can never be referenced again.
              The method gives an object a chance to perform any cleanup
              operations that are necessary before it is destroyed by the
              garbage collector.

              The finalize() method of Object does nothing. A subclass
              overrides the finalize() method to perform any necessary
              cleanup operations. The overriding method should call
              super.finalize() as the very last thing it does, so that any
              finalize() method in the superclass is called.

              When the garbage collector calls an object's finalize()
              method, the garbage collector does not immediately destroy
              the object because the finalize() method might do some-
              thing that results in a reference to the object. Thus the garbage
              collector waits to destroy the object until it can again prove it is
              safe to do so. The next time the garbage collector decides it is
              safe to destroy the object, it does so without calling finalize()
              again. In other words, the garbage collector never calls the
              finalize() method more than once for a particular object.

              A finalize() method can throw any kind of exception. An
              exception causes the finalize() method to stop running. The
              garbage collector then catches and ignores the exception, so it
              has no further effect on a program.

See Also

Equality Comparison Operators 4.9; Exceptions 9.4.1; Object Destruction 5.3.4; The finalize method 5.4.8; String 10.20; Threads 8; Throwable 10.25

10.15   Process

Synopsis

Class Name: java.lang.Process
Superclass: java.lang.Object
Immediate Subclasses: None that are provided on all platforms. However, a platform-specific version of Java should include at least one operating-system-specific subclass.
Interfaces Implemented: None
Availability: JDK 1.0 or later

Description

The Process class describes processes that are started by the exec() method in the Runtime class. A Process object controls a process and gets information about it.

The Process class is an abstract class; therefore, it cannot be instantiated. The actual Process objects created by the exec() method belong to operating-system-specific subclasses of Process that implement the Process methods in platform-dependent ways.

Note that losing all references to a Process object, thereby making it garbage collectable, does not result in the underlying Process object dying. It merely means that there is no longer a Java object to control the process. The process itself continues to run asynchronously. In addition, no guarantees are made as to whether a controlled process will be able to continue after its parent process dies.

Class Summary

```
public abstract class java.lang.Process extends java.lang.Object {
    // Constructors
    public Process();

    // Instance Methods
    public abstract void destroy();
    public abstract int exitValue();
    public abstract InputStream getErrorStream();
    public abstract InputStream getInputStream();
```

```
public abstract OutputStream getOutputStream();
public abstract int waitFor();
}
```

Constructors

Process

public Process()

    Description   Creates a Process object.

Instance Methods

destroy

abstract public void destroy()

    Description   This method kills the process controlled by this object.

exitValue

abstract public int exitValue()

    Returns   The exit value of the process controlled by this object.

    Throws   IllegalThreadStateException

            If the process is still running and the exit value is not yet available.

    Description   This method returns the exit value of the process that this object is controlling.

            The waitFor() method is a similar method that waits for the controlled process to terminate and then returns its exit value.

getErrorStream

abstract public InputStream getErrorStream()

    Returns   An InputStream object connected to the error stream of the process.

    Description   This method returns an InputStream object that can read from the error stream of the process.

            Although it is suggested that this InputStream not be buffered, the Java specification does not forbid such an implementation. In other words, although error output from programs is traditionally unbuffered, there is no guarantee that it won't be buffered. This means that error output written by the process may not be received immediately.

getInputStream

abstract public InputStream getInputStream()

Returns	An InputStream object that is connected to the standard output stream of the process.
Description	This method returns an InputStream object that can read from the standard output stream of the process.

This InputStream is likely to be buffered, which means that output written by the process may not be received immediately.

getOutputStream

abstract public OutputStream getOutputStream()

Returns	An OutputStream object that is connected to the standard input stream of the process.
Description	This method returns an OutputStream object that can write to the standard input stream of the process.

This OutputStream is likely to be buffered, which means that input sent to the process may not be received until the buffer fills up or a new line or carriage-return character is sent.

waitFor

abstract public int waitFor()

Returns	The exit value of the process controlled by this object.
Throws	InterruptedException
	If another thread interrupts this thread while it is waiting for the process to exit.
Description	This method returns the exit value of the process that this object is controlling. If the process is still running, the method waits until the process terminates and its exit value is available.

The exitValue() method is a similar method that does not wait for the controlled process to terminate.

Inherited Methods

Method	Inherited From	Method	Inherited From
clone()	Object	equals(Object)	Object
finalize()	Object	getClass()	Object
hashCode()	Object	notify()	Object
notifyAll()	Object	toString()	Object
wait()	Object	wait(long)	Object
wait(long, int)	Object		

See Also

Exceptions 9.4.1; Object 10.14; Runtime 10.17

10.16   Runnable

Synopsis

Interface Name: `java.lang.Runnable`
Super-interface: None
Immediate Sub-interfaces:
                         None
Implemented By: `java.lang.Thread`
Availability: JDK 1.0 or later

Description

The `Runnable` interface declares the `run()` method that is required for use with the `Thread` class. Any class that implements the `Runnable` interface must define a `run()` method. This method is the top-level code that is run by a thread.

Interface Declaration

```
public interface java.lang.Runnable {
    // Methods
    public abstract void run();
}
```

Methods

run

`public abstract void run()`

Description   When a `Thread` object starts running a thread, it associates executable code with the thread by calling a `Runnable` object's `run()` method. The subsequent behavior of the thread is controlled by the `run()` method. Thus, a class that wants to perform certain operations in a separate thread should implement the `Runnable` interface and define an appropriate `run()` method. When the `run()` method called by a `Thread` object returns or throws an exception, the thread dies.

See Also

Thread 10.23; ThreadGroup 10.24; Threads 8

10.17 Runtime

Synopsis

Class Name:	java.lang.Runtime
Superclass:	java.lang.Object
Immediate Subclasses:	None
Interfaces Implemented:	None
Availability:	JDK 1.0 or later

Description

The Runtime class provides access to various information about the environment in which a program is running. The Java run-time environment creates a single instance of this class that is associated with a program. The Runtime class does not have any public constructors, so a program cannot create its own instances of the class. A program must call the getRuntime() method to get a reference to the current Runtime object.

Information about operating system features is accessible through the System class.

Class Summary

```
public class java.lang.Runtime extends java.lang.Object {
    // Class Methods
    public static Runtime getRuntime();
    public static void runFinalizersOnExit(boolean value);  // New in 1.1

    // Instance Methods
    public Process exec(String command);
    public Process exec(String command, String envp[]);
    public Process exec(String cmdarray[]);
    public Process exec(String cmdarray[], String envp[]);
    public void exit(int status);
    public native long freeMemory();
    public native void gc();
    public InputStream
        getLocalizedInputStream(InputStream in);       // Deprecated in 1.1
    public OutputStream
        getLocalizedOutputStream(OutputStream out);    // Deprecated in 1.1
    public synchronized void load(String filename);
    public synchronized void loadLibrary(String libname);
    public native void runFinalization();
```

```
    public native long totalMemory();
    public native void traceInstructions(boolean on);
    public native void traceMethodCalls(boolean on);
}
```

Class Methods

getRuntime

public static Runtime getRuntime()

Returns	A reference to the current Runtime object.
Description	This method returns a reference to the current Runtime object. Because the other methods of the Runtime class are not static, a program must call this method first in order to get a reference to a Runtime object that can be used in calling the other methods.

runFinalizersOnExit

public static void runFinalizersOnExit(boolean value)

Availability	New as of JDK 1.1	
Parameters	value	A boolean value that specifies whether or not finalization occurs on exit.
Throws	SecurityException	
		If the checkExit() method of the SecurityManager throws a SecurityException.
Description	This method specifies whether or not the finalize() methods of all objects that have finalize() methods are run before the Java virtual machine exits. By default, the finalizers are not run on exit.	

Instance Methods

exec

public Process exec(String command) throws IOException

Parameters	command	A string that contains the name of an external command and any arguments to be passed to it.
Returns	A Process object that controls the process started by this method.	
Throws	IOException	If there is a problem finding or accessing the specified external command.
	SecurityException	
		If the checkExec() method of the SecurityManager throws a SecurityException.

Description | This method starts a new process to execute the given external command. The standard input, standard output, and standard error streams from the process are redirected to OutputStream and InputStream objects that are accessible through the Process object returned by this method.

Calling this method is equivalent to:

```
exec(command, null)
```

public Process exec(String command, String[] envp)
        throws IOException

Parameters | command | A string that contains the name of an external command and any arguments to be passed to it.

| envp | An array of strings that specifies the values for the environment variables of the new process. Each String in the array should be of the form *variableName=value*. If envp is null, the values of the environment variables in the current process are copied to the new process.

Returns | A Process object that controls the process started by this method.

Throws | IOException | If there is a problem finding or accessing the specified external command.

SecurityException

If the checkExec() method of the SecurityManager throws a SecurityException.

Description | This method starts a new process to execute the given external command. The standard input, standard output, and standard error streams from the process are redirected to OutputStream and InputStream objects that are accessible through the Process object returned by this method.

The method parses the command string into words that are separated by whitespace. It creates a String object for each word and places word String objects into an array. If that array is called commandArray, calling this method is equivalent to:

```
exec(commandArray, envp)
```

public Process exec(String[] commandArray) throws IOException

Parameters | commandArray

An array of strings that contains separate strings for the name of an external command and any arguments to be passed to it. The first string in the array must be the command name.

Returns
: A `Process` object that controls the process started by this method.

Throws
: `IOException` If there is a problem finding or accessing the specified external command.

`SecurityException`
: If the `checkExec()` method of the `SecurityMan-ager` throws a `SecurityException`.

Description
: This method starts a new process to execute the given external command. The standard input, standard output, and standard error streams from the process are redirected to `OutputStream` and `InputStream` objects that are accessible through the `Pro-cess` object returned by this method.

Calling this method is equivalent to:

```
exec(commandArray, null)
```

```
public Process exec(String[] commandArray, String[] envp)
        throws IOException
```

Parameters
: `commandArray`
: An array of strings that contains separate strings for the name of an external command and any arguments to be passed to it. The first string in the array must be the command name.

`envp`
: An array of strings that specifies the values for the environment variables of the new process. Each `String` in the array should be of the form *variableName=value*. If `envp` is `null`, the values of the environment variables in the current process are copied to the new process.

Returns
: A `Process` object that controls the process started by this method.

Throws
: `IOException` If there is a problem finding or accessing the specified external command.

`SecurityException`
: If the `checkExec()` method of the `SecurityMan-ager` throws a `SecurityException`.

Description
: This method starts a new process to execute the given external command. The standard input, standard output, and standard error streams from the process are redirected to `OutputStream` and `InputStream` objects that are accessible through the `Pro-cess` object returned by this method.

exit

public void exit(int status)

Parameters	status	The exit status code to use.
Throws	SecurityException	
		If the checkExit() method of the SecurityManager throws a SecurityException.
Description		This method causes the Java virtual machine to exit with the given status code. By convention, a nonzero status code indicates abnormal termination. This method never returns.

freeMemory

public native long freeMemory()

Returns	An estimate of the number of free bytes in system memory.
Description	This method returns an estimate of the number of free bytes in system memory. The value returned by this method is always less than the value returned by totalMemory(). Additional memory may be freed by calling the gc() method.

gc

public native void gc()

Description	This method causes the Java virtual machine to run the garbage collector in the current thread.
	The garbage collector finds objects that will never be used again because there are no live references to them. After it finds these objects, the garbage collector frees the storage occupied by these objects.
	The garbage collector is normally run continuously in a thread with the lowest possible priority, so that it works intermittently to reclaim storage. The gc() method allows a program to invoke the garbage collector explicitly when necessary.

getLocalizedInputStream

public InputStream getLocalizedInputStream(InputStream in)

Availability	Deprecated as of JDK 1.1	
Parameters	in	An InputStream object that is to be localized.
Returns	The localized InputStream.	
Description	This method returns an InputStream object that converts characters from the local character set to Unicode. For example, if the InputStream uses an 8-bit character set with values less than 128 representing Cyrillic letters, this method maps those char-	

acters to the corresponding Unicode characters in the range
'\u0400' to '\u04FF'.

This method is deprecated as of JDK 1.1. You should instead
use the new InputStreamReader and BufferedReader classes to
convert characters from the local character set to Unicode.

getLocalizedOutputStream

public OutputStream getLocalizedOutputStream(OutputStream out)

Availability	Deprecated as of JDK 1.1	
Parameters	out	An OutputStream object that is to be localized.
Returns	The localized OutputStream.	
Description	This method returns an OutputStream object that converts characters from Unicode to the local character set. For example, if the local character set is an 8-bit character set with values less than 128 representing Cyrillic letters, this method maps Unicode characters in the range '\u0400' to '\u04FF' to the appropriate characters in the local character set.	

This method is deprecated as of JDK 1.1. You should instead
use the new OutputStreamWriter and BufferedWriter classes
to convert characters from Unicode to the local character set.

load

public synchronized void load(String filename)

Parameters	filename	A string that specifies the complete path of the file to be loaded.
Throws	SecurityException	
		If the checkLink() method of the SecurityManager throws a SecurityException.
	UnsatisfiedLinkError	
		If the method is unsuccessful in loading the specified dynamically linked library.
Description	This method loads the specified dynamically linked library. It is often more convenient to call the load() method of the System class because it does not require getting a Runtime object.	

loadLibrary

public synchronized void loadLibrary(String libname)

Parameters	libname	A string that specifies the name of a dynamically linked library.

Throws	SecurityException
	If the checkLink() method of the SecurityManager throws a SecurityException.
	UnsatisfiedLinkError
	If the method is unsuccessful in loading the specified dynamically linked library.
Description	This method loads the specified dynamically linked library. It looks for the specified library in a platform-specific way.

It is often more convenient to call the loadLibrary() method of the System class because it does not require getting a Runtime object.

runFinalization

public native void runFinalization()

Description	This method causes the Java virtual machine to run the finalize() methods of any objects in the finalization queue in the current thread.

When the garbage collector discovers that there are no references to an object, it checks to see if the object has a finalize() method that has never been called. If the object has such a finalize() method, the object is placed in the finalization queue. While there is a reference to the object in the finalization queue, the object is no longer considered garbage-collectable.

Normally, the objects in the finalization queue are handled by a separate finalization thread that runs continuously at a very low priority. The finalization thread removes an object from the queue and calls its finalize() method. As long as the finalize() method does not generate a reference to the object, the object again becomes available for garbage collection.

Because the finalization thread runs at a very low priority, there may be a long delay from the time that an object is put on the finalization queue until the time that its finalize() method is called. The runFinalization() method allows a program to run the finalize() methods explicitly. This can be useful when there is a shortage of some resource that is released by a finalize() method.

totalMemory

public native long totalMemory()

Returns   The total number of bytes in system memory.

Description   This method returns the total number of bytes in system memory in the Java virtual machine. The total includes the number of bytes of memory being used by allocated objects, as well as the number of free bytes available for allocating additional objects. An estimate of the number of free bytes in system memory is available through the freeMemory() method.

traceInstructions

public native void traceInstructions(boolean on)

Parameters   on   A boolean value that specifies if instructions are to be traced. true if instructions are to be traced; otherwise false.

Description   This method controls whether or not the Java virtual machine outputs a detailed trace of each instruction that is executed. The boolean parameter causes tracing to be turned on or off. The tracing of instructions is only possible in a Java virtual machine that was compiled with the tracing option enabled. Production releases of the Java virtual machine are generally not compiled with tracing enabled.

traceMethodCalls

public native void traceMethodCalls(boolean on)

Parameters   on   A boolean value that specifies if method calls are to be traced. true if instructions are to be traced; otherwise false.

Description   This method controls whether or not the Java virtual machine outputs a detailed trace of each method that is invoked. The boolean parameter causes tracing to be turned on or off. The tracing of instructions is only possible in a Java virtual machine that was compiled with the tracing option enabled. Production releases of the Java virtual machine are generally not compiled with tracing enabled.

Inherited Methods

Method	Inherited From	Method	Inherited From
clone()	Object	equals(Object)	Object
finalize()	Object	getClass()	Object
hashCode()	Object	notify()	Object
notifyAll()	Object	toString()	Object
wait()	Object	wait(long)	Object
wait(long, int)	Object		

See Also

Errors 9.4.2; Exceptions 9.4.1; Object 10.14; Object Destruction 5.3.4; Process 10.15; SecurityManager 10.18; System 10.22

10.18   SecurityManager

Synopsis

Class Name:	java.lang.SecurityManager
Superclass:	java.lang.Object
Immediate Subclasses:	None
Interfaces Implemented:	None
Availability:	JDK 1.0 or later

Description

The SecurityManager class provides a way of implementing a comprehensive security policy for a Java program. As of this writing, SecurityManager objects are used primarily by Web browsers to establish security policies for applets. However, the use of a SecurityManager object is appropriate in any situation where a hosting environment wants to limit the actions of hosted programs.

The SecurityManager class contains methods that are called by methods in other classes to ask for permission to do something that can affect the security of the system. These permission methods all have names that begin with check. If a check method does not permit an action, it throws a SecurityException or returns a value that indicates the lack of permission. The SecurityManager class provides default implementations of all of the check methods. These default implementations are the most restrictive possible implementations; they simply deny permission to do anything that can affect the security of the system.

The SecurityManager class is an abstract class. A hosting environment should define a subclass of SecurityManager that implements an appropriate security policy. To give the subclass of SecurityManager control over security, the hosting environment creates an instance of the class and installs it by passing it to the setSecurityManager() method of the System class. Once a SecurityManager object is installed, it cannot be changed. If the setSecurityManager() method is called any additional times, it throws a SecurityException.

The methods in other classes that want to ask the SecurityManager for permission to do something are able to access the SecurityManager object by calling the getSecurityManager() method of the System class. This method returns the SecurityManager object, or null to indicate that there is no SecurityManager installed.

Class Summary

```
public abstract class java.lang.SecurityManager extends java.lang.Object {
    // Constructors
    protected SecurityManager();

    // Variables
    protected boolean inCheck;

    // Instance Methods
    public void checkAccept(String host, int port);
    public void checkAccess(Thread t);
    public void checkAccess(ThreadGroup g);
    public void checkAwtEventQueueAccess();                     // New in 1.1
    public void checkConnect(String host, int port);
    public void checkConnect(String host, int port, Object context);
    public void checkCreateClassLoader();
    public void checkDelete(String file);
    public void checkExec(String cmd);
    public void checkExit(int status);
    public void checkLink(String libname);
    public void checkListen(int port);
    public void checkMemberAccess(Class clazz, int which);    // New in 1.1
    public void checkMulticast(InetAddress maddr);            // New in 1.1
    public void checkMulticast(InetAddress maddr, byte ttl); // New in 1.1
    public void checkPackageAccess();
    public void checkPackageDefinition();
    public void checkPrintJobAccess();                        // New in 1.1
    public void checkPropertiesAccess();
    public void checkPropertyAccess(String key);
    public void checkRead(int fd);
    public void checkRead(String file);
    public void checkRead(String file, Object context);
    public void checkSecurityAccess(String action);           // New in 1.1
    public void checkSetFactory();
    public void checkSystemClipboardAccess();                 // New in 1.1
```

```
    public boolean checkTopLevelWindow();
    public void checkWrite(int fd);
    public void checkWrite(String file);
    public boolean getInCheck();
    public Object getSecurityContext();
    public ThreadGroup getThreadGroup();                    // New in 1.1

    // Protected Instance Methods
    protected int classDepth(String name);
    protected int classLoaderDepth();
    protected ClassLoader currentClassLoader();
    protected Class currentLoadedClass();                   // New in 1.1
    protected Class[] getClassContext();
    protected boolean inClass(String name);
    protected boolean inClassLoader();
}
```

Variables

inCheck

protected boolean inCheck = false

Description   This variable indicates whether or not a security check is in progress. A subclass of SecurityManager should set this variable to true while a security check is in progress.

This variable can be useful for security checks that require access to resources that a hosted program may not be permitted to access. For example, a security policy might be based on the contents of a permissions file. This means that the various check methods need to read information from a file to decide what to do. Even though a hosted program may not be allowed to read files, the check methods can allow such reads when inCheck is true to support this style of security policy.

Constructors

SecurityManager

protected SecurityManager()

Throws   SecurityException

If a SecurityManager object already exists. In other words, if System.getSecurityManager() returns a value other than null.

Description   Creates a new SecurityManager object. This constructor cannot be called if there is already a current SecurityManager installed for the program.

Public Instance Methods

checkAccept

```
public void checkAccept(String host, int port)
```

Parameters   host   The name of the host machine.

                port   A port number.

Throws   SecurityException

                                If the caller does not have permission to accept
                                the connection.

Description   This method decides whether or not to allow a connection
                from the given host on the given port to be accepted. An imple-
                mentation of the method should throw a SecurityException to
                deny permission to accept the connection. The method is
                called by the accept() method of the java.net.ServerSocket
                class.

                The checkAccept() method of SecurityManager always throws
                a SecurityException.

checkAccess

```
public void checkAccess(Thread g)
```

Parameters   g   A reference to a Thread object.

Throws   SecurityException

                                If the current thread does not have permission
                                to modify the specified thread.

Description   This method decides whether or not to allow the current
                thread to modify the specified Thread. An implementation of
                the method should throw a SecurityException to deny permis-
                sion to modify the thread. Methods of the Thread class that call
                this method include stop(), suspend(), resume(), setPrior-
                ity(), setName(), and setDaemon().

                The checkAccess() method of SecurityManager always throws
                a SecurityException.

```
public void checkAccess(ThreadGroup g)
```

Parameters   g   A reference to a ThreadGroup object.

Throws   SecurityException

                                If the current thread does not have permission
                                to modify the specified thread group.

Description   This method decides whether or not to allow the current
                thread to modify the specified ThreadGroup. An implementa-
                tion of the method should throw a SecurityException to deny
                permission to modify the thread group. Methods of the
                ThreadGroup class that call this method include setDaemon(),

setMaxPriority(), stop(), suspend(), resume(), and destroy().

The checkAccess() method of SecurityManager always throws a SecurityException.

checkAwtEventQueueAccess

public void checkAwtEventQueueAccess()

Availability   New as of JDK 1.1

Throws   SecurityException

If the caller does not have permission to access the AWT event queue.

Description   This method decides whether or not to allow access to the AWT event queue. An implementation of the method should throw a SecurityException to deny permission to access the event queue. The method is called by the getSystemEventQueue() method of the java.awt.Toolkit class.

The checkAwtEventQueueAccess() method of SecurityManager always throws a SecurityException.

checkConnect

public void checkConnect(String host, int port)

Parameters   host   The name of the host.

                port   A port number. A value of -1 indicates an attempt to determine the IP address of given hostname.

Throws   SecurityException

If the caller does not have permission to open the socket connection.

Description   This method decides whether or not to allow a socket connection to the given host on the given port to be opened. An implementation of the method should throw a SecurityException to deny permission to open the connection. The method is called by the constructors of the java.net.Socket class, by the send() and receive() methods of the java.net.DatagramSocket class, and the getByName() and getAllByName() methods of the java.net.InetAddress class.

The checkConnect() method of SecurityManager always throws a SecurityException.

```
public void checkConnect(String host, int port,
                         Object context)
```
    Parameters   `host`   The name of the host.

                     `port`   A port number. A value of −1 indicates an attempt to determine the IP address of given host name.

                     `context`   A security context object returned by this object's `getSecurityContext()` method.

    Throws   `SecurityException`

                           If the specified security context does not have permission to open the socket connection.

    Description   This method decides whether or not to allow a socket connection to the given host on the given port to be opened for the specified security context. An implementation of the method should throw a `SecurityException` to deny permission to open the connection.

                  The `checkConnect()` method of `SecurityManager` always throws a `SecurityException`.

checkCreateClassLoader

```
public void checkCreateClassLoader()
```
    Throws   `SecurityException`

                           If the caller does not have permission to create a `ClassLoader` object.

    Description   This method decides whether or not to allow a `ClassLoader` object to be created. An implementation of the method should throw a `SecurityException` to deny permission to create a `ClassLoader`. The method is called by the constructor of the `ClassLoader` class.

                  The `checkCreateClassLoader()` method of `SecurityManager` always throws a `SecurityException`.

checkDelete

```
public void checkDelete(String file)
```
    Parameters   `file`   The name of a file.

    Throws   `SecurityException`

                           If the caller does not have permission to delete the specified file.

Description This method decides whether or not to allow a file to be deleted. An implementation of the method should throw a SecurityException to deny permission to delete the specified file. The method is called by the delete() method of the java.io.File class.

The checkDelete() method of SecurityManager always throws a SecurityException.

checkExec

public void checkExec(String cmd)

Parameters   cmd   The name of an external command.

Throws   SecurityException

                If the caller does not have permission to execute the specified command.

Description This method decides whether or not to allow an external command to be executed. An implementation of the method should throw a SecurityException to deny permission to execute the specified command. The method is called by the exec() methods of the Runtime and System classes.

The checkExec() method of SecurityManager always throws a SecurityException.

checkExit

public void checkExit(int status)

Parameters   status   An exit status code.

Throws   SecurityException

                If the caller does not have permission to exit the Java virtual machine with the given status code.

Description This method decides whether or not to allow the Java virtual machine to exit with the given status code. An implementation of the method should throw a SecurityException to deny permission to exit with the specified status code. The method is called by the exit() methods of the Runtime and System classes.

The checkExit() method of SecurityManager always throws a SecurityException.

checkLink

```
public void checkLink(String lib)
```

Parameters	lib	The name of a library.
Throws	SecurityException	
		If the caller does not have permission to load the specified library.
Description		This method decides whether to allow the specified library to be loaded. An implementation of the method should throw a SecurityException to deny permission to load the specified library. The method is called by the load() and loadLibrary() methods of the Runtime and System classes.

The checkLink() method of SecurityManager always throws a SecurityException.

checkListen

```
public void checkListen(int port)
```

Parameters	port	A port number.
Throws	SecurityException	
		If the caller does not have permission to listen on the specified port.
Description		This method decides whether or not to allow the caller to listen on the specified port. An implementation of the method should throw a SecurityException to deny permission to listen on the specified port. The method is called by the constructors of the java.net.ServerSocket class and by the constructor of the java.net.DatagramSocket class that takes one argument.

The checkListen() method of SecurityManager always throws a SecurityException.

checkMemberAccess

```
public void checkMemberAccess(Class clazz, int which)
```

Availability	New as of JDK 1.1	
Parameters	clazz	A Class object.
	which	The value java.lang.reflect.Member.PUBLIC for the set of all public members including inherited members or the value java.lang.reflect.Member.DECLARED for the set of all declared members of the specified class or interface.

Throws   SecurityException

                    If the caller does not have permission to access the members of the specified class or interface.

Description   This method decides whether or not to allow access to the members of the specified Class object. An implementation of the method should throw a SecurityException to deny permission to access the members. Methods of the Class class that call this method include getField(), getFields(), getDeclared-Field(), getDeclaredFields(), getMethod(), getMethods(), getDeclaredMethod(), getDeclaredMethods(), getConstructor(), getConstructors(), getDeclaredConstructor(), getDeclaredConstructors(), and getDeclaredClasses().

                The checkMemberAccess() method of SecurityManager always throws a SecurityException.

checkMulticast

public void checkMulticast(InetAddress maddr)

Availability   New as of JDK 1.1

Parameters   maddr   An InetAddress object that represents a multicast address.

Throws   SecurityException

                If the current thread does not have permission to use the specified multicast address.

Description   This method decides whether or not to allow the current thread to use the specified multicast InetAddress. An implementation of the method should throw a SecurityException to deny permission to use the multicast address. The method is called by the send() method of java.net.DatagramSocket if the packet is being sent to a multicast address. The method is also called by the joinGroup() and leaveGroup() methods of java.net.MulticastSocket.

                The checkMulticast() method of SecurityManager always throws a SecurityException.

public void checkMulticast(InetAddress maddr, byte ttl)

Availability   New as of JDK 1.1

Parameters   maddr   An InetAddress object that represents a multicast address.

                ttl   The time-to-live (TTL) value.

Throws   SecurityException

If the current thread does not have permission to use the specified multicast address and TTL value.

Description   This method decides whether or not to allow the current thread to use the specified multicast InetAddress and TTL value. An implementation of the method should throw a SecurityException to deny permission to use the multicast address. The method is called by the send() method of java.net.MulticastSocket.

The checkMulticast() method of SecurityManager always throws a SecurityException.

checkPackageAccess

public void checkPackageAccess(String pkg)

Parameters   pkg   The name of a package.
Throws   SecurityException

If the caller does not have permission to access the specified package.

Description   This method decides whether or not to allow the specified package to be accessed. An implementation of the method should throw a SecurityException to deny permission to access the specified package. The method is intended to be called by implementations of the loadClass() method in subclasses of the ClassLoader class.

The checkPackageAccess() method of SecurityManager always throws a SecurityException.

checkPackageDefinition

public void checkPackageDefinition(String pkg)

Parameters   pkg   The name of a package.
Throws   SecurityException

If the caller does not have permission to define classes in the specified package.

Description   This method decides whether or not to allow the caller to define classes in the specified package. An implementation of the method should throw a SecurityException to deny permission to create classes in the specified package. The method is intended to be called by implementations of the loadClass() method in subclasses of the ClassLoader class.

The checkPackageDefinition() method of SecurityManager always throws a SecurityException.

checkPrintJobAccess

public void checkPrintJobAccess()

Availability   New as of JDK 1.1

Throws   SecurityException

If the caller does not have permission to initiate a print job request.

Description   This method decides whether or not to allow the caller to initiate a print job request. An implementation of the method should throw a SecurityException to deny permission to initiate the request.

The checkPrintJobAccess() method of SecurityManager always throws a SecurityException.

checkPropertiesAccess

public void checkPropertiesAccess()

Throws   SecurityException

If the caller does not have permission to access the system properties.

Description   This method decides whether or not to allow the caller to access and modify the system properties. An implementation of the method should throw a SecurityException to deny permission to access and modify the properties. Methods of the System class that call this method include getProperties() and setProperties().

The checkPropertiesAccess() method of SecurityManager always throws a SecurityException.

checkPropertyAccess

public void checkPropertyAccess(String key)

Parameters   key   The name of an individual system property.

Throws   SecurityException

If the caller does not have permission to access the specified system property.

Description   This method decides whether or not to allow the caller to access the specified system property. An implementation of the method should throw a SecurityException to deny permission to access the property. The method is called by the getProperty() method of the System class.

The checkPropertyAccess() method of SecurityManager always throws a SecurityException.

checkRead

public void checkRead(FileDescriptor fd)

Parameters	fd	A reference to a FileDescriptor object.
Throws	SecurityException	
		If the caller does not have permission to read from the given file descriptor.
Description		This method decides whether or not to allow the caller to read from the specified file descriptor. An implementation of the method should throw a SecurityException to deny permission to read from the file descriptor. The method is called by the constructor of the java.io.FileInputStream class that takes a FileDescriptor argument.

The checkRead() method of SecurityManager always throws a SecurityException.

public void checkRead(String file)

Parameters	file	The name of a file.
Throws	SecurityException	
		If the caller does not have permission to read from the named file.
Description		This method decides whether or not to allow the caller to read from the named file. An implementation of the method should throw a SecurityException to deny permission to read from the file. The method is called by constructors of the java.io.FileInputStream and java.io.RandomAccessFile classes, as well as by the canRead(), exists(), isDirectory(), isFile(), lastModified(), length(), and list() methods of the java.io.File class.

The checkRead() method of SecurityManager always throws a SecurityException.

public void checkRead(String file, Object context)

Parameters	file	The name of a file.
	context	A security context object returned by this object's getSecurityContext() method.
Throws	SecurityException	
		If the specified security context does not have permission to read from the named file.

Description   This method decides whether or not to allow the specified security context to read from the named file. An implementation of the method should throw a SecurityException to deny permission to read from the file.

The checkRead() method of SecurityManager always throws a SecurityException.

checkSecurityAccess

public void checkSecurityAccess(String action)
    Availability   New as of JDK 1.1
    Parameters   action   A string that specifies a security action.
    Throws   SecurityException
                        If the caller does not have permission to perform the specified security action.
    Description   This method decides whether to allow the caller to perform the specified security action. An implementation of the method should throw a SecurityException to deny permission to perform the action. The method is called by many of the methods in the java.security.Identity and java.security.Security classes.

The checkSecurityAccess() method of SecurityManager always throws a SecurityException.

checkSetFactory

public void checkSetFactory()
    Throws   SecurityException
                        If the caller does not have permission to set the factory class to be used by another class.
    Description   This method decides whether to allow the caller to set the factory class to be used by another class. An implementation of the method should throw a SecurityException to deny permission to set the factory class. The method is called by the setSocketFactory() method of the java.net.ServerSocket class, the setSocketImplFactory() method of the java.net.Socket class, the setURLStreamHandlerFactory() method of the java.net.URL class, and the setContentHandlerFactory() method of the java.net.URLConnection class.

The checkSetFactory() method of SecurityManager always throws a SecurityException.

checkSystemClipboardAccess

```
public void checkSystemClipboardAccess()
```
Availability   New as of JDK 1.1

Throws   SecurityException

                 If the caller does not have permission to access the system clipboard.

Description   This method decides whether or not to allow the caller to access the system clipboard. An implementation of the method should throw a SecurityException to deny permission to access the system clipboard.

                The checkSystemClipboardAccess() method of SecurityManager always throws a SecurityException.

checkTopLevelWindow

```
public boolean checkTopLevelWindow(Object window)
```
Parameters   window   A window object.

Returns   true if the caller is trusted to put up the specified top-level window; otherwise false.

Description   This method decides whether or not to trust the caller to put up the specified top-level window. An implementation of the method should return false to indicate that the caller is not trusted. In this case, the hosting environment can still decide to display the window, but the window should include a visual indication that it is not trusted. If the caller is trusted, the method should return true, and the window can be displayed without any special indication.

                The checkTopLevelWindow() method of SecurityManager always returns false.

checkWrite

```
public void checkWrite(FileDescriptor fd)
```
Parameters   fd   A FileDescriptor object.

Throws   SecurityException

                 If the caller does not have permission to write to the given file descriptor.

Description   This method decides whether or not to allow the caller to write to the specified file descriptor. An implementation of the method should throw a SecurityException to deny permission to write to the file descriptor. The method is called by the constructor of the java.io.FileOutputStream class that takes a FileDescriptor argument.

The checkWrite() method of SecurityManager always throws a SecurityException.

public void checkWrite(String file)

Parameters	file	The name of a file.
Throws	SecurityException	
		If the caller does not have permission to read from the named file.
Description		This method decides whether or not to allow the caller to write to the named file. An implementation of the method should throw a SecurityException to deny permission to write to the file. The method is called by constructors of the java.io.FileOutputStream and java.io.RandomAccessFile classes, as well as by the canWrite(), mkdir(), and renameTo() methods of the java.io.File class.

The checkWrite() method of SecurityManager always throws a SecurityException.

getInCheck

public boolean getInCheck()

Returns	true if a security check is in progress; otherwise false.
Description	This method returns the value of the SecurityManager object's inCheck variable, which is true if a security check is in progress and false otherwise.

getSecurityContext

public Object getSecurityContext()

Returns	An implementation-dependent object that contains enough information about the current execution environment to perform security checks at a later time.
Description	This method is meant to create an object that encapsulates information about the current execution environment. The resulting security context object is used by specific versions of the checkConnect() and checkRead() methods. The intent is that such a security context object can be used by a trusted method to determine whether or not another, untrusted method can perform a particular operation.

The getSecurityContext() method of SecurityManager simply returns null. This method should be overridden to return an appropriate security context object for the security policy that is being implemented.

getThreadGroup

`public ThreadGroup getThreadGroup()`

Availability	New as of JDK 1.1
Returns	A `ThreadGroup` in which to place any threads that are created when this method is called.
Description	This method returns the appropriate parent `ThreadGroup` for any threads that are created when the method is called. The `getThreadGroup()` method of `SecurityManager` simply returns the `ThreadGroup` of the current thread. This method should be overridden to return an appropriate `ThreadGroup`.

Protected Instance Methods

classDepth

`protected native int classDepth(String name)`

Parameters	name The fully qualified name of a class.
Returns	The number of pending method invocations from the top of the stack to a call to a method of the given class; -1 if no stack frame in the current thread is associated with a call to a method in the given class.
Description	This method returns the number of pending method invocations between this method invocation and an invocation of a method associated with the named class.

classLoaderDepth

`protected native int classLoaderDepth()`

Returns	The number of pending method invocations from the top of the stack to a call to a method that is associated with a class that was loaded by a `ClassLoader` object; -1 if no stack frame in the current thread is associated with a call to such a method.
Description	This method returns the number of pending method invocations between this method invocation and an invocation of a method associated with a class that was loaded by a `ClassLoader` object.

currentClassLoader

`protected native ClassLoader currentClassLoader()`

Returns	The most recent `ClassLoader` object executing on the stack.
Description	This method finds the most recent pending invocation of a method associated with a class that was loaded by a `ClassLoader` object. The method then returns the `ClassLoader` object that loaded that class.

currentLoadedClass

`protected Class currentLoadedClass()`

Availability	New as of JDK 1.1
Returns	The most recent `Class` object loaded by a `ClassLoader`.
Description	This method finds the most recent pending invocation of a method associated with a class that was loaded by a `ClassLoader` object. The method then returns the `Class` object for that class.

getClassContext

`protected native Class[] getClassContext()`

Returns	An array of `Class` objects that represents the current execution stack.
Description	This method returns an array of `Class` objects that represents the current execution stack. The length of the array is the number of pending method calls on the current thread's stack, not including the call to `getClassContext()`. Each element of the array references a `Class` object that describes the class associated with the corresponding method call. The first element of the array corresponds to the most recently called method, the second element is that method's caller, and so on.

inClass

`protected boolean inClass(String name)`

Parameters	name	The fully qualified name of a class.
Returns		true if there is a pending method invocation on the stack for a method of the given class; otherwise false.
Description		This method determines whether or not there is a pending method invocation that is associated with the named class.

inClassLoader

`protected boolean inClassLoader()`

Returns	true if there is a pending method invocation on the stack for a method of a class that was loaded by a `ClassLoader` object; otherwise false.
Description	This method determines whether or not there is a pending method invocation that is associated with a class that was loaded by a `ClassLoader` object. The method returns true only if the `currentClassLoader()` method does not return null.

Inherited Methods

Method	Inherited From	Method	Inherited From
clone()	Object	equals(Object)	Object
finalize()	Object	getClass()	Object
hashCode()	Object	notify()	Object
notifyAll()	Object	toString()	Object
wait()	Object	wait(long)	Object
wait(long, int)	Object		

See Also

Class 10.4; ClassLoader 10.5; Exceptions 9.4.1; Object 10.14; Runtime 10.17; System 10.22; Thread 10.23; ThreadGroup 10.24

10.19   Short

Synopsis

Class Name:	java.lang.Short
Superclass:	java.lang.Number
Immediate Subclasses:	None
Interfaces Implemented:	None
Availability:	New as of JDK 1.1

Description

The Short class provides an object wrapper for a short value. This is useful when you need to treat a short value as an object. For example, there are a number of utility methods that take a reference to an Object as one of their arguments. You cannot specify a short value for one of these arguments, but you can provide a reference to a Short object that encapsulates the short value. Furthermore, the Short class is necessary as of JDK 1.1 to support the Reflection API and class literals.

The Short class also provides a number of utility methods for converting short values to other primitive types and for converting short values to strings and vice-versa.

Class Summary

```
public final class java.lang.Short extends java.lang.Number {
    // Constants
    public static final short MAX_VALUE;
    public static final short MIN_VALUE;
    public static final Class TYPE;

    // Constructors
    public Short(short value);
    public Short(String s);

    // Class Methods
    public static Short decode(String nm);
    public static short parseShort(String s);
    public static short parseShort(String s, int radix);
    public static String toString(short s);
    public static Short valueOf(String s, int radix);
    public static Short valueOf(String s);

    // Instance Methods
    public byte byteValue();
    public double doubleValue();
    public boolean equals(Object obj);
    public float floatValue();
    public int hashCode();
    public int intValue();
    public long longValue();
    public short shortValue();
    public String toString();
}
```

Constants

MAX_VALUE

```
public static final short MAX_VALUE = 32767
```
The largest value that can be represented by a short.

MIN_VALUE

```
public static final byte MIN_VALUE = -32768
```
The smallest value that can be represented by a short.

TYPE

```
public static final Class TYPE
```
The Class object that represents the primitive type short. It is always true that Short.TYPE == short.class.

Constructors

Short

`public Short(short value)`

Parameters	value	The short value to be encapsulated by this object.
Description		Creates a Short object with the specified short value.

`public Short(String s) throws NumberFormatException`

Parameters	s	The string to be made into a Short object.
Throws		NumberFormatException
		If the sequence of characters in the given String does not form a valid short literal.
Description		Constructs a Short object with the value specified by the given string. The string should consist of one or more digit characters. The digit characters can be preceded by a single '–' character. If the string contains any other characters, the constructor throws a NumberFormatException.

Class Methods

decode

`public static Short decode(String nm) throws NumberFormatException`

Parameters	nm	A String representation of the value to be encapsulated by a Short object. If the string begins with # or 0x, it is a radix 16 representation of the value. If the string begins with 0, it is a radix 8 representation of the value. Otherwise, it is assumed to be a radix 10 representation of the value.
Returns		A Short object that encapsulates the given value.
Throws		NumberFormatException
		If the String contains any non-digit characters other than a leading minus sign, or if the value represented by the String is less than Short.MIN_VALUE or if it is greater than Short.MAX_VALUE.
Description		This method returns a Short object that encapsulates the given value.

parseByte

```
public static short parseShort(String s)
                throws NumberFormatException
```

Parameters | s | The String to be converted to a short value.
Returns | The numeric value of the short represented by the String object.
Throws | NumberFormatException

If the String does not contain a valid representation of a short or the value represented by the String is less than Short.MIN_VALUE or greater than Short.MAX_VALUE.

Description | This method returns the numeric value of the short represented by the contents of the given String object. The String must contain only decimal digits, except that the first character may be a minus sign.

```
public static short parseShort(String s, int radix)
                throws NumberFormatException
```

Parameters | s | The String to be converted to a short value.
radix | The radix used in interpreting the characters in the String as digits. This value must be in the range Character.MIN_RADIX to Character.MAX_RADIX. If radix is in the range 2 through 10, only characters for which the Character.isDigit() method returns true are considered to be valid digits. If radix is in the range 11 through 36, characters in the ranges 'A' through 'Z' and 'a' through 'z' are considered valid digits.

Returns | The numeric value of the short represented by the String object in the specified radix.
Throws | NumberFormatException

If the String does not contain a valid representation of a short, radix is not in the appropriate range, or the value represented by the String is less than Short.MIN_VALUE or greater than Short.MAX_VALUE.

Description | This method returns the numeric value of the short represented by the contents of the given String object in the specified radix. The String must contain only valid digits of the specified radix, except that the first character may be a minus sign. The digits are parsed in the specified radix to produce the numeric value.

toString

```
public String toString(short s)
```
Parameters   s   The short value to be converted to a string.

Returns   The string representation of the given value.

Description   This method returns a String object that contains the decimal representation of the given value.

This method returns a string that begins with '–' if the given value is negative. The rest of the string is a sequence of one or more of the characters '0', '1', '2', '3', '4', '5', '6', '7', '8', and '9'. This method returns "0" if its argument is 0. Otherwise, the string returned by this method does not begin with "0" or "-0".

valueOf

```
public static Short valueOf(String s) throws NumberFormatException
```
Parameters   s   The string to be made into a Short object.

Returns   The Short object constructed from the string.

Throws   NumberFormatException

If the String does not contain a valid representation of a short or the value represented by the String is less than Short.MIN_VALUE or greater than Short.MAX_VALUE.

Description   Constructs a Short object with the value specified by the given string. The string should consist of one or more digit characters. The digit characters can be preceded by a single '–'. If the string contains any other characters, the method throws a NumberFormatException.

```
public static Short valueOf(String s, int radix)
            throws NumberFormatException
```
Parameters   s   The string to be made into a Short object.

                 radix   The radix used in converting the string to a value. This value must be in the range Character.MIN_RADIX to Character.MAX_RADIX.

Returns   The Short object constructed from the string.

Throws   NumberFormatException

If the String does not contain a valid representation of a short, radix is not in the appropriate range, or the value represented by the String is less than Short.MIN_VALUE or greater than Short.MAX_VALUE.

Description   Constructs a Short object with the value specified by the given
                string in the specified radix. The string should consist of one
                or more digit characters or characters in the range 'A' to 'Z' or
                'a' to 'z' that are considered digits in the given radix. The digit
                characters can be preceded by a single '-' character. If the
                string contains any other characters, the method throws a Num-
                berFormatException.

Instance Methods

byteValue

```
public byte byteValue()
```
   Returns   The value of this object as a byte. The high order bits of the
                 value are discarded.
   Overrides   Number.byteValue()
   Description   This method returns the value of this object as a byte.

doubleValue

```
public double doubleValue()
```
   Returns   The value of this object as a double.
   Overrides   Number.doubleValue()
   Description   This method returns the value of this object as a double.

equals

```
public boolean equals(Object obj)
```
   Parameters   obj   The object to be compared with this object.
   Returns   true if the objects are equal; false if they are not.
   Overrides   Object.equals()
   Description   This method returns true if obj is an instance of Short and it
                  contains the same value as the object this method is associated
                  with.

floatValue

```
public float floatValue()
```
   Returns   The value of this object as a float.
   Overrides   Number.floatValue()
   Description   This method returns the value of this object as a float.

hashCode

```
public int hashCode()
```

Returns   A hashcode based on the short value of the object.

Overrides   Object.hashCode()

Description   This method returns a hash code computed from the value of this object.

intValue

```
public int intValue()
```

Returns   The value of this object as an int.

Overrides   Number.intValue()

Description   This method returns the value of this object as an int.

longValue

```
public long longValue()
```

Returns   The value of this object as a long.

Overrides   Number.longValue()

Description   This method returns the value of this object as a long.

shortValue

```
public short shortValue()
```

Returns   The value of this object as a short.

Overrides   Number.shortValue()

Description   This method returns the value of this object as a short.

toString

```
public String toString()
```

Returns   The string representation of the value of this object.

Overrides   Object.toString()

Description   This method returns a String object that contains the decimal representation of the value of this object.

                This method returns a string that begins with '–' if the value is negative. The rest of the string is a sequence of one or more of the characters '0', '1', '2', '3', '4', '5', '6', '7', '8', and '9'. This method returns "0" if the value of the object is 0. Otherwise, the string returned by this method does not begin with "0" or "-0".

Inherited Methods

Method	Inherited From	Method	Inherited From
clone()	Object	finalize()	Object
getClass()	Object	notify()	Object
notifyAll()	Object	wait()	Object
wait(long)	Object	wait(long, int)	Object

See Also

Byte 10.2; Character 10.3; Class 10.4; Double 10.8; Exceptions 9.4.1; Float 10.9; Integer literals 2.2.3.1; Integer types 3.1.1.1; Integer 10.10; Long 10.11; Number 10.13; String 10.20

10.20   String

Synopsis

Class Name:	java.lang.String
Superclass:	java.lang.Object
Immediate Subclasses:	None
Interfaces Implemented:	java.io.Serializable
Availability:	JDK 1.0 or later

Description

The String class represents sequences of characters. Once a String object is created, it is immutable. In other words, the sequence of characters that a String represents cannot be changed after it is created. The StringBuffer class, on the other hand, represents a sequence of characters that can be changed. StringBuffer objects are used to perform computations on String objects.

The String class includes a number of utility methods, such as methods for fetching individual characters or ranges of contiguous characters, for translating characters to upper- or lowercase, for searching strings, and for parsing numeric values in strings.

String literals are compiled into String objects. Where a String literal appears in an expression, the compiled code contains a String object. If s is declared as String, the following two expressions are identical:

```
s.equals("ABC")
"ABC".equals(s)
```

The string concatenation operator implicitly creates String objects.

Class Summary

```
public final class java.lang.String extends java.lang.Object {
    // Constructors
    public String();
    public String(byte[] bytes);                        // New in 1.1
    public String(byte[] bytes, String enc);            // New in 1.1
    public String(byte[] bytes, int offset, int length); // New in 1.1
    public String(byte[] bytes, int offset,
                  int length, String enc);              // New in 1.1
    public String(byte[] lowbytes, int hibyte);         // Deprecated in 1.1
    public String(byte[] lowbytes, int hibyte,
                  int offset, int count);               // Deprecated in 1.1
    public String(char[] value);
    public String(char[] value, int offset, int;
    public String(String value);
    public String(StringBuffer buffer);

    // Class Methods
    public static String copyValueOf(char data[]);
    public static String copyValueOf(char data[], int offset, int count);
    public static String valueOf(boolean b);
    public static String valueOf(char c);
    public static String valueOf(char[] data);
    public static String valueOf(char[] data, int offset, int count);
    public static String valueOf(double d);
    public static String valueOf(float f);
    public static String valueOf(int i);
    public static String valueOf(long l);
    public static String valueOf(Object obj);

    // Instance Methods
    public char charAt(int index);
    public int compareTo(String anotherString);
    public String concat(String str);
    public boolean endsWith(String suffix);
    public boolean equals(Object anObject);
    public boolean equalsIgnoreCase(String anotherString);
    public byte[] getBytes();                           // New in 1.1
    public byte[] getBytes(String enc);                 // New in 1.1
    public void getBytes(int srcBegin, int srcEnd,
                         byte[] dst, int dstBegin);     // Deprecated in 1.1
    public void getChars(int srcBegin, int srcEnd, char[] dst, int dstBegin);
    public int hashCode();
    public int indexOf(int ch);
    public int indexOf(int ch, int fromIndex);
    public int indexOf(String str);
    public int indexOf(String str, int fromIndex);
```

```
    public native String intern();
    public int lastIndexOf(int ch);
    public int lastIndexOf(int ch, int fromIndex);
    public int lastIndexOf(String str);
    public int lastIndexOf(String str, int fromIndex;
    public int length();
    public boolean regionMatches(boolean ignoreCase, int toffset,
                                 String other, int ooffset, int len);
    public boolean regionMatches(int toffset, String other,
                                 int ooffset, int len);
    public String replace(char oldChar, char newChar);
    public boolean startsWith(String prefix);
    public boolean startsWith(String prefix, int toffset);
    public String substring(int beginIndex);
    public String substring(int beginIndex, int endIndex);
    public char[] toCharArray();
    public String toLowerCase();
    public String toLowerCase(Locale locale);          // New in 1.1
    public String toString();
    public String toUpperCase();
    public String toUpperCase(Locale locale);          // New in 1.1
    public String trim();
}
```

Constructors

String

`public String()`

    Description   Creates a new String object that represents the empty string (i.e., a string with zero characters).

`public String(byte[] bytes)`

    Availability   New as of JDK 1.1

    Parameters   bytes   An array of byte values.

    Description   Creates a new String object that represents the sequence of characters stored in the given byte array. The bytes in the array are converted to characters using the system's default character encoding scheme.

`public String(byte[] bytes, String enc)`

    Availability   New as of JDK 1.1

    Parameters   bytes   An array of byte values.

                      enc   The name of an encoding scheme.

    Throws   UnsupportedEncodingException

                            If enc is not a supported encoding scheme.

Description   Creates a new String object that represents the sequence of characters stored in the given byte array. The bytes in the array are converted to characters using the specified character encoding scheme.

public String(byte[] bytes, int offset, int length)

Availability   New as of JDK 1.1

Parameters
bytes	An array of byte values.
offset	An offset into the array.
length	The number of bytes to be included.

Throws   StringIndexOutOfBoundsException
If offset or length indexes an element that is outside the bounds of the bytes array.

Description   Creates a new String object that represents the sequence of characters stored in the specified portion of the given bytes array. The bytes in the array are converted to characters using the system's default character encoding scheme.

public String(byte[] bytes, int offset, int length,
             String enc)

Availability   New as of JDK 1.1

Parameters
bytes	An array of byte values.
offset	An offset into the array.
length	The number of bytes to be included.
enc	The name of an encoding scheme.

Throws   StringIndexOutOfBoundsException
If offset or length indexes an element that is outside the bounds of the bytes array.

UnsupportedEncodingException
If enc is not a supported encoding scheme.

Description   Creates a new String object that represents the sequence of characters stored in the specified portion of the given bytes array. The bytes in the array are converted to characters using the specified character encoding scheme.

public String(byte[] lowbytes, int hibyte)

Availability   Deprecated as of JDK 1.1

Parameters
lowbytes	An array of byte values.
hibyte	The value to be put in the high-order byte of each 16-bit character.

Description   Creates a new String object that represents the sequence of characters stored in the given lowbytes array. The type of the array elements is byte, which is an 8-bit data type, so each element must be converted to a char, which is a 16-bit data type.

The value of the `hibyte` argument is used to provide the value of the high-order byte when the `byte` values in the array are converted to `char` values.

More specifically, for each element i in the array `lowbytes`, the character at position i in the created `String` object is:

```
((hibyte & 0xff)<<8) | lowbytes[i]
```

This method is deprecated as of JDK 1.1 because it does not convert bytes into characters properly. You should instead use one of the constructors that takes a specific character encoding argument or that uses the default encoding.

```
public String(byte[] lowbytes, int hibyte, int offset,
              int count)
```

Availability	Deprecated as of JDK 1.1	
Parameters	lowbytes	An array of `byte` values.
	hibyte	The value to be put in the high-order byte of each 16-bit character.
	offset	An offset into the array.
	count	The number of bytes from the array to be included in the string.
Throws	StringIndexOutOfBoundsException	
		If `offset` or `count` indexes an element that is outside the bounds of the `lowbytes` array.
Description	Creates a new `String` object that represents the sequence of characters stored in the specified portion of the `lowbytes` array. That is, the portion of the array that starts at `offset` elements from the beginning of the array and is `count` elements long.	

The type of the array elements is `byte`, which is an 8-bit data type, so each element must be converted to a `char`, which is a 16-bit data type. The value of the `hibyte` argument is used to provide the value of the high-order byte when the `byte` values in the array are converted to `char` values.

More specifically, for each element i in the array `lowbytes` that is included in the `String` object, the character at position i in the created `String` is:

```
((hibyte & 0xff)<<8) | lowbytes[I]
```

This method is deprecated as of JDK 1.1 because it does not convert bytes into characters properly. You should instead use one of the constructors that takes a specific character encoding argument or that uses the default encoding.

```
public String(char[] value)
```
    Parameters   value   An array of char values.

    Description   Creates a new String object that represents the sequence of characters stored in the given array.

```
public String(char[] value, int offset, int count)
```
    Parameters   value   An array of char values.

                    offset   An offset into the array.

                    count   The number of characters from the array to be included in the string.

    Throws   StringIndexOutOfBoundsException

                                  If offset or count indexes an element that is outside the bounds of the value array.

    Description   Creates a new String object that represents the sequence of characters stored in the specified portion of the given array. That is, the portion of the given array that starts at offset elements from the beginning of the array and is count elements long.

```
public String(String value)
```
    Parameters   value   A String object.

    Description   Creates a new String object that represents the same sequence of characters as the given String object.

```
public String(StringBuffer value)
```
    Parameters   value   A StringBuffer object.

    Description   Creates a new String object that represents the same sequence of characters as the given object.

Class Methods

copyValueOf

```
public static String copyValueOf(char data[])
```
    Parameters   data   An array of char values.

    Returns   A new String object that represents the sequence of characters stored in the given array.

    Description   This method returns a new String object that represents the character sequence contained in the given array. The String object produced by this method is guaranteed not to refer to the given array, but instead to use a copy. Because the String object uses a copy of the array, subsequent changes to the array do not change the contents of this String object.

                  This method is now obsolete. The same result can be obtained using the valueOf() method that takes an array of char values.

```
public static String copyValueOf(char data[], int offset,
                                 int count)
```

Parameters   data   An array of char values.

offset   An offset into the array.

count   The number of characters from the array to be included in the string.

Returns   A new String object that represents the sequence of characters stored in the specified portion of the given array.

Throws   StringIndexOutOfBoundsException

If offset or count indexes an element that is outside the bounds of the data array.

Description   This method returns a new String object that represents the character sequence contained in the specified portion of the given array. That is, the portion of the given array that starts at offset elements from the beginning of the array and is count elements long. The String object produced by this method is guaranteed not to refer to the given array, but instead to use a copy. Because the String object uses a copy of the array, subsequent changes to the array do not change the contents of this String object.

This method is obsolete. The same result can be obtained by using the valueOf() method that takes an array of char values, an offset, and a count.

valueOf

```
public static String valueOf(boolean b)
```

Parameters   b   A boolean value.

Returns   A new String object that contains "true" if b is true or "false" if b is false.

Description   This method returns a string representation of a boolean value. In other words, it returns "true" if b is true or "false" if b is false.

```
public static String valueOf(char c)
```

Parameters   c   A char value.

Returns   A new String object that contains just the given character.

Description   This method returns a string representation of a char value. In other words, it returns a String object that contains just the given character.

```
public static String valueOf(char[] data)
```

Parameters   data   An array of char values.

Returns   A new String object that contains the sequence of characters stored in the given array.

Description   This method returns a string representation of an array of char values. In other words, it returns a String object that contains the sequence of characters stored in the given array.

```
public static String valueOf(char[] data, int offset,
                             int count)
```

Parameters   data   An array of char values.

                offset   An offset into the array.

                count   The number of characters from the array to be included in the string.

Returns   A new String object that contains the sequence of characters stored in the specified portion of the given array.

Throws   StringIndexOutOfBoundsException

                                If offset or count indexes an element that is outside the bounds of the data array.

Description   This method returns a string representation of the specified portion of an array of char values. In other words, it returns a String object that contains the sequence of characters in the given array that starts offset elements from the beginning of the array and is count elements long.

```
public static String valueOf(double d)
```

Parameters   d   A double value.

Returns   A new String object that contains a string representation of the given double value.

Description   This method returns a string representation of a double value. In other words, it returns the String object returned by Double.toString(d).

```
public static String valueOf(float f)
```

Parameters   f   A float value.

Returns   A new String object that contains a string representation of the given float value.

Description   This method returns a string representation of a float value. In other words, it returns the String object returned by Float.toString(f).

```
public static String valueOf(int i)
```
    Parameters   `i`   An int value.

    Returns   A new `String` object that contains a string representation of the given int value.

    Description   This method returns a string representation of an int value. In other words, it returns the `String` object returned by `Integer.toString(i)`.

```
public static String valueOf(long l)
```
    Parameters   `l`   A long value.

    Returns   A new `String` object that contains a string representation of the given long value.

    Description   This method returns a string representation of a long value. In other words, it returns the `String` object returned by `Long.toString(l)`.

```
public static String valueOf (Object obj)
```
    Parameters   `obj`   A reference to an object.

    Returns   A new `String` that contains a string representation of the given object.

    Description   This method returns a string representation of the given object. If `obj` is `null`, the method returns `"null"`. Otherwise, the method returns the `String` object returned by the `toString()` method of the object.

Instance Methods

charAt

```
public char charAt(int index)
```
    Parameters   `index`   An index into the string.

    Returns   The character at the specified position in this string.

    Throws   `StringIndexOutOfBoundsException`

                      If `index` is less than zero or greater than or equal to the length of the string.

    Description   This method returns the character at the specified position in the `String` object; the first character in the string is at position 0.

compareTo

```
public int compareTo(String anotherString)
```
    Parameters   `anotherString`

                      The `String` object to be compared.

Returns	A positive value if this string is greater than anotherString, 0 if the two strings are the same, or a negative value if this string is less than anotherString.
Description	This method lexicographically compares this String object to anotherString.

Here is how the comparison works: the two String objects are compared character-by-character, starting at index 0 and continuing until a position is found in which the two strings contain different characters or until all of the characters in the shorter string have been compared. If the characters at k are different, the method returns:

```
this.charAt(k)-anotherString.charAt(k)
```

Otherwise, the comparison is based on the lengths of the strings and the method returns:

```
this.length()-anotherString.length()
```

concat

```
public String concat(String str)
```

Parameters	str	The String object to be concatenated.
Returns		A new String object that contains the character sequences of this string and str concatenated together.
Description		This method returns a new String object that concatenates the characters from the argument string str onto the characters from this String object. Although this is a good way to concatenate two strings, concatenating more than two strings can be done more efficiently using a StringBuffer object.

endsWith

```
public boolean endsWith(String suffix)
```

Parameters	suffix	The String object suffix to be tested.
Returns		true if this string ends with the sequence of characters specified by suffix; otherwise false.
Description		This method determines whether or not this String object ends with the specified suffix.

equals

```
public boolean equals(Object anObject)
```

Parameters	anObject	The Object to be compared.

Returns   true if the objects are equal; false if they are not.

Overrides   Object.equals()

Description   This method returns true if anObject is an instance of String and it contains the same sequence of characters as this String object.

Note the difference between this method and the == operator, which only returns true if both of its arguments are references to the same object.

equalsIgnoreCase

public boolean equalsIgnoreCase(String anotherString)

Parameters   anotherString

The String object to be compared.

Returns   true if the strings are equal, ignoring case; otherwise false.

Description   This method determines whether or not this String object contains the same sequence of characters, ignoring case, as anotherString. More specifically, corresponding characters in the two strings are considered equal if any of the following conditions are true:

- The two characters compare as equal using the == operator.
- The Character.toUppercase() method returns the same result for both characters.
- The Character.toLowercase() method returns the same result for both characters.

getBytes

public byte[] getBytes()

Availability   New as of JDK 1.1

Returns   A byte array that contains the characters of this String.

Description   This method converts the characters in this String object to an array of byte values. The characters in the string are converted to bytes using the system's default character encoding scheme.

public byte[] getBytes(String enc)

Availability   New as of JDK 1.1

Parameters   enc   The name of an encoding scheme.

Returns   A byte array that contains the characters of this String.

Throws   UnsupportedEncodingException

If enc is not a supported encoding scheme.

Description   This method converts the characters in this String object to an array of byte values. The characters in the string are converted to bytes using the specified character encoding scheme.

```
public void getBytes(int srcBegin, int srcEnd,
               byte[] dst, int dstBegin)
```

Availability   Deprecated as of JDK 1.1

Parameters   srcBegin   The index of the first character to be copied.

srcEnd   The index after the last character to be copied.

dst   The destination byte array.

dstBegin   An offset into the destination array.

Throws   StringIndexOutOfBoundsException

If srcBegin, srcEnd, or dstBegin is out of range.

Description   This method copies the low-order byte of each character in the specified range of this String object to the given array of byte values. More specifically, the first character to be copied is at index srcBegin; the last character to be copied is at index srcEnd-1. The low-order bytes of these characters are copied into dst, starting at index dstBegin and ending at index:

```
dstBegin + (srcEnd-srcBegin) - 1
```

This method is deprecated as of JDK 1.1 because it does not convert characters into bytes properly. You should instead use the getBytes() method that takes a specific character encoding argument or the one that uses the default encoding.

getChars

```
public void getChars(int srcBegin, int srcEnd,
               char[] dst, int dstBegin)
```

Parameters   srcBegin   The index of the first character to be copied.

srcEnd   The index after the last character to be copied.

dst   The destination char array.

dstBegin   An offset into the destination array.

Throws   StringIndexOutOfBoundsException

If srcBegin, srcEnd, or dstBegin is out of range.

Description   This copies each character in the specified range of this String object to the given array of char values. Specifically, the first character to be copied is at index srcBegin; the last character to be copied is at index srcEnd-1. These characters are copied into dst, starting at index dstBegin and ending at index:

```
dstBegin + (srcEnd-srcBegin) - 1
```

hashCode

`public int hashCode()`

Returns	A hashcode based on the sequence of characters in this string.
Overrides	`Object.hashCode()`
Description	This method returns a hashcode based on the sequence of characters this `String` object represents.

More specifically, one of two algorithms is used to compute a hash code for the string, depending on its length. If n is the length of the string and S_i is the character at position i in the string, then if $n = 15$ the method returns:

$$\sum_{i=0}^{n-1} 37^i \cdot S_i$$

If $n > 15$, the method returns:

$$\sum_{i=0}^{\left\lceil \frac{n}{k} \right\rceil} 39^i \cdot S_{i \cdot k} \text{ where } k = \left\lfloor \frac{n}{8} \right\rfloor$$

indexOf

`public int indexOf(int ch)`

Parameters	ch	A char value.
Returns		The index of the first occurrence of the given character in this string or –1 if the character does not occur.
Description		This method returns the index of the first occurrence of the given character in this `String` object. If there is no such occurrence, the method returns the value –1.

`public int indexOf(int ch, int fromIndex)`

Parameters	ch	A char value.
	fromIndex	The index where the search is to begin.
Returns		The index of the first occurrence of the given character in this string after `fromIndex` or –1 if the character does not occur.
Description		This method returns the index of the first occurrence of the given character in this `String` object after ignoring the first `fromIndex` characters. If there is no such occurrence, the method returns the value –1.

`public int indexOf(String str)`

Parameters	str	A `String` object.
Returns		The index of the first occurrence of `str` in this string or –1 if the substring does not occur.

Description   This method returns the index of the first character of the first occurrence of the substring str in this String object. If there is no such occurrence, the method returns the value –1.

public int indexOf(String str, int fromIndex)

Parameters   str   A String object.

fromIndex   The index where the search is to begin.

Returns   The index of the first occurrence of str in this string after from-Index or –1 if the substring does not occur.

Description   This method returns the index of the first character of the first occurrence of the substring str in this String object after ignoring the first fromIndex characters. If there is no such occurrence, the method returns the value –1.

intern

public native String intern()

Returns   A String object that is guaranteed to be the same object for every String that contains the same character sequence.

Description   This method returns a canonical representation for this String object. The returned String object is guaranteed to be the same String object for every String object that contains the same character sequence. In other words, if:

```
s1.equals(s2)
```

then:

```
s1.intern() == s2.intern()
```

The intern() method is used by the Java environment to ensure that String literals and constant-value String expressions that contain the same sequence of characters are all represented by a single String object.

lastIndexOf

public int lastIndexOf(int ch)

Parameters   ch   A char value.

Returns   The index of the last occurrence of the given character in this string or –1 if the character does not occur.

Description   This method returns the index of the last occurrence of the given character in this String object. If there is no such occurrence, the method returns the value –1.

```
public int lastIndexOf(int ch, int fromIndex)
```
    Parameters   ch   A char value.
                  fromIndex   The index where the search is to begin.
    Returns   The index of the last occurrence of the given character in this
                  string after fromIndex or –1 if the character does not occur.
    Description   This method returns the index of the last occurrence of the
                  given character in this String object after ignoring the first
                  fromIndex characters. If there is no such occurrence, the
                  method returns the value –1.

```
public int lastIndexOf(String str)
```
    Parameters   str   A String object.
    Returns   The index of the last occurrence of str in this string or –1 if
                  the substring does not occur.
    Description   This method returns the index of the first character of the last
                  occurrence of the substring str in this String object. If there is
                  no such occurrence, the method returns the value –1.

```
public int lastIndexOf(String str, int fromIndex)
```
    Parameters   str   A String object.
                  fromIndex   The index where the search is to begin.
    Returns   The index of the last occurrence of str in this string after
                  from-Index or –1 if the substring does not occur.
    Description   This method returns the index of the first character of the last
                  occurrence of the substring str in this String object after
                  ignoring the first fromIndex characters. If there is no such
                  occurrence, the method returns the value –1.

length

```
public int length()
```
    Returns   The length of the character sequence represented by this
                  string.
    Description   This method returns the number of characters in the character
                  sequence represented by this String object.

regionMatches

```
public boolean regionMatches(int toffset, String other,
                             int ooffset, int len)
```
    Parameters   toffset   The index of the first character in this string.
                  other   The String object to be used in the comparison.
                  ooffset   The index of the first character in other.

len	The length of the sub-sequences to be compared.
Returns	true if the sub-sequences are identical; otherwise false.
Description	This method determines whether or not the specified subsequences in this String object and other are identical. The method returns false if toffset is negative, if ooffset is negative, if toffset+len is greater than the length of this string, or if ooffset+len is greater than the length of other. Otherwise, the method returns true if for all nonnegative integers k less than len it is true that:

```
this.charAt(toffset+k) == other.charAt(ooffset+k)
```

```
public boolean regionMatches(boolean ignoreCase, int toffset,
                             String other, int ooffset,
                             int len)
```

Parameters	ignoreCase	A boolean value that indicates whether case should be ignored.
	toffset	The index of the first character in this string.
	other	The String object to be used in the comparison.
	ooffset	The index of the first character in other.
	len	The length of the sub-sequences to be compared.
Returns		true if the sub-sequences are identical; otherwise false. The ignoreCase argument controls whether or not case is ignored in the comparison.
Description		This method determines whether or not the specified subsequences in this String object and other are identical. The method returns false if toffset is negative, if ooffset is negative, if toffset+len is greater than the length of this string, or if ooffset+len is greater than the length of other. Otherwise, if ignoreCase is false, the method returns true if for all nonnegative integers k less than len it is true that:

```
this.charAt(toffset+k) == other.charAt(ooffset+k)
```

If ignoreCase is true, the method returns true if for all nonnegative integers k less than len it is true that:

```
Character.toLowerCase(this.charAt(toffset+k))
  == Character.toLowerCase(other.charAt(ooffset+k))
```

or:

```
Character.toUpperCase(this.charAt(toffset+k))
  == Character.toUpperCase(other.charAt(ooffset+k))
```

replace

```
public String replace(char oldChar, char newChar)
```
Parameters | oldChar | The character to be replaced.
| newChar | The replacement character.

Returns | A new String object that results from replacing every occurrence of oldChar in the string with newChar.

Description | This method returns a new String object that results from replacing every occurrence of oldChar in this String object with newChar. If there are no occurrences of oldChar, the method simply returns this String object.

startsWith

```
public boolean startsWith(String prefix)
```
Parameters | prefix | The String object prefix to be tested.

Returns | true if this string begins with the sequence of characters specified by prefix; otherwise false.

Description | This method determines whether or not this String object begins with the specified prefix.

```
public boolean startsWith(String prefix, int toffset)
```
Parameters | prefix | The String object prefix to be tested.
| toffset | The index where the search is to begin.

Returns | true if this string contains the sequence of characters specified by prefix starting at the index toffset; otherwise false.

Description | This method determines whether or not this String object contains the specified prefix at the index specified by toffset.

substring

```
public String substring(int beginIndex)
```
Parameters | beginIndex | The index of the first character in the substring.

Returns | A new String object that contains the sub-sequence of this string that starts at beginIndex and extends to the end of the string.

Throws | StringIndexOutOfBoundsException
| | If beginIndex is less than zero or greater than or equal to the length of the string.

Description | This method returns a new String object that represents a sub-sequence of this String object. The sub-sequence consists of the characters starting at beginIndex and extending through the end of this String object.

```
public String substring(int beginIndex, int endIndex)
```
Parameters   `beginIndex`   The index of the first character in the substring.

                          `endIndex`   The index after the last character in the substring.

Returns   A new `String` object that contains the sub-sequence of this string that starts at `beginIndex` and extends to the character at `endindex-1`.

Throws   `StringIndexOutOfBoundsException`

                          If `beginIndex` or `endIndex` is less than zero or greater than or equal to the length of the string.

Description   This method returns a new `String` object that represents a sub-sequence of this `String` object. The sub-sequence consists of the characters starting at `beginIndex` and extending through `endIndex-1` of this `String` object.

toCharArray

```
public char[] toCharArray()
```
Returns   A new `char` array that contains the same sequence of characters as this string.

Description   This method returns a new `char` array that contains the same sequence of characters as this `String`object. The length of the array is the same as the length of this `String` object.

toLowerCase

```
public String toLowerCase()
```
Returns   A new `String` object that contains the characters of this string converted to lowercase.

Description   This method returns a new `String` that represents a character sequence of the same length as this `String` object, but with each character replaced by its lowercase equivalent if it has one. If no character in the string has a lowercase equivalent, the method returns this `String` object.

```
public String toLowerCase(Locale locale)
```
Availability   New as of JDK 1.1

Parameters   `locale`   The `Locale` to use.

Returns   A new `String` object that contains the characters of this string converted to lowercase using the rules of the specified locale.

Description   This method returns a new `String` that represents a character sequence of the same length as this `String` object, but with each character replaced by its lowercase equivalent if it has one according to the rules of the specified locale. If no character in

the string has a lowercase equivalent, the method returns this
String object.

toString

public String toString()

Returns	This String object.
Overrides	Object.toString()
Description	This method returns this String object.

toUpperCase

public String toUpperCase()

Returns	A new String object that contains the characters of this string converted to uppercase.
Description	This method returns a new String that represents a character sequence of the same length as this String object, but with each character replaced by its uppercase equivalent if it has one. If no character in the string has an uppercase equivalent, the method returns this String object.

public String toUpperCase(Locale locale)

Availability	New as of JDK 1.1	
Parameters	locale	The Locale to use.
Returns	A new String object that contains the characters of this string converted to uppercase using the rules of the specified locale.	
Description	This method returns a new String that represents a character sequence of the same length as this String object, but with each character replaced by its uppercase equivalent if it has one according to the rules of the specified locale. If no character in the string has an uppercase equivalent, the method returns this String object.	

trim

public String trim()

Returns	A new String object that represents the same character sequence as this string, but with leading and trailing whitespace and control characters removed.
Description	If the first and last character in this String object are greater than '\u0020' (the space character), the method returns this String object. Otherwise, the method returns a new String object that contains the same character sequence as this String object, but with leading and trailing characters that are less than '\u0020' removed.

Inherited Methods

Method	Inherited From	Method	Inherited From
clone()	Object	finalize()	Object
getClass()	Object	notify()	Object
notifyAll()	Object	wait()	Object
wait(long)	Object	wait(long, int)	Object

See Also

Character 10.3; Class 10.4; Double 10.8; Exceptions 9.4.1; Float 10.9; Integer 10.10; Long 10.11; Object 10.14; StringBuffer 10.21; String Concatenation Operator + 4.6.3; String literals 2.2.3.5

10.21   StringBuffer

Synopsis

Class Name:	java.lang.StringBuffer
Superclass:	java.lang.Object
Immediate Subclasses:	None
Interfaces Implemented:	java.io.Serializable
Availability:	JDK 1.0 or later

Description

The StringBuffer class represents a variable-length sequence of characters. StringBuffer objects are used in computations that involve creating new String objects. The StringBuffer class provides a number of utility methods for working with StringBuffer objects, including append() and insert() methods that add characters to a StringBuffer and methods that fetch the contents of String-Buffer objects.

When a StringBuffer object is created, the constructor determines the initial contents and capacity of the StringBuffer. The capacity of a StringBuffer is the number of characters that its internal data structure can hold. This is distinct from the length of the contents of a StringBuffer, which is the number of characters that are actually stored in the StringBuffer object. The capacity of a String-Buffer can vary. When a StringBuffer object is asked to hold more characters than its current capacity allows, the StringBuffer enlarges its internal data structure. However, it is more costly in terms of execution time and memory when a StringBuffer has to repeatedly increase its capacity than when a StringBuffer object is created with sufficient capacity.

Because the intended use of StringBuffer objects involves modifying their contents, all methods of the StringBuffer class that modify StringBuffer objects are synchronized. This means that is it safe for multiple threads to try to modify a StringBuffer object at the same time.

StringBuffer objects are used implicitly by the string concatenation operator. Consider the following code:

```
String s, s1, s2;
s = s1 + s2;
```

To compute the string concatenation, the Java compiler generates code like:

```
s = new StringBuffer().append(s1).append(s2).toString();
```

Class Summary

```
public class java.lang.StringBuffer extends java.lang.Object {
    // Constructors
    public StringBuffer();
    public StringBuffer(int length);
    public StringBuffer(String str);

    // Instance Methods
    public StringBuffer append(boolean b);
    public synchronized StringBuffer append(char c);
    public synchronized StringBuffer append(char[] str);
    public synchronized StringBuffer append(char[] str, int offset, int len);
    public StringBuffer append(double d);
    public StringBuffer append(float f);
    public StringBuffer append(int i);
    public StringBuffer append(long l);
    public synchronized StringBuffer append(Object obj);
    public synchronized StringBuffer append(String str);
    public int capacity();
    public synchronized char charAt(int index);
    public synchronized void ensureCapacity(int minimumCapacity);
    public synchronized void getChars(int srcBegin, int srcEnd,
                            char[] dst, int dstBegin);
    public StringBuffer insert(int offset, boolean b);
    public synchronized StringBuffer insert(int offset, char c);
    public synchronized StringBuffer insert(int offset, char[] str);
    public StringBuffer insert(int offset, double d);
    public StringBuffer insert(int offset, float f);
    public StringBuffer insert(int offset, int i);
    public StringBuffer insert(int offset, long l);
    public synchronized StringBuffer insert(int offset, Object obj);
    public synchronized StringBuffer insert(int offset, String str);
    public int length();
    public synchronized StringBuffer reverse();
    public synchronized void setCharAt(int index, char ch);
```

```
    public synchronized void setLength(int newLength);
    public String toString();
}
```

Constructors

StringBuffer

  public StringBuffer()

    Description   Creates a StringBuffer object that does not contain any characters and has a capacity of 16 characters.

  public StringBuffer(int capacity)

    Parameters   capacity   The initial capacity of this StringBufffer object.

    Throws   NegativeArraySizeException

                          If capacity is negative.

    Description   Creates a StringBuffer object that does not contain any characters and has the specified capacity.

  public StringBuffer(String str)

    Parameters   str   A String object.

    Description   Creates a StringBuffer object that contains the same sequence of characters as the given String object and has a capacity 16 greater than the length of the String.

Instance Methods

append

  public StringBuffer append(boolean b)

    Parameters   b   A boolcan value.

    Returns   This StringBuffer object.

    Description   This method appends either "true" or "false" to the end of the sequence of characters stored in ths StringBuffer object, depending on the value of b.

  public synchronized StringBuffer append(char c)

    Parameters   c   A char value.

    Returns   This StringBuffer object.

    Description   This method appends the given character to the end of the sequence of characters stored in this StringBuffer object.

  public synchronized StringBuffer append(char str[])

    Parameters   str   An array of char values.

    Returns   This StringBuffer object.

    Description   This method appends the characters in the given array to the end of the sequence of characters stored in this StringBuffer object.

```
public synchronized StringBuffer append(char str[], int offset,
                                         int len)
```

Parameters   str   An array of char values.

                 offset   An offset into the array.

                 len   The number of characters from the array to be appended.

Returns   This StringBuffer object.

Throws   StringIndexOutOfBoundsException

                       If offset or len are out of range.

Description   This method appends the specified portion of the given array to the end of the character sequence stored in this String-Buffer object. The portion of the array that is appended starts offset elements from the beginning of the array and is len elements long.

```
public StringBuffer append(double d)
```

Parameters   d   A double value.

Returns   This StringBuffer object.

Description   This method converts the given double value to a string using Double.toString(d) and appends the resulting string to the end of the sequence of characters stored in this StringBuffer object.

```
public StringBuffer append(float f)
```

Parameters   f   A float value.

Returns   This StringBuffer object.

Description   This method converts the given float value to a string using Float.toString(f) and appends the resulting string to the end of the sequence of characters stored in this StringBuffer object.

```
public StringBuffer append(int i)
```

Parameters   i   An int value.

Returns   This StringBuffer object.

Description   This method converts the given int value to a string using Integer.toString(i) and appends the resulting string to the end of the sequence of characters stored in this StringBuffer object.

```
public StringBuffer append(long l)
```

Parameters   l   A long value.

Returns   This StringBuffer object.

Description   This method converts the given long value to a string using
                   Long.toString(1) and appends the resulting string to the end
                   of the sequence of characters stored in this StringBuffer
                   object.

public synchronized StringBuffer append(Object obj)
    Parameters   obj   A reference to an object.
    Returns   This StringBuffer object.
    Description   This method gets the string representation of the given object
                   by calling String.valueOf(obj) and appends the resulting
                   string to the end of the character sequence stored in this
                   StringBuffer object.

public synchronized StringBuffer append(String str)
    Parameters   str   A String object.
    Returns   This StringBuffer object.
    Description   This method appends the sequence of characters represented
                   by the given String to the characters in this StringBuffer
                   object. If str is null, the string "null" is appended.

capacity

public int capacity()
    Returns   The capacity of this StringBuffer object.
    Description   This method returns the current capacity of this object. The
                   capacity of a StringBuffer object is the number of characters
                   that its internal data structure can hold. A StringBuffer object
                   automatically increases its capacity when it is asked to hold
                   more characters than its current capacity allows.

charAt

public synchronized char charAt(int index)
    Parameters   index   An index into the StringBuffer.
    Returns   The character stored at the specified position in this String-
                   Buffer object.
    Throws   StringIndexOutOfBoundsException
                                    If index is less than zero or greater than or equal
                                    to the length of the StringBuffer object.
    Description   This method returns the character at the specified position in
                   the StringBuffer object. The first character in the String-
                   Buffer is at index 0.

ensureCapacity

```
public synchronized void ensureCapacity(int minimumCapacity)
```
Parameters   minimumCapacity

The minimum desired capacity.

Description   This method ensures that the capacity of this StringBuffer object is at least the specified number of characters. If necessary, the capacity of this object is increased to the greater of minimumCapacity or double its current capacity plus two.

It is more efficient to ensure that the capacity of a String-Buffer object is sufficient to hold all of the additions that will be made to its contents, rather than let the StringBuffer increase its capacity in multiple increments.

getChars

```
public synchronized void getChars(int srcBegin, int srcEnd,
                                  char dst[], int dstBegin)
```
Parameters   srcBegin   The index of the first character to be copied.

srcEnd   The index after the last character to be copied.

dst   The destination char array.

dstBegin   An offset into the destination array.

Throws   StringIndexOutOfBoundsException

If srcBegin, srcEnd, or dstBegin is out of range.

Description   This method copies each character in the specified range of this StringBuffer object to the given array of char values. More specifically, the first character to be copied is at index srcBegin; the last character to be copied is at index srcEnd-1.

These characters are copied into dst, starting at index dstBegin and ending at index:

```
dstBegin + (srcEnd-srcBegin) - 1
```

insert

```
public StringBuffer insert(int offset, boolean b)
```
Parameters   offset   An offset into the StringBuffer.

b   A boolean value.

Returns   This StringBuffer object.

Throws   StringIndexOutOfBoundsException

If offset is out of range.

Description   This method inserts either "true" or "false" into the sequence of characters stored in this StringBuffer object, depending on the value of b. The string is inserted at a position offset characters from the beginning of the sequence. If offset is 0, the string is inserted before the first character in the StringBuffer.

public synchronized StringBuffer insert(int offset, char c)

Parameters	offset	An offset into the StringBuffer.
	c	A char value.
Returns	This StringBuffer object.	
Throws	StringIndexOutOfBoundsException	
		If offset is less than zero or greater than or equal to the length of the StringBuffer object.
Description	This method inserts the given character into the sequence of characters stored in this StringBuffer object. The character is inserted at a position offset characters from the beginning of the sequence. If offset is 0, the character is inserted before the first character in the StringBuffer.	

public synchronized StringBuffer insert(int offset, char str[])

Parameters	offset	An offset into the StringBuffer.
	str	An array of char values.
Returns	This StringBuffer object.	
Throws	StringIndexOutOfBoundsException	
		If offset is less than zero or greater than or equal to the length of the StringBuffer object.
Description	This method inserts the characters in the given array into the sequence of characters stored in this StringBuffer object. The characters are inserted at a position offset characters from the beginning of the sequence. If offset is 0, the characters are inserted before the first character in the StringBuffer.	

public StringBuffer insert(int offset, double d)

Parameters	offset	An offset into the StringBuffer.
	d	A double value.
Returns	This StringBuffer object.	
Throws	StringIndexOutOfBoundsException	
		If offset is less than zero or greater than or equal to the length of the StringBuffer object.
Description	This method converts the given double value to a string using Double.toString(d) and inserts the resulting string into the sequence of characters stored in this StringBuffer object. The string is inserted at a position offset characters from the beginning of the sequence. If offset is 0, the string is inserted before the first character in the StringBuffer.	

```
public StringBuffer insert(int offset, float f)
```

Parameters	offset	An offset into the StringBuffer.
	f	A float value.
Returns	This StringBuffer object.	
Throws	StringIndexOutOfBoundsException	
		If offset is less than zero or greater than or equal to the length of the StringBuffer object.
Description	This method converts the given float value to a string using Float.toString(f) and inserts the resulting string into the sequence of characters stored in this StringBuffer object. The string is inserted at a position offset characters from the beginning of the sequence. If offset is 0, the string is inserted before the first character in the StringBuffer.	

```
public StringBuffer insert(int offset, int i)
```

Parameters	offset	An offset into the StringBuffer.
	i	An int value.
Returns	This StringBuffer object.	
Throws	StringIndexOutOfBoundsException	
		If offset is less than zero or greater than or equal to the length of the StringBuffer object.
Description	This method converts the given int value to a string using Integer.toString(i) and inserts the resulting string into the sequence of characters stored in this StringBuffer object. The string is inserted at a position offset characters from the beginning of the sequence. If offset is 0, the string is inserted before the first character in the StringBuffer.	

```
public StringBuffer insert(int offset, long l)
```

Parameters	offset	An offset into the StringBuffer.
	l	A long value.
Returns	This StringBuffer object.	
Throws	StringIndexOutOfBoundsException	
		If offset is less than zero or greater than or equal to the length of the StringBuffer object.
Description	This method converts the given long value to a string using Long.toString(l) and inserts the resulting string into the sequence of characters stored in this StringBuffer object. The string is inserted at a position offset characters from the beginning of the sequence. If offset is 0, the string is inserted before the first character in the StringBuffer.	

```
public synchronized StringBuffer insert(int offset, Object obj)
```
Parameters	offset	An offset into the StringBuffer.
	obj	A reference to an object.
Returns	This StringBuffer object.	
Throws	StringIndexOutOfBoundsException	
		If offset is less than zero or greater than or equal to the length of the StringBuffer object.
Description	This method gets the string representation of the given object by calling String.valueOf(obj) and inserts the resulting string into the sequence of characters stored in this StringBuffer object. The string is inserted at a position offset characters from the beginning of the sequence. If offset is 0, the string is inserted before the first character in the StringBuffer.	

```
public synchronized StringBuffer insert(int offset, String str)
```
Parameters	offset	An offset into the StringBuffer.
	str	A String object.
Returns	This StringBuffer object.	
Throws	StringIndexOutOfBoundsException	
		If offset is less than zero or greater than or equal to the length of the StringBuffer object.
Description	This method inserts the sequence of characters represented by the given String into the sequence of characters stored in this StringBuffer object. If str is null, the string "null" is inserted. The string is inserted at a position offset characters from the beginning of the sequence. If offset is 0, the string is inserted before the first character in the StringBuffer.	

length

```
public int length()
```
Returns	The number of characters stored in this StringBuffer object.
Description	This method returns the number of characters stored in this StringBuffer object. The length is distinct from the capacity of a StringBuffer, which is the number of characters that its internal data structure can hold.

reverse

```
public synchronized StringBuffer reverse()
```
Returns	This StringBuffer object.

Description   This method reverses the sequence of characters stored in this `StringBuffer` object.

setCharAt

```
public synchronized void setCharAt(int index, char ch)
```

Parameters   index   The index of the character to be set.

               ch   A char value.

Throws   StringIndexOutOfBoundsException

                     If index is less than zero or greater than or equal to the length of the `StringBuffer` object.

Description   This method modifies the character located index characters from the beginning of the sequence of characters stored in this `StringBuffer` object. The current character at this position is replaced by the character ch.

setLength

```
public synchronized void setLength(int newLength)
```

Parameters   newLength   The new length for this `StringBuffer`.

Throws   StringIndexOutOfBoundsException

                     If index is less than zero.

Description   This method sets the length of the sequence of characters stored in this `StringBuffer` object. If the length is set to be less than the current length, characters are lost from the end of the character sequence. If the length is set to be more than the current length, NUL characters (\u0000) are added to the end of the character sequence.

toString

```
public String toString()
```

Returns   A new `String` object that represents the same sequence of characters as the sequence of characters stored in this `StringBuffer` object.

Overrides   Object.toString()

Description   This method returns a new `String` object that represents the same sequence of characters as the sequence of characters stored in this `StringBuffer` object.

             Note that any subsequent changes to the contents of this `StringBuffer` object do not affect the contents of the `String` object created by this method.

Inherited Methods

Method	Inherited From	Method	Inherited From
clone()	Object	equals(Object)	Object
finalize()	Object	getClass()	Object
hashCode()	Object	notify()	Object
notifyAll()	Object	wait()	Object
wait(long)	Object	wait(long, int)	Object

See Also

Character 10.3; Double 10.8; Exceptions 9.4.1; Float 10.9; Integer 10.10; Long 10.11; Object 10.14; String 10.20; String Concatenation Operator + 4.6.3

10.22   System

Synopsis

Class Name:	java.lang.System
Superclass:	java.lang.Object
Immediate Subclasses:	None
Interfaces Implemented:	None
Availability:	JDK 1.0 or later

Description

The System class provides access to various information about the operating system environment in which a program is running. For example, the System class defines variables that allow access to the standard I/O streams and methods that allow a program to run the garbage collector and stop the Java virtual machine.

All of the variables and methods in the System class are static. In other words, it is not necessary to create an instance of the System class in order to use its variables and methods. In fact, the System class does not define any public constructors, so it cannot be instantiated.

The System class supports the concept of system properties that can be queried and set.

The properties in the following table are guaranteed always to be defined.

Property Name	Description
file.encoding	The character encoding for the default locale (Java 1.1 only)
file.encoding.pkg	The package that contains converters between local encodings and Unicode (Java 1.1 only)
file.separator	File separator ("/" on UNIX, "\" on Windows)
java.class.path	The class path
java.class.version	Java class version number
java.compiler	The just-in-time compiler to use, if any (Java 1.1 only)
java.home	Java installation directory
java.vendor	Java vendor-specific string
java.vendor.url	Java vendor URL
java.version	Java version number
line.separator	Line separator(" \n" on UNIX, " \r\n" on Windows)
os.arch	Operating system architecture
os.name	Operating system name
os.version	Operating system version
path.separator	Path separator (":" on UNIX, "," on Windows)
user.dir	User's current working directory when the properties were initialized
user.home	User's home directory
user.language	The two-letter language code of the default locale (Java 1.1 only)
user.name	User's account name
user.region	The two-letter country code of the default locale (Java 1.1 only)
user.timezone	The default time zone (Java 1.1 only)

Additional properties may be defined by the run-time environment. The –D command-line option can be used to define system properties when a program is run.

The Runtime class is related to the System class; it provides access to information about the environment in which a program is running.

Class Summary

```
public final class java.lang.System extends java.lang.Object {
    // Constants
    public static final PrintStream err;
    public static final InputStream in;
    public static final PrintStream out;

    // Class Methods
    public static void arraycopy(Object src, int srcOffset,
                                Object dst, int dstOffset, int length);
    public static long currentTimeMillis();
    public static void exit(int status);
    public static void gc();
    public static Properties getProperties();
```

```
    public static String getProperty(String key);
    public static String getProperty(String key, String default);
    public static SecurityManager getSecurityManager();
    public static String getenv(String name);            // Deprecated in 1.1
    public static native int identityHashCode(Object x);   // New in 1.1
    public static void load(String filename);
    public static void loadLibrary(String libname);
    public static void runFinalization();
    public static void runFinalizersOnExit(boolean value); // New in 1.1
    public static void setErr(PrintStream err);            // New in 1.1
    public static void setIn(InputStream in);              // New in 1.1
    public static void setOut(PrintStream out);            // New in 1.1
    public static void setProperties(Properties props);
    public static void setSecurityManager(SecurityManager s);
}
```

Variables

err

public static final PrintStream err

Description   The standard error stream. In an application environment, this variable refers to a java.io.PrintStream object that is associated with the standard error output for the process running the Java virtual machine. In an applet environment, the PrintStream is likely to be associated with a separate window, although this is not guaranteed.

The value of err can be set using the setErr() method. The value of err can only be set if the currenly installed SecurityManager does not throw a SecurityException when the request is made.

Prior to to Java 1.1, err was not final. It has been made final as of Java 1.1 because the unchecked ability to set err is a security hole.

in

public static final InputStream in

Description   The standard input stream. In an application environment, this variable refers to a java.io.InputStream object that is associated with the standard input for the process running the Java virtual machine.

The value of in can be set using the setIn() method. The value of in can only be set if the currently installed SecurityManager does not throw a SecurityException when the request is made.

Prior to to Java 1.1, in was not `final`. It has been made `final` as of Java 1.1 because the unchecked ability to set `in` is a security hole.

out

```
public static final PrintStream out
```
Description   The standard output stream. In an application environment, this variable refers to a `java.io.PrintStream` object that is associated with the standard output for the process running the Java virtual machine. In an applet environment, the `PrintStream` is likely to be associated with a separate window, although this is not guaranteed.

out is the most commonly used of the three I/O streams provided by the `System` class. Even in GUI-based applications, sending output to this stream can be useful for debugging. The usual idiom for sending output to this stream is:

```
System.out.println("Some text");
```

The value of `out` can be set using the `setOut()` method. The value of `out` can only be set if the currently installed `Security-Manager` does not throw a `SecurityException` when the request is made.

Prior to to Java 1.1, out was not `final`. It has been made `final` as of Java 1.1 because the unchecked ability to set `out` is a security hole.

Class Methods

arraycopy

```
public static void arraycopy(Object src, int src_position,
                             Object dst, int dst_position,
                             int length)
```
Parameters   src   The source array.

src_position

                              An index into the source array.

dst   The destination array.

dst_position

                              An index into the destination array.

length   The number of elements to be copied.

Throws   `ArrayIndexOutOfBoundsException`

> If the values of the `src_position`, `dst_position`, and `length` arguments imply accessing either array with an index that is less than zero or an index greater than or equal to the number of elements in the array.

`ArrayStoreException`

> If the type of value stored in the `src` array cannot be stored in the `dst` array.

`NullPointerException`

> If `src` or `dst` is `null`.

Description   This method copies a range of array elements from the `src` array to the `dst` array. The number of elements that are copied is specified by `length`. The elements at positions `src_position` through `src_position+length-1` in `src` are copied to the positions `dst_position` through `dst_position+length-1` in `dst`, respectively.

If `src` and `dst` refer to the same array, the copying is done as if the array elements were first copied to a temporary array and then copied to the destination array.

Before this method does any copying, it performs a number of checks. If either `src` or `dst` are `null`, the method throws a `NullPointerException` and `dst` is not modified.

If any of the following conditions are true, the method throws an `ArrayStoreException`, and `dst` is not modified:

- Either `src` or `dst` refers to an object that is not an array.
- `src` and `dst` refer to arrays whose element types are different primitive types.
- `src` refers to an array that has elements that contain a primitive type, while `dst` refers to an array that has elements that contain a reference type, or vice versa.

If any of the following conditions are true, the method throws an `ArrayIndexOutOfBoundsException`, and `dst` is not modified:

- `srcOffset`, `dstOffset`, or `length` is negative.
- `srcOffset+length` is greater than `src.length()`.
- `dstOffset+length` is greater than `dst.length()`.

Otherwise, if an element in the source array being copied cannot be converted to the type of the destination array using the rules of the assignment operator, the method throws an

ArrayStoreException when the problem occurs. Since the problem is discovered during the copy operation, the state of the dst array reflects the incomplete copy operation.

currentTimeMillis

public static native long currentTimeMillis()

Returns   The current time as the number of milliseconds since 00:00:00 UTC, January 1, 1970.

Description This method returns the current time as the number of milliseconds since 00:00:00 UTC, January 1, 1970. It will not overflow until the year 292280995.

The java.util.Date class provides more extensive facilities for dealing with times and dates.

exit

public static void exit(int status)

Parameters status   The exit status code to use.

Throws   SecurityException

If the checkExit() method of the SecurityManager throws a SecurityException.

Description This method causes the Java virtual machine to exit with the given status code. This method works by calling the exit() method of the current Runtime object. By convention, a nonzero status code indicates abnormal termination. This method never returns.

gc

public static void gc()

Description This method causes the Java virtual machine to run the garbage collector in the current thread. This method works by calling the gc() method of the current Runtime object.

The garbage collector finds objects that will never be used again because there are no live references to them. After it finds these objects, the garbage collector frees the storage occupied by these objects.

The garbage collector is normally run continuously in a thread with the lowest possible priority, so that it works intermittently to reclaim storage. The gc() method allows a program to invoke the garbage collector explicitly when necessary.

getProperties

`public static Properties getProperties()`

Returns	A `Properties` object that contains the values of all the system properies.
Throws	`SecurityException`
	If the `checkPropertiesAccess()` method of the `SecurityManager` throws a `SecurityException`.
Description	This method returns all of the defined system properties encapsulated in a `java.util.Properties` object. If there are no system properties currently defined, a set of default system properties is created and initialized. As discussed in the description of the `System` class, some system properties are guaranteed always to be defined.

getProperty

`public static String getProperty(String key)`

Parameters	`key`	The name of a system property.
Returns	The value of the named system property or `null` if the named property is not defined.	
Throws	`SecurityException`	
	If the `checkPropertyAccess()` method of the `SecurityManager` throws a `SecurityException`.	
Description	This method returns the value of the named system property. If there is no definition for the named property, the method returns `null`. If there are no system properties currently defined, a set of default system properties is created and initialized. As discussed in the description of the `System` class, some system properties are guaranteed always to be defined.	

`public static String getProperty(String key, String def)`

Parameters	`key`	The name of a system property.
	`def`	A default value for the property.
Returns	The value of the named system property, or the default value if the named property is not defined.	
Throws	`SecurityException`	
	If the `checkPropertyAccess()` method of the `SecurityManager` throws a `SecurityException`.	
Description	This method returns the value of the named system property. If there is no definition for the named property, the method returns the default value as specified by the `def` parameter. If there are no system properties currently defined, a set of default system properties is created and initialized. As discussed	

earlier in the description of the System class, some system properties are guaranteed to always be defined.

getSecurityManager

public static SecurityManager getSecurityManager()

Returns A reference to the installed SecurityManager object or null if there is no SecurityManager object installed.

Description This method returns a reference to the installed SecurityManager object. If there is no SecurityManager object installed, the method returns null.

getenv

public static String getenv(String name)

Availability Deprecated as of JDK 1.1

Parameters name The name of a system-dependent environment variable.

Returns The value of the environment variable or null if the variable is not defined.

Description This method is obsolete; it always throws an error. Use getProperties() and the -D option instead.

identityHashCode

public static native int identityHashCode(Object x)

Availability New as of JDK 1.1

Parameters x An object.

Returns The identity hashcode value for the specified object.

Description This method returns the same hashcode value for the specified object as would be returned by the default hashCode() method of Object, regardless of whether or not the object's class overrides hashCode().

load

public void load(String filename)

Parameters filename A string that specifies the complete path of the file to be loaded.

Throws SecurityException

    If the checkLink() method of the SecurityManager throws a SecurityException.

  UnsatisfiedLinkError

    If the method is unsuccessful in loading the specified dynamically linked library.

Description   This method loads the specified dynamically linked library. This method works by calling the load() method of the current Runtime object.

loadLibrary

```
public void loadLibrary(String libname)
```
Parameters   libname   A string that specifies the name of a dynamically linked library.

Throws   SecurityException
          If the checkLink() method of the SecurityManager throws a SecurityException.

          UnsatisfiedLinkError
          If the method is unsuccessful in loading the specified dynamically linked library.

Description   This method loads the specified dynamically linked library. It looks for the specified library in a platform-specific way. This method works by calling the loadLibrary() method of the current Runtime object.

runFinalization

```
public static void runFinalization()
```
Description   This method causes the Java virtual machine to run the finalize() methods of any objects in the finalization queue in the current thread. This method works by calling the runFinalization() method of the current Runtime object.

When the garbage collector discovers that there are no references to an object, it checks to see if the object has a finalize() method that has never been called. If the object has such a finalize() method, the object is placed in the finalization queue. While there is a reference to the object in the finalization queue, the object is no longer considered garbage collectable.

Normally, the objects in the finalization queue are handled by a separate finalization thread that runs continuously at a very low priority. The finalization thread removes an object from the queue and calls its finalize() method. As long as the finalize() method does not generate a reference to the object, the object again becomes available for garbage collection.

Because the finalization thread runs at a very low priority, there may be a long delay from the time that an object is put on the finalization queue until the time that its finalize() method is called. The runFinalization() method allows a program to run the finalize() methods explicitly. This can be useful when there is a shortage of some resource that is released by a finalize() method.

runFinalizersOnExit

public static void runFinalizersOnExit(boolean value)

Availability	New as of JDK 1.1	
Parameters	value	A boolean value that specifies whether or not finalization occurs on exit.
Throws	SecurityException	
		If the checkExit() method of the SecurityManager throws a SecurityException.
Description		This method specifies whether or not the finalize() methods of all objects that have finalize() methods are run before the Java virtual machine exits. By default, the finalizers are not run on exit. This method works by calling the runFinalizersOnExit() method of the current Runtime object.

setErr

public static void setErr(PrintStream err)

Availability	New as of JDK 1.1	
Parameters	err	A PrintStream object to use for the standard error stream.
Throws	SecurityException	
		If the checkExec() method of the SecurityManager throws a SecurityException.
Description		This method sets the standard error stream to be this PrintStream object.

setIn

public static void setIn(InputStream in)

Availability	New as of JDK 1.1	
Parameters	in	A InputStream object to use for the standard input stream.
Throws	SecurityException	
		If the checkExec() method of the SecurityManager throws a SecurityException.
Description		This method sets the standard input stream to be this InputStream object.

setOut

`public static void setOut(PrintStream out)`

Availability	New as of JDK 1.1
Parameters	out	A `PrintStream` object to use for the standard output stream.
Throws	`SecurityException`
	If the `checkExec()` method of the `SecurityManager` throws a `SecurityException`.
Description	This method sets the standard output stream to be this `PrintStream` object.

setProperties

`public static void setProperties(Properties props)`

Parameters	props	A reference to a `Properties` object.
Throws	`SecurityException`
	If the `checkPropertiesAccess()` method of the `SecurityManager` throws a `SecurityException`.
Description	This method replaces the current set of system property definitions with a new set of system property definitions that are encapsulated by the given `Properties` object. As discussed in the description of the `System` class, some system properties are guaranteed to always be defined.

setSecurityManager

`public static void setSecurityManager(SecurityManager s)`

Parameters	s	A reference to a `SecurityManager` object.
Throws	`SecurityException`
	If a `SecurityManager` object has already been installed.
Description	This method installs the given `SecurityManager` object. If s is null, then no `SecurityManager` object is installed. Once a `SecurityManager` object is installed, any subsequent calls to this method throw a `SecurityException`.

Inherited Methods

Method	Inherited From	Method	Inherited From
clone()	Object	equals(Object)	Object
finalize()	Object	getClass()	Object
hashCode()	Object	notify()	Object
notifyAll()	Object	toString()	Object

Method	Inherited From	Method	Inherited From
wait()	Object	wait(long)	Object
wait(long, int)	Object		

See Also

Assignment Compatibility 4.13.1; Errors 9.4.2; Exceptions 9.4.1; Object 10.14; Object Destruction 5.3.4; Process 10.15; Runtime 10.17; SecurityManager 10.18

10.23   Thread

Synopsis

Class Name:	java.lang.Thread
Superclass:	java.lang.Object
Immediate Subclasses:	None
Interfaces Implemented:	java.lang.Runnable
Availability:	JDK 1.0 or later

Description

The Thread class encapsulates all of the information about a single thread of control running in a Java environment. Thread objects are used to control threads in a multithreaded program.

The execution of Java code is always under the control of a Thread object. The Thread class provides a static method called currentThread() that can be used to get a reference to the Thread object that controls the current thread of execution.

In order for a Thread object to be useful, it must be associated with a method that it is supposed to run. Java provides two ways of associating a Thread object with a method:

- Declare a subclass of Thread that defines a run() method. When such a class is instantiated and the object's start() method is called, the thread invokes this run() method.
- Pass a reference to an object that implements the Runnable interface to a Thread constructor. When the start() method of such a Thread object is called, the thread invokes the run() method of the Runnable object.

After a thread is started, it dies when one of the following things happens:

- The run() method called by the Thread returns.

- An exception is thrown that causes the run() method to be exited.
- The stop() method of the Thread is called.

Class Summary

```
public class java.lang.Thread extends java.lang.Object
                            implements java.lang.Runnable {
    // Constants
    public final static int MAX_PRIORITY;
    public final static int MIN_PRIORITY;
    public final static int NORM_PRIORITY;

    // Constructors
    public Thread();
    public Thread(Runnable target);
    public Thread(Runnable target, String name);
    public Thread(String name);
    public Thread(ThreadGroup group, Runnable target);
    public Thread(ThreadGroup group, Runnable target, String name);
    public Thread(ThreadGroup group, String name);

    // Class Methods
    public static int activeCount();
    public static native Thread currentThread();
    public static void dumpStack();
    public static int enumerate(Thread tarray[]);
    public static boolean interrupted();
    public static native void sleep(long millis);
    public static void sleep(long millis, int nanos);
    public static native void yield();

    // Instance Methods
    public void checkAccess();
    public native int countStackFrames();
    public void destroy();
    public final String getName();
    public final int getPriority();
    public final ThreadGroup getThreadGroup();
    public void interrupt();
    public final native boolean isAlive();
    public final boolean isDaemon();
    public boolean isInterrupted();
    public final void join();
    public final synchronized void join(long millis);
    public final synchronized void join(long millis, int nanos);
    public final void resume();
    public void run();
    public final void setDaemon(boolean on);
    public final void setName(String name);
    public final void setPriority(int newPriority);
```

```
    public synchronized native void start();
    public final void stop();
    public final synchronized void stop(Throwable o);
    public final void suspend();
    public String toString();
}
```

Constants

MAX_PRIORITY

public final static int MAX_PRIORITY = 10

Description   The highest priority a thread can have.

MIN_PRIORITY

public final static int MIN_PRIORITY = 1

Description   The lowest priority a thread can have.

NORM_PRIORITY

public final static int NORM_PRIORITY = 5

Description   The default priority assigned to a thread.

Constructors

Thread

public Thread()

Throws   SecurityException

If the checkAccess() method of the Security-
Manager throws a SecurityException.

Description   Creates a Thread object that belongs to the same ThreadGroup
object as the current thread, has the same daemon attribute as
the current thread, has the same priority as the current thread,
and has a default name.

A Thread object created with this constructor invokes its own
run() method when the Thread object's start() method is
called. This is not useful unless the object belongs to a subclass
of the Thread class that overrides the run() method.

Calling this constructor is equivalent to:

```
Thread(null, null, genName)
```

genName is an automatically generated name of the form
"Thread-"+n, where n is an integer incremented each time a
Thread object is created.

`public Thread(String name)`

Parameters	name	The name of this `Thread` object.
Throws	`SecurityException`	
		If the `checkAccess()` method of the `Security-Manager` throws a `SecurityException`.
Description		Creates a `Thread` object that belongs to the same `ThreadGroup` object as the current thread, has the same daemon attribute as the current thread, has the same priority as the current thread, and has the specified name.

A `Thread` object created with this constructor invokes its own `run()` method when the `Thread` object's `start()` method is called. This is not useful unless the object belongs to a subclass of the `Thread` class that overrides the `run()` method.

Calling this constructor is equivalent to:

```
Thread(null, null, name)
```

The uniqueness of the specified `Thread` object's name is not checked, which may be a problem for programs that attempt to identify `Thread` objects by their name.

`public Thread(ThreadGroup group, Runnable target)`

Parameters	group	The `ThreadGroup` object that this `Thread` object is to be added to.
	target	A reference to an object that implements the `Runnable` interface.
Throws	`SecurityException`	
		If the `checkAccess()` method of the `Security-Manager` throws a `SecurityException`.
Description		Creates a `Thread` object that belongs to the specified `ThreadGroup` object, has the same daemon attribute as the current thread, has the same priority as the current thread, and has a default name.

A `Thread` object created with this constructor invokes the `run()` method of the specified `Runnable` object when the `Thread` object's `start()` method is called.

Calling this constructor is equivalent to:

```
Thread(group, target, genName)
```

`genName` is an automatically generated name of the form `"Thread-"+n`, where n is an integer that is incremented each time a `Thread` object is created.

```
public Thread(ThreadGroup group, Runnable target, String name)
```

Parameters	group	The ThreadGroup object that this Thread object is to be added to.
	target	A reference to an object that implements the Runnable interface.
	name	The name of this Thread object.
Throws	SecurityException	
		If the checkAccess() method of the Security-Manager throws a SecurityException.
Description		Creates a Thread object that belongs to the specified Thread-Group object, has the same daemon attribute as the current thread, has the same priority as the current thread, and has the specified name.

A Thread object created with this constructor invokes the run() method of the specified Runnable object when the Thread object's start() method is called.

The uniqueness of the specified Thread object's name is not checked, which may be a problem for programs that attempt to identify Thread objects by their names.

```
public Thread(ThreadGroup group, String name)
```

Parameters	group	The ThreadGroup object that this Thread object is to be added to.
	name	The name of this Thread object.
Throws	SecurityException	
		If the checkAccess() method of the Security-Manager throws a SecurityException.
Description		Creates a Thread object that belongs to the specified Thread-Group object, has the same daemon attribute as the current thread, has the same priority as the current thread, and has the specified name.

A Thread object created with this constructor invokes its own run() method when the Thread object's start() method is called. This is not useful unless the object belongs to a subclass of the Thread class that overrides the run() method. Calling this constructor is equivalent to:

```
Thread(group, null, name)
```

The uniqueness of the specified Thread object's name is not checked, which may be a problem for programs that attempt to identify Thread objects by their name.

Class Methods

activeCount

    public static int activeCount()

Returns	The current number of threads in the ThreadGroup of the currently running thread.
Description	This method returns the number of threads in the ThreadGroup of the currently running thread for which the isAlive() method returns true.

currentThread

    public static native Thread currentThread()

Returns	A reference to the Thread object that controls the currently executing thread.
Description	This method returns a reference to the Thread object that controls the currently executing thread.

dumpStack

    public static void dumpStack()

Description	This method outputs a stack trace of the currently running thread.

enumerate

    public static int enumerate(Thread tarray[])

Parameters	tarray	A reference to an array of Thread objects.
Returns		The number of Thread objects stored in the array.
Description		This method stores a reference in the array for each of the Thread objects in the ThreadGroup of the currently running thread for which the isAlive() method returns true.

                Calling this method is equivalent to:

```
currentThread().getThreadGroup().enumerate(tarray)
```

                If the array is not big enough to contain references to all the Thread objects, only as many references as will fit are put into the array. No indication is given that some Thread objects were left out, so it is a good idea to call activeCount() before calling this method, to get an idea of how large to make the array.

interrupted

`public static boolean interrupted()`

Returns   true if the currently running thread has been interrupted; otherwise false.

Description   This method determines whether or not the currently running thread has been interrupted.

sleep

`public static native void sleep(long millis)`

Parameters   millis   The number of milliseconds that the currently running thread should sleep.

Throws   InterruptedException

If another thread interrupts the currently running thread.

Description   This method causes the currently running thread to sleep. The method does not return until at least the specified number of milliseconds have elapsed.

While a thread is sleeping, it retains ownership of all locks. The Object class defines a method called wait() that is similar to sleep() but causes the currently running thread to temporarily relinquish its locks.

`public static void sleep(long millis, int nanos)`

Parameters   millis   The number of milliseconds that the currently running thread should sleep.

nanos   An additional number of nanoseconds to sleep.

Throws   InterruptedException

If another thread interrupts the currently running thread.

Description   This method causes the currently running thread to sleep. The method does not return until at least the specified number of milliseconds have elapsed.

While a thread is sleeping, it retains ownership of all locks. The Object class defines a method called wait() that is similar to sleep() but causes the currently running thread to temporarily relinquish its locks.

Note that Sun's reference implementation of Java does not attempt to implement the precision implied by this method. Instead, it rounds to the nearest millisecond (unless millis is 0, in which case it rounds up to 1 millisecond) and calls sleep(long).

yield

public static native void yield()

Description   This method causes the currently running thread to yield control of the processor so that another thread can be scheduled.

Instance Methods

checkAccess

public void checkAccess()

Throws   SecurityException

If the checkAccess() method of the Security-Manager throws a SecurityException.

Description   This method determines if the currently running thread has permission to modify this Thread object.

countStackFrames

public native int countStackFrames()

Returns   The number of pending method invocations on this thread's stack.

Description   This method returns the number of pending method invocations on this thread's stack.

destroy

public void destroy()

Description   This method is meant to terminate this thread without any of the usual cleanup (i.e., any locks held by the thread are not released). This method provides a last-resort way to terminate a thread. While a thread can defeat its stop() method by catching objects thrown from it, there is nothing that a thread can do to stop itself from being destroyed.

Note that Sun's reference implementation of Java does not implement the documented functionality of this method. Instead, the implementation of this method just throws a NoSuchMethodError.

getName

public final String getName()

Returns   The name of this thread.

Description   This method returns the name of this Thread object.

getPriority

public final int getPriority()

Returns	The priority of this thread.
Description	This method returns the priority of this Thread object.

getThreadGroup

public final ThreadGroup getThreadGroup()

Returns	The ThreadGroup of this thread.
Description	This method returns a reference to the ThreadGroup that this Thread object belongs to.

interrupt

public void interrupt()

Description	This method interrupts this Thread object.

Note that prior to version 1.1, Sun's reference implementation of Java does not implement the documented functionality of this method. Instead, the method just sets a private flag that indicates that an interrupt has been requested. None of the methods that should throw an InterruptedException currently do. However, the interrupted() and isInterrupted() methods do return true after this method has been called.

isAlive

public final native boolean isAlive()

Returns	true if this thread is alive; otherwise false.
Description	This method determines whether or not this Thread object is alive. A Thread object is alive if it has been started and has not yet died. In other words, it has been scheduled to run before and can still be scheduled to run again. A thread is generally alive after its start() method is called and until its stop() method is called.

isDaemon

public final boolean isDaemon()

Returns	true if the thread is a daemon thread; otherwise false.
Description	This method determines whether or not this thread is a daemon thread, based on the value of the daemon attribute of this Thread object.

isInterrupted

public boolean isInterrupted()

Returns   true if this thread has been interrupted; otherwise false.

Description   This method determines whether or not this Thread object has been interrupted.

join

public final void join()

Throws   InterruptedException

If another thread interrupts this thread.

Description   This method allows the thread that calls it to wait for the Thread associated with this method to die. The method returns when the Thread dies. If this thread is already dead, then this method returns immediately.

public final synchronized void join(long millis)

Parameters   millis   The maximum number of milliseconds to wait for this thread to die.

Throws   InterruptedException

If another thread interrupts this thread.

Description   This method causes a thread to wait to die. The method returns when this Thread object dies or after the specified number of milliseconds has elapsed, whichever comes first. However, if the specified number of milliseconds is zero, the method will wait forever for this thread to die. If this thread is already dead, the method returns immediately.

public final synchronized void join(long millis, int nanos)

Parameters   millis   The maximum number of milliseconds to wait for this thread to die.

              nanos   An additional number of nanoseconds to wait.

Throws   InterruptedException

If another thread interrupts this thread.

Description   This method causes a thread to wait to die. The method returns when this Thread object dies or after the specified amount of time has elapsed, whichever comes first. However, if millis and nanos are zero, the method will wait forever for this thread to die. If this thread is already dead, the method returns immediately.

Note that Sun's reference implementation of Java does not attempt to implement the precision implied by this method. Instead, it rounds to the nearest millisecond (unless millis is 0,

in which case it rounds up to 1 millisecond) and calls
`join(long)`.

resume

`public final void resume()`

Throws	SecurityException
	If the `checkAccess()` method of the Security-Manager throws a SecurityException.
Description	This method resumes a suspended thread. The method causes this Thread object to once again be eligible to be run. Calling this method for a thread that is not suspended has no effect.

run

`public void run()`

Implements	Runnable.run()
Description	A Thread object's start() method causes the thread to invoke a run() method. If this Thread object was created without a specified Runnable object, the Thread object's own run() method is executed. This behavior is only useful in a subclass of Thread that overrides this run() method, since the run() method of the Thread class does not do anything.

setDaemon

`public final void setDaemon(boolean on)`

Parameters	on	The new value for this thread's daemon attribute.
Throws	IllegalThreadStateException	
		If this method is called after this thread has been started and while it is still alive.
	SecurityException	
		If the checkAccess() method of the Security-Manager throws a SecurityException.
Description		This method sets the daemon attribute of this Thread object to the given value. This method must be called before the thread is started. If a thread dies and there are no other threads except daemon threads alive, the Java virtual machine stops.

setName

public final void setName(String name)

Parameters	name	The new name for this thread.
Throws	SecurityException	
		If the checkAccess() method of the Security-Manager throws a SecurityException.
Description		This method sets the name of this Thread object to the given value. The uniqueness of the specified Thread object's name is not checked, which may be a problem for programs that attempt to identify Thread objects by their name.

setPriority

public final void setPriority(int newPriority)

Parameters	newPriority	The new priority for this thread.
Throws	IllegalArgumentException	
		If the given priority is less than MIN_PRIORITY or greater than MAX_PRIORITY.
	SecurityException	
		If the checkAccess() method of the Security-Manager throws a SecurityException.
Description		This method sets the priority of this Thread to the given value.

start

public synchronized native void start()

Throws	IllegalThreadStateException	
		If this Thread object's start() method has been called before.
Description		This method starts this Thread object, allowing it to be scheduled for execution. The top-level code that is executed by the thread is the run() method of the Runnable object specified in the constructor that was used to create this object. If no such object was specified, the top-level code executed by the thread is this object's run() method.

It is not permitted to start a thread more than once.

stop

public final void stop()

Throws	SecurityException	
		If the checkAccess() method of the Security-Manager throws a SecurityException.

Description   This method causes this Thread object to stop executing by throwing a ThreadDeath object. The object is thrown in this thread, even if the method is called from a different thread. This thread is forced to stop whatever it is doing and throw a newly created ThreadDeath object. If this thread was suspended, it is resumed; if it was sleeping, it is awakened. Normally, you should not catch ThreadDeath objects in a try statement. If you need to catch ThreadDeath objects to detect a Thread is about to die, the try statement that catches ThreadDeath objects should rethrow them.

When an object is thrown out of the run() method associated with a Thread, the uncaughtException() method of the ThreadGroup for that Thread is called. The uncaughtException() method normally outputs a stack trace. However, uncaughtException() treats a ThreadDeath object as a special case by not outputting a stack trace. When the uncaughtException() method returns, the thread is dead. The thread is never scheduled to run again.

If this Thread object's stop() method is called before this thread is started, the ThreadDeath object is thrown as soon as the thread is started.

```
public final synchronized void stop(Throwable o)
```
Parameters   o   The object to be thrown.

Throws   SecurityException

                  If the checkAccess() method of the Security-Manager throws a SecurityException.

Description   This method causes this Thread object to stop executing by throwing the given object. Normally, the stop() method that takes no arguments and throws a ThreadDeath object should be called instead of this method. However, if it is necessary to stop a thread by throwing some other type of object, this method can be used.

The object is thrown in this thread, even if the method is called from a different thread. This thread is forced to stop whatever it is doing and throw the Throwable object o. If this thread was suspended, it is resumed; if it was sleeping, it is awakened.

When an object is thrown out of the run() method associated with a Thread, the uncaughtException() method of the ThreadGroup for that Thread is called. If the thrown object is not an instance of the ThreadDeath class, uncaughtException()

calls the thrown object's printStackTrace() method and then the thread dies. The thread is never scheduled to run again.

If this Thread object's stop() method is called before this thread is started, the ThreadDeath object is thrown as soon as the thread is started.

suspend

public final void suspend()

Throws	SecurityException
	If the checkAccess() method of the Security-Manager throws a SecurityException.
Description	This method suspends a thread. The method causes this Thread object to temporarily be ineligible to be run. The thread becomes eligible to be run again after its resume() method is called. Calling this method for a thread that is already suspended has no effect.

toString

public String toString()

Returns	A string representation of this Thread object.
Overrides	Object.toString()
Description	This method returns a string representation of this Thread object.

Inherited Methods

Method	Inherited From	Method	Inherited From
clone()	Object	equals(Object)	Object
finalize()	Object	getClass()	Object
hashCode()	Object	notify()	Object
notifyAll()	Object	wait()	Object
wait(long)	Object	wait(long, int)	Object

See Also

Exceptions 9.4.1; Object 10.14; Runnable 10.16; SecurityManager 10.18; Thread-Group 10.24, Threads 8

10.24　*ThreadGroup*

Synopsis

Class Name:　　　　　　　java.lang.ThreadGroup
Superclass:　　　　　　　java.lang.Object
Immediate Subclasses:　　None
Interfaces Implemented:　None
Availability:　　　　　　　JDK 1.0 or later

Description

The ThreadGroup class implements a grouping scheme for threads. A ThreadGroup object can own Thread objects and other ThreadGroup objects. The ThreadGroup class provides methods that allow a ThreadGroup object to control its Thread and ThreadGroup objects as a group. For example, suspend() and resume() methods of a ThreadGroup object call the suspend() and resume() methods of each of the Thread and ThreadGroup objects that belong to the particular ThreadGroup.

When a Java program starts, a ThreadGroup object is created to own the first Thread. Any additional ThreadGroup objects are explicitly created by the program.

Class Summary

```
public class java.lang.ThreadGroup extends java.lang.Object {
    // Constructors
    public ThreadGroup(String name);
    public ThreadGroup(ThreadGroup parent, String name;

    // Instance Methods
    public int activeCount();
    public int activeGroupCount();
    public boolean allowThreadSuspension(boolean b);        // New in 1.1
    public final void checkAccess();
    public final void destroy();
    public int enumerate(Thread list[]);
    public int enumerate(Thread list[], boolean recurse);
    public int enumerate(ThreadGroup list[]);
    public int enumerate(ThreadGroup list[], boolean recurse);
    public final int getMaxPriority();
    public final String getName();
    public final ThreadGroup getParent();
    public final boolean isDaemon();
    public synchronized boolean isDestroyed();              // New in 1.1
    public void list();
    public final boolean parentOf(ThreadGroup g);
    public final void resume();
    public final void setDaemon(boolean daemon);
    public final void setMaxPriority(int pri);
```

```
    public final void stop();
    public final void suspend();
    public String toString();
    public void uncaughtException(Thread t, Throwable e);
}
```

Constructors

ThreadGroup

public ThreadGroup(String name)

Parameters	name	The name of this ThreadGroup object.
Throws	SecurityException	
		If the checkAccess() method of the Security-Manager throws a SecurityException.
Description		Creates a ThreadGroup object that has the specified name and the same parent ThreadGroup as the current thread.

public ThreadGroup(ThreadGroup parent, String name)

Parameters	parent	The ThreadGroup object that this ThreadGroup object is to be added to.
	name	The name of this ThreadGroup object.
Throws	SecurityException	
		If the checkAccess() method of the Security-Manager throws a SecurityException.
Description		Creates a ThreadGroup object with the specified name and parent ThreadGroup object.

Instance Methods

activeCount

public int activeCount()

Returns	An approximation of the current number of threads in this ThreadGroup object and any child ThreadGroup objects.
Description	This method returns an approximation of the number of threads that belong to this ThreadGroup object and any child ThreadGroup objects. The count is approximate because a thread can die after it is counted, but before the complete count is returned. Also, after a child ThreadGroup is counted but before the total count is returned, additional Thread and ThreadGroup objects can be added to a child ThreadGroup.

activeGroupCount

`public int activeGroupCount()`

Returns	An approximation of the current number of child ThreadGroup objects in this ThreadGroup object.
Description	This method returns an approximation of the number of child ThreadGroup objects that belong to this ThreadGroup object. The count is approximate because after a child ThreadGroup is counted but before the total count is returned, additional ThreadGroup objects can be added to a child ThreadGroup.

allowThreadSuspension

`public boolean allowThreadSuspension(boolean b)`

Availability	New as of JDK 1.1	
Parameters	b	A boolean value that specifies whether or not the run-time system is allowed to suspend threads due to low memory.
Returns	The boolean value true.	
Description	This method specifies whether or not the Java virtual machine is allowed to suspend threads due to low memory.	

checkAccess

`public final void checkAccess()`

Throws	SecurityException	
		If the checkAccess() method of the Security-Manager throws a SecurityException.
Description	This method determines if the currently running thread has permission to modify this ThreadGroup object.	

destroy

`public final void destroy()`

Throws	IllegalThreadStateException	
		If this ThreadGroup object is not empty, or if it has already been destroyed.
	SecurityException	
		If the checkAccess() method of the Security-Manager throws a SecurityException.
Description	This method destroys this ThreadGroup object and any child ThreadGroup objects. The ThreadGroup must not contain any Thread objects. This method also removes the ThreadGroup object from its parent ThreadGroup object.	

enumerate

    public int enumerate(Thread list[])

Parameters	list	A reference to an array of Thread objects.
Returns		The number of Thread objects stored in the array.
Description		This method stores a reference in the array for each of the Thread objects that belongs to this ThreadGroup or any of its child ThreadGroup objects.

If the array is not big enough to contain references to all the Thread objects, only as many references as will fit are put into the array. No indication is given that some Thread objects were left out, so it is a good idea to call activeCount() before calling this method, to get an idea of how large to make the array.

    public int enumerate(Thread list[], boolean recurse)

Parameters	list	A reference to an array of Thread objects.
	recurse	A boolean value that specifies whether or not to include Thread objects that belong to child ThreadGroup objects of this ThreadGroup object.
Returns		The number of Thread objects stored in the array.
Description		This method stores a reference in the array for each of the Thread objects that belongs to this ThreadGroup object. If recurse is true, the method also stores a reference for each of the Thread objects that belongs to a child ThreadGroup object of this ThreadGroup.

If the array is not big enough to contain references to all the Thread objects, only as many references as will fit are put into the array. No indication is given that some Thread objects were left out, so it is a good idea to call activeCount() before calling this method, to get an idea of how large to make the array.

    public int enumerate(ThreadGroup list[])

Parameters	list	A reference to an array of ThreadGroup objects.
Returns		The number of ThreadGroup objects stored in the array.
Description		This method stores a reference in the array for each Thread-Group object that belongs to this ThreadGroup or any of its child ThreadGroup objects.

If the array is not big enough to contain references to all the ThreadGroup objects, only as many references as will fit are put into the array. No indication is given that some ThreadGroup objects were left out, so it is a good idea to call activeGroup-Count() before calling this method, to get an idea of how large to make the array.

```
public int enumerate(Thread list[], boolean recurse)
```
    Parameters   list   A reference to an array of ThreadGroup objects.

                       recurse   A boolean value that specifies whether or not to include ThreadGroup objects that belong to child ThreadGroup objects of this ThreadGroup object.

    Returns   The number of ThreadGroup objects stored in the array.

    Description   This method stores a reference in the array for each of the ThreadGroup objects that belongs to this ThreadGroup object. If recurse is true, the method also stores a reference for each of the ThreadGroup objects that belongs to a child ThreadGroup object of this ThreadGroup.

                    If the array is not big enough to contain references to all the ThreadGroup objects, only as many references as will fit are put into the array. No indication is given that some ThreadGroup objects were left out, so it is a good idea to call activeGroup-Count() before calling this method, to get an idea of how large to make the array.

getMaxPriority

```
public final int getMaxPriority()
```
    Returns   The maximum priority that can be assigned to Thread objects that belong to this ThreadGroup object.

    Description   This method returns the maximum priority that can be assigned to Thread objects that belong to this ThreadGroup object.

                    It is possible for a ThreadGroup to contain Thread objects that have higher priorities than this maximum, if they were given that higher priority before the maximum was set to a lower value.

getName

```
public final String getName()
```
    Returns   The name of this ThreadGroup object.

    Description   This method returns the name of this ThreadGroup object.

getParent

```
public final ThreadGroup getParent()
```
    Returns   The parent ThreadGroup object of this ThreadGroup, or null if this ThreadGroup is the root of the thread group hierarchy.

Description   This method returns the parent ThreadGroup object of this ThreadGroup object. If this ThreadGroup is at the root of the thread group hierarchy and has no parent, the method returns null.

isDaemon

```
public final boolean isDaemon()
```
Returns   true if this ThreadGroup is a daemon thread group; otherwise false.

Description   This method determines whether or not this ThreadGroup is a daemon thread group, based on the value of daemon attribute of this ThreadGroup object. A daemon thread group is destroyed when the last Thread in it is stopped, or the last ThreadGroup in it is destroyed.

isDestroyed

```
public synchronized boolean isDestroyed()
```
Availability   New as of JDK 1.1

Returns   true if this ThreadGroup has been destroyed; otherwise false.

Description   This method determines whether or not this ThreadGroup has been destroyed.

list

```
public void list()
```
Description   This method outputs a listing of the contents of this Thread-Group object to System.out.

parentOf

```
public final boolean parentOf(ThreadGroup g)
```
Parameters   g   A ThreadGroup object.

Returns   true if this ThreadGroup object is the same ThreadGroup, or a direct or indirect parent of the specified ThreadGroup; otherwise false.

Description   This method determines if this ThreadGroup object is the same as the specified ThreadGroup or one of its ancestors in the thread-group hierarchy.

resume

```
public final void resume()
```
Throws   SecurityException
                    If the checkAccess() method of the Security-Manager throws a SecurityException.

Description   This method resumes each `Thread` object that directly or indirectly belongs to this `ThreadGroup` object by calling its `resume()` method.

setDaemon

```
public final void setDaemon(boolean daemon)
```

Parameters   `daemon`   The new value for this `ThreadGroup` object's daemon attribute.

Throws   `SecurityException`

                  If the `checkAccess()` method of the `Security-Manager` throws a `SecurityException`.

Description   This method sets the daemon attribute of this `ThreadGroup` object to the given value. A daemon thread group is destroyed when the last `Thread` in it is stopped, or the last `ThreadGroup` in it is destroyed.

setMaxPriority

```
public final void setMaxPriority(int pri)
```

Parameters   `pri`   The new maximum priority for `Thread` objects that belong to this `ThreadGroup` object.

Description   This method sets the maximum priority that can be assigned to `Thread` objects that belong to this `ThreadGroup` object.

                  It is possible for a `ThreadGroup` to contain `Thread` objects that have higher priorities than this maximum, if they were given that higher priority before the maximum was set to a lower value.

stop

```
public final void stop()
```

Throws   `SecurityException`

                  If the `checkAccess()` method of the `Security-Manager` throws a `SecurityException`.

Description   This method stops each `Thread` object that directly or indirectly belongs to this `ThreadGroup` object by calling its `stop()` method.

suspend

```
public final void suspend()
```

Throws   SecurityException

                      If the checkAccess() method of the Security-
                      Manager throws a SecurityException.

Description   This method suspends each Thread object that directly or indi-
                rectly belongs to this ThreadGroup object by calling its sus-
                pend() method.

toString

  public String toString()

Returns   A string representation of this ThreadGroup object.

Overrides   Object.toString()

Description   This method returns a string representation of this Thread-
                Group object.

uncaughtException

  public void uncaughtException(Thread t, Throwable e)

Parameters   t   A reference to a Thread that just died because of
                                an uncaught exception.

                e   The uncaught exception.

Description   This method is called when a Thread object that belongs to this
                ThreadGroup object dies because of an uncaught exception. If
                this ThreadGroup object has a parent ThreadGroup object, this
                method just calls the parent's uncaughtException() method.
                Otherwise, this method must determine whether the uncaught
                exception is an instance of ThreadDeath. If it is, nothing is
                done. If it is not, the method calls the printStackTrace()
                method of the exception object.

                If this method is overridden, the overriding method should end
                with a call to super.uncaughtException().

Inherited Methods

Method	Inherited From	Method	Inherited From
clone()	Object	equals(Object)	Object
finalize()	Object	getClass()	Object
hashCode()	Object	notify()	Object
notifyAll()	Object	wait()	Object
wait(long)	Object	wait(long, int)	Object

See Also

Exceptions 9.4.1; Object 10.14; Runnable 10.16; SecurityManager 10.18; Thread 10.23; Threads 8; Throwable 10.25

10.25　Throwable

Synopsis

Class Name:	`java.lang.Throwable`
Superclass:	`java.lang.Object`
Immediate Subclasses:	`java.lang.Error, java.lang.Exception`
Interfaces Implemented:	`java.io.Serializable`
Availability:	JDK 1.0 or later

Description

The `Throwable` class is the superclass of all objects that can be thrown by the `throw` statement in Java. This is a requirement of the `throw` statement.

A `Throwable` object can have an associated message that provides more detail about the particular error or exception that is being thrown.

The `Throwable` class provides a method that outputs information about the state of the system when an exception object is created. This method can be useful in debugging Java programs.

The subclasses of `Throwable` that are provided with Java do not add functionality to `Throwable`. Instead, they offer more specific classifications of errors and exceptions.

Class Summary

```
public class java.lang.Throwable extends java.lang.Object
                            implements java.lang.Serializable {
    // Constructors
    public Throwable();
    public Throwable(String message);

    // Instance Methods
    public native Throwable fillInStackTrace();
    public String getLocalizedMessage();              // New in 1.1
    public String getMessage();
    public void printStackTrace();
    public void printStackTrace(PrintStream s);
    public void printStackTrace(PrintWriter s);       // New in 1.1
    public String toString();
}
```

Constructors

Throwable

    public Throwable()

     Description   Creates a Throwable object with no associated message. This constructor calls fillInStackTrace() so that information is available for printStackTrace().

    public Throwable(String message)

     Parameters   message   A message string to be associated with the object.

     Description   Create a Throwable object with an associated message. This constructor calls fillInStackTrace() so that information is available for printStackTrace().

Instance Methods

fillInStackTrace

    public native Throwable fillInStackTrace()

     Returns   A reference to this object.

     Description   This method puts stack trace information in this Throwable object. It is not usually necessary to explicitly call this method, since it is called by the constructors of the class. However, this method can be useful when rethrowing an object. If the stack trace information in the object needs to reflect the location that the object is rethrows from, fillInStackTrace() should be called.

getLocalizedMessage

    public String getLocalizedMessage()

     Availability   New as of JDK 1.1

     Returns   A localized version of the String object associated with this Throwable object, or null if there is no message associated with this object.

     Description   This method creates a localized version of the message that was associated with this object by its constructor.

                The getLocalizedMessage() method in Throwable always returns the same result as getMessage(). A subclass must override this method to produce a locale-specific message.

getMessage

`public String getMessage()`

Returns   The `String` object associated with this `Throwable` object, or `null` if there is no message associated with this object.

Description   This method returns any string message that was associated with this object by its constructor.

printStackTrace

`public void printStackTrace()`

Description   This method outputs the string representation of this `Throwable` object and a stack trace to `System.err`.

`public void printStackTrace(PrintStream s)`

Parameters   s   A `java.io.PrintStream` object.

Description   This method outputs the string representation of this `Throwable` object and a stack trace to the specified `PrintStream` object.

`public void printStackTrace(PrintStream w)`

Availability   New as of JDK 1.1

Parameters   s   A `java.io.PrintWriter` object.

Description   This method outputs the string representation of this `Throwable` object and a stack trace to the specified `PrintWriter` object.

toString

`public String toString()`

Returns   A string representation of this object.

Overrides   `Object.toString()`

Description   This method returns a string representation of this `Throwable` object.

Inherited Methods

Method	Inherited From	Method	Inherited From
clone()	Object	equals(Object)	Object
finalize()	Object	getClass()	Object
hashCode()	Object	notify()	Object
notifyAll()	Object	wait()	Object
wait(long)	Object	wait(long, int)	Object

See Also

Errors 9.4.2; Exceptions 9.4.1; Object 10.14

10.26   Void

Synopsis

Class Name: `java.lang.Void`
Superclass: `java.lang.Object`
Immediate Subclasses: None
Interfaces Implemented: None
Availability   New as of JDK 1.1

Description

The `Void` class is an uninstantiable wrapper for the primitive type void. The class contains simply a reference to the `Class` object that represents the primitive type void. The `Void` class is necessary as of JDK 1.1 to support the Reflection API and class literals.

Class Summary

```
public final class java.lang.Void extends java.lang.Object {
    // Constants
    public static final Class TYPE;
}
```

Constants

TYPE

`public static final Class TYPE`

The `Class` object that represents the primitive type void. It is always true that `Void.TYPE == void.class`.

Inherited Methods

Method	Inherited From	Method	Inherited From
clone()	Object	equals(Object)	Object
finalize()	Object	getClass()	Object
hashCode()	Object	notify()	Object
notifyAll()	Object	toString()	Object
wait()	Object	wait(long)	Object
wait(long, int)	Object		

See Also

Byte 10.2; Character 10.3; Class 10.4; Double 10.8; Float 10.9; Integer 10.10; Long 10.11; Short 10.19

A

The Unicode 2.0 Character Set

Characters	Description
\u0000 – \u1FFF	Alphabets
\u0020 – \u007F	Basic Latin
\u0080 – \u00FF	Latin-1 supplement
\u0100 – \u017F	Latin extended-A
\u0180 – \u024F	Latin extended-B
\u0250 – \u02AF	IPA extensions
\u02B0 – \u02FF	Spacing modifier letters
\u0300 – \u036F	Combining diacritical marks
\u0370 – \u03FF	Greek
\u0400 – \u04FF	Cyrillic
\u0530 – \u058F	Armenian
\u0590 – \u05FF	Hebrew
\u0600 – \u06FF	Arabic
\u0900 – \u097F	Devanagari
\u0980 – \u09FF	Bengali
\u0A00 – \u0A7F	Gurmukhi
\u0A80 – \u0AFF	Gujarati
\u0B00 – \u0B7F	Oriya
\u0B80 – \u0BFF	Tamil
\u0C00 – \u0C7F	Telugu
\u0C80 – \u0CFF	Kannada
\u0D00 – \u0D7F	Malayalam
\u0E00 – \u0E7F	Thai
\u0E80 – \u0EFF	Lao
\u0F00 – \u0FBF	Tibetan

Characters	Description
\u10A0 - \u10FF	Georgian
\u1100 - \u11FF	Hangul Jamo
\u1E00 - \u1EFF	Latin extended additional
\u1F00 - \u1FFF	Greek extended
\u2000 - \u2FFF	Symbols and punctuation
\u2000 - \u206F	General punctuation
\u2070 - \u209F	Superscripts and subscripts
\u20A0 - \u20CF	Currency symbols
\u20D0 - \u20FF	Combining diacritical marks for symbols
\u2100 - \u214F	Letterlike symbols
\u2150 - \u218F	Number forms
\u2190 - \u21FF	Arrows
\u2200 - \u22FF	Mathematical operators
\u2300 - \u23FF	Miscellaneous technical
\u2400 - \u243F	Control pictures
\u2440 - \u245F	Optical character recognition
\u2460 - \u24FF	Enclosed alphanumerics
\u2500 - \u257F	Box drawing
\u2580 - \u259F	Block elements
\u25A0 - \u25FF	Geometric shapes
\u2600 - \u26FF	Miscellaneous symbols
\u2700 - \u27BF	Dingbats
\u3000 - \u33FF	CJK auxiliary
\u3000 - \u303F	CJK symbols and punctuation
\u3040 - \u309F	Hiragana
\u30A0 - \u30FF	Katakana
\u3100 - \u312F	Bopomofo
\u3130 - \u318F	Hangul compatibility Jamo
\u3190 - \u319F	Kanbun
\u3200 - \u32FF	Enclosed CJK letters and months
\u3300 - \u33FF	CJK compatibility
\u4E00 - \u9FFF	CJK unified ideographs: Han characters used in China, Japan, Korea, Taiwan, and Vietnam
\uAC00 - \uD7A3	Hangul syllables
\uD800 - \uDFFF	Surrogates
\uD800 - \uDB7F	High surrogates
\uDB80 - \uDBFF	High private use surrogates
\uDC00 - \uDFFF	Low surrogates
\uE000 - \uF8FF	Private use
\uF900 - \uFFFF	Miscellaneous
\uF900 - \uFAFF	CJK compatibility ideographs
\uFB00 - \uFB4F	Alphabetic presentation forms
\uFB50 - \uFDFF	Arabic presentation forms-A

Characters	Description
\uFE20 – \uFE2F	Combing half marks
\uFE30 – \uFE4F	CJK compatibility forms
\uFE50 – \uFE6F	Small form variants
\uFE70 – \uFEFE	Arabic presentation forms-B
\uFEFF	Specials
\uFF00 – \uFFEF	Halfwidth and fullwidth forms
\uFFF0 – \uFFFF	Specials

Index

Symbols

& (ampersand)
  & (bitwise AND) operator, 94
  && (boolean AND) operator, 97
* (asterisk)
  * (multiplication) operator, 73–74
  in import directive, 203
@ tags, javadoc, 204
\ (backslash), 20
  \u escapes (see Unicode characters)
! (bang)
  ! (unary negation) operator, 68
  != (not-equal-to) operator, 93
[ ] (brackets)
  array allocation expressions, 61
  in array type declarations, 35, 174
^ (bitwise exclusive OR) operator, 95
, (comma), 22, 187
= (equal sign)
  = (assignment) operator, 101
  == (equal-to) operator, 91–92
- (hyphen)
  - (arithmetic subtraction) operator,
    79–80
  - (unary minus) operator, 67
  -- (decrement) operator, 46, 64–66
< (left angle bracket)
  < (less-than) operator, 86
  <= (less-than-or-equal-to) operator, 87
  << (left shift) operator, 83

( ) (parentheses), 43
  cast operations, 69–72
  object allocation expressions, 58
% (remainder) operator, 76–77
+ (plus)
  + (arithmetic addition) operator, 78–79
  + (string concatenation) operator, 43,
    80–83
  + (unary plus) operator, 67
  ++ (increment) operator, 46, 64–66
?: (conditional) operator, 99–101
> (right angle bracket)
  > (greater-than) operator, 89
  >= (greater-than-or-equal-to) operator,
    88
  >> (right shift) operator, 84
  >>> (unsigned right shift) operator, 85
; (semicolon), 149
/ (slash)
  / (division) operator, 74–76
  /* */ C-style comments, 3, 23
  /** */ documentation comments, 23,
    204
  // single-line comments, 3, 23
~ ((bitwise negation) operator, 68
| (vertical bar)
  | (bitwise include OR) operator, 96
  || (boolean OR) operator, 98

About the Author

Mark Grand (*mgrand@mindspring.com*) is a Java consultant, speaker, and instructor. He teaches classes on Java, develops Java-based software, and advises companies on how to best use Java-related technology with databases, networks, and electronic commerce. In addition to writing the *Java Language Reference*, Mark is the author of *Java Fundamental Classes Reference*. Prior to his involvement with Java, Mark worked for ten years as a designer and implementor of fourth-generation programming languages. His most recent role in this vein was as the architect of an electronic data interchange product. More information about Mark is available on his Web page at *http://www.mindspring.com/~mgrand/*.

Colophon

Our look is the result of reader comments, our own experimentation, and feedback from distribution channels. Distinctive covers complement our distinctive approach to technical topics, breathing personality and life into potentially dry subjects.

The image of binoculars on the cover of *Java Language Reference* is from the CMCD PhotoCD Collection. It was manipulated by Edie Freedman using Adobe Photoshop 3.0 and Adobe Gallery Effects filters. The cover layout was produced with Quark XPress 3.3 using the Bodoni Black font from URW Software.

The inside layout was designed by Nancy Priest. Text was prepared by Erik Ray in SGML DocBook 2.4 DTD. The print version of this book was created by translating the SGML source into a set of gtroff macros using a filter developed at ORA by Norman Walsh. Steve Talbott designed and wrote the underlying macro set on the basis of the GNU troff -gs macros; Lenny Muellner adapted them to SGML and implemented the book design. The GNU groff text formatter version 1.09 was used to generate PostScript output. The heading font is Bodoni BT; the text font is New Baskerville. The illustrations that appear in the book were created in Macromedia Freehand 5.0 by Chris Reilley and Robert Romano.

 # *More Titles from O'Reilly*

Java Programming

Exploring Java, Second Edition

By Patrick Niemeyer & Joshua Peck
2nd Edition June 1997 (est.)
500 pages (est.), ISBN 1-56592-271-9

The second edition of *Exploring Java*, fully revised to cover Version 1.1 of the JDK, introduces the basics of Java, the object-oriented programming language for networked applications. The ability to create animated World Wide Web pages sparked the rush to Java. But what also makes this language so important is that it's truly portable. The code runs on any machine that provides a Java interpreter, whether Windows 95, Windows NT, the Macintosh, or any flavor of UNIX.

Java in a Nutshell, Second Edition

By David Flanagan
2nd Edition May 1997
650 pages, ISBN 1-56592-262-X

The bestselling Java book just got better. Java programmers migrating to 1.1 find this second edition of Java in a Nutshell contains everything they need to get up to speed.

Newcomers find it still has all of the features that have made it the Java book most often recommended on the Internet. This complete quick reference contains descriptions of all of the classes in the core Java 1.1 API, making it the only quick reference that a Java programmer needs.

Java Virtual Machine

By Troy Downing & Jon Meyer
1st Edition March 1997
440 pages, ISBN 1-56592-194-1

This book is a comprehensive programming guide for the Java Virtual Machine (JVM). It gives readers a strong overview and reference of the JVM so that they may create their own implementations of the JVM or write their own compilers that create Java object code. A Java assembler is provided with the book, so the examples can all be compiled and executed.

Java Language Reference, Second Edition

By Mark Grand
2nd Edition July 1997 (est.)
448 pages, ISBN 1-56592-326-X

The second edition of the *Java Language Reference* is an invaluable tool for Java programmers, especially those who have migrated to Java 1.1. Part of O'Reilly's Java documentation series, this complete reference describes all aspects of the Java language plus new features in Version 1.1, such as inner classes, final local variables and method parameters, anonymous arrays, class literals, and instance initializers.

Java Fundamental Classes Reference

By Mark Grand
1st Edition May 1997
1152 pages, ISBN 1-56592-241-7

The *Java Fundamental Classes Reference* provides complete reference documentation for the Java fundamental classes.

This book takes you beyond what you'd expect from a standard reference manual. Classes and methods are, of course, described in detail. It offers tutorial-style explanations of the important classes in the Java Core API and includes lots of sample code to help you learn by example.

Java AWT Reference

By John Zukowski
1st Edition March 1997
1100 pages, ISBN 1-56592-240-9

With AWT, you can create windows, draw, work with images, and use components like buttons, scrollbars, and pulldown menus. *Java AWT Reference* covers the classes that comprise the java.awt, java.awt.image, and java.applet packages. These classes provide the functionality that allows a Java application to provide user interaction in a graphical environment. It offers a comprehensive explanation of how AWT components fit together with easy-to-use reference material on every AWT class and lots of sample code to help you learn by example.

Java Programming *continued*

Java Threads

By Scott Oaks and Henry Wong
1st Edition January 1997
252 pages, ISBN 1-56592-216-6

Java Threads is a comprehensive guide to the intricacies of threaded programming in Java, covering everything from the most basic synchronization techniques to advanced topics like writing your own thread scheduler.

Java Threads uncovers the one tricky but essential aspect of Java programming and provides techniques for avoiding deadlock, lock starvation, and other topics.

Java Network Programming

By Elliotte Rusty Harold
1st Edition February 1997
448 pages, ISBN 1-56592-227-1

Java Network Programming is a complete introduction to developing network programs, both applets and applications, using Java; covering everything from networking fundamentals to remote method invocation (RMI).

It also covers what you can do without explicitly writing network code, how you can accomplish your goals using URLs and the basic capabilities of applets.

Developing Java Beans

By Rob Englander
1st Edition June 1997 (est.)
300 pages (est.), ISBN 1-56592-289-1

With *Developing Java Beans,* you'll learn how to create components that can be manipulated by tools like Borland's Latte or Symantec's Visual Cafe, enabling others to build entire applications by using and reusing these building blocks. Beyond the basics, *Developing Java Beans* teaches you how to create Beans that can be saved and restored properly; how to take advantage of introspection to provide more information about a Bean's capabilities; how to provide property editors and customizers that manipulate a Bean in sophisticated ways; and how to integrate Java Beans into ActiveX projects.

Java in a Nutshell, DELUXE EDITION

By various authors
1st Edition June1997 (est.)
ISBN 1-56592-304-9
includes CD-ROM and books.

Java in a Nutshell, Deluxe Edition, is a Java programmer's dream come true in one small package. The heart of this Deluxe Edition is the Java reference library on CD-ROM, which brings together five indispensable volumes for Java developers and programmers, linking related info across books. It includes: *Exploring Java 2nd Edition*, *Java Language Reference, 2nd Edition*, *Java Fundamental Classes Reference*, *Java AWT Reference*, and *Java in a Nutshell, 2nd Edition*, included both on the CD-ROM and in a companion desktop edition. This deluxe library gives you everything you need to do serious programming with Java 1.1.

Database Programming with JDBC and Java

By George Reese
1st Edition July 1997 (est.)
300 pages (est.), ISBN 1-56592-270-0

Java and databases make a powerful combination. Getting the two sides to work together, however, takes some effort—largely because Java deals in objects while most databases do not.

This book describes the standard Java interfaces that make portable,object-oriented access to relational databases possible, and offers a robust model for writing applications that are easy to maintain. It introduces the JDBC and RMI packages and uses them to develop three-tier applications (applications divided into a user interface, an object-oriented logic component, and an information store). Covers Java 1.1.

Developing Web Content

Building Your Own WebSite

By Susan B. Peck & Stephen Arrants
1st Edition July 1996
514 pages, ISBN 1-56592-232-8

This is a hands-on reference for Windows® 95 and Windows NT™ desktop users who want to host their own site on the Web or on a corporate intranet. You'll also learn how to connect your web to information in other Windows applications, such as word processing documents and databases. Packed with examples and tutorials on every aspect of Web management. Includes the highly acclaimed WebSite™ 1.1 on CD-ROM.

Web Client Programming with Perl

By Clinton Wong
1st Edition March 1997
250 pages, ISBN 1-56592-214-X

Web Client Programming with Perl teaches you how to extend scripting skills to the Web. This book teaches you the basics of how browsers communicate with servers and how to write your own customized Web clients to automate common tasks. It is intended for those who are motivated to develop software that offers a more flexible and dynamic response than a standard Web browser.

JavaScript: The Definitive Guide, Regular Edition

By David Flanagan
2nd Edition January 1997
672 pages, ISBN 1-56592-234-4

In this second edition, the author of the best-selling, *Java in a Nutshell* describes the server-side JavaScript application, LiveWire, developed by Netscape and Sun Microsystems.

The book describes the version of JavaScript shipped with Navigator 2.0, 2.0.1, and 2.0.2, and also the much-changed version of JavaScript shipped with Navigator 3.0. LiveConnect, used for communication between JavaScript and Java applets, and addresses commonly encountered bugs on JavaScript objects.

HTML: The Definitive Guide, Second Edition

By Chuck Musciano & Bill Kennedy
2nd Edition April 1997
520 pages, ISBN 1-56592-235-2

The second edition covers the most up-to-date version of the HTML standard (the proposed HTML version 3.2), Netscape 4.0 and Internet Explorer 3.0, plus all the common extensions, especially Netscape extensions. The authors address all the current version's elements, explaining how they work and interact with each other. Includes a style guide that helps you to use HTML to accomplish a variety of tasks, from simple online documentation to complex marketing and sales presentations.

Designing for the Web: Getting Started in a New Medium

By Jennifer Niederst with Edie Freedman
1st Edition April 1996
180 pages, ISBN 1-56592-165-8

Designing for the Web gives you the basics you need to hit the ground running. Although geared toward designers, it covers information and techniques useful to anyone who wants to put graphics online. It explains how to work with HTML documents from a designer's point of view, outlines special problems with presenting information online, and walks through incorporating images into Web pages, with emphasis on resolution and improving efficiency.

WebMaster in a Nutshell

By Stephen Spainhour & Valerie Quercia
1st Edition October 1996
378 pages, ISBN 1-56592-229-8

Web content providers and administrators have many sources of information, both in print and online. *WebMaster in a Nutshell* pulls it all together into one slim volume — for easy desktop access. This quick-reference covers HTML, CGI, Perl, HTTP, server configuration, and tools for Web administration.

O'REILLY™

TO ORDER: **800-998-9938** • order@ora.com • *http://www.ora.com/*
OUR PRODUCTS ARE AVAILABLE AT A BOOKSTORE OR SOFTWARE STORE NEAR YOU.
FOR INFORMATION: **800-998-9938** • **707-829-0515** • info@ora.com

World Wide Web Journal

Fourth International World Wide Web Conference Proceedings

A publication of O'Reilly & Associates and the World Wide Web Consortium (W3C) Winter 1995/96 748 pages, ISBN 1-56592-169-0

The *World Wide Web Journal,* published quarterly, provides timely, in-depth coverage of the W3C's technological developments, such as protocols for security, replication and caching, HTML and SGML, and content labeling. This issue contains 57 refereed technical papers presented at the Fourth International World Wide Web Conference, held December 1995 in Boston, Massachusetts. It also includes the two best papers from regional conferences.

Key Specifications of the World Wide Web

A publication of O'Reilly & Associates and the World Wide Web Consortium (W3C) Spring 1996 356 pages, ISBN 1-56592-190-9

The key specifications that describe the architecture of the World Wide Web and how it works are maintained online at the World Wide Web Consortium. This issue of the *World Wide Web Journal* collects these key papers in a single volume as an important reference for the Webmaster, application programmer, or technical manager with definitive specifications for the core technologies in the Web.

The Web After Five Years

A publication of O'Reilly & Associates and the World Wide Web Consortium (W3C) Summer 1996, 226 pp, ISBN 1-56592-210-7

This issue is a reflection on the web after five years. In an interview with Tim Berners-Lee, the inventor of the Web and Director of the W3C, we learn that the Web was built to be an interactive, inter-creative, two-way medium from the beginning. These issues are addressed in selections from the MIT/W3C Workshop on Web Demographics and Internet Survey Methodology, along with commerce-related papers selected from the Fifth International World Wide Web Conference, which took place from May 6–10 in Paris.

Building an Industrial Strength Web

A publication of O'Reilly & Associates and the World Wide Web Consortium (W3C) Fall 1996, 244 pp, ISBN 1-56592-211-5

Issue 4 focuses on the infrastructure needed to create and maintain an "Industrial Strength Web," from network protocols to application design. Included are the first standard versions of core Web protocols: HTTP/1.1, Digest Authentication, State Management (Cookies), and PICS. This issue also provides guides to the specs, highlighting new features, papers explaining modifications to 1.1 (sticky and compressed headers), extensibility, support for collaborative authoring, and using distributed objects.

Advancing HTML: Style and Substance

A publication of O'Reilly & Associates and the World Wide Web Consortium (W3C) Winter 1996/97 254 pages, ISBN 1-56592-264-6

This issue is a guide to the specifications and tools that buttress the user interface to the World Wide Web. It includes the latest HTML 3.2 and CSS1 specs, papers on gif animation, JavaScript, Web accessibility, usability engineering, multimedia design, and a report on Amaya.

Scripting Languages: Automating the Web

A publication of O'Reilly & Associates and the World Wide Web Consortium (W3C) By Lincoln Stein, Clint Wong, Ron Petrusha, Shishir Gundavaram, etc. Spring 1997, 244 pages, 1-56592-265-4

In spite of all the power built into popular web utilities, the informality, ease, and rapid development cycle of scripting languages make them well suited to the constant change common to most web sites. *Scripting Languages: Automating the Web* guides users and developers in choosing and deploying scripting solutions.

In addition, this issue examines the web-wide impact of Perl as the scripting language of choice for webmasters everywhere, with an in-depth article featuring Perl developers Larry Wall and Tom Christiansen.

How to stay in touch with O'Reilly

1. Visit Our Award-Winning Web Site

http://www.ora.com/

★"Top 100 Sites on the Web" —*PC Magazine*
★"Top 5% Web sites" —*Point Communications*
★"3-Star site" —*The McKinley Group*

Our web site contains a library of comprehensive product information (including book excerpts and tables of contents), downloadable software, background articles, interviews with technology leaders, links to relevant sites, book cover art, and more. File us in your Bookmarks or Hotlist!

2. Join Our Email Mailing Lists

New Product Releases

To receive automatic email with brief descriptions of all new O'Reilly products as they are released, send email to:
listproc@online.ora.com
Put the following information in the first line of your message (*not* in the Subject field):
subscribe ora-news "Your Name" of "Your Organization" (for example: subscribe ora-news Kris Webber of Fine Enterprises)

O'Reilly Events

If you'd also like us to send information about trade show events, special promotions, and other O'Reilly events, send email to: **listproc@online.ora.com**
Put the following information in the first line of your message (*not* in the Subject field):
subscribe ora-events "Your Name" of "Your Organization"

3. Get Examples from Our Books via FTP

There are two ways to access an archive of example files from our books:

Regular FTP

* ftp to:
  ftp.ora.com
  (login: anonymous
  password: your email address)
* Point your web browser to:
  ftp://ftp.ora.com/

FTPMAIL

* Send an email message to:
  ftpmail@online.ora.com
  (Write "help" in the message body)

4. Visit Our Gopher Site

* Connect your gopher to:
  gopher.ora.com

* Point your web browser to:
  gopher://gopher.ora.com/

* Telnet to:
  gopher.ora.com
  login: gopher

5. Contact Us via Email

order@ora.com
To place a book or software order online. Good for North American and international customers.

subscriptions@ora.com
To place an order for any of our newsletters or periodicals.

books@ora.com
General questions about any of our books.

software@ora.com
For general questions and product information about our software. Check out O'Reilly Software Online at **http://software.ora.com/** for software and technical support information. Registered O'Reilly software users send your questions to: **website-support@ora.com**

cs@ora.com
For answers to problems regarding your order or our products.

booktech@ora.com
For book content technical questions or corrections.

proposals@ora.com
To submit new book or software proposals to our editors and product managers.

international@ora.com
For information about our international distributors or translation queries. For a list of our distributors outside of North America check out:
http://www.ora.com/www/order/country.html

O'Reilly & Associates, Inc.
101 Morris Street, Sebastopol, CA 95472 USA
TEL 707-829-0515 or 800-998-9938
(6am to 5pm PST)
FAX 707-829-0104

Titles from O'Reilly

Please note that upcoming titles are displayed in italic.

WEB PROGRAMMING

Apache: The Definitive Guide
Building Your Own Web Conferences
Building Your Own Website
CGI Programming for the World Wide Web
Designing for the Web
HTML: The Definitive Guide, 2nd Ed.
JavaScript: The Definitive Guide, 2nd Ed.
Learning Perl
Programming Perl, 2nd Ed.
Mastering Regular Expressions
WebMaster in a Nutshell
Web Security & Commerce
Web Client Programming with Perl
World Wide Web Journal

USING THE INTERNET

Smileys
The Future Does Not Compute
The Whole Internet User's Guide & Catalog
The Whole Internet for Win 95
Using Email Effectively
Bandits on the Information Superhighway

JAVA SERIES

Exploring Java
Java AWT Reference
Java Fundamental Classes Reference
Java in a Nutshell
Java Language Reference, 2nd Edition
Java Network Programming
Java Threads
Java Virtual Machine

SOFTWARE

WebSite™ 1.1
WebSite Professional™
Building Your Own Web Conferences
WebBoard™
PolyForm™
Statisphere™

SONGLINE GUIDES

NetActivism
Net Law
NetLearning
Net Lessons
NetResearch
NetSuccess
NetTravel

SYSTEM ADMINISTRATION

Building Internet Firewalls
Computer Crime: A Crimefighter's Handbook
Computer Security Basics
DNS and BIND, 2nd Ed.
Essential System Administration, 2nd Ed.
Getting Connected: The Internet at 56K and Up
Linux Network Administrator's Guide
Managing Internet Information Services
Managing NFS and NIS
Networking Personal Computers with TCP/IP
Practical UNIX & Internet Security, 2nd Ed.
PGP: Pretty Good Privacy
sendmail, 2nd Ed.
sendmail Desktop Reference
System Performance Tuning
TCP/IP Network Administration
termcap & terminfo
Using & Managing UUCP
Volume 8: X Window System Administrator's Guide
Web Security & Commerce

UNIX

Exploring Expect
Learning VBScript
Learning GNU Emacs, 2nd Ed.
Learning the bash Shell
Learning the Korn Shell
Learning the UNIX Operating System
Learning the vi Editor
Linux in a Nutshell
Making TeX Work
Linux Multimedia Guide
Running Linux, 2nd Ed.
SCO UNIX in a Nutshell
sed & awk, 2nd Edition
Tcl/Tk Tools
UNIX in a Nutshell: System V Edition
UNIX Power Tools
Using csh & tsch
When You Can't Find Your UNIX System Administrator
Writing GNU Emacs Extensions

WEB REVIEW STUDIO SERIES

Gif Animation Studio
Shockwave Studio

WINDOWS

Dictionary of PC Hardware and Data Communications Terms
Inside the Windows 95 Registry
Inside the Windows 95 File System
Windows Annoyances
Windows NT File System Internals
Windows NT in a Nutshell

PROGRAMMING

Advanced Oracle PL/SQL Programming
Applying RCS and SCCS
C++: The Core Language
Checking C Programs with lint
DCE Security Programming
Distributing Applications Across DCE & Windows NT
Encyclopedia of Graphics File Formats, 2nd Ed.
Guide to Writing DCE Applications
lex & yacc
Managing Projects with make
Mastering Oracle Power Objects
Oracle Design: The Definitive Guide
Oracle Performance Tuning, 2nd Ed.
Oracle PL/SQL Programming
Porting UNIX Software
POSIX Programmer's Guide
POSIX.4: Programming for the Real World
Power Programming with RPC
Practical C Programming
Practical C++ Programming
Programming Python
Programming with curses
Programming with GNU Software
Pthreads Programming
Software Portability with imake, 2nd Ed.
Understanding DCE
Understanding Japanese Information Processing
UNIX Systems Programming for SVR4

BERKELEY 4.4 SOFTWARE DISTRIBUTION

4.4BSD System Manager's Manual
4.4BSD User's Reference Manual
4.4BSD User's Supplementary Documents
4.4BSD Programmer's Reference Manual
4.4BSD Programmer's Supplementary Documents
X Programming
Vol. 0: X Protocol Reference Manual
Vol. 1: Xlib Programming Manual
Vol. 2: Xlib Reference Manual
Vol. 3M: X Window System User's Guide, Motif Edition
Vol. 4M: X Toolkit Intrinsics Programming Manual, Motif Edition
Vol. 5: X Toolkit Intrinsics Reference Manual
Vol. 6A: Motif Programming Manual
Vol. 6B: Motif Reference Manual
Vol. 6C: Motif Tools
Vol. 8 : X Window System Administrator's Guide
Programmer's Supplement for Release 6
X User Tools
The X Window System in a Nutshell

CAREER & BUSINESS

Building a Successful Software Business
The Computer User's Survival Guide
Love Your Job!
Electronic Publishing on CD-ROM

TRAVEL

Travelers' Tales: Brazil
Travelers' Tales: Food
Travelers' Tales: France
Travelers' Tales: Gutsy Women
Travelers' Tales: India
Travelers' Tales: Mexico
Travelers' Tales: Paris
Travelers' Tales: San Francisco
Travelers' Tales: Spain
Travelers' Tales: Thailand
Travelers' Tales: A Woman's World

O'REILLY™

TO ORDER: **800-998-9938** • *order@ora.com* • *http://www.ora.com/*
OUR PRODUCTS ARE AVAILABLE AT A BOOKSTORE OR SOFTWARE STORE NEAR YOU.
FOR INFORMATION: **800-998-9938** • **707-829-0515** • *info@ora.com*

International Distributors

UK, Europe, Middle East and Northern Africa (except France, Germany, Switzerland, & Austria)

INQUIRIES
International Thomson Publishing
Europe
Berkshire House
168-173 High Holborn
London WC1V 7AA, United Kingdom
Telephone: 44-171-497-1422
Fax: 44-171-497-1426
Email: itpint@itps.co.uk

ORDERS
International Thomson Publishing
Services, Ltd.
Cheriton House, North Way
Andover, Hampshire SP10 5BE,
United Kingdom
Telephone: 44-264-342-832
 (UK orders)
Telephone: 44-264-342-806
 (outside UK)
Fax: 44-264-364418 (UK orders)
Fax: 44-264-342761 (outside UK)
UK & Eire orders: itpuk@itps.co.uk
International orders: itpint@itps.co.uk

France

Editions Eyrolles
61 bd Saint-Germain
75240 Paris Cedex 05
France
Fax: 33-01-44-41-11-44

FRENCH LANGUAGE BOOKS
All countries except Canada
Phone: 33-01-44-41-46-16
Email: geodif@eyrolles.com

ENGLISH LANGUAGE BOOKS
Phone: 33-01-44-41-11-87
Email: distribution@eyrolles.com

Australia

WoodsLane Pty. Ltd.
7/5 Vuko Place, Warriewood NSW 2102
P.O. Box 935, Mona Vale NSW 2103
Australia
Telephone: 61-2-9970-5111
Fax: 61-2-9970-5002
Email: info@woodslane.com.au

Germany, Switzerland, and Austria

INQUIRIES
O'Reilly Verlag
Balthasarstr. 81
D-50670 Köln
Germany
Telephone: 49-221-97-31-60-0
Fax: 49-221-97-31-60-8
Email: anfragen@oreilly.de

ORDERS
International Thomson Publishing
Königswinterer Straße 418
53227 Bonn, Germany
Telephone: 49-228-97024 0
Fax: 49-228-441342
Email: order@oreilly.de

Asia (except Japan & India)

INQUIRIES
International Thomson Publishing Asia
60 Albert Street #15-01
Albert Complex
Singapore 189969
Telephone: 65-336-6411
Fax: 65-336-7411

ORDERS
Telephone: 65-336-6411
Fax: 65-334-1617
thomson@signet.com.sg

New Zealand

WoodsLane New Zealand Ltd.
21 Cooks Street (P.O. Box 575)
Wanganui, New Zealand
Telephone: 64-6-347-6543
Fax: 64-6-345-4840
Email: info@woodslane.com.au

Japan

O'Reilly Japan, Inc.
Kiyoshige Building 2F
12-Banchi, Sanei-cho
Shinjuku-ku
Tokyo 160 Japan
Telephone: 81-3-3356-5227
Fax: 81-3-3356-5261
Email: kenji@ora.com

India

Computer Bookshop (India) PVT. LTD.
190 Dr. D.N. Road, Fort
Bombay 400 001
India
Telephone: 91-22-207-0989
Fax: 91-22-262-3551
Email: cbsbom@giasbm01.vsnl.net.in

The Americas

O'Reilly & Associates, Inc.
101 Morris Street
Sebastopol, CA 95472 U.S.A.
Telephone: 707-829-0515
Telephone: 800-998-9938 (U.S. &
Canada)
Fax: 707-829-0104
Email: order@ora.com

Southern Africa

International Thomson Publishing
Southern Africa
Building 18, Constantia Park
138 Sixteenth Road
P.O. Box 2459
Halfway House, 1685 South Africa
Telephone: 27-11-805-4819
Fax: 27-11-805-3648

O'REILLY™

O'REILLY™

O'Reilly & Associates, Inc.
101 Morris Street
Sebastopol, CA 95472-9902
1-800-998-9938

Visit us online at:
http://www.ora.com/
orders@ora.com

O'REILLY WOULD LIKE TO HEAR FROM YOU

Which book did this card come from?

_____

Where did you buy this book?
- ❏ Bookstore   ❏ Computer Store
- ❏ Direct from O'Reilly ❏ Class/seminar
- ❏ Bundled with hardware/software
- ❏ Other _____

What operating system do you use?
- ❏ UNIX   ❏ Macintosh
- ❏ Windows NT   ❏ PC(Windows/DOS)
- ❏ Other _____

What is your job description?
- ❏ System Administrator   ❏ Programmer
- ❏ Network Administrator   ❏ Educator/Teacher
- ❏ Web Developer
- ❏ Other _____

❏ Please send me O'Reilly's catalog, containing
a complete listing of O'Reilly books and
software.

Name _____   Company/Organization _____

Address _____

City _____   State _____   Zip/Postal Code _____   Country _____

Telephone _____   Internet or other email address (specify network) _____

Nineteenth century wood engraving
of a bear from the O'Reilly &
Associates Nutshell Handbook®
Using & Managing UUCP.

POST CARD

BUSINESS REPLY MAIL
FIRST CLASS MAIL   PERMIT NO. 80   SEBASTOPOL, CA

Postage will be paid by addressee

O'Reilly & Associates, Inc.
101 Morris Street
Sebastopol, CA 95472-9902